W9-DBJ-854

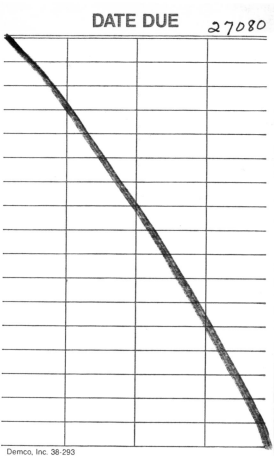

DATE DUE   27080

The Rebirth of Europe

ELIZABETH POND

The Rebirth
of Europe

BROOKINGS INSTITUTION PRESS
Washington, D.C.

ABOUT BROOKINGS

Copyright © 1999
THE BROOKINGS INSTITUTION
1775 Massachusetts Avenue, N.W., Washington, D.C. 20036
www.brookings.edu

Library of Congress Cataloging-in-Publication data

Pond, Elizabeth.
    The rebirth of Europe / Elizabeth Pond.
    p.   cm.
    Includes bibliographical references and index.

    ISBN 0-8157-7157-6 (alk. paper)
    ISBN 0-8157-7158-4 (pbk. : alk. paper)
    1. European Union. 2. Europe—Politics and government—1945–
3. Europe—Economic integration. 4. Europe—Foreign relations—1945–
5. World politics—945– I. Title.
    JN30 .P66   1998   98-58114
    327.4—dc21   CIP

                    9 8 7 6 5 4 3 2 1

The paper used in this publication meets minimum requirements of the American National Standard for Information Sciences—Permanence of Paper for Printed Library Materials: ANSI Z39.48-1984.

Typeset in Sabon

Composition by Cynthia Stock
Silver Spring, Maryland

Printed by R. R. Donnelley and Sons
Harrisonburg, Virginia

Acknowledgments

This book benefited greatly from suggestions by J. D. Bindenagel, Robert Cooper, Hans-Joachim Falenski, Michael Mertes, Virginia Nordin, Hans-Friedrich von Ploetz, Wilhelm Schönfelder, Peggy Simpson, Elisabeth Wendt, and three Brookings reviewers, as well as from a seminar at the Brookings Institution in March 1998 on my initial concept. Any failure to meet the high standards these readers set is my own. Financial support came from the John D. and Catherine T. MacArthur Foundation in a research and writing grant (1991–93); from the Woodrow Wilson International Center for Scholars, where I was a Fellow in 1994–95; and from the German Marshall Fund of the United States (1998).

Permission to use substantial portions of my essays in the following magazines is gratefully acknowledged: "Letter from Bonn: Visions of the European Dream," *Washington Quarterly*, vol. 20, no. 3 (Summer 1997), pp. 53-72, ©1997 by the Center for Strategic and International Studies (CSIS) and the Massachusetts Institute of Technology; "Letter from Kiev: Crisis, 1997 Style," *Washington Quarterly*, vol. 20, no. 4 (Autumn 1997), pp. 79-87, ©1997 by the Center for Strategic and International Studies (CSIS) and the Massachusetts Institute of Technology; "Miracle on the Vistula," *Washington Quarterly*, vol. 21, no. 3 (Summer 1998), pp. 209-30, ©1998 by the Center for Strategic and International Studies (CSIS) and the Massachusetts Institute of Technology; and "The Escape from History," *World Link*, January/February 1998, pp. 64-68. *World Link* is the magazine of the World Economic Forum.

I am also most appreciative of the editorial guidance I received from Nancy Davidson and Deborah Styles.

To Mary Vance Trent

Contents

Glossary of Abbreviations and Terms

acquis communautaire—the 80,000 pages of laws and regulations already adopted by the EU that every new entrant must endorse

Amsterdam Treaty of 1997—follow-on agreement to the Maastricht Treaty of the European Union

Baltic Sea Region Accord—agreement signed in 1998 for cooperation between Poland, Denmark, Sweden, Kaliningrad, Latvia, and Lithuania

Benelux—Belgium, Netherlands, and Luxembourg

Bundesbank—the powerful German central bank that the ECB is modeled on

CAP—EU's common agricultural policy

CEFTA—Central European Free Trade Agreement; grouping of Poland, Hungary, Czech Republic, Romania, Bulgaria, Slovakia, and Slovenia that aims to remove all tariffs in trade between them by 2002 as a step toward EU membership

CFE—treaty limiting conventional forces in Europe, signed in 1990 and subsequently modified

CFSP—common foreign and security policy, the distant EU goal

CIS—Commonwealth of Independent States, the Russian-led grouping of former Soviet states, excluding the Baltics

CJTF—Combined Joint Task Force, or WEU forces that would borrow NATO assets for operations to be run without direct American participation

CNAD—Conference of National Armaments Directors of NATO countries

Contact Group—the steering committee for dealing with Yugoslavia set up in 1994; members are the United States, Russia, France, Germany, Britain

Council of Europe—organization to promote and certify observation of democratic norms and human rights in Europe (not to be confused with the EU's European Council)

Council of Ministers—see European Council

Coreper—Committee of Permanent Representatives of EU heads of government (and state, in the case of France) that do the bulk of the European Council's work between summits

Coreu—Correspondant Europeen (communications system linking EU foreign ministries)

CSCE—Conference on Security and Cooperation in Europe based on the 1975 Helsinki Agreement (after 1995, OSCE)

DG—Directorate General, division in the European Commission corresponding to a national cabinet ministry

EAPC—Euro-Atlantic Partnership Council that brings together ambassadors from NATO members and from the Partnership for Peace countries

EBRD—European Bank for Reconstruction and Development to help Central and East European economies

EC—European Communities (or European Community); after 1993, European Union

ECB—European Central Bank

ECJ—European Court of Justice

Ecofin—Council of Economic and Finance Ministers

EEA—European Economic Area, establishing the same rules for, initially, the EC and EFTA countries

EEC—European Economic Community (later just EC)

EFTA—European Free Trade Association between Western European nations not in the EEC; merged (except for Switzerland) with the EC to form the European Economic Area in 1992; after Sweden, Finland, and Austria left to join the EU in 1995, EFTA consisted of Iceland, Liechtenstein, Norway, and Switzerland

EIB—European Investment Bank, set up in 1958 to provide long-term development financing in Europe

EMI—European Monetary Institute (forerunner of the ECB)

EMU—European Economic and Monetary Union

EPC—European Political Cooperation, the more modest forerunner of CFSP agreed on in 1969

ESDI—European Security and Defense Identity—the hardest part of the CFSP goal to achieve; to be realized in cooperation with NATO

EU—European Union, the 1993 successor to the EC

Euratom—European Atomic Energy Community

Eurocorps—multilateral European force (with troops from France, Germany, Belgium, Spain, and Luxembourg)

Eurogroup—European group within NATO from 1970 on

Euroland/Eurozone/euro-11—the eleven EU members that are members of EMU (Austria, Benelux, Finland, France, Germany, Ireland, Italy, Portugal, Spain)

European Agreements—agreements between the EU and candidates that are promised eventual membership

European Commission—EU president, with the collegium of twenty commissioners and the administrative bureaucracy under them

European Council—summits of EU heads of government (and state, in the case of France), meeting at least twice annually; supplemented by Council of Ministers' meetings of EU ministers in a single competence, such as foreign or interior ministers

European Parliament—Strasbourg-based parliament of directly elected deputies from all EU member countries

E-15—all EU members before eastern enlargement (as distinct from the eleven members of EMU)

G-3—the informal inner grouping of the United States, Germany, and Japan on financial and economic policy

G-7—Group of seven leading industrial democracies—the United States, Canada, Germany, France, Britain, Italy, and Japan (plus the EU president)—that meet in annual summits

G-8—see P-8

G-10—(actually 11) G-7 plus Belgium, the Netherlands, Sweden, and Switzerland; these finance ministers meet informally at the fringes of IMF or World Bank meetings

G-22 of "systemically significant economies"—G-7 plus key emerging economies in Asia and Latin America; membership creep actually brought it up to twenty-seven by December 1998

G-24—Group of twenty-four states that joined forces in 1989 to support economic and democratic reforms in Eastern Europe; the fifteen EU members plus Iceland, Norway, Switzerland, Turkey, Australia, New Zealand, Japan, the United States, and Canada

GATT—General Agreement on Tariffs and Trade (succeeded in 1995 by the WTO)

GDP—gross domestic product

IEPG—Independent European Program Group of all European NATO members except Iceland; aims at cooperation in arms procurement

IFOR—Implementation Force (UN–mandated, NATO–led peacekeepers in Bosnia from December 1995)

IMF—International Monetary Fund

NAC—North Atlantic Council of ambassadors permanently stationed at NATO headquarters in Brussels

NACC—North Atlantic Cooperation Council

NAFTA—North American Free Trade Area

NATO—North Atlantic Treaty Organization

NGO—nongovernmental organization

Occar—the joint defense procurement agency set up by Britain, France, Germany, and Italy in 1998

OECD—Organization for Economic Cooperation and Development; grew out of the cooperative administration of the Marshall Plan; current members are all west European market democracies, including Iceland, Turkey, the Czech Republic, Hungary, and Poland, plus the United States, Canada, Mexico, Japan, South Korea, Australia, and New Zealand

OSCE—Organization for Security and Cooperation in Europe; (before 1995, CSCE)

P-8—"political 8," the G-7 nations plus Russia

PfP —NATO's Partnership for Peace with nonmembers of the alliance

PHARE—Poland and Hungary: Aid for the Restructuring of Economies (later extended to aid other central European states too)

QUAD—group of United States, EU, Canada, and Japan in GATT and WTO

Rome Treaty—the 1957 founding treaty of the EEC

Schengen Agreements—1985 and subsequent agreements between the inner EU core to scrap border controls; implemented so far (partially) by Germany, France, Benelux, Spain, Portugal, Austria, Italy, and Greece

SFOR—Stabilization Force in Bosnia (succeeded IFOR at the end of 1996)

SHAPE—Supreme Headquarters Allied Powers Europe, in Mons, Belgium

Single European Act—the amendment to the Rome Treaty adopted in 1986 that led to the single market of 1992

TACIS—EU technical assistance for Soviet successor states

TEU (Maastricht) Treaty on European Union, 1992

Trevi—EU police cooperation on terrorism, radicalism, extremism, violence, and information

Troika—the EU steering team of the states holding the previous, current, and incoming EU presidency

UNPROFOR—UN Protection Force in Croatia and Bosnia, 1992–95

Visegrad states—Poland, Hungary, and Czechoslovakia (later the two states of the Czech Republic and Slovakia)

WEU—Western European Union, the European-only security alliance that predated NATO in the Brussels Treaty of 1948, but has no troops or military structure

World Bank—bank to "reduce poverty and improve living standards by promoting sustainable growth and investments in people," in the bank's self description; cooperates closely with European Commission, EBRD, and the EIB in supporting accession to the EU by central European countries

WTO—World Trade Organization (succeeded GATT in 1995)

Prologue

Europe matters. It mattered enough for the United States to sacrifice half a million men and women in World Wars I and II. It mattered enough for American forces to stay on the old continent for half a century thereafter to keep the cold war cold.

Now, at this beginning of a new millennium, Europe still matters. Its spreading zone of peace and prosperity is, at the least, a bastion against spillover from the new Russian turmoil or, at the most, a conveyor of some of its own stability to the former superpower and continuing nuclear power to its east.

Its $8 trillion output matches that of the United States and is the other engine for world growth in the current financial turbulence. In our globalized era, it absorbs more U.S. overseas investment than any other region. Reciprocally, Europe contributes the most foreign investment to the United States as a whole and to virtually every single state. Europe's economic clout will only grow with the advent of European Monetary Union. Early in the next century the euro will probably equal the dollar as a reserve currency. For the first time Europe's equity markets will grow to rival America's. As more investment then flows to Europe and less to the United States, the world's biggest debtor will have to find new ways to fund its record trade deficits.

Politically, too, Europe is experimenting in ways that should interest us. A congenitally war-prone continent has, with our help, turned into one of the safest and most humane places on earth—and is now reinventing itself. It is pioneering a postnational, postmodern "pooling of sovereignty" that is supplanting the nation-state system of the past three centuries. The European Union is not and probably never will be a united federation, but it is already far more than a loose

1

confederation. It is asserting, in Americanesque fashion, that history is not destiny. It is renouncing the hereditary enmity between French and Germans. It is rejecting the repeated crushing of Poles between aggressive Russians and aggressive Germans and is inviting Warsaw—after a thousand years of Polish striving—to join the Western family. In a leap of faith, it is converting the mark, the franc, and the guilder—e pluribus unum—into one euro. It is, after a justly pessimistic century, importing America's optimistic sense of possibility. Remarkably, it is doing so at a time of financial vicissitudes that some are calling the most dangerous since the Great Depression of the 1930s.

Europe's transformation will challenge us economically and psychologically. The world's sole superpower is not yet prepared for the shock to come.

This book is one attempt to begin the preparation necessary for the new century. Its genesis goes back a decade, to a summer day in 1987.

I had already lived in Europe for some years. But like every other American reporter, I avoided covering the boring European Community as much as possible. If I visited the European capital of Brussels at all, it was only to look into the hot (and now forgotten) issue of theater nuclear missiles. Then, at the height of a stagnation in the EC that had earned the nickname "Eurosclerosis," I attended an omnibus conference in a Bavarian castle.

One of the first speakers was a University of Virginia professor who described in gripping detail the birth of the American Constitution two centuries earlier. The convention of Benjamin Franklin, James Madison, and their friends and foes audaciously exceeded its mandate. It struck unhappy compromises between small and large states; it wrestled with issues of how to control commerce; in the end it turned a failed confederation into an enduring federation. Many states were suspicious of the resulting document, fearing loss of their powers. In a cliffhanger roll call, the New York legislature approved ratification by one vote. Until the last minute, what Americans now accept as the bedrock of their nation was touch and go.

The next speaker was a pollster for the European Community, who analyzed public opinion about European integration. To the surprise of everyone around the table, his results showed a large majority—ranging up to percentiles in the 60s—in all EC member countries except Britain and Denmark in favor of more integration. Specific issues were still controversial, of course—clashes of interest between the small and large states, the precise control of commerce, and confederal competence. But the basic desire for more joint European governance was constant.

The juxtaposition was electrifying. It was as if a cartoon light bulb went on over the heads of all the participants. The eccentric thought coursed around the room: *Maybe we are not as far away from a united Europe as we all assume.*

From that day on I tracked the European Community. I watched as the goal of forming a real single European market by 1992 took hold. I saw the business community begin to make investment decisions as if this union would actually come to pass. And of course I stared transfixed as the Berlin Wall fell and Chancellor Helmut Kohl swore that German unification must lead to European unification.

Kohl's correlation was not coincidental. Once it became clear that West and East Germany would merge, "the German question" again reared its head. How could the old, sometimes terrifying Teutonic energies be channeled into constructive rather than destructive uses as Germany became overnight one-third larger than the other big European nations of Britain, France, and Italy? How could this third rise of Germany in a century avoid being as disastrous as the first and second times, with the carnage of World War I and the Holocaust?

Kohl's answer was to embed Germany so thoroughly in a European structure that it could never again dream of national solutions. In the chancellor's words, the integration of Europe must be made "irreversible" before another generation came to power that would not personally remember the horror of World War II and would therefore see less urgency in the pan-European enterprise. The result, he said, borrowing Thomas Mann's phrase, must be a European Germany, and not a German Europe.

This compulsion explained Kohl's drive for European political union and then, as political union foundered, for a monetary union that would itself impel further integration. It also explained Bonn's determination to get Poland into the EU so that Germany would no longer be the frontline to the east, but would be totally surrounded by allies.

This inner dynamic is poorly understood by Americans. European integration has repeatedly been dismissed in the United States; observers have often let the manifest difficulties of each step toward greater union blind them to the fact that the steps were actually being taken. Since a major cause of the American failure of perception seems to have been a disproportionate focus on Britain (which has consistently opposed EC "deepening" to any political or economic integration beyond a simple free-trade zone) and on France (which for years opposed EC "widening" to Germany's backyard in central Europe), this book aims to compensate. It tells the story of the past decade from the point of view of the main movers of "deepening" and "widening," Germany and Poland.

Here, then, is the thesis of this book.

On the eve of the twenty-first century, a miracle occurred. Europe was reborn.

For the first time since 1648, nation-states became convinced that they had more to gain than to lose by surrendering fundamental attributes of sovereignty to a supranational body. For the longest period since the Middle Ages, Europeans suddenly realized, they have enjoyed continuous peace. For the first time since the Age of Exploration (or at least since the nineteenth-century belief in inevitable progress), they have recovered a sense of purpose.

On a bloody continent, in which every other generation has gone to war as far back as folk memory extends, every one of these impulses was astonishing. For three centuries the idealists, the ambitious, and the defeated of Europe had fled to the New World to escape the old, to outwit pogroms and poverty, habit and hierarchy. America, not Europe, was where one could get a second chance, could begin anew, could homestead land, worship according to conscience, invent telephones and mail-order houses and a new identity. Europeans loved the cowboy and, later, the on-the-road biker. They might find Americans naive or shallow, but they envied American exuberance. America was the land of promise.

Europe, by contrast, was the land of the Thirty Years' War, the Napoleonic wars, the potato famine, inherited social status, slaughter in the trenches of World War I, genocide in World War II, the despair of Nietzsche and of Kafka.

There was no sudden inversion of this dismal self-image. There were, rather, a tectonic shift as the cold war ended and, in parallel, a series of incremental pragmatic advances that accrued to metamorphosis.

In this context the tale is less a whodunit than a howdunit. Kohl, with the assistance of EC president Jacques Delors and French president François Mitterrand, is the obvious protagonist. But just how did the German chancellor get a population that was two-thirds opposed to European Monetary Union to give up its cherished deutsche mark? How did the project of EMU survive the worst recession since the 1930s? How did Kohl get reelected in 1994 on the heels of that recession before being dumped by voters in 1998? How did deepening and widening come to be seen by others, as well as by the Germans, as not only compatible, but even complementary? How did happy-go-lucky Italy manage to meet the strict "convergence criteria" of top economic performance and qualify for EMU? How have the Poles managed to produce 5 or 6 percent growth for four years running, without overheating?

How was the lowest common denominator that one might expect from fifteen very different European Union states turned into "benchmarking," in which the best achievement becomes the standard for the rest?

How, in sum, was Europe reborn? And will this new Europe prove strong enough to survive the current storms?

CHAPTER ONE

Images of Europe: Skeptics versus Skeptical Optimists

Heartland Europe is finally escaping from its past slaughter and division. Francis Fukuyama's thesis that liberalism's victory over absolutism means the end of history is demonstrably true for this part of the globe.[1] To be sure, optimism is tempered by all the contrary scenarios of the disaster that looms if the European enterprise does not go forward. No Frenchman struggling to adapt to the post–cold war primacy of a united Germany—and to the Bundesbank's no-inflation credo—would interpret his lot as rosy. And every upstanding German, horrified by the accusation that he or she might actually be a closet optimist, would recoil from the very suspicion of such weakness of character.

Yet Europe's postnational change of consciousness and activism at this end of a millennium would be unthinkable if Europeans were not braced by a new self-confidence. Most fundamentally, members of the European Union trust each other in a way they never have before. No matter how often they have fought in the past, they have no doubt today that they have banished war among themselves. More and more they are surrendering, or "pooling," once sacrosanct sovereignty and now allow a full 50 percent of their domestic legislation and 80 percent of their economic legislation to be written in Brussels. And they are leaping into the unknowns of monetary union and of enlarging the European Union to absorb the fledgling, unproven central European democracies.

There are, of course, rational motivations for all of these innovations in an era of globalization and interdependence; ozone holes and instantaneous worldwide transfers of billions of dollars make every European state too small to cope alone.[2] But such motivations at any previous point in history would have been swamped by all the opposing impulses of nationalism, habit, and fear. Today they are not.

Probably never before in history has a transformation of such magnitude been so little remarked as it occurred. The assumption of the divine right of kings fell in battle. The transatlantic slave trade ended only after a titanic struggle. Today, by contrast, the maturing beyond nineteenth-century nationalism that is occurring in central as well as western Europe has been undramatic—and obscured by countervailing wars in the Balkans and the Caucasus. It flouts conventional wisdom to note that what is most striking about the savagery in these fringes of Europe in the 1990s is that it is in fact the exception, a phenomenon occurring at Europe's periphery but not its core. The heartland—and today this heartland already goes well beyond Carolingian Europe to include the whole space of the old Holy Roman Empire—is already postnational and no longer inclined to solve its problems through war. Against all the probabilities of history, the core Europe of prosperity and peace has already spread hundreds of miles to the east in just the decade following the fall of the Berlin Wall.

Europe's postnational change of consciousness is most pronounced, of course, among Germans, who recoiled from Hitler's atrocities by initially seeking to submerge their dishonored German identity in a larger European identity. The Christian Democratic party chairman, Wolfgang Schäuble, speaks for many when he says, "What is our national interest? Our overriding interest is stability in Europe, political, economic, and social stability. And this can be achieved only through the Atlantic Community and the EU. . . . It is not an act of altruism, but perhaps the result of a certain process of maturing or learning from earlier experience."[3]

The new cooperative mindset powerfully attracts non-Germans as well, as a way not only to avoid old-style German national domination, but also to maintain economic competitiveness in an age based on knowledge and loosed from geopolitics. Italy and Spain strove mightily to meet the criteria to become founding members of monetary union in 1999. Spain is joining the integrated military command of the North Atlantic Treaty Organization (NATO). Sweden, Finland,

and Austria, following the collapse of communism, have formally joined the commonwealth of the European Community/European Union (EC/EU) that for decades was in fact determining their economic environment. Austria, despite its neutral status, may be working up to entering NATO as well, and even Switzerland, while still eschewing membership in the United Nations, is participating in NATO Partnership for Peace exercises. Farther east, the central Europeans are clamoring to be admitted to both blue-ribbon western clubs, the EU and NATO.

Because they have generated neither telegenic bloodshed nor eight-second sound bites, these startling departures from centuries of more confrontational intercourse in international relations have gone largely unnoticed in the United States—but historically they are far more novel and significant than the resort to archaic chauvinism that is going on at Europe's margins. Voters in Poland deliberately rejected irredentism and right-wing anti-Europeanism in the 1990s—and, despite financial evidence to the contrary, rate themselves in opinion polls to be as much middle class as did Americans in the 1950s. Similarly, voters in Hungary, the country that was left with the largest number of compatriots outside its borders after the murders and dislocations of World War II, have rejected notions of the kind of greater Hungary their forebears claimed. And even the apparatchik Romanian government that ruled with anything but liberal leanings in the early 1990s agreed with Budapest on rights for the Hungarian minority in Transylvania. Repeatedly, these conciliatory choices resulted from the yearning by governments and citizens to qualify for admission to the magic circle of the EU and NATO.

In Bonn and Warsaw, then, the vision of the twenty-first century is one in which the western European nations progressively cede sovereignty to the EU and European Monetary Union (EMU), then look east to integrate central European states into their commonwealth. As it did for western Europe in the second half of the twentieth century, NATO, the European Union's military analog, provides the assurance of security—partly against any possible resurgence of Russian imperialism, partly against petty Balkan or other tyrants. And this assurance fosters in an ever widening circle the kind of trust and cooperation that developed in western Europe during the cold-war threat and has now become routine.

From this point of view the main task of European politics today is to institutionalize the expanding cooperation so that it will endure.

Just as post–World War II statesmen like Dean Acheson and Jean Monnet seized the opportunity to force the hitherto warring western European states to work together in the European Community and NATO, so today's leaders need to seize the opportunity to intensify west European collaboration and bring those willing and able central European states into the privileged community. This requires a new kind of self-confidence and a willingness to take political and economic risks.

Thus, in the case of European monetary union, no philosopher, historian, or economist can say whether or not the experiment will really work. But it was launched anyway in 1999. A critical mass of politicians, whose very livelihood depends on healthy caution, is daring this leap and bringing to the gamble the kind of political will that is usually associated with gung-ho Americans. EMU must work, the logic goes, or else we incur catastrophe. Therefore we will make it work. End of discussion.

Moreover, although monetary union is an elite project carried out despite popular disapproval, various ordinary Europeans are coming to share the spirit. Well before the 1999 inauguration, shopkeepers in Finland, Spain, and Italy were proudly advertising their countries' inclusion as founder-members of EMU by posting prices of goods in euros as well as in markka, pesetas, and lira. Even those conservative German voters who reelected Chancellor Helmut Kohl twice in the 1990s on the strength of his Adenauer-like promise of no experiments—and did not notice that he was plunging them into the biggest experiment of all—seem to be taking the surrender of their beloved deutsche mark in stride.[4] And certainly the Social Democrat who ousted Kohl in a landslide vote in 1998, Gerhard Schröder, dropped his misgivings about the euro when he became chancellor.

Much the same could be said about Europe's second grand project, enlargement of the EU and the North Atlantic Treaty Organization in the ambitious reuniting of a continent that was split at Yalta in 1945. In its own way this enterprise is just as bold, and just as unprecedented, as monetary union. No central European country, with the exception of the Czech lands, was a practicing democracy or had reached western European economic levels before World War II.[5] And all suffered from dysfunctional economies and politics in the half century of Soviet hegemony. Yet the optimism of Poland especially, the largest of the central European nations, is striking. Their tragic history has inclined Poles to fatalism. But today an upbeat mood is prevalent as they lead the reforms and economic recovery in the region. Their centuries-old inferiority complex toward the Germans is gone—in part, because they have compared themselves with the east German recipients of Bonn's largesse and have realized proudly that although they are poor, their 6 percent–plus growth is the result of their own efforts, with no charity from others. This self-assurance has enabled them at last to feel at ease with the surrounding Germans, Ukrainians, and even Russians.

Escape from History

In 1990 neither the western nor the central European success was foreordained. Serious commentators warned that the post–World War II era of EC (and transatlantic) cooperation was an aberration, no more than an emergency response to the existential and ahistorical Soviet threat. With that Soviet threat gone, defense would now be "renationalized"—that is, revert from routine NATO–alliance cooperation to fierce nineteenth-century style national clashes. Transatlantic trade wars would have nothing to constrain them. In the turbulence following the certainties of the cold war, the Europeans would revert to nasty balance-of-power free-for-alls. France and Germany would no longer be held to their marriage of convenience. The United States might well bring the GIs home and fall back into traditional isolationism. The United States's abdication of its role as mediator would aggravate old intra-European antagonisms—between Britain and Germany, between the rich north and the poor Mediterranean, certainly between Greece and Turkey.

Predictions about nations to the east were even more dire as the new would-be democracies underwent impossible instant economic, political, social, and institutional revolutions, at a dizzying speed that no Western nation ever had to match during the slow evolution of complex democratic and free-market practices. These nations of central and eastern Europe had to build capitalist economies from scratch, with suspicious peasantries but no stable middle class, at a time when western Europe itself had sunk into recession and could offer no saving market. Given the wrenching change, skyrocketing prices, ruined savings, and loss of meager but steady social benefits in the early transition, there was a high risk that disoriented voters would equate de-

mocracy with misery rather than with plenty and would turn to popu-
lists for salvation. Many observers feared the spread of Yugoslav-style
xenophobia as the Soviet lid was removed, releasing passions from
the pressure cooker of central Europe's old rival nationalisms.

In the case of Poland, the largest central European country, there
was also grave doubt that the heroic streak that was so magnificent
during the century of Polish partition could assimilate the contrary
art of democratic compromise. Indeed, Solidarity saint Lech Walesa
became president by inciting a baleful "war at the top" and running
against Solidarity prime minister Tadeusz Mazowiecki. The resultant
clash within Solidarity temporarily threatened to vault Stanislaw
Tyminski, an unknown populist émigré interloper, into the presidency;
and the first fully free parliamentary elections seated twenty-nine squab-
bling mini-parties in the Polish parliament, the Sejm.

Nevertheless, western Europe discovered that its European Community was in fact more than just an anomaly. Even after the Soviet
Union collapsed in 1991, the West did not revert to Hobbesian anarchy; the greatly feared renationalization of trade and security issues
never took place. The benefits of European Community cooperation
and of NATO's shared defense proved far too attractive to discard.
Both organizations turned out to be hardy enough to survive even the
loss of the enemy.

France had forfeited the most influence of any country as a result
of German unification and the subsequent devaluation of nuclear
weapons, revaluation of the deutsche mark, and extension of Europe
proper to the east. Nonetheless, France concluded that the only way
to beat the rising Germans was to stay joined to them. The quaint
French notion of the 1960s and 1970s that the French political rider
would steer the German economic workhorse dissipated. At the same
time, the small countries that have had such a disproportionately large
say in the EC and the EU became resigned to lowering their voices so
as to preserve the EU's ability to act.

United Germany, alone for a long time in the conviction that deepening and widening of the EU are not only compatible but complementary, drove both processes by sheer political will. Chancellor Kohl,
with his first dream of German unification fulfilled, single-mindedly
pursued his second dream of making European integration irreversible.[6] This was, he preached melodramatically, "a question of war and
peace."[7] To be sure, he had to give up his goal of European political

union. But with time he expected EMU to create its own pressures for more political integration—and he also expected the threat of gridlock as the EU doubles in size to create its own pressures for more veto-proof majority voting. In this context, timing did not matter so much, despite the artificial debate in the United States about whether NATO or the EU would admit new members first. What was important was to get EMU and EU expansion started and let the central Europeans know they could count on eventual EU membership.

Moreover, the transatlantic alliance has endured. President Bill Clinton and a bipartisan congressional leadership bridged the period when the United States might have withdrawn into itself after the cold war was won; Congress finally approved the rescue of NATO even at the cost of stationing GIs in Bosnia. The United States shares its burden as a superpower and magnifies its influence by steady engagement in Europe, Clinton argued successfully. So firmly did he commit a new generation of politicians to the alliance that the Senate's big debate about NATO enlargement hardly raised the fundamental question of whether GIs should be in Europe at all half a century after World War II. And for their part, the West Europeans—despite periodic irritation with American know-it-alls—concluded yet again that they prefer U.S. leadership in security matters to sorting out European leadership among themselves.

Contemplating the new phenomena, senior British diplomat Robert Cooper concludes radically that we are witnessing the end, not only of the cold war, but of the whole continental system that has prevailed since the Peace of Westphalia in 1648. In our "post-modern" world European nation-states no longer pursue exclusive national interests with a heedless zero-sum reckoning. In an electronic age in which territory hardly matters, nations have little desire—except in the Balkans and the Caucasus—to acquire each other's terrain. As a consequence, the stunning new fact is, as Cooper says, that "Western European countries no longer want to fight each other." This approach goes well beyond the "crude" hope of earlier decades "that states which merge their industries cannot fight each other." It rests on the realization that war and conquest in Europe are no longer useful in the present era.[8] It sanctions unprecedented outside interference in members' domestic affairs. It presumes a new relationship mixing both cooperation and competition in what the business world is already calling "coopetition." And it is simultaneously bringing the central Europeans into the family and enabling them to catch up with the West's prosperity and new-found peace for the first time in a millennium.

Oddly, the bipolar cold war—which Cooper regards not as an exception, but rather as an extreme form of the nineteenth-century balance of power—froze political Europe long enough for the new realization about the virtues of the West's transnational cooperation to sink in. The EC's four decades of teamwork proved to have been habit-forming. And the Community's sister organization, NATO—though it first seemed to be no more than a traditional defense alliance against a powerful adversary—also transformed relations among the allies themselves. In the 1950s it introduced a permanent integrated multinational command. In the 1960s it supplemented this with a mutual review of each member's medium-term defense planning that let every nation see clearly its allies' military capabilities and intentions. The resulting transparency strongly inhibited aggression or any slide into hostilities, while promoting progressive transnational collaboration, even in the sensitive realm of weapons manufacture. By now, no NATO member could possibly launch a surprise attack even on an outside country—as Britain and France did in 1956 in trying to recapture the nationalized Suez Canal from Egypt—without the previous knowledge of its partners.

If the rhetoric of current leaders does not reflect this extraordinary transformation and evoke a United States of Europe as Winston Churchill did after World War II, the reason may be found in the twentieth century's disillusionment with all utopias. Post–cold war Europe is wary of grand designs. Modesty, not charisma, is the hallmark of this new beginning. Contemporary statesmen see themselves as carpenters, not as architects. And there is virtue in such diffidence, argues Michael Mertes, domestic adviser to Chancellor Kohl in the 1990s. It demonstrates the loss of a Hegelian trust in a dialectic of progress of the nineteenth-century variety. It shows a healthy skepticism and sobriety after the failure of utopian visions, which are in any case superfluous in the presence of vigorous pragmatic action. "We are in a phase in which we are implementing the great projects conceived at the end of the 1980s and the beginning of the 1990s," asserts Mertes. European monetary union, the first project, will itself compel further needed changes in EU institutions. And "widening to the east, the second grand task," will not only bring added security to Germany and central Europe, but will increasingly spread stability from Poland to its east. "It's a kind of reverse domino theory," he concludes. "You might say that the lack of great visions is a good sign, because at the moment there is so much to do."[9]

The perspective of Mertes—as of the bulk of the German political and bureaucratic elite—offers hope for the future. But a century ago Europe also exhibited optimism in expecting constant progress, only to have this faith shattered by the carnage of World Wars I and II. Are the twentieth century's five decades of peace, then, just as much a false dawn as the four decades of peace before the guns of August 1914?

No, because of the A-bomb above all, thinks Dominique Moisi, deputy director of the French Institute of International Relations, savoring the irony of this blackest of reasons for hope. "The big difference today is that, to a large extent because of nuclear weapons, the return of war in a classical sense, if not excluded, is at least very far-fetched. It's a totally new phenomenon in world history."[10]

Besides, adds Wladyslaw Bartoszewski, Polish foreign minister in the mid-1990s, people have learned caution precisely because twentieth-century history was so terrible. He declares, "I am a practicing Christian, and I have faith in the capacity of people to change." He speaks as both a historian of the twentieth century and a participant in that history, a veteran of Nazi and Communist jails, and the only central European member of the commission that tracked Nazi gold in Swiss banks. Delving into the past, he compares the current metamorphosis with the first birth of a European consciousness in the Middle Ages. And he believes the current Polish foreign minister, distinguished medieval historian Bronislaw Geremek, has the best possible training for that job.[11]

Europe's Miracles

Geremek, less shy than his Western counterparts about using romantic language, seizes every opportunity to hark back to the eleventh-century east-west summit in Krakow between Otto III of the Holy Roman Empire and Boleslaw the Brave of Poland. The wish of these two rulers to unite their empires was not realized, Geremek notes, until a thousand years later, as part of the miracle of the present chain reaction of reconciliation in Europe.

In this chain, the first miracle was the French-German rapprochement, after almost two centuries of bitter enmity. So successful was the personal reconciliation that today's young French and Germans take it for granted and find incomprehensible their great-grandparents' assumption that contests between these two neighbors would periodically burst into war. So solid is the political fraternity that it now prevails, time and again, even over major bilateral differences over the European Central Bank, economic pump-priming, and the very goals of European Union.

The second miracle, perhaps, was the rejuvenation of the European Community in the mid-1980s, as it roused itself from Eurosclerosis to aim for that real single market by 1992. This new momentum ensured that subsequent German unification could be embedded in a larger European framework rather than bursting that framework. Unlike 1871, 1914, or 1939, this latest rise of German power has been peaceful. Today we are finally getting Thomas Mann's European Germany, and not a German Europe. Or, rather, it is a German Europe as forged by a very European Germany.

The third miracle was the annus mirabilis itself, 1989, and its aftermath. Against all the odds of history, the world's last great empire, the Soviet Union, collapsed without bloodshed, except in Romania. There were many to thank for this: the stubborn Polish Solidarity free trade union, American deterrence, Soviet president Mikhail Gorbachev, the 70,000 Leipzigers who expected to get shot but still turned out to demonstrate for freedom on October 9 and foreshadowed the opening of the Berlin Wall a month later. The Czechs—concluding that in Gorbachev's world, if enough demonstrators gathered, the police would not shoot—came next. The Bulgarians and Romanians—and then the Lithuanians and Muscovites—followed with their own street protests that toppled communist governments. Russia's internal as well as external empire disintegrated. And the central Europeans, with the democratic Germans as their new tribunes for admission into the Western organizations, began modernizing and escaped their perennial suspension between a big, predatory Russia and a big, predatory Germany.

The cornerstone of the benign central European evolution was the reconciliation that had long been pending between Germany and Poland, the country that had suffered the highest per capita death rate of any large nation under Nazi occupation. The two countries signed treaties pledging friendship and recognizing as permanent the post–World War II border realignment that awarded German Silesia and parts of East Prussia to Poland. Kohl gambled on opening the Polish-German frontier, despite all the fears about a flood of immigrants from a region with wages only a tenth of those in western Europe.[12] And Germany, determined not to be western Europe's border on the East any longer, joined the United States in prodding their allies to help the Poles and other central Europeans join the West by providing them with financial aid, technology, managerial know-how, and institutional models.

Most of all, of course, in the new climate the central Europeans helped themselves by emulating the golden West. They craved membership in the EU and NATO, and they altered their behavior significantly in order to qualify. In varying degree they instituted rule of law, with protection of human rights, minorities, and commercial contracts. They set up independent judiciaries and allowed robust media to emerge. They privatized business. They accepted World Bank and International Monetary Fund conditions of austerity and did not make the IMF the scapegoat for the agony of modernization. They passed legislation to align themselves with EU requirements. They nurtured an incipient civil society. And the central European governments were not even deterred by the prospect of subordinating much of their newly acquired full sovereignty to the EU and a European Court of Justice empowered to sit in judgment over national laws.

To show their readiness for NATO membership, the governments raced to establish civilian control of their militaries and to open their defense planning to outside scrutiny. Poland began exporting stability, in part by donating weapons to the infant Lithuanian army, in part by forming joint peacekeeping units with its Ukrainian and Baltic neighbors, and generally blurring the new line between East and West as much as possible. Even noncandidate Ukraine, eager to have the alliance's nimbus radiate beyond the designated candidates for NATO membership, set aside disputed claims to Serpent Island to sign a friendship treaty with Romania and made the most of its opportunities under NATO's Partnership for Peace program.

Central Europeans are already reaping the rewards for their strenuous efforts. They have begun the march toward EU prosperity. They regard NATO membership as insurance against any imperial recidivism on the part of Russia and against any military contagion from the Balkans. Most fundamentally, they regard their admission to the West's premier clubs as certification, at last, of their Western identity. For them, this signifies deliverance from centuries of being the passive victims of history to becoming codeterminants of their own destiny.

Europe's final contemporary miracle might be identified as the new energy on the continent. To be sure, Europeans agonize about ruthless globalization, about their 17 million unemployed, their loss of competitiveness to American rivals, and the crippling costs of their social welfare. But the dynamism is real. So is the intuition that one must use to the full the rare historical gift of choice in an era when old institutions have dissolved but new ones have not yet solidified. The propitious moment must now be seized, to build a European Union that can save Germans from themselves and Europeans from themselves. "Such a historic opportunity doesn't come often," warns one senior German diplomat. "And if we give it up frivolously for a return to nationalism and protectionism, coming generations will never forgive us."[13]

And so European monetary union is proceeding, with an unanticipated normative and disciplining power to force down inflation rates and budget deficits across the continent. After prodigious efforts, even Italy and Spain are participating from the beginning, and Greece intends to qualify in a few years. At the same time, central Europe is beginning to get the payoff from austerity during its painful first transition years. Northern central Europe, at least, has finally rebuilt the quantitative gross domestic product (GDP) it had when the communist systems collapsed, on a much sounder qualitative base. Poland, with close to the fastest growth in Europe today, should essentially catch up with the western European standard of living in a generation or two—for the first time in a thousand years.

That is the European self-image.

American Skepticism

American observers have a more jaundiced view of Europe. In a capsule, elite conventional wisdom reads like this:

Henry Kissinger's famous taunt—What telephone number do I call for Europe? —is as justified as ever. Without the Soviet threat to compel unity, Europe is relapsing into nationalism and war and the natural anarchy of international relations. Yugoslavia is a harbinger. The Europeans had their chance to deal with Bosnia, and fumbled it, as they are fumbling the Kosovo crisis. Deepening and widening are irreconcilable, and the Europeans are acting either hypocritically or irresponsibly in trying to do both. And small central European countries must still be the object, not the subject, of policy, subordinate to the West's more important relations with the former superpower, Russia.

Internally, Europeans squabble over mad cows. While the United States has the lowest unemployment in memory, Europe has 17 million unemployed officially (and maybe 27 million in real numbers) and has forgotten how to create new jobs or venture capital. The exorbitant welfare entitlements of European countries smother initiative. The old continent is in crisis and will not admit it. Monetary union is an incantation; it is going ahead, but probably should not. There is a public backlash against the 1992 Maastricht Treaty establishing the European Union; Helmut Kohl had to give up his chimera of European political union.[14] Europe plunged ahead in an upbeat mood as it pulled out of recession in the mid-1990s, but in the present world financial crisis, true to form, European integration will again stagnate or regress. The consensus system of fifteen very different members produces only stasis. Europe is a museum of the past.

This is a simplification, but not a falsification, of much mainstream writing about Europe in the United States.[15]

The rebuttal from Bonn and Warsaw, equally compressed, would read something like this: You Americans have been misled by the neorealist school into expecting only Hobbesian contests among European nations in the wake of cold-war bipolarity. Conversely, you are setting up a straw man when you measure European integration against some imagined United States of Europe and conclude that it is failing. The new hybrid we are developing pragmatically does not fit on any hypothetical charts. It falls well short of your federation, but it also goes well beyond what you understand as a confederation, in which commonalities have to be thrashed out anew with each fresh transaction. It lets national identity and idiosyncrasies flourish, but it also authorizes a growing area of pre-agreed united action in trade negotiations and in the whole acquis communautaire, the 80,000 pages of laws and regulations already adopted. However ungainly it may appear, the EU continues to function because it brings tangible benefit to its members. The old Westphalian nation-state is no longer an option in Europe; it is simply too small to be viable. The megadeaths of World Wars I and II, the existential nuclear threat, Chernobyl, and today's digital globalization have all impressed this truth on central Europeans and even on the French, if not yet fully the British. We are already pooling our sovereignty to a remarkable degree. And in synergy with you in NATO, we are performing the historic task of drawing central Europe into the West's circumference of peace and prosperity.

Yes, Europe (like America) did fail the test of Yugoslav breakup. But in the end the Balkan atrocities and humiliations finally compelled the West to do the right thing there and in the process to reorient NATO for twenty-first-century crisis management.

Yes, European unemployment is a blight, and it will not be easy for us to regain the competitiveness lost in the past decade. But our business cycles differ. While we applaud your record in job creation and will try to emulate you, we regard the 1990s more as your turn to surge than as evidence of our permanent inferiority. We may all be in for a difficult time for a few years as we ride out the Asian, Russian, and Latin American crises, but Europe has already begun its own round of boosting productivity. And in the interim, before we liberalize our labor markets and reduce long-term unemployment, our compassionate social net will enable the jobless to lead decent lives even in the midst of wrenching change; we have no explosive underclass. Currency union is focusing minds on fiscal discipline throughout Europe and will make our bottlenecks obvious so we can correct them.

Europe is indeed in a structural crisis, the Europeans continue—but this very crisis is impelling unprecedented cooperation. It is a high-risk venture. But not acting together would pose even greater risk. And the present course promises high reward, if competitiveness can be restored and if this war-prone continent can banish mass bloodshed in an ever-widening arc. Central Europe, with its low wages, well-educated workers, and pent-up consumer demand, will help the whole European continent. Already Poland, with its fast growth, expects to produce half as much as output in the much larger Russian Federation by the early twenty-first century, points out former finance minister Grzegorz Kolodko.[16]

Birth Pangs and Birth

What accounts, then, for the stark difference in the view of Europe on the two sides of the Atlantic? Why do Americans see only the birth pangs, while the Europeans experience the birth?

Again, from the point of view of Bonn and Warsaw, Americans would seem to be prisoners of previous patterns in their stereotypes, even as the old patterns are dissolving. They seek to squeeze the emerging Europe into a nineteenth-century mold of nationalism, into old cold-war definitions of power, or perhaps into Gaullist expectations. They have been strongly influenced—especially before Prime Minister Tony Blair brought a friendlier view of the continent to 10 Downing Street—by British Tory fears about being sucked into some homogenized, bureaucratic Europe. And, it must be added, they have been reinforced in their dismissal of the EU by the absence in Brussels of staff reporters for any major American periodical other than the *Wall Street Journal*. No journalist for a general quality newspaper or news magazine in the United States scrutinizes the increasingly central institution of the EU the way, say, the *Financial Times* does. The American political class therefore lacks the osmosis of the European system that it might acquire from daily exposure to it.

Judged by traditional categories, of course, Europe is ineffectual. It lacks the glue of any single nationalism or any other overarching purpose beyond the dry rationality of cooperation in an era of interdependence. Ever since Hitler's terrible abuse of patriotic loyalty, Europe's more responsible politicians have eschewed emotional appeals. In consequence, Europe as a whole has a "myth deficit," as Munich historian Wolfgang Schmale points out.[17] It has never articulated the goals of integration in a way that would stir the hearts of its citizens, let alone convince outsiders of its dynamism.

Besides, a superpower with the fierce national pride of the United States can hardly credit the willing surrender of sovereignty by smaller nation-states that is now occurring in Europe. Many American commentators argue, on the contrary, that resurgent nationalism is the key that explains everything since the dissolution of Soviet hegemony in eastern Europe. As proof, they point to the war in Chechnya, the war of the Yugoslav succession, and Abkhazian (and Flemish and Walloonian) separatism. Nationalism is patently growing, not shrinking, they assert. So why—they asked until a scant few months before EMU became a reality—should a reunited, newly sovereign Germany, with the third-largest economy in the world, voluntarily denationalize the Bundesbank and cede its might to a less predictable and more diffuse European Central Bank? Or, obversely, why should countries surrounding Germany rush to melt their identities into a greater Europe that the economic giant of Germany must necessarily dominate?

Furthermore, superpower America knows that Europe cannot make its military weight felt without the support of American airlift and intelligence and nuclear umbrella. Even if it could, Europe has no single political authority to apply that capability. Oddly enough, for the country that invented the "soft power" of persuasion and example, the United States does not seem to recognize the potency of agenda-setting or the habit-forming nature of daily consultation and compromise across Europe on everything from drug running to passports.[18] These matters are low politics, Americans argue; when push comes to shove in high politics, only the British and French, acting as nations—and certainly not the poor man's NATO of the Western European Union— are capable of dispatching troops and pilots to restore peace and order.

An additional reason for U.S. dismissal of confederation-plus consensus politics within the EU follows from American incomprehension of the consensual style of national politics in the Germanic and Low Countries. For all of their similarities, each democracy has its own peculiar mixture of cooperation and confrontation. The United States favors a robust clash of opposing interests until compromise is finally hammered out. Many Europeans, by contrast, practice a consensus or even corporatist style of politics that translates easily into the backroom give-and-take of EU tradeoffs.[19]

The U.S. sense of European impotence is only enhanced by a widespread continued fixation on the one-time superpower adversary, even though Russia's army is in disarray and Russia's GDP is now less than Spain's. The preoccupation is understandable. The central Europeans do not have nuclear weapons to claim Western attention, and all Soviet successor states other than Russia that inherited Soviet nuclear missiles have renounced them. Besides, in Russia itself nuclear weapons are in some ways more dangerous now than during the cold war, since controls on them have slackened and since Moscow is compensating for its current weakness in conventional military forces with a new military doctrine of first nuclear use.[20] These circumstances— plus the need to avoid stoking resentment and humiliating a weak Russia as Germany was humiliated after World War I—require extra solicitude of Moscow, the argument runs, even at the expense of central European concerns. The overriding priority must be to ensure Russian adherence to START II arms control, and this requires sublimation of central European interests.

One final explanation for the downbeat American reading of European integration is perhaps psychological. Intellectually, it is less risky to be pessimistic than to be optimistic. It is always easier to reconstruct old shapes than to decipher new ones, in any case—and the old European configurations of hegemonic totalitarianism in this century and balance of power in the last certainly invite pessimism. Then, too, predictions of failure take a long time to be proven wrong (rather than simply delayed in impact), while predictions of success, which presume that all key elements will succeed together, can be confounded momentarily by any single spoiler. Finally—since the German movers and shakers of European integration unconsciously use pessimism the way Americans use optimism, to galvanize corrective action—periodic German alarums can be overinterpreted by onlookers.

In the aggregate, these instincts colored U.S. commentary on Europe until the very eve of the launch of monetary union. In late 1997 Martin Feldstein, president of the National Bureau of Economic Research, went so far as to ask whether Europe's quest for a common currency might not unleash a new war.[21] Veteran diplomatic analyst John Newhouse still expected Germany to lurch in an anti–EU direction, saw EMU as a "massive distraction" that would very likely produce "economic chaos," believed that eastern enlargement was "unlikely in the foreseeable future," and called the whole sorry mess "a collective nervous breakdown."[22] Noting these and other "funereal" warnings, a *Financial Times* columnist rued the "intellectual gulf" between European perceptions and the American obsession with the "famine, pestilence, and war" that European monetary union would supposedly set off.[23] In February 1998 Irving Kristol, the dean of American neoconservatives, still expected the combination of a common European currency and statist continental economies to generate crisis and perpetuate high unemployment, thus "subverting the political institutions of the nations in the [European] union," leading to "ultimate impoverishment," and reinforcing the "hedonistic" refusal of young Europeans to procreate in adequate numbers.[24] *New York Times* columnist William Safire added his disapproval of "Alice in Euroland" as EU heads of government gathered to found the European Central Bank in May of 1998.[25]

By then straight news coverage, as distinct from commentary, in the United States turned at least neutral or even positive.[26] The shift came far too late, however, to prepare the general American reader intelligently for the realities of monetary union.

Despite the widespread "funereal" U.S. perception of Europe, the real surprise at this end of a terrible century is not the atavistic wars at the margins of Europe, but rather the absence of war in all those other places where blind, repetitive history might have decreed it. Today the magnetic attraction of the voluntary Western system of peace and prosperity for those states in the cursed space between the Germans and the Russians has a benign effect, subduing chauvinism and reinforcing moderation. Europe's blessed zone of peace and prosperity is expanding—and thereby enhancing American security. The new paradigm is not, after all, the atrocities of the former Yugoslavia, or even the old nineteenth-century balance-of-power jostling. It is an unaccustomed reconciliation in the heart of Europe, between France and Germany, Germany and Poland, Poland and Ukraine, Romania and Hungary, Germany and the Netherlands. In Bartoszewski's simile, Europe is indeed experiencing, after a millennium, its second birth.

CHAPTER TWO

The European Community during the Cold War

In the beginning was the cold war. Or so it must have seemed to the generation of leaders who governed in the 1980s. U.S. president George Bush had come of age as the youngest combat pilot in the U.S. Navy in World War II and become a congressman in 1967 at the height of the Vietnam War. Chancellor Helmut Kohl had lost a brother in Hitler's war, had pulled corpses out of bombed buildings as a teenager, and never forgot the chocolate distributed by GIs in occupied Germany. Soviet president Mikhail Gorbachev had attended university after Stalin's death, but rose through the nomenklatura communist elite that took Leninist struggle with the West as a given. Polish president Wojciech Jaruzelski, despite the repressions his own parents had endured at the hands of the Soviet regime, was still a janissary in the Warsaw Pact machine as a general of the Polish army.

In retrospect, the cold war years were good ones for Western Europe. To be sure, they began with some of the coldest winters and one of the worst droughts in memory, with near famine, cramped living space, shortages of everything, cities in ruins. There were millions of displaced persons. Manufacturing, trade, and societies themselves had broken down. The black market rewarded the criminal and punished the honest. Italy and France looked vulnerable to communist pied pipers. Even Britain, spared the worst ravages of World War II, had to ration bread after the war, for the first time—and to ration tea, its national drink, until 1951. Grain acreage in France was 25 percent below prewar levels, and the balance-of-payments deficit of Britain, France, Italy, and the British and American sectors of Germany was $5 billion, for a subminimal standard of living.[1] The most terrible weapon known to man foreshadowed the very annihilation of the human race. Edvard Munch's painting "The Scream" was the emblem of the age.

In Germany, Dresden was so thoroughly firebombed that not even the old city blocks were discernible. Daily diets in the British zone of occupation were 1,150 calories, less than half the League of Nations norm of 3,000. The average weight for men in the better-supplied American sector was 112 pounds. Beyond the war dead, at least 1 million persons died after the war in the revenge expulsion of ethnic Germans from Silesia and the Sudetenland. The 10 million who lived through the trek and now constituted a sixth of the West German population had to be fed, clothed, and given jobs in a nonfunctioning economy in the Federal Republic. Inflation, while not reaching the wheelbarrow levels of the 1920s, made the Reichsmark so valueless that cigarettes and even cigarette butts were the more reliable currency. Bread cost 30 to 40 times its official price, butter and cooking oil more than 100 times. Well into the 1970s, photos of World War II survivors were displayed on public bulletin boards in an effort to bring separated families together again. And for an increasing number of Germans, there was shame and horror at the genocide of the Jews in the land of Immanuel Kant and Johann Wolfgang von Goethe.

But the slaughter of 45 million was over. In the American zone military governor General Lucius D. Clay basically ignored his orders to punish Germany and prevent it from ever rising again. On second thought the United States launched the Marshall Plan to help pump dollars into the system, restore trade and distribution of food, and help even Germany to recover by providing once again producer goods for the continent. The International Monetary Fund (IMF), the World Bank, and the General Agreement on Tariffs and Trade (GATT) were invented to kick-start the world system of finance and commerce. And in the incredible eleven-month airlift after the Soviet Union blocked land routes to beleaguered West Berlin, Allied cargo planes landed every ninety seconds to keep the half-city alive with 8,000 daily tons of meat, milk, vegetables, coal, raisins for the children—and, on one memorable occasion, a live camel. West Berliners lived without electricity, gas, or public transport, listened for the comforting drone of the aircraft, suddenly viewed their Western occupiers as protectors, and occasionally visited Tempelhof airport to bestow heirlooms on the pilots in gratitude. The North Atlantic Treaty Organization was founded; American troops came back to the continent to reassure Europeans that this time the United States would stay engaged and defend them against the Soviet empire; a unique peacetime integrated command was formed. And, in one of many ingenious innovations (this one after the United States thwarted the British and French expedition to recapture the Suez canal in 1956 following its nationalization by Egypt), NATO effected military transparency among its members by allowing them to review each other's detailed medium-term defense plans. The intent was to apply peer pressure to hold nations to common infrastructure and readiness goals in a season of budget cuts—but the result was unprecedented military openness among allies.

No such robust reconstruction awaited the East Europeans. The Soviets plundered East German industry lock, stock, and barrel. The Poles, Czechs, and Hungarians were forbidden by the Soviets to accept any Marshall Plan largesse. Czechoslovakia's model light industry and respectable prewar democracy were crushed by Soviet central planning of both economics and politics. Poland had to accept a Russian as its defense minister. Prague's imitative show trials exhibited both tragedy and farce as prosecutor and witnesses mangled the lines dictated to them by their Soviet masters—and the victims were executed anyway. Eastern Europe stagnated in the two generations in which Western Europe recovered, grew rich, and spread its wealth across a large and growing middle class.

For France, treated as a victorious ally despite the Vichy regime's collaboration with Hitler, the cold war was cozy. Charles de Gaulle again gave the country coherence and even a bit of glory. France's German problem seemed to have been solved by the division and political delegitimization of its powerful neighbor. As author François Mauriac is famously quoted as saying, "I love Germany so much, it makes me happy to have two of them."[2] France had a privileged role as one of the permanent members of the United Nations Security Council, an occupying power in Germany along with the United States, Britain, and the Soviet Union, and one of only five nuclear states in the world. It could anticipate, in the commonly voiced simile, that an increasingly prosperous Germany would be the economic horse, but France would be the political rider that determined the course of Europe. The buffer zone of West Germany and NATO's nuclear guarantee of the Federal Republic gave France the security behind which it could occasionally flirt with the Soviet Union and tweak Uncle Sam's nose.

The Federal Republic of Germany, too, for all the existential angst of living in the nuclear front line, led a comfortable life in the cold war. NATO, as Lord Ismay noted pithily, was designed to keep the Soviets out, the Americans in, and the Germans down. Yet that "down"— after fierce domestic controversy Germany rearmed and joined the alliance in 1955—was as much blessing as curse. Often enough it allowed the Germans the luxury of abdicating from messy security situations in their environs. And above all, it neatly solved the dilemma of European leadership in which no Belgian would defer to France, no Irish to the United Kingdom, and certainly no other European to Germany. The Europeans found that they liked having the outsider United States lead them (as long, of course, as it was in the direction they wanted to go). Often enough, they also liked the very fact that the United States was big enough to cut through prolonged debate and force a decision—even if they did not agree with specific policies. And relief from excess burdens of defense freed the Germans to concentrate on their new economic miracle and social market contract, according entrepreneurs low profits but promising them as compensation labor stability and generous pensions when they finally retired.

Behind the NATO shield, then, France, Germany, and the rest of Western Europe could begin their unprecedented integration. The United States pushed them in this direction by requiring recipients of Marshall Plan aid to administer the funds jointly. Visionaries like French foreign minister Robert Schuman and planning commissar Jean Monnet went further in proposing the European Coal and Steel Community (ECSC)—and France endorsed this as a way to ensure that Germany would never again be able to build a war machine on the basis of its mining and heavy industry in the Saar and Ruhr valleys. France, Germany, Italy, and the Benelux countries duly formed the ECSC in 1951, and two years later instituted a common market for coal, iron ore, scrap, and steel. In the mid-1950s they added nuclear collaboration in EURATOM. In 1957 they signed the Treaty of Rome, establishing the European Economic Community (EEC), which would aim for a common market with the "four freedoms" of unhindered movement of goods, services, capital, and people.

At the heart of this new experiment was an explicit attempt to solve the recurring problem of a Germany that was bigger and, all too often, more aggressive and efficient than its neighbors. Memory of the wars of 1870, 1914, and 1939 hung in the air as Belgian foreign minister Paul-Henri Spaak praised Germany's "passionately pro-European" founding father, Konrad Adenauer, and advocated European institutions' embracing Germany as "the most effective, and perhaps the only means to defend Germany from itself. . . . European integration gives Germany a framework to limit its expansion, and creates a community of interests that gives it security, while securing us against certain probes and adventures."[3]

Specifically, the Treaty of Rome resulted in a French-German deal and a small–big deal. In the former, Paris got subsidies for its farmers, while Bonn got an open market in Europe for its industrial goods (and also profited, especially in Bavaria, from agricultural support). In the latter bargain Belgium, Luxembourg, and the Netherlands got augmented votes in EEC decisions out of proportion to their tiny populations and were also ensured one commissioner each (as against two each for France, Germany, and Italy) in the quasi cabinet and secretariat that was to write agendas, run daily operations, and generally represent common rather than national interests. With time, the small states would come to regard the European Commission as their special shield against any directorate by the large states.

The other new EEC institutions were the European Council, the European Court of Justice, and the European Parliament. Of these, the European Parliament started out as—and has continued to be—the weakest. The European Council, consisting of the roving summits of the leaders of the still sovereign member states, was and is the dominant body. It shares executive powers with the commission and legislative powers with both the commission and the parliament, but always from a commanding position.[4] The council had no permanent structure but constituted itself in ad hoc meetings among all six finance or agricultural ministers or, at summit level, of all six heads of government or state. It was and is "a more or less permanent negotiating forum and recurrent international conference, yet its primary members are ministers drawn from the member states," according to the best single study of it. It is "unashamedly national," directly accountable not to the commission, but "to national parliaments and national electorates."[5] With time, the council would come to operate on a day-

to-day level through the powerful Committee of Permanent Representatives (Coreper) in Brussels, which officially prepares for the ministerial council meetings, but in fact itself thrashes out solutions to
perhaps two-thirds of issues without having to pass them up to ministerial level.

Efforts to form a European defense community to parallel the economic community failed, rejected by the French National Assembly.
Efforts to imitate the European Economic Community in surrounding countries succeeded, as Denmark, Sweden, Norway, Britain, Austria, Switzerland, and Portugal formed their own European Free Trade
Association (EFTA).

No sooner had the EEC been founded than Berlin entered its last
great crisis of the cold war. In 1958 the new Soviet premier and Communist party general-secretary, Nikita Khrushchev, demanded that
(West) Berlin be demilitarized. He threatened to abandon Soviet guar-
antees for the city by formally turning over its sector to the (East)
German Democratic Republic (GDR), which would not be bound by
earlier Soviet pledges. In that same year Charles de Gaulle returned to
public life to save a France rent by colonial wars in Algeria and
Indochina and by weak, shifting governments. In 1960 John F. Kennedy
was elected president of the United States; in 1961 he was bullied at
his maiden superpower summit by a Khrushchev who thought the
first cosmonaut in space demonstrated the superiority that would enable the Soviet Union to "bury" the West. In August of that year the
Berlin wall went up overnight to seal off half of the city; in October
American and Soviet tanks confronted each other nose to nose at
Checkpoint Charlie. Only later did it become clear that the three-year
Berlin crisis was actually over now, with West Berlin's rights preserved
and with East Berlin's wall having stopped the hemorrhage of the GDR's
best and brightest to the West.

The French-German Tandem

The French-German special relationship grew out of the Berlin crisis—and stumbled almost immediately. Adenauer worried at first that
Paris might be tempted to make a separate deal with Moscow in order
to remove Soviet support for Algerian rebels, and de Gaulle worried
reciprocally that Bonn might make a separate deal with Moscow in

order to ease the pressure on West Berlin. In the event, neither wavered. Throughout the three years of Soviet probes, de Gaulle stood firm against any encroachment on the enclave of West Berlin in a way the British did not—and the Americans might not—Adenauer thought. De Gaulle, the French "prince of ambiguity," did upset Adenauer by secretly sounding out the Americans and the British about developing a permanent three-power directorate for Europe that would exclude Bonn. But in the end Adenauer and de Gaulle needed each other too much to let their mutual wariness stand in the way. The defeated and discredited Germany craved the legitimacy conferred by France; Paris craved the homage to French leadership in Europe that neither the British nor the Americans would grant. After a hundred hours of private talks, the two grand old men signed the French-German Treaty of Friendship in January of 1963.

A week earlier de Gaulle had vetoed what he called the Anglo-Saxon "Trojan horse" of British entry into the Common Market. That veto, along with de Gaulle's anti-American reading of the French-German treaty, set off alarm bells among leading politicians in Adenauer's Christian Democratic Union. The redoubtable Franz Josef Strauss of the CDU's junior Bavarian sister, the Christian Social Union, was willing to toy with a Gaullist course for Germany, and Adenauer himself thought he could play the field shrewdly enough to keep special relationships with both Paris and Washington. But Ludwig Erhard, the father of Germany's economic miracle, vehemently opposed any tilt toward France. Other CDU lieutenants were already in the process of forcing the octogenarian Adenauer to resign for other reasons, and they combined to write a unilateral preamble to the treaty that was a slap in de Gaulle's face. As passed unanimously by the Bundestag in the ratification process, the preamble called for "a close partnership between Europe and the United States of America"; integration in NATO; unification of Europe, with British admission to the EEC as the next step; and even support for the Kennedy Round of tariff cuts talks that the protectionist French loathed. "Now the adoption of the treaty conceived by both Adenauer and de Gaulle as the basis of a German-French entente cordiale turned into a public triumph of Atlanticism in Bonn," concluded historian Hans-Peter Schwarz.[6] De Gaulle's own judgment, three year after signature of the treaty, was, "It's not our fault if the ties with Washington that Bonn preferred and constantly nurtured robbed this German-French treaty of its spirit and substance."[7]

After this contretemps the vaunted French-German relationship remained in limbo until Social Democratic chancellor Helmut Schmidt and conservative French president Valéry Giscard d'Estaing reactivated the partnership a decade and a half later.

In the meantime de Gaulle displayed French grandeur by boycotting EEC summits in 1965 and by withdrawing France from NATO's integrated military command in 1966. With his "policy of the empty chair" in the EEC, he forced his five partners to accept the "Luxembourg compromise" in which members could veto any item touching on what they deemed vital national interests. With French departure from the NATO military command, Paris asserted its independence from the United States, but also lost the touchstone of constant rehearsal and comparison with other armies and the boost this gave to readiness.

By 1970 the six members of the EEC gave up national competence for trade negotiations, ceding this authority to the European Community (EC), as the organization was called after 1967. In 1972 free trade was introduced among all EC and EFTA countries. In 1973 (after de Gaulle's departure from the political scene) the United Kingdom was finally admitted to the EC, along with Ireland and Denmark. In 1974 the European Council of nine members began meeting regularly. In 1975 the European Commission got its own budget and set up regional funds—and the Tindemans Report argued that, for further integration, the EC would need to develop "two-speed" possibilities to prevent blockage by slower countries of those wishing to integrate faster. In 1977 all tariffs were removed among the nine members. In 1978 Schmidt and Giscard, as a defense against any new oil shocks and the now floating and fluctuating dollar, pushed through the European Monetary System, with exchange rates held within narrow bands. In 1979 the first direct elections to the European Parliament were held. In 1981 Greece entered the EC, and six years later Spain and Portugal joined, making an even dozen members.

The EC and the Single Market

After its inception, the EC settled into useful but low-key economic tasks. The venue of high politics remained the national capitals. Beginning in the 1970s an attempt was made to expand the domain of coordination to include foreign policy in what was called "European political cooperation," but this was only moderately successful. It failed the first test of forging a united approach to the oil crisis of the early 1970s, worked better as a motor for the Helsinki Conference on Security and Cooperation in Europe, and in 1976 gave birth to the TREVI cooperation among national police and antiterrorist agencies.[8] In that period it also backed West Germany's new "Ostpolitik" of détente with the Soviet bloc—and it regularized contacts among foreign ministry political directors and working groups in phone calls, meetings, and thousands of annual "coreu" ("European correspondence") telegrams over a secure communications network. In the sharp judgment of Anthony Forster and William Wallace, however, the talking shop of European Political Cooperation, lacking resources and any commitment to common action, produced only "procedures without policy [and] activity without output."[9] That left the European Community, many complained, as little more than a forum for arguing about groceries and apportionment of subsidies for the mountains of wheat and lakes of wine that were devouring two-thirds of the entire EC budget.

Through the early 1980s Eurosclerosis reigned, with one little-noticed exception—the European Court of Justice. Unobtrusively, the very activist court asserted more and more power, curbing national sovereignty to a far greater extent than did any other European organ in the EC's first quarter century. The court did not confine itself to interpreting existing treaties or legislation, but set out general principles of European law, including "proportionality, equality, legal certainty, fundamental rights," and the "mutual recognition" that has underpinned harmonization and market liberalization. It "endorsed a set of values to underpin European governance" and strengthened the autonomous role of the European Commission as against the European Council.[10] Even with no pan-European enforcement agency behind it, it assumed that the national courts and police of EC member states would enforce its "preliminary rulings"—and they did so with remarkably few exceptions, even in the case of such sensitive issues as Irish prohibition of divorce; German bans on radicals in the civil service and import of beer that did not meet German "purity" laws; a proscription on registry of Spanish fishing boats in the United Kingdom; the French government's liability for French farmers' destruction of imported produce; and EU quotas on banana imports.[11] It established that European law takes precedence over national law. It required governments to pay retroactive damages to individuals for violation of European law. And it arrogated to itself the authority to decide which appeals it may adjudicate, including cases brought by individuals as well as by states.[12] So critical has the role of the European Court of Justice been in expanding the EC/EU writ that it is often compared with the role of the U.S. Supreme Court in interpreting the U.S. Constitution's interstate commerce clause to expand Washington's federal powers over the states.

By the early 1980s European judicial activism had run its course and was encountering the first backlash as national governments (and courts) noticed what was happening and objected. By the early 1990s the objections led to formal delimitation of the court's powers in the Maastricht Treaty. And the German Constitutional Court felt constrained to declare in its 1993 ruling on the constitutionality of the Maastricht Treaty that the German high court and not the European Court of Justice would decide whether EU institutions were staying within their proper bounds.[13] But at this point, for a variety of reasons, the politicians roused themselves from their slumbers to take over the European initiative from the Court.

The new political movement was first manifest in the Schengen Agreement, in the decision to turn the spotty common market into a real single market, and in the European Commission's competition and environment policy. The Schengen Agreement on open borders actually started as a bilateral initiative by France and Germany to relax controls on their common frontier. Out of fear that exclusive agreements among a few EC members might destroy the commonality of the European Community, however, the Benelux countries pressed France and Germany to open the inner club to them, too. The Schengen Agreement of 1985 among these five states was the result—as was the pressure on the respective national police forces to coordinate their activities more, lest open borders give a free hand to terrorists, drug-runners, smugglers of illegal immigrants, and other transnational criminals.

The goal of tearing down the many remaining trade barriers to establish a real European single market was revived in the mid-1980s—and changed the entire character of the community. The primary aims were to stimulate the slumped European economy, reverse high trade deficits, combat Eurosclerosis, and recover the competitiveness that was being lost to American and Japanese firms. The Federal Republic, exporting a third of its GDP, was eager to improve its markets. And since most of these exports went to European partners, Bonn was especially keen on countering, in this time of recession, the new trend of protectionism and erection of nontariff barriers among other EC states. The cause was also a perfect one for the liberal United Kingdom, which was only too happy to steer the EC away from grand political designs and toward a free-trade zone pure and simple. And it suited the incoming French president of the European Commission, Jacques Delors, an activist who from his first day in office in January 1985 deployed the issue to make the presidency, for the first time, a major player on the European scene.

By December 1985 the Single European Act was agreed on by the European Council and given the target date of 1992 for its completion. It committed EC members to pass 282 pieces of detailed harmonized legislation to produce at last the proclaimed "four freedoms" of capital, goods, services, and people. It incarnated a broad European swing away from the Social Democratic-conservative consensus of the 1960s and 1970s on the social responsibility of business and governments and toward a conservative-Social Democratic consensus on neoliberalism. It blurred the distinction between government and the private sector as the EC's use of consultants mushroomed to meet new demands, and various think tanks that were in part advocacy groups received contracts to help the EC work out the modalities of adjustment. It revolutionized business strategy as executives began to think not of segmented Swedish or Spanish markets, but of a huge transnational market of 320 million consumers. And it would generate a momentum toward what would soon be called "deepening" of the community, or a strengthening of its political commonality.

Delors's first initiative was to issue two documents on budget reform that became known as the Delors Package, then simply Delors-1. As adopted in 1987, the package consisted of a classic trade-off. The poor Mediterranean states and Ireland approved the single market that would end their protectionism. In return, they got their financial aid doubled between 1988 and 1993, as the EC's earmarked "structural" fund rose to strengthen "economic and social cohesion" between northern and southern members. Simultaneously, a ceiling was put on farm support. Predictably, national finance ministers welcomed the limits on agricultural subsidies, while farm ministers, including Bonn's, protested. The European Parliament—which had rejected the commission's 1980 and 1985 draft budgets as too miserly for the parliament's desired social and other projects—accepted the Delors bargain. Paymaster Kohl then brokered a deal that gave rebates to British prime minister Margaret Thatcher in 1988, and budgetary peace reigned for the next decade. The commission, it calculated, got 90 percent of what it had first laid out; Delors became a man to be reckoned with.[14]

In another way the commission also turned into a force to be reckoned with through the maneuvering of a person who was very different from Delors—Sir Leon Brittan, the commissioner for competition from the late 1980s to the early 1990s. Sir Leon was as much a believer in the British liberal hands-off tradition as Jacques Delors was in the French dirigiste tradition of active government intervention, and Sir Leon was said to be the one commissioner who could stand up to Delors. Certainly the Englishman did not blanch at taking on both Delors and various EC governments to establish the commission's authority in trust-busting and in setting limits on just how much aid governments could give their national industrial champions.

The latter issue had already come before the European Court of Justice in 1981; the Court had ruled that the European Commission was justified in outlawing Dutch special benefits for the Philip Morris company, and even egged the commission on to take a tougher line. Sir Leon did so, going so far as to insist that such stars as Renault and Rover pay back excessive national subsidies they had already received. His successor would later carry on the same row with east German state premier Kurt Biedenkopf over Saxon subsidies to Volkswagen.

In the case of mergers, there was nothing in the Treaty of Rome that gave explicit oversight to the European Commission. The treaty did forbid *abuse* of a dominant position, but not monopolies per se. If anything, this implied possible ex post facto, not prior, restraint. But Sir Leon leapfrogged the EEC Treaty and based his claims on the original European Coal and Steel Community, which allowed the High Authority to declare a merger in that specific branch illegal. The unspoken intent in the ECSC was in fact not to prevent monopolies as such, but to prevent any reassertion of German dominance—but Sir Leon interpreted the provision in the broadest possible sense. He deliberately sought out a large merger that he could prohibit and found it in barring the French-Italian ATR firm from acquiring the Canadian de Havilland aircraft producer. Against the objections of the French and Italians—and the abstention of Delors, who did not want to be on the losing side—Sir Leon successfully pushed the ban through with a 9-to-7 vote in the commission. The precedent of premerger approval by the commission was established, and Sir Leon moved on to take on even the "natural monopolies" in energy and related sectors. Later, as commissioner for External Economic Relations in the seven-year-long Uruguay negotiations to lower tariff and nontariff barriers, he would similarly arrogate powers to speak for all of the EC/ EU, even in the highly sensitive area of agriculture.[15]

In the 1980s EC environmental policy also gathered momentum. German ecologists, sensitized by dying forests and frustrated by the domestic resistance to thorough clean-up by large chemical and other firms, hoped they could circumvent national industrial lobbies by taking their case up to the European level. And as Germany's own anti-pollution laws were in fact made tougher, German business, too, joined in the European environmental campaign, partly because it feared loss of competitiveness if rival firms did not have to incur the same purification costs. The whole issue was a tricky area at first, since the Treaty of Rome did not assign environmental affairs to the community, but the proactive European Court of Justice ruled in 1985 that "environmental protection was one of the Community's essential objectives." With support from Denmark and the Netherlands, Germany led the successful fight for EC legislation limiting sulfur dioxide emissions from large combustion plants in 1982—and for a general European tilt toward preventive rather than remedial action thereafter. Once the Single European Act explicitly gave the community authority in environmental affairs, a burst of European antipollution legislation followed.[16]

Simultaneously, the French-German "alliance within the alliance" also shook itself out of its lethargy. The agents were the odd couple of new German chancellor Helmut Kohl and new French president François Mitterrand. The two men were utterly different. Mitterrand was short, elegant, intellectual, sphynx-like, with a personal history of working for the Vichy regime before settling on socialism as his philosophy and then, as president, moving France away from its time-honored exceptionalism to become "more like the others" in a shrinking Europe. Kohl, by contrast, was huge, bluff, folksy, and suspicious of intellectuals as lacking common sense. His personal history was a straight, less spectacular, middle-of-the-road line from student days in the Christian Democratic youth wing to party leader to chancellor of received conservative verities.

The one thing the two shared, however, they shared deeply: they were contemporaries in the tragic history of their age. When they stood at Verdun and clasped hands in memory of the dead, the gesture may have seemed embarrassing in its contrivance—but it was real. Whatever their stylistic differences, whatever their many policy quarrels, both were determined above all to prevent another Verdun from ever arising, even in the subconscious of their respective nations. Their generation, they felt in their bones, was bound in a *Schicksalsgemeinschaft*—a community of shared fate. The British, by their own choice, were not part of that community.[17] Nor would Kohl ever develop the same bond with Mitterrand's successor, Jacques Chirac, despite their shared position on the conservative side of the political spectrum.

This kinship explained much in the Kohl-Mitterrand relationship. It gave the French-German tie a stability that outlasted day-to-day lurches of interest. It would allow Kohl to excuse even Mitterrand's attempted conspiracy in 1989 with Soviet president Mikhail Gorbachev and East German leader Egon Krenz to block German unity.[18]

In the heightened East-West tension in the early 1980s after the Soviet invasion of Afghanistan, the first arena for the odd couple's joint action was security. For Mitterrand, the primary motivation was concern about a possible German drift toward accommodation with the Soviet Union. In particular, he feared that the hundreds of thousands of German nuclear pacifists who were marching in the streets against deployment of new NATO nuclear missiles might succeed in blocking that deployment. For Kohl's defense ministry, by contrast, a primary motivation was the wish to nudge Paris away from funding expensive and useless nuclear forces at the expense of the French infantry that alone could give Germany the ground reserves it would need to feel confident that it could repel any Soviet surprise attack.

In an anomalous role for the socialist leader of a nation that was still refusing to rejoin NATO's integrated command, Mitterrand traveled to Bonn to tell parliamentarians in a special session that they must stand firm and deploy the alliance's Pershing and Cruise missiles. Kohl's center-right German government indeed did so. Shortly thereafter, the French and Germans formed a joint brigade that would later be supplemented by troops from Belgium, Spain, and Luxembourg to become the "Eurocorps." They also held bilateral maneuvers in Bavaria, in which French units conspicuously operated east of the restrictive mid-German line that de Gaulle had earlier drawn as the outer limit for French deployment. At the time, the French veto on official NATO observers at the exercise grabbed the headlines. The real news, however, was the publicity Mitterrand was now willing to grant to his generals, who chafed at the French aloofness from NATO and from the alliance's advances, and had long used discreet French-German defense collaboration as a conduit for catching up on NATO experience.[19]

Less dramatic but even more significant for bilateral relations was the quiet abandonment by Mitterrand and the French Socialist party in the early 1980s of Keynesian pump-priming. With this shift Paris implemented a "franc fort"—strong franc—policy that pegged the franc to the deutsche mark and adopted, at least cerebrally, the Bundesbank's anti-inflation target as its own highest goal.

Now economic convergence could really begin. Paris and Bonn would become the motor of Europe; thereafter, what the two proposed jointly would set Europe's agenda.[20]

The timing was auspicious. Throughout Europe the consensus was growing—even during the kind of snail-like growth that in the past traditionally induced backsliding from European integration—that nation-states are simply too small today to cope with the challenges of globalized production, electronic currency flows, crime, and pollution. In the new jargon, the only hope for coping with the problems at the end of the millennium was pooled sovereignty.

CHAPTER THREE

German Unification and Maastricht, 1989–93

Pooled sovereignty was not the first thought of those who witnessed the extraordinary night of November 9, 1989, in Berlin. Maybe bananas were, if you were one of the tropical fruit–starved East Berliners streaming through the accidentally opened Berlin Wall into the West's cornucopia.[1] Perhaps alarm was your primary reaction, if you were the commandant in the British sector and had no idea what provocations a desperate Stasi secret police might resort to, or what flare-up of tempers might spark an incident. Or perhaps it all seemed like "insanity," if you shared the unanimous slang judgment of events by those thousands of tear-streaked, ecstatic East Berliners interviewed by journalists as they crossed to the other side of the city for the first time in twenty-eight years and mixed and danced and sang and scaled the wall together all night with their West Berlin cousins.

Pooled sovereignty was not even the second thought of Margaret Thatcher, whose nightmare was German unification. But it quickly became the preoccupation of Chancellor Kohl, precisely because his very different nightmare was that of his famous nineteenth-century predecessor, Otto von Bismarck—a Germany surrounded by a hostile coalition of neighbors. His method of warding off this danger was to bind his countrymen irrevocably to a pan-European structure and preclude "renationalization" of defense and foreign policy on the continent. Kohl was above all a master politician, a doer and not a thinker, a man who deliberately avoided detailed knowledge of the work of the ministries under him, sat out decisions whenever he could, and was reassuring to German voters in this time of dizzying change precisely because he seemed to embody the folk wisdom of the *Stammtisch*, or table of regulars in the local pub.[2] But he held two strong policy convictions: at some point Germany must be unified, and Europe must be integrated. The one was the obverse of the other. His monologues explaining the need for the continent to come together were laced with personal reminiscences about having pulled down toll barriers on the French-German border in his youth—and with detailed allusions to the successive tragedies as Spanish, Bavarian, Swedish, and French troops swept across his native Palatinate in the seventeenth, eighteenth, and nineteenth centuries.

Younger Germans who had not personally experienced war and holocaust might not share his European drive, Kohl feared; therefore he had to lock the Federal Republic as soon as he could into European institutions that could not be easily dismantled. Again and again he preached that German unification must not be a barrier to, but a catalyst for, European integration. Characteristically, the last sentence in his quasi autobiography closes with the chancellor's musings on the heady day of German unification in 1990: "I was also aware, of course, that we had realized only half of our vision after the war. Before us lay—and still lies—the realization of the other half: the unification of Europe."[3]

In this aspiration he had the general backing of Germans, whose nationalism had been totally discredited by Hitler's atrocities—and whose formidable economic success in the previous three decades had been achieved in the benign framework of the European Community. Yet in what would soon shape up as the crucial policy issue of the decade, he would encounter strong popular opposition to yielding the deutsche mark to an unknown European currency, since the deutsche mark was itself the denationalized badge of German success, prosperity, and even good behavior in a way that the German flag or national anthem never again could be.

Initially French president François Mitterrand did not share Kohl's vision of the future. After the wall fell, Mitterrand's first instinct, like Thatcher's, was to revert to nineteenth-century balance-of-power national games, to try to make common cause with Soviet president Mikhail Gorbachev to block German unification, and to slip into East

Germany to court the new premier, Hans Modrow, before Kohl could get there. Within two months Mitterrand and Thatcher called a four-power meeting in Berlin—including the Soviets—to discuss the future of the absent Germans, and they would have continued to exclude the Germans from deciding their own fate had not Washington vetoed the idea and forced Paris and London to accept swift German union.

Yet Mitterrand's hand was greatly weakened by the end of the cold war. Unification might not greatly increase German territory; the Federal Republic would grow only from the size of Oregon to the size of Montana. But German union, along with the regrafting of central Europe onto western Europe, would move the heart of the continent from the Rhineland and the thousand-year-old "French hexagon" to Berlin. It would multiply Germans from the 61 million inhabiting the old Federal Republic—roughly equal to the French, British, or Italian populations—to a dominant 81 million. It would enhance Germany's already preeminent economic power once the obsolescent eastern German plants had been replaced. Germany's forthcoming full sovereignty would rob France of the prestige of being an occupying power in Berlin. And it would eradicate Bonn's reliance on cooperation with Paris for legitimacy in foreign policy.

Psychologically, too, the central Europeans' rebellion against state-run socialism in 1989 was calling into question the first glorious French revolution just in the midst of its gala 200th anniversary.[4] And with Gorbachev's promised withdrawal of Soviet divisions from east Germany and central Europe by 1994, Paris's vaunted nuclear weapons were suddenly worthless politically. The old Gaullist dream of France as the brain to Germany's economic brawn in Europe died. And, if it chose go-it-alone nationalism, France could not hope to win against this more powerful Germany.[5]

As the two Germanys raced toward unification in 1990, other Europeans faced the same dilemma that Mitterrand faced. Once again, the memory of all the destabilizing ascents of German power in the past century haunted them. Would the Germans again become assertive? And now that the Soviet threat was gone, what could hold the West Europeans together? Had their ahistorical suspension of national quarrels and cooperation in the EC during the half century of cold war been no more than an emergency response to existential nuclear jeopardy? Did this not foreordain a return to history and to Hobbesian anarchy?[6] How could the dynamic Germans be tamed this time?

Jacques Delors, president of the European Commission, was among the first Europeans to say that the only possible answer to these questions was to embrace the post–World War II German democrats and not to demonize them in expecting the worst. He interpreted the Federal Republic's membership in the EC as instantly including its new eastern German citizens, without requiring any demeaning process of accession that would set the other Europeans in judgment over the Germans. Mitterrand eventually followed his compatriot's example, revisiting his own realization of the early 1980s, "If you can't lick 'em, you might as well join 'em." But in the coming decade the French would repeatedly face the same agonizing choice. Always the ultimate answer would be that the one thing worse than domination by the Germans within the EC would be domination by them outside of the EC.

If the project for a single market by 1992 had not already broken the EC's two-decade-long stagnation, it is doubtful whether embedding a united Germany in European institutions could have worked.[7] The structure of the old EC before the single market was far too weak to have contained German energies, and the political deals and coalition building (and misjudgments) that went into the single-market enterprise would probably have been impossible to strike in the postwall atmosphere of disorientation and latent suspicion. A Europe that was in fact well on its way to "1992," however, would prove capable, just, of turning the fourth rise of Germany in 120 years to creative rather than destructive uses.

The means first seemed to be combined monetary and political union, but soon this would be narrowed to monetary union alone. The goal of currency union, which had been around for decades, had been revived with the Single European Act of 1986. The intent was to get beyond mere lowered trade barriers to establish a fully open single market. Capital was to move freely by 1990 and would subsequently evolve into a common EC currency as the final step in achieving a genuine common market. The concept of monetary union was promoted especially by German foreign minister Hans-Dietrich Genscher at various Council meetings in the two years following adoption of the 1986 act, though it was initially regarded with indifference by Kohl.

As it became clear in 1989 and 1990 that Germany was going to unify rapidly, however, it was President Mitterrand who seized on the project as a way to tame the Germans. It was, of course, a two-edged sword. Since they had linked their money to the deutsche mark seven years earlier as a way to beat inflation, the French had had to abide by terms dictated by the Bundesbank, and they now welcomed a chance to secure at least some shared decision with the German central bank by getting a seat of their own on a new European Central Bank (ECB).[8] Obversely, though, a powerful new ECB might magnify the power of Germany as the leading economy in Europe and the third largest in the world. Mitterrand weighed the pros and cons and chose monetary union as the lesser evil.

Despite conventional wisdom to the contrary both inside and outside Germany, Kohl was not opposed to the scheme at this point. To be sure, he did not yet regard it politically as the key development that would make European integration irrevocable. Tactically, he wanted to avoid monetary union's becoming a major issue before the 1990 election among German voters wedded to the deutsche mark. Strategically, he would not make a final commitment to EMU until he was assured of his one absolute condition, independence of the European Central Bank from politicians. But already he favored monetary union as one additional tie binding Europe together.[9]

Kohl, of course, did not mind letting France think that Paris would have to pay a price to get German assent to monetary union. As Kohl met with Mitterrand in April of 1990 to prepare bilateral initiatives for the next council summit, the price that he asked for was concomitant political union. The two asserted, "It is necessary to accelerate the political construction of the Europe of the Twelve" and effect political union, "which is close to citizens and corresponds with its federal vocation."[10]

As Kohl elaborated on October 3, 1990, on the occasion of German unification,

> The coming years will show that unified Germany means a victory for all of Europe. . . . Even in the future France and Germany will remain the motor of European unification. [The EC] should remain a firm foundation for the growing together of all Europe and form its core. . . . But there must be no doubt: We want political union; we do not want a glorified free-trade zone, but the political unification of Europe in the sense of the Treaties of Rome.[11]

The new Rome summit in December (after Kohl's reelection) duly endorsed both currency and political union, even if few apart from the Germans were enthusiastic about the political goal. With greater zeal (or perhaps desperation, given the bank's resistance to a common European currency), Bundesbank president Hans Tietmeyer took to promoting political union as a guarantee that monetary union would work and would be backed by governance with compatible fiscal policies.

The Maastricht Conference

By the end of 1991, EC members were ready to open the conference at Maastricht in the Netherlands that would conduct the first major overhaul of the 1957 Treaty of Rome and chart the future course. The most controversial issue on the agenda was German pressure on its allies to recognize Croatian and Slovenian independence from Yugoslavia. Bonn argued that such recognition would escape the taboo against interfering in a sovereign nation's internal affairs and allow the newly recognized states to call for outside assistance. Paris and London saw the issue very differently, especially since Bonn would still labor under its own domestic taboo against sending German armed forces abroad, and any intervention would in practice have to be done by the French and British. Under the circumstances, they interpreted Bonn's pressure as the reassertion of a heavyweight Germany that wanted to recreate Hitler's old sphere of influence in the Balkans. They further regarded premature acceptance of Croatian independence as the trigger that would extend the terrible bloodshed to Bosnia, and they blamed Bonn for heartless indifference to this certain consequence of recognition. Yet they went along with recognition, in part for the sake of promoting agreement on other issues at Maastricht.

In the end no agreement was reached on the hot issue of deepening—intensifying the formal and informal practices that served the six well but were already strained in a community of twelve. The Germans could not win their hoped-for reforms of more majority voting in the council, pruning of the burgeoning number of commissioners, more democratic powers for the European Parliament, and greater continuity in the EC presidency, which rotated every six months. Nor was the issue of widening the EC to take in fledgling central European democracies seriously addressed. In the early 1990s the Germans were still alone in Europe in believing that deepening and widening were in fact compatible.[12]

Yet even if its political aims remained vague, Maastricht was a watershed. The summit dared to give the EC the ambitious new name of European Union. And it meddled in the formerly forbidden areas of currency, defense, and foreign policy.

The Treaty of European Union itself, hammered out in thirty exhausting hours of final summit negotiations at Maastricht, was a potpourri. It established the Court of Auditors—court in the sense of a watchdog office, not a judicial court—which, astonishingly, had never before existed. It instituted the new Committee of the Regions in recognition of the growing sense of subnational and local identity that cut across existing political boundaries. It envisioned establishment of an effective Europol police agency by 1994.[13] It set up three "pillars"— the first a Community pillar of economic powers delegated to Brussels by member-states, the second and third "intergovernmental" pillars for foreign policy and home and justice matters that would be coordinated among the several national ministers in meetings of the Council of Ministers. It set up, in addition to the structural aid to Greece, Spain, Portugal, and Ireland, the new Cohesion Fund to promote environmental cleanup and transportation lines in these poorer member-states. It wrote a "social charter"—with an opt-out for Britain that for the first time officially endorsed differentiation within the EC. At the paradoxical insistence of the British, who ran a highly centralized domestic polity, it also endorsed "subsidiarity," or devolving all powers to the lowest possible level. It bravely called for a European "common foreign and security policy," even though there was little sign of any common response to the barbarity in Yugoslavia or even the dramatic contemporary collapse of the Soviet Union. The treaty modestly accorded the European Parliament more rights of "codecision" with the Commission and confirmed a future increase by eighteen seats of the united Germans' representation in the European Parliament. And it deferred issues of political union by setting up yet another intergovernmental conference to look at the question beginning in 1996.

Kohl considered the results a resounding success. In his euphoric report to the Bundestag he declared, "The way to European Union is irreversible. . . . The German-French partnership and friendship was, is, and remains decisive for Europe. Above all, we are united with France in the vision that Europe grow together not only economically, but also politically."[14] Given his own regret that the summit achieved little in the way of political union—and the German public's opposition to exchanging deutsche marks for an invented currency—Kohl did not brag about the centerpiece of the conference, monetary union. But at Maastricht he secured agreement on his two nonnegotiable conditions for surrendering the deutsche mark. The future European Central Bank, the treaty stipulated, would be independent of national governments, and the Bank's commandment would be stability approaching zero inflation. Moreover, the central banks of every founding member of European Monetary Union—including the Banque de France—would also have to be freed from government interference by the time they became part of the ECB system at the beginning of monetary union. With this foundation, the Germans were convinced, the ECB would be just as strict as the Bundesbank—even if a German were not its chief—since any good central bankers, whether French, Dutch, or Italian, would obviously think exactly like the Bundesbank.

The Maastricht Treaty thus represented "an absolute novum," said Jürgen Stark, the state secretary in the German Finance Ministry responsible for preparing G-7 summits and monetary union in the 1990s and subsequently vice president of the Bundesbank. "We [Germans] have something to lose. For the first time in history a good currency is being given up," and there must be firm measures to ensure that its replacement will have the same credibility and value. For this reason, again for the first time in history, the independence of a central bank "is now anchored in international law" and can be changed only unanimously by the signatories of Maastricht. Euroland will henceforth have "a centralized monetary policy, but decentralized fiscal and economic policy." The system will require closer cooperation among participating governments and more flexibility in capital and especially labor markets. But "if everything works well, out of it will come a policy mix that does not need fine tuning." And already the "convergence process has established a stable, healthy basis on which we can build this project."[15]

Concretely, five convergence criteria corresponding to Germany's "stability culture" were agreed on in Maastricht as the tough measure defining which states would qualify: inflation no higher than 1.5 percent above the average of the EC's three best performers; long-term interest rates no higher than 2 percent above the average of the three best performers; budget deficits no higher than 3 percent of GDP (with some wiggle room); public debt no higher than 60 percent of GDP (with some wiggle room); and exchange-rate adherence to the European Monetary System's bandwidths for two years. There would be no collective bailout of any EMU member's debts. Britain and later Denmark, at their request, were granted opt-outs. What turned out to be the most innovative aspect of these guidelines was the concept of "benchmarking," by which the achievements of the stars would not be dragged down to a mediocre average, but would instead set the standard for others to reach.

While Kohl was still cheering, the backlash hit. The chancellor had been right in his premonition that Germans would protest the loss of their deutsche mark—but even he was not prepared for the shock as the *Bild* boulevard newspaper trumpeted, "Our lovely money/The mark is being abolished."[16] Bavarian premier Edmund Stoiber called the planned currency "esperanto money." *Der Spiegel* agreed. Various German economists joined in to savage the whole idea of currency union; some of them filed a challenge to the constitutionality of EMU with the German Constitutional Court.[17]

Elsewhere in the obligatory process of unanimous ratification, the Danes rejected the treaty in a referendum, threatening to reopen all the intricate 2 a.m. deals that had been reached, as usual, only under pressure of the Maastricht deadline. This setback was bad enough, but it was at least understandable in a nation that resembled Britain in its suspicion of European "federalism"—and had grave doubts about splitting off from Scandinavian nonmembers of the EC. The bare favorable majority in the French referendum was almost more disheartening in occurring in a country that was one of the motors of integration.

Moreover, France's closest ally, Germany, was the negative target of much of the plebiscite campaign in France, on both sides. Opponents charged that the EU Treaty's "ever closer union" gave Germany a vehicle to magnify its preeminence. Recent defense minister Jean-Pierre Chevènement objected that the agreement would bind France more than Germany. Jacques Chirac, the head of the neogaullist Rassemblement pour la République and soon to be the president of France, accused fellow conservatives allied with Valéry Giscard d'Estaing of being too sympathetic to foreigners. Philippe Séguin, his party colleague, went further and wrote a bestseller castigating Maastricht and branding the negotiators there worthy successors to Hitler. "Almost fifty years after the collapse of the Third Reich, will

Hitler's dream be resurrected in another form, and will Germany dominate Europe?" asked the newspaper *Le Point* in the same vein.[18]

Nor were the arguments of the Maastricht proponents in France any more flattering to Germany. Basically, their position was that it would be much safer to have the regional giant constrained by having to work within pan-European institutions than to allow the dynamic Germans once again to become a dangerous loose cannon.

In exasperation, writer Alain Finkielkraut reproached his fellow French for a two-faced policy that he deemed far more dangerous than the old "German question." In *Liberation* he wrote, "Everybody in France fears Germany. Some allege that the Europe of Maastricht is the German Europe; the others say that if we really want to keep an eye on, anchor, and westernize German power, we must vote for the Treaty of European Union. And it does not occur to anyone that there are good reasons today to watch out for France itself. In the eyes of the French, only Germany is disturbing, only Germany has evil demons."[19]

To add to the strife, at this point a bitter quarrel over interest rates arose between the German and French (and other European) elites. It compounded resentment of the German pressure to recognize Croatia and called into question some of the fundamental assumptions of monetary union. Bonn, rather than taxing its own citizens to pay for the resuscitation of eastern Germany, borrowed the money for much of its $100 billion annual transfers to the east, vacuuming investment away from its neighbors. To neutralize the inflationary pressures thus generated, the Bundesbank raised interest rates by six points in five years, even as the continent's economy sagged; other EU countries could not then cut their own interest rates to stimulate growth. European partners complained that Germany was prolonging recession and thus taxing them without their consent, just as the monetary superpower, the United States, had exported its deficit financing of the Vietnam War in the 1960s. The French implored the Bundesbank to lower interest rates and, if it did not do so, threatened to abandon the "franc fort" and their own earlier abandonment of Kenyesian inflation. To those chafing under the Bundesbank yoke, European monetary union looked more necessary—and more unattainable—than ever.

Yet to the German population EMU looked all too attainable and threatening. The folk memory of hauling wheelbarrows full of Reichsmarks to the local bakery in the 1920s—and losing savings again in the 1948 currency reform—had given Germans a fear of inflation second to none in the industrialized world. And the phobia was only reinforced by the groundswell of "deutsche mark patriotism"—pride in the strong currency that had been so good to Germans for four decades—as the politically correct substitute for nationalism.

Kohl's response to the popular malaise was not at all the public relations blitz that one might expect in a similar situation in the United States. Instead, the chancellor adopted tactics designed for a society that operates by elite consensus. Scorning populism, he deliberately imitated Konrad Adenauer's earlier defiance of overwhelmingly negative public opinion (and fierce Social Democratic opposition) to bind the Federal Republic to the West, form an army, join the EC—and win the gratitude of later generations. To this list Kohl added his own successful defiance in the 1980s of the hundreds of thousands of demonstrators arrayed against stationing medium-range missiles in Germany.[20] It is the job of the statesman, Kohl asserted repeatedly, not to cater to voters when they are wrong, but to lead them in the right direction even if they do not want to go that way. Afterward they will appreciate this tutelage.

Kohl's main target audience was thus not the public as such, but the Bundesbank. This revered keeper of the deutsche mark grail enjoyed the kind of political prestige and popular trust that less revered and more technical central banks in other countries could only marvel at. If the Bundesbank could be persuaded that the new pan-European currency would be almost as hard as the deutsche mark, Kohl reasoned—not a foregone conclusion, by any means—then the Bundesbank would reassure the little savings banks in every town and village, and they, in turn, would reassure their depositors. As a corollary, the Kohl team determined to blame the unavoidable belt tightening in the next few years only on the challenge of globalization—and never on EMU—in order not to brand monetary union a job killer. In this it would be astonishingly successful, especially in contrast to France.

Kohl's secondary audience was the German political class. Here—remarkably, given the bitter past feuds over European and foreign policy—the conservatives, the Social Democrats, the Liberals, and the Greens' parliamentary caucus all united behind the chancellor's leap of faith. Later, when planning for the EMU was back on course and sniping at it was cost free, the premiers of Bavaria, Saxony, and Lower Saxony would all air doubts about EMU or its tempo. But in the trough of Europessimism in the early 1990s, it was only outsiders like Manfred Brunner who did so. And Brunner's anti–EMU League of Free Citizens, like all new single-purpose parties in the Federal Republic with the exception of the Greens, would sink without a trace.

A Maastricht Hangover, 1992–93

In the early 1990s Europe slumped into its worst recession since the 1930s. The European Monetary System, even though it was far less demanding than full monetary union would be, succumbed to speculative market attack in September of 1992, forcing the British pound and the Italian lira to devalue by one quarter, and obliging Spain, Portugal, Ireland, and Denmark to devalue their currencies by a lesser extent inside the system. The French franc too would have plunged out of the agreed exchange bands but for massive intervention by the Bundesbank—and stretching of the bandwidths so far that by August of 1993 the new elasticity was initially regarded as collapse of the system.[21]

Then, as recession continued in 1993, the long-awaited inaugural year of the single European market, the economy, far from quickening as advocates had prophesied, fell into an absolute decline of 1.1 percent for Germany and 0.3 percent for the continent, with 10.5 percent unemployment. The ground was laid for the widespread social unrest that would later break out in France. And even after growth eventually resumed, structural unemployment would continue to rise inexorably.

Under the circumstances, plans for monetary union looked ludicrous. A few short years before the hoped-for launch of a single currency, only the tiny bankers' paradise of Luxembourg met the stiff Maastricht criteria. Outstanding central bankers were notably reluctant to take on the job of president of the European Central Bank's forerunner, the European Monetary Institute, apparently out of doubts that the project would ever get off the ground. Only Kohl, it seemed, maintained the confidence that the ambitious plans would proceed as scheduled, if not in 1997, then in the fallback year of 1999.

As had happened so often before in the history of the EC, when recession hit, momentum ground to a halt. The institutional and budgetary reforms that were essential if the EU was to double its members were postponed. There was no movement to increase majority voting, to rectify the cumbersome distribution of Commission posts, or to change the erratic leadership of half-year presidencies rotating among all members of the EU. No initiatives were forthcoming to readjust the bias favoring small members, who could outvote the largest countries if their numbers were extended by a dozen tiny new entrants. Yet without change, doubling the dozen members would clearly freeze up institutions designed for the cozy interaction of the original six signatories of the Treaty of Rome. Talk of Eurosclerosis was revived, not least in the American media. The demoralization was profound. Everything conspired to confound the disciples of Jean Monnet and Robert Schuman.

In pocketbook issues, France (and Germany) still resisted any more meddling with the farm subsidies that even after the increase in other EU spending still ate up half of EU budgets. Spain, Portugal, Greece, and Ireland accepted their fresh cohesion funds and prepared to defend these new entitlements against any future sharing out with the east. Yet calculations indicated that extending existing EU programs to the four Visegrad states alone would increase EU spending by an untenable half or more.[22] And milk cow Germany, staggering under its annual $100 billion transfers to its new eastern Länder (states), began declaring that it would not continue indefinitely to pay 60 percent of net EU outlays. The first step in Bonn's campaign to ease its financial burden was to leak to the German public the scale of its contributions, which had previously been kept quiet, and to publicize the country's drop in ranking, after absorbing east Germany, to only the fifth-richest EU country per capita.[23]

Domestically, all the large EU nations were in trouble. Italy was wracked by a systemic breakdown, as scandals revealed pervasive official corruption and collusion with the mafia, and had little spare time to contemplate Europe at large. France, with a new conservative prime minister at odds with its socialist president, was distracted by the vicissitudes of "cohabitation." Nor was it certain how well the more European-minded prime minister, Edouard Balladur, might cohabit with his more nationalist neogaullist leader, Jacques Chirac. Nor was the specter of the xenophobic right banished; Jean-Marie Le Pen's National Front claimed an influential and rising 14 percent in the general election. In Britain, Prime Minister John Major was reaping the whirlwind after Margaret Thatcher, and, despite his promise to bring the United Kingdom into "the heart of Europe," he was failing to unite a Tory party in which Euroskeptics were in full cry.

For their part, the Germans were discovering just how many economic and psychological barriers still hindered them from becoming the "one people" the Leipzig demonstrators had dreamed of in the heady fall days of 1989. True unification, it turned out, would take much longer and be far more painful than anyone had imagined. Many an (eastern) "Ossi" accused (western) "Wessis" of arrogance. Many a Wessi resented being compelled to pay a surtax for charity to the east. A hangover of cynicism and disgust with politics and parties settled in that was palpable enough for the Zeitgeist to win the unmistakably Germanic nickname of "Politikverdrossenheit," or "political sulkiness."[24]

Most alarming of all, right-wing extremists were lethally tormenting third-world foreigners who sought refuge under the constitution's generous promise of asylum. In 1992 some 700,000 new foreigners entered Germany—and the death toll of outsiders from arson and beatings rose to seventeen. Improved police work, stiff jail sentences, and popular outrage at such behavior stopped the wave of murders in 1993. But politically, antiforeign resentment brought the xenophobic right into three state legislatures in 1993, with an alarmingly high vote of 11 percent in Baden-Württemberg. Surveys suggested that the far right might even win enough in the next general election to put extremists into the Bundestag for the first time since adoption of the 5 percent minimum requirement.

At the same time, Germany was going through the agony of shedding one more layer of post-Hitler constraints as the issue arose of sending Bundeswehr units abroad on UN and NATO peacekeeping operations. The broad choice was between, on the one hand, assuming a full role in common European and transatlantic actions commensurate with Germany's new full sovereignty and continuing economic might, or, on the other hand, abdicating and remaining a Switzerland writ large—the course that much of the left still saw as Germany's history-ordained penance.

Though it went largely unremarked at the time, Germany's semipacifist reticence had in fact already been breached when Iraqi Scud missiles hit Israel in the Gulf War of 1991.[25] Fierce polemics rent the intellectual left as supporters of the Gulf intervention, some of them Jewish, accused the more doctrinaire of their old anti–Vietnam War comrades of knee-jerk anti-Americanism and hidden anti-

Semitism.[26] The mounting atrocities in Croatia and especially in Bosnia then strengthened the argument that there might be a higher morality than pacifism; the Kohl government, turning the historical argument on its head, argued that precisely because of its past, Germany had a special responsibility to protect defenseless neighbors against their persecutors. By April of 1993, in one of the more bizarre twists of German wrestling with the past, the junior Liberal members of the ruling coalition sued their own government in court over the presumed unconstitutionality of assigning Bundeswehr units or members of multinational flight crews to operations in or over the former Yugoslavia.[27] They lost, as they had hoped to do; thereafter Germany, too, dispatched peacekeeping forces to Bosnia and reconfigured its army to produce rapid reaction forces suitable for such missions. Witnessing these throes, London and Paris ceased to worry that Germany would disrupt Europe by its strength and assertiveness—but began to worry instead that Germany would disrupt Europe by proving too weak to cope with the new burdens heaped on it.[28]

Nor did prospects look much better in the "widening" half of the European enterprise, righting the historic wrongs of the division of Europe accomplished at Yalta by welcoming the new central European democracies into the EC/EU. In both its own programs and those of the G-24 group of states aiding reform in central and eastern Europe, the European Union was providing substantial financial and technical assistance for development of new institutions and markets, along with ready commercial, administrative, and other models to help smooth transformation. And with prodding from Bonn and the European Commission (with the help, surprisingly, of Italy and Spain), the EC summit in Copenhagen in June 1993 did conclude "Europe Agreements" with the central Europeans. For the first time this promised future membership in binding form and provided a political framework that advocates could cite in trying to make the single market more hospitable to central European imports.[29]

Yet in this most crucial area of opening its markets to the east, the EC was dragging its feet. It did offer progressive lowering of tariffs aiming at free trade in industrial goods from 1995, steel from 1996, and textiles in 1997—but its own weak demand hardly sucked in central European imports. And in response to west European lobbyists who were much more adept at playing the fragmented Brussels bureaucracy than were the central European neophytes, the EC kept imposing ad hoc quotas on Polish cherries or Ukrainian tablecloths or Slovak steel in precisely those sectors in which the central and east Europeans had a comparative advantage.[30] Even the central Europeans' champion, Germany, with a crisis in its own downsizing steel industry, showed no eagerness to expand imports in this branch.

The Poles, profiting from their open border with Germany, initially made huge unrecorded sales to consumers across the Oder River of gasoline, ceramic garden dwarfs, and prostitutes' services, and thus kept their real trade balance in the black. But overall, the EC/EU registered an official trade surplus of 5.6 billion European currency units (ecus) in 1993 ($6.1 billion), with 8 percent of this arising from food exports that by logic should have been flowing in the other direction. And France, which never had been keen on magnifying German influence by extending the EU into Berlin's backyard, now proposed as a precondition for candidates a minimum GDP that would long bar entry to central Europeans living at a third of EU levels. Moreover, while Rome, Paris, and Bonn fiddled, the former Yugoslavia continued to burn.

In the face of these multiple tribulations, the European allies displayed only grudging solidarity. Even the hallowed French-German alliance within the alliance suffered. The two partners were still jockeying for position in the post–cold war world; Germany still continued to honor France, but Kohl was becoming less malleable, even as he continued to regard the bilateral relationship as the sine qua non for Europe. And divergent perceived interests split the two on trade issues, in residual French dirigiste instincts, and in shaping the new European Central Bank (ECB). After it was outvoted on the issue in the EU, Bonn had to yield to the French desire to protect the insatiable German banana market against Chiquita and Dole and ensure large sales for the blander fruit from former French colonies.[31] It went along with Paris, too, in setting bureaucratic rather than market standards for European color TV—though it did not agree to let the European Commission guide the invisible hand more broadly by picking and promoting industrial winners.

Kohl also deferred to his friend Mitterrand in rejecting American urgings to press Paris to reduce EU subsidies for agricultural exports and to lower barriers against audiovisual imports in the Uruguay round negotiations that were then in their seventh interminable year of bargaining. In the end the French did accept a complex intra–EU formula that managed to trim EU outlays largely because of the high world price for cereals; another bruising trade war was averted with the United States before the American president's fast-track authorization lapsed, and Kohl maintained his balancing act between Paris and Washington.

Even for the sake of French and European harmony, however, there was one central issue on which Kohl would not and could not compromise. In April 1990 his acceptance of the ultimate sacrifice of the deutsche mark in agreeing with Mitterrand to enact monetary union was premised on the condition that the European Central Bank must be totally independent of political influence. Again and again, up to the very last moment of instituting EMU, Kohl would return to this standard; again and again Paris would challenge it. Yet only on this bedrock, the chancellor believed, could he sell the loss of the deutsche mark to his suspicious voters. He therefore insisted not only that the institutional autonomy of the European Central Bank must be guaranteed, but also that the ECB and its forerunner European Monetary Institute (EMI) must be located in the same city as the Bundesbank— and that the common currency must not carry the name of the old ecu.

These were no mere whims. Kohl believed that EMI officials must have their backbone strengthened by daily contact with Bundesbank officials as they drafted all the ECB's detailed regulations and procedures in the brief half decade of preparation for launch. And the new coin of the realm must not be tarnished in the public mind by association with the bureaucratic basket currency ecu, which had devalued against the deutsche mark in its two decades of notional existence.

Ironically, for all of Kohl's ardor, Germany was the last state in the European Community to ratify the Maastricht Treaty. On October 11, 1993, the German Constitutional Court finally approved German acceptance of the Maastricht Treaty and entry into monetary union, contingent on the Bundestag's democratic approval. The Bundestag promptly voted for ratification. On November 1, 1993, the European Union staggered into existence. No one could have accused it of excessive euphoria.

CHAPTER FOUR

Present at the Second Creation: NATO

The North Atlantic Treaty Organization emerged from the cold war with glory and perplexity. Its deterrence had produced the longest peace on the European continent in history, and it had never fired a shot in anger.[1] Yet it appeared to many to have put itself out of business, now that Moscow's troops had retreated a thousand miles to the east and the democratic Germans had regained unity and full sovereignty. Especially after the Warsaw Pact dissolved in 1990, the Soviet Union dissolved in 1991, and the no-longer-Soviet army completed its withdrawal from Germany in 1994, NATO no longer seemed necessary to keep the Russians out or to keep the Germans down.

The U.S. Engagement

Its strongest remaining rationale, then, was to keep the Americans in Europe—and various European and American voices argued that a prolongation of Pax Americana would be no more than bureaucratic self-perpetuation.[2] Other organizations that did not embody outdated U.S. hegemony, like the Conference on Security and Cooperation in Europe (CSCE), were proposed for the continent's security architecture in the dawning era of peace. So strong was this sentiment that President George Bush testily warned the Europeans in 1991, "If your ultimate aim is to provide independently for your own defense, the time to tell us is today." If so, he implied, the United States would happily go home and leave the Europeans to be hoist with their own petard.[3]

As they took a second look at the uncertain world about them, however, NATO governments and the new central European democracies saw an urgent need for the United States to stay engaged in Europe—and saw NATO as the only possible instrument of this engagement. In its desire to reap a peace dividend so that it could focus on neglected domestic needs, the U.S. Congress was hardly in a mood to approve some new defense commitment to foreign allies. But after four successful decades, Americans felt comfortable with NATO; they might be willing to preserve its existence and even, the central Europeans devoutly hoped, extend its reach.

Essentially there were three reasons for the wish to keep the United States as a major player in Europe. The most important was reinsurance against any imperial recidivism by a Russia still armed with nuclear weapons. Three episodes contributed to European nervousness.

The initial scare came with the attempted hard-line putsch against President Mikhail Gorbachev in mid-1991. The second scare, after Soviet collapse, came when the Russian 14th Army intervened in Moldova on behalf of separatist ethnic Russians to secure the breakaway of the newly invented Trans-Dniestr Republic. Subsequently, all thirteen blocs in parliament and the Russian government itself affirmed the Russian Federation's "great power" interests in the "near abroad"—the Baltic and other newly independent states that had emerged out of Soviet collapse—and implicitly sanctioned Russian military action there.

The third fright came in the fall of 1993, as President Boris Yeltsin and his former vice president, Alexander Rutskoi, engaged in a proxy shootout, with Yeltsin ordering troops to fire on parliament while CNN cameras covered the events live. Within months voters protested against price rises and the new chaos by giving the most seats in the Duma to the party of Vladimir Zhirinovsky, an out-and-out chauvinist who wanted to reconstitute the Soviet Union, irradiate Lithuania, and even reclaim Alaska. Shortly thereafter Yeltsin, who had initially condoned the concept of a more civic and less ethnic Russian state, turned more nationalist in viewing the 25 million Russian speakers in the near abroad as an integral part of the Russian nation.[4] By April of

1994 the Russian government indeed announced establishment of thirty military bases in the "CIS and Latvia." The CIS, or Commonwealth of Independent States, was the organization of Soviet successor states that nominally resembled the voluntary European Union, but that Moscow saw increasingly as a vehicle for reconsolidating Russia's hegemony over the near abroad.[5] Moscow also pointedly refused to recognize the borders of the second-largest Slav scion of the Soviet Union, Ukraine. And at the turn of 1994–95, the Russian army started what it thought would be a brief campaign to suppress Chechen secessionists by brutally razing civilian districts in Grozny, the capital of Chechnya.[6] A new Time of Troubles loomed.

None of this posed any direct threat to western Europe, of course, especially after the Russian army failed disastrously in Chechnya and deteriorated to only two combat-ready divisions, according to Western intelligence. And the West, however much it might deplore Russian deviations from the common understanding of democracy, essentially refrained from criticizing Yeltsin out of fear of weakening him against more hard-line rivals. Yet every new reminder of the old Soviet imperial policy made the NATO security blanket look more comforting to the western Europeans, and doubly so to the central Europeans and Balts, who were much more exposed to the erratic Russian army. Only the United States, with its airlift, intelligence, and real-time, state-of-the-art battlefield technology—and, ultimately, nuclear guarantee—was in a position to counterbalance every possible military risk should things lurch out of control in Moscow.

The second reason for embracing NATO was the conspicuous preference (on the part of Germans as well as other Europeans) for American security leadership over the alternatives of German leadership or no leadership. Even two generations after World War II, the British, French, and Danes still balked more at deferring to a big Germany than deferring to an even bigger United States. And some kind of strong leadership was often needed to force inconclusive allied debates into decision and action.

The third reason, which became clear as the atrocities mounted in the former Yugoslavia, was the need for credible force—which only the Americans could provide—to constrain local bullies on the peripheries of Europe. As television brought the bloodletting on Europe's southern doorstep to living rooms every night, a remarkably broad consensus about the need to defend the weak overcame the European left's residual suspicion of the United States. The antinuclear (and anti-American) demonstrations by hundreds of thousands during the 1980s were forgotten. And even the French, however much they might bridle as American officials called the United States a European power, concurred in these broad judgments.

On the U.S. side, President George Bush continued the transatlantic connection in the early post–cold war years and helped steer the adaptation to the new environment that was essential if NATO was to remain viable. Even before the Soviet Union fell apart, the alliance modified NATO doctrine, downgraded nuclear missiles to "truly weapons of last resort," sharply cut forces and especially "forward deployment" on the eastern border of NATO, offered cooperation instead of confrontation to Moscow, and began thinning out American troops in Europe to a politically sustainable 100,000 or less.[7] Washington, its allies, and Moscow concluded the long-drawn-out negotiations on major reductions in Conventional Forces in Europe (CFE) with the agreement in late 1990 to melt down 33,000 tanks, artillery, and other heavy weapons, and thus bring the Soviet bloc down to NATO levels.

In 1991 President Bush, relying on NATO infrastructure in Europe while not engaging the NATO organization itself in such an operation outside alliance territory, led a coalition of the willing to deny Saddam Hussein's takeover of Kuwait. At the time Washington regarded the action as a likely model for the "new world order" that would now prevail, with the United States as the only superpower, and with NATO Europe as the solid logistical base for Western operations in the Middle East. Within NATO territory the alliance maintained collective defense, at reduced military levels, with small, mobile rapid reaction forces and heavy reliance on reinforcements—but it put more emphasis on political tasks, establishing the North Atlantic Cooperation Council for dialogue with the Soviet Union and the new central European democracies only weeks before the Soviet Union fell apart. Then in 1992 Washington steered NATO to revise its basic "strategic concept." NATO still saw itself as the continent's primary defense organization, but it now welcomed the "European defense identity" the western Europeans desired.

More fundamental questions about U.S. interest in Europe arose once Bill Clinton became president in 1993, deliberately subordinated foreign policy to domestic concerns, and largely ignored Europe in his first year in favor of the more fashionable Pacific Rim. The Europeans waited and would take his measure in three tests: trade negotiations, NATO enlargement, and war in the former Yugoslavia.

Trade negotiations came to a head at the end of 1993. The president's fast-track authority was about to expire, and before it did, Clinton had to win ratification of the North American Free Trade Agreement, as well as settle on the final bargain of the long-running Uruguay Round of General Agreement on Tariff and Trade (GATT) negotiations to cut nontariff barriers. In both cases, to the cheers of the Europeans, Clinton won against strong protectionist sentiment in Congress. He then took his first, triumphal tour of Europe. Once he finally noticed the old continent, his instincts paralleled Bush's. He arrived in Brussels for the NATO summit at the beginning of 1994 and told the western Europeans what they wanted to hear in committing his administration to continued alliance and European engagement. He traveled on to central Europe to tell the Poles, Czechs, and Hungarians what they wanted to hear by promising them admission to NATO. Illustrating the sort of thing the United States could do that Europeans could not, he also cajoled Ukraine into making the continent a safer place by giving up the nuclear weapons it had inherited from the Soviet Union. Within NATO, too, even the long rift between France and the United States looked as if it might be resolved, as Paris joined contingency planning for Bosnia and returned for the first time since 1966 to participate in NATO's Military Committee (if not the Defense Planning Committee).

Bosnia

On the fighting in the former Yugoslavia, however, Clinton remained silent, and quarrels on this issue would risk the very breakup of the transatlantic alliance. The new president had come into office criticizing the Bush administration for its passivity as the Serbs swept beyond conquering ethnic Serb parts of Croatia to dismembering (in collusion with the Croats) the long-time Bosnian model of multicultural tolerance. Yet in his first two years as president, Clinton himself took no more action than his predecessor. Within the alliance, American aloofness was initially welcomed; Luxembourg's foreign minister, Jacques Poos, famously announced, "The hour of Europe has dawned."[8] Even the British told Washington that Yugoslavia was Europe's business.

Secretary of State Warren Christopher made one half-hearted attempt in allied capitals to promote the American idea of "lift and strike"—lifting the arms embargo on the outgunned (Muslim) Bosniaks and striking their Serb besiegers from the air without putting any GIs in harm's way on the ground—but when he met a lukewarm response, he retreated.

As the United States approached mid-term elections in 1994, the Bosniaks had been pushed back into vulnerable enclaves. The Bosnian capital of Sarajevo, best known to the outside world as the site of the winter Olympics a decade earlier, had been besieged and shelled by Bosnian Serbs for two years, with one bombardment killing sixty-eight civilians in a single hit. Both the Serbs and the Croats were practicing "ethnic cleansing," brutally driving other nationalities out of their conquered villages, murdering old people and children, setting up prison camps reminiscent of Nazi concentration camps, and, in the case of the Serbs in particular, raping captive Bosniak women serially for months on end to produce Serb babies and defile the women for Bosniak husbands.

Anguished by the brutality, the United Nations for the first time provided food and medicine to civilians in the midst of a war, and some 10,000 to 25,000 French, British, Dutch, and other United Nations Protection Force (UNPROFOR) troops were deployed to guard these relief operations, then later to guarantee Bosnian "safe areas." The UNPROFOR troops had strict orders to be "neutral." In practice, this euphemism meant they never intervened to protect defenseless civilians. On the contrary, they abetted ethnic cleansing by transporting women and children out of Bosniak towns while leaving the men to be massacred, or else they themselves became de facto hostages. When Bosniaks pleaded for allied air strikes against Bosnian Serb warlords who were shelling them, UN commanders and civilian officials repeatedly refused, in order to avoid partiality toward one side, but also to avoid retaliation against exposed UNPROFOR troops.[9]

In early 1994 the United States had at least managed to get the Croats and Bosniaks to stop fighting each other and to establish a federation in the 30 percent of Bosnia not controlled by the Serbs. And a "Contact Group" of the four largest European nations, plus the United States and Russia, had been established to make both Washington and Moscow accept some responsibility for a settlement and not let Serbs play the Russian card or Bosniaks play the American card in rejecting European peace proposals. But NATO, the world's most powerful security alliance, was a minor actor, doing no more than monitoring sanctions together with the Western European Union, conducting overflights on invitation in Hungarian airspace (and thus stopping Yugoslav bombing of Hungarian border towns), enforcing a no-fly zone in Bosnia mandated by the United Nations, and conducting pinprick retaliatory strikes against Bosnian Serb besiegers of Sarajevo and other Bosniak enclaves.

To be sure, everyone had a reason for not acting or for acting timidly. As war broke out in the Balkans, the Germans were preoccupied with unification, and the conviction that had characterized discourse on the German left ever since the Vietnam War—that peace constituted the highest morality—had not yet been challenged as sometimes condoning evil. European coordination of foreign policy was still in its infancy, and before the breakup of Yugoslavia the taboo, under the nuclear balance of terror, against intervening within the borders of a sovereign country remained absolute. Britain—besides having great awe of the Serb partisans' legendary resistance to Hitler's legions and holding a certain romantic view of the Serbs derived from the bible of Rebecca West's *Black Lamb and Gray Falcon*—calculated cynically that since Serbia was the regional strongman, the sooner it finished conquering the Croats and the Bosniaks, the sooner stability would return.

Across the Atlantic, Washington viewed the former Yugoslavia as a far-off land and a distraction from more pressing issues. Bush's secretary of state, James Baker, noted pungently in 1992 that the United States had no "dog in this fight."[10] Clinton still saw himself as a domestic, not a foreign-policy, president, and he recalled this priority ever more vividly as the 1994 and 1996 elections drew closer. For its part, the U.S. military hierarchy, vividly recalling Vietnam and, later, the TV shots of a GI's naked corpse being dragged through the streets of Mogadishu, shrank from any assignment that might produce "mission creep" and did not entail a sure "exit strategy." Various northern democrats in both the United States and Europe, seeing the barbarity that was practiced by all sides in the south Slav lands, simply washed their hands of the affair. Indeed, many dismissed the Balkan tribes as incorrigibly bellicose and—despite the fact that it took Serbian president Slobodan Milosevic two long years to stoke nationalist hatreds up to the passions of war—viewed such a reversion to chauvinism as the natural recycling of history after the removal of the artificial constraints of the cold war.[11]

As the horror mounted in 1995, so did recriminations among NATO allies. The Americans castigated the French and especially the British for their studied neutrality between the heavily armed Serbs (and, increasingly, Croats) and the poorly armed Bosniaks and for blocking air strikes against those Serbs who were bombarding civilians in the Bosniak enclaves. The French and especially the British castigated the United States for threatening to drop unilaterally the UN arms embargo on Bosnia and for preaching morality to others when it would not risk a single GI on the ground. As they feuded, up to 8,000 Bosniak men were executed in Srebrenica, the largest single mass murder in Europe since World War II. Despite American satellite photography of the atrocity at the time, neither American planes nor European infantry intervened. The word genocide again made the rounds in a Europe that thought it had banished that demon.

The Bosnian Serbs, emboldened by the lack of opposition to their savagery, this time took UNPROFOR soldiers as literal hostages against NATO air strikes, chaining them to lampposts in front of the international corps of photographers. The French, who for some time had wanted to suppress the heavy Serb weapons, now insisted on forming rapid reaction forces with real combat capability. The Europeans as a whole now regarded their UNPROFOR mission to date as having only delayed final Serb victory, thereby increasing the total death and destruction.

As the lightly armed UNPROFOR troops appeared to be increasingly at risk, Clinton reluctantly pledged that American ground troops would help extricate them if it became necessary—without realizing the potential scope of casualties to which the NATO contingency process committed the United States.[12] And this time, unlike the aftermath of Suez, there was no overarching Soviet threat to force the Western allies back together again after their split. On the one hand, if Clinton delivered on his promise, and dozens or hundreds of American lives were lost in nothing more than ignominious retreat, Congress might order all the troops home, from Germany as well as from Bosnia. On the other hand, if Clinton left allied forces to fight their own way out against both Serbs and the deserted Bosniaks—and the president seemed to think he still had a choice—the whole American security guarantee and process of NATO consultation would be exposed as a sham. Either way, in the view of Assistant Secretary of State Richard Holbrooke, "It was not an overstatement to say that America's post–World War II security role in Europe was at stake."[13] Stanley R. Sloan, the Congressional Research Service's specialist on NATO, worried, "Neither the United States nor the Europeans have been willing to risk the sacrifices that could have been required to impose and enforce a peace in Bosnia. Now there is a growing tendency on both sides of the Atlantic to blame each other and NATO for the consequent policy failure."[14]

The only way, then, to avoid a humiliating withdrawal, unacceptable loss of American soldiers' lives, or the death of NATO was to up the ante. The Croats suddenly helped by applying the weapons they had been quietly accumulating with tacit American approval. In a mini-blitzkrieg they won back not only the Serb-conquered parts of Croatia, but also 20 percent of Bosnian territory, effecting a more even 51–49 percent division of terrain between the Bosnian Serbs and the Croat-Bosniak "federation." NATO aircraft for the first time responded disproportionately to Serb bombardments of Bosniak enclaves, flying 3,400 sorties in two weeks and destroying Serb heavy weapons ringing the enclaves.

Holbrooke seized the opportunity. He all but imprisoned the three Yugoslav parties (and Washington's European allies) in "proximity talks" at a Dayton airbase and bored in on Milosevic, who by now had abandoned his Bosnian Serb protégés in order to end Western economic sanctions on Belgrade.[15] An uneasy deal was cut; the hypnotism of war was broken long enough for participants to realize their own war exhaustion. The four years of battles and massacres had claimed some 200,000 lives, made refugees of half of the Bosnian population of 4.3 million, and displaced the largest number of children since World War II.

As part of the settlement, some 60,000 Implementation Forces (IFOR), a third of them now American, were sent into Bosnia with supporting firepower and robust rules of engagement to impound (primarily Serb) heavy weapons and police the peace. IFOR functioned for a year, to be succeeded by the smaller Stabilization Force (SFOR). NATO suddenly became the core of a multinational operation, with Russian, Ukrainian, central European, and other military units from twenty-one non–NATO countries cooperating under the alliance's new

Partnership for Peace program.[16] And a new war crimes court was opened in the Hague to try the few low- and medium-level Yugoslav thugs delivered to it as defendants.

The jury is still out as to whether the NATO–led truce enforcers can produce a peace that can outlast their armed presence, in Bosnia or in Kosovo. But they did at least stop the bloodshed, and they did provide the space for more moderate politicians to surface in Montenegro and the Srpska Republic in Bosnia.

Poland and Enlargement

Enlarging NATO to take in new members to the east followed a less stormy course than did Western policy on the former Yugoslavia. Initially the West cheered on the new democracies without promising them membership in NATO or offering any timetable for joining the EC. It was not until early 1993 that the first senior Western politician, German defense minister Volker Rühe, proposed that central European countries be welcomed into the defense alliance. Concern was rising in the West at that point about the more belligerent voices in Moscow that were starting to call for a Russian sphere of influence not only over the whole territory of the former Soviet Union, but also in the entire former Soviet bloc. And the central Europeans again felt as if they were falling into a power vacuum of the sort that throughout history had pulled belligerent neighbors in to war over them.[17]

Into this breach leaped Rühe, declaring, "Eastern Europe must not become a conceptual 'no-man's land.' . . . I cannot see one good reason for denying future members of the European Union membership in NATO." And since qualifying for membership in the fiercely competitive and complex EU would be far more difficult for fledgling market economies and polities than would qualifying for NATO, the defense minister further floated the notion that NATO membership might even precede EU membership.[18]

He spoke of central Europe generically, but he was thinking of Poland specifically; the Polish question was the problem that animated widening of both the EU and NATO, as fully as the German question animated deepening of the EU. With a population of 39 million, Poland was by far the largest of the central European countries—and over three centuries it had repeatedly been buffeted between assertive

Germans and assertive Russians. Eighteenth-century partition among Russia, Prussia, and Austria set the pattern; Hitler's attack on Poland, triggering World War II, and what Poles viewed as a half-century of occupation by the Soviet Union, were only the latest examples. In the early 1990s, Poles still recited the number of times they felt abandoned by the West—in their doomed periodic revolts against Russian rule under the partition, in the German attack in 1939, and in the Warsaw uprising in 1944, then in 1945 as the East-West lines drawn at the Yalta conference of the great powers once again delivered them to Moscow. With bitterness some Poles anticipated a new betrayal by the West in relegating Poland to a post–cold war limbo and subjection to pressure from the Russians.

Making the same point more positively about Poland's thousand-year yearning to be accepted as part of the West, Janusz Onyszkiewicz asserted in an interview, "Our aspirations to join the European Union and NATO are two sides of the same coin." Speaking with the authority he acquired as Solidarity spokesman in 1980–81 and as defense minister twice in the 1990s, he continued, "We simply want to join the community of democratic countries of the northern hemisphere."[19]

Foreign Minister Bronislaw Geremek, accepting the 1998 Charlemagne Prize, expressed the same sentiment. Europe and Poland have a common "Judeo-Christian and humanist tradition," he proclaimed, that is finally asserting itself in a twenty-first-century Europe that is both whole and free. Geremek welcomed today's belated coming together as expressing a "geocultural" commonweal that should now replace the geopolitics, chauvinism, and national and class "egoism" of the past. He praised in particular Germany's rapprochement with Poland in 1990 and Germany's role today in helping Poles and other central Europeans enter the Western clubs. This "surprising and wonderful change" in bilateral relations, he declared, is "one of the greatest events of our century. . . . Thanks to the reunification of Germany Poland could become free, and thanks to the freedom of Poland wrested in the great epic of Solidarity, Germany could achieve reunification."[20]

Despite this new bilateral warmth, Rühe remained a lone prophet for almost a year in calling for NATO expansion. Kohl displayed little interest in the subject. And unlike Rühe and Geremek, Washington saw many compelling reasons for not enlarging NATO. The most important consideration was to avoid provoking Moscow and strengthening all the Russian Zhirinovskys who resented their abrupt loss of empire.

Two incidents in 1993 changed America's view, however. The first occurred during Russian president Boris Yeltsin's visit to Poland on the invitation of Polish president Lech Walesa. In Warsaw the old Solidarity electrician-hero, using a time-honored ploy of diplomacy, got his guest drunk and let him say publicly, No, it would not bother Russia if Poland joined NATO. Back home, Russian officials quickly corrected their chief, and eventually Yeltsin himself changed his position. But by then he was too late; what had previously been the universal assumption that NATO expansion would be utterly unacceptable to Moscow had been cast into doubt.

The second incident occurred in Washington, where Walesa and Czech president Vaclav Havel used their participation in the opening of the Holocaust Museum to press their case personally with Clinton. Against the somber memory of Auschwitz, their pleas that history should be rectified—and central Europeans given the chance to create the prosperity and security that their more fortunate west European cousins had been granted half a century earlier—sounded persuasive to the American president. The central Europeans had paid the penalty of being on the wrong side of the Iron Curtain for two generations. The courage of the Poles in particular—who had gone on mass strike against their communist government and its Russian masters in the 1980s and in the end brought down Moscow's whole internal as well as external empire—deserved reward. The prospect of the very rich reward of NATO and EU membership would buttress the still shaky central European democracies and market economies, give citizens the patience to endure painful short-term adjustments in order to attain the larger goal, and refute extremist demagogues. By September of 1993, National Security Adviser Anthony Lake, in his first major foreign-policy speech, was urging replacement of the old strategy of containment with a "strategy of enlargement—enlargement of the world's free community of market democracies." This would offer the Poles, Czechs, and others "an essential collective security."[21]

The Pentagon balked. It feared that expansion would dilute NATO, spreading the alliance too thin—especially in a period of sharp defense budget cuts—and bringing in new members whose militaries would be far below alliance standards in equipment and training. In part to deflect enlargement, in late 1993 the Defense Department and its allies in the civilian bureaucracies launched a far weaker substitute, the Partnership for Peace program, under which any eastern partner who wished to do so could join NATO officers and troops in individually tailored exercises and exchanges.

For the next two-and-a-half years a tug of war ensued within the Washington bureaucracies and on the op-ed pages of U.S. newspapers. Those who opposed NATO enlargement argued that it was unnecessary in the more benign post–cold war environment, that it would be self-fulfilling in presuming Russia as the adversary, and that it catered only to ethnic politics in the United States and to American arms manufacturers who wanted to sell their jets and electronics in new central European markets.[22]

Those who favored expansion contended that the reinsurance of NATO membership would enlarge the west European zone of peace and stability, deter threats from any quarter at an early stage (including disputes between candidate countries themselves, on the Greek-Turkish model), and thus make it less likely that NATO would ever have to use force ex post facto to restore peace in the region. They argued further that expansion could be sold politically in the United States as an appeal to ethnic voters. Moreover, they asserted, the central Europeans should no longer be regarded as pawns of the superpowers, but as sovereign countries with a right to choose their own alliances. The carrot of NATO membership would help the young democracies meet the membership preconditions of military transparency and civilian control of the military, and defense would cost them less cooperatively than it would individually.[23]

The bureaucratic victory for enlargement in Washington was signaled by the appearance of an essay on its behalf by no less than Strobe Talbott, the Russo-centric deputy secretary of state.[24] After William Perry became secretary of defense, the Defense Department also shifted to favor this policy. And when Madeleine Albright became secretary of state, she was especially vigorous in promoting admission of Poland, Hungary, and her native Czech Republic into NATO.[25]

Once the United States had decided its course, the Europeans followed. The Germans were delighted to have the United States take the lead in a policy that so clearly served their desire to have NATO allies to their east as well as to their west. Other Europeans did not have strong opinions on the question; the only real disagreement pitted

France against the United States over the tactical issue of whether to include Romania in the first tranche of new admissions. Given the urgent need to secure two-thirds' U.S. Senate approval for every new member, Washington won that fight; only Poland, Hungary, and the Czech Republic would be admitted in the first cut.

With the political debate closed, the main diplomatic task became damage control in Moscow. With Polish membership, the alliance would border Russia for the first time, along the Baltic exclave of Kaliningrad (Königsberg) that the Soviet Union had wrested from Germany in 1945.[26] And even though NATO, in the wake of the cold war, had sharply reduced its total troops, deployed the troops in a defensive pattern, and promised to place no outside units or nuclear weapons in Poland under the contemporary lack of threat, the psychological stress on the former superpower would be great.

Nor could the West expect a smooth transition for alliance expansion just because the Soviet Union had tolerated eastern Germany's leaving the Warsaw Pact and immediately becoming a member of NATO as a result of the GDR's merger with the Federal Republic. In one sense, East Germany had been Moscow's biggest prize from World War II and was the hardest for it to give up. Yet ever since the time of Catherine the Great, the Russians had been in awe of the Germans' technological and military prowess. The one thing they did not want to have happen was for a dynamic reunited Germany to "renationalize" its defense and foreign policy, go it alone without the constraints of its allies, and possibly become more assertive. On balance, binding the Germans into the Western alliance looked like the lesser of two evils.

No such considerations applied to Poland in the late 1990s. The Russians had no comparable awe of Poland, which Moscow regarded not as a major player like Germany, but only as a subordinate buffer zone insulating Russia from the West. Nor could Moscow hope to receive any financial compensation for the "loss" of Poland equal to the largesse Bonn bestowed on it as recompense for the "loss" of the German Democratic Republic.

Nonetheless, the West still proceeded from the assumption that with enough diplomatic effort it could expand NATO in cooperation rather than confrontation with Moscow—and calculated in any case that the West's foreign policy would have little political impact on a Russia absorbed in its own economic troubles. The oligarchs who held both economic and political power in Russia would want to preserve their profitable deals with the West rather than force a clash, Washington concluded, while the disillusioned and struggling Ivan Ivanich would not easily be mobilized against the West on abstract questions of superpower status.

Out of deference to Moscow as well as out of internal policy disagreement, then, the West moved only slowly to take in new NATO members; it avoided surprises and signaled each step to Russia well in advance. While helping to train the tiny new armies in Estonia, Latvia, and Lithuania, and signing a charter anticipating future NATO membership for the Baltic states, the West postponed this especially sensitive question to the twenty-first century and left its implied security engagement in this militarily indefensible region to discreet joint Scandinavian or Partnership for Peace exercises. It made the unilateral pledge to refrain from nuclear or NATO troop deployments on the territory of Poland and other new alliance members under the existing low threat.[27] And it established the NATO–Russian Permanent Joint Council to give Moscow, as the shorthand had it, "a voice but not a veto" in alliance policy debates. In addition, the Group of Seven leading industrial powers conferred prestige on Russia by taking it in as the eighth member at its annual summits. And this package helped secure a mild Russian reaction when NATO did make the formal decision in summer of 1997 to admit the first new central European members. Noting the Russian equanimity, Western proponents of NATO expansion said I told you so, while opponents who had predicted more dire consequences observed tartly that history sometimes forgives mistakes.

The West, with some arm-twisting of Ukraine and Turkey by the United States, further offered Moscow the adjustments Russia sought in easing CFE conventional weapons restrictions on its flanks. NATO secretary-general Javier Solana argued forcefully in Moscow that NATO enlargement should actually help Russia by consolidating democracy, stability, and peaceful behavior to its west. A country that had its hands full with unrest in the Caucasus and central Asia, he suggested, should welcome having a peaceful border it did not need to worry about.

As the key new NATO candidate, Poland said that the promise of membership would actually give it the confidence to improve relations with Russia, since with NATO backing it need not fear that its overtures might be misunderstood as subservience. In 1997, shortly before he became defense minister for the second time—and shortly before Poland went on NATO's short list—Onyszkiewicz explained the paradox:

Because we were more or less accepted as viable applicants to NATO, we could try to intensify cooperation with Russia. In 1989, or 1991 even, we would have run a certain risk that if we did try to make some opening to Russia, this could have sent the wrong signal to the Russians—that Poland is hesitating or has still not decided where our place is. So before we were able to embark on this policy, to develop our "Ostpolitik" [détente with the east], we had not only to define our position but also to get acceptance from the West.

He ticked off the areas of rapid improvement already appearing in bilateral relations, including contracts for delivery of Russian gas and Poland's rise to become Russia's fourth-largest trading partner, after the United States, Japan, and China. "In that context, if new Zhirinovskys came up, [with NATO membership] we could afford to give them the benefit of the doubt" and not react with countermoves that might increase tension, he continued. "If not, we would be too jumpy to do so. Look who has the worst relations with Russia—Estonia, just because it is so vulnerable."[28]

Assessing the situation in mid-1998, a year after NATO's firm promise of admission and a year before formal induction, Bartolomiej Sienkiewicz, director of the Polish Eastern Studies Center, echoed Onyszkiewicz's observation. The Russian foreign policy elite has now begun treating Poland with new "normality" and "equality of rights," he found, and has dropped the old "imperial superpower" arrogance toward an inferior. President Yeltsin, far from regarding Polish activism in the region as trespassing on Russia's sphere of influence, even complimented visiting Polish president Alexander Kwasniewski, marveled Sienkiewicz, about Poland's policy toward Ukraine, the Baltic states, and Belarus.[29] The Balts also sense a new respect in Russia's treatment of them, despite the continuing Russian feuds with Latvia and Estonia about ethnic Russians in those countries.[30]

The Poles are thus convinced that the three new central European members will neither sour relations between Russia and the West nor—in the contrary fear of prominent U.S. opponents of enlargement—

weaken the alliance. Hungary already contributes positively to NATO by providing important bases for its operations in the former Yugoslavia. (The Czech Republic does not figure in the criticism, since it is a small country located south of the historic arena of East-West confrontation and therefore does not cost the alliance anything in its defense commitment.) Poland, the main actor, contributes above all the traditional esprit that distinguished its pilots in the Battle of Britain and its foot soldiers at Monte Cassino, suggests Nicholas Rey, U.S. ambassador to Poland in the mid-1990s.[31] Poland would also provide, in the unlikely event of any return to East-West military confrontation, the depth for maneuver that NATO lacked throughout the cold war—and in peacetime it certainly provides shooting ranges where live ammunition can be used without provoking citizen petitions against the practice. Nor is there any doubt that Polish home territory would be defended by forces that are no longer massed for attack on the west as in the old Warsaw Pact days, but are now deployed more evenly throughout the country.

In equipment, the Poles have better tanks than the Greeks, Turks, and even Italians and French, says Defense Minister Onyszkiewicz. Under its $2.3 billion upgrading plan, Poland will essentially be wired into NATO's air defense by 2003; its fighter planes will mostly be equipped with alliance IFF (identification friend or foe) electronics; communications will be essentially compatible with NATO's; and military maps will have been redrawn according to alliance specifications. While they will long remain as far behind the west Europeans as the west Europeans are behind the United States in advanced battlefield technology, with the prod of Target Force Goals assigned by NATO, they are at least heading toward compatibility, or, in NATO jargon, "interoperability," of their and NATO's main weapons by about 2010.

Ukraine and Other Neighbors

Poland's accession to NATO poses the question of how to deal with Ukraine as well as with Russia, of course. Ukraine, with a territory and population matching those of France, has never had any lasting sovereignty of its own, and for the past three centuries it has been essentially a province of Russia. Its new independence of 1991 was widely considered illegitimate and temporary by Russians, even those

of a liberal persuasion; the common expectation was that Ukraine would prove to be too immature to govern itself and would therefore fall back into Russia's lap fairly soon.

Yet any attempt by Russians to reclaim Ukraine—and Moscow mayor and likely Russian presidential candidate Yuri Luzhkov already claims the Crimean port of Sevastopol, 800 miles away, as a Moscow municipal district—would be the first step to restoring the Russian empire and would probably be accompanied by an antidemocratic backlash in Russia. A stable, independent Ukraine, by contrast, would be not only a buffer for Poland, but also a brake on reversion to an imperial mentality in Russia. As Volodymyr Vernadsky, the first president of the Ukrainian Academy of Sciences, warned almost a century ago, "Russian democracy ends where the Ukrainian question begins."[32] More positively, a senior Polish diplomat put it this way today: "If Ukraine stays independent, Russia has a chance to become a normal nation-state."[33]

Kyiv was acutely aware of the dangers, and various foreign-policy strategists in the entourage of Ukrainian president Leonid Kuchma campaigned hard for a NATO guarantee of Ukrainian independence— or, as second best, a "special relationship" with NATO that might exhibit alliance interest in Ukraine's continuing independence much as it did in the Baltics. In nonprovocative tandem with the NATO– Russian relationship, in the spring of 1997 the Ukrainians finally attained what NATO cautiously called a "distinctive" partnership—and the Ukrainians translated as their greatly desired "special" partnership. The showcase of the agreement was a joint NATO–Ukrainian commission that would parallel the new NATO–Russian council.

The impact of this symbol of NATO–Ukraine rapprochement on bilateral Russian-Ukrainian relations was immediate. Within a week of Moscow's acceptance of the NATO–Russian Permanent Joint Council and tacit acquiescence in Polish entry into NATO—and concurrent signing of the NATO–Ukraine partnership—Yeltsin reversed his six-year-long refusal to regularize relations between the two largest Slav states. He suddenly flew to Kyiv in May of 1997, signed a comprehensive treaty of friendship, and agreed on the final Ukrainian and Russian shares of the Soviet Black Sea Fleet. Moreover, he acknowledged Ukrainian sovereignty over the previously contested Crimean Peninsula by paying Kyiv rent for berthing the Russian ships that would continue to be based in Sevastopol.[34] In the eyes of the Ukrainians, this more benign Russian policy was the direct result of NATO's willingness to guarantee the security of neighboring Poland and to embrace Ukraine, even if not to guarantee its borders.[35] Linkage was sealed with the first multilateral Partnership for Peace maneuvers in western Ukraine and with a bilateral Ukrainian-American naval exercise off the Crimean coast. For the cash-strapped Ukrainian navy, it was a godsend to have Washington foot the bill every now and then for joint exercises that got the Ukrainian ships out of their docks.

A further accomplishment of NATO enlargement, long before the first accession of new members, came from the prophylactic effect of the very hope of admission to NATO. The alliance categorically bars entry to any candidates with unsettled territorial or other disputes with neighbors. And this precondition for EU as well as NATO membership—plus the compelling contrast between French-German reconciliation and shared prosperity on the one hand and the Yugoslav vortex of self-perpetuating war and impoverishment on the other— combines to form a powerful incentive to peaceful resolution of conflicts. Between 1996 and 1998, NATO secretary-general Solana points out, in a series of "bilateral agreements the central and east Europeans have solved problems that have been with them since [before] World War II: Romania-Hungary, Romania-Moldova, Ukraine-Russia—all the century-old issues have been solved. Why?" he asks. "Because we said very clearly, you have no chance of being in this club [unless you make a real effort to solve] minority problems."[36]

The most arresting examples of NATO's preventive peacemaking are to be found in Hungarian-Romanian and in Polish-Ukrainian rapprochement. Hungary is the one country that ended up after the terrible genocide, forced migrations, and border changes of World War II with many of its countrymen—3 million, or close to 30 percent of the state's present population—still outside its national borders. The largest portion of these live in Transylvania, which was awarded to Romania by the Trianon Treaty of 1920. In any earlier period (or in the Balkans today) such a condition would have justified irredentism and belligerence toward neighbors; and some nationalist demagogues in Hungary indeed sought to exploit this grievance in the early 1990s, as did some Romanian nationalists. Yet in both cases the chauvinists lost to moderates in elections—primarily because both countries craved NATO membership and did not want to spoil their chances of admission by bad behavior. There are still strains over the ethnic Hungarian demand for a Hungarian-language university in Cluj, but Budapest is now seeking joint solutions with both Bucharest and local Transylvanian communities rather than enflaming disputes. And the reformist Romanian government that took office in 1996 is not only protecting Hungarian language rights in Transylvania, but also for the first time includes a Hungarian ethnic party in its coalition.

The second major example of NATO's prophylactic effect—rapprochement between the two largest nations in the region—is even more striking. For centuries Ukrainian peasants rebelled periodically against Polish landlords in the region they cohabited between the Vistula and the Dnepr rivers. The two were still butchering each other throughout World War II, and hostility continued after the postwar settlement awarded this territory to Soviet Ukraine (and awarded compensatory German lands in the west to Poland). At the end of the war Poles avenged themselves by brutally expelling millions of Germans from the area around Breslau (Wroclaw), a city that had been German for centuries; in mirror image, Ukrainians brutally expelled Poles from Lviv (Lvov), a city that for centuries had been essentially Polish and Jewish. Additionally, Polish authorities scattered the Ukrainian minority in Poland throughout the country and broke up its social networks. There was, in sum, far more historical tinder to kindle conflict between Poles and Ukrainians than between the Serbs and Bosniaks who for generations had lived together in mutual tolerance and intermarriage.

Yet in the post–cold war world both Warsaw and Kyiv decided that traditional enmity is dysfunctional and that they could only gain by adopting Western norms of peaceful cooperation. And although the phenomenon is largely ignored by journalists with a professional bias toward strife and violence, the record suggests that the really startling news on this once bloodthirsty continent is not the atavistic chain reaction of savagery and war in the former Yugoslavia. It is instead the unprecedented chain reaction of reconciliation among old enemies in central Europe. In an arc spreading east from western Europe, war is becoming as obsolete as feather boas or ruling monarchs. "Poland and Ukraine have a window of historic opportunity to repeat what has been achieved by France and Germany after the Second World War," commented Ambassador Ihor Kharchenko of the Ukrainian Foreign Ministry during the run-up to Polish acceptance into NATO. And a senior Polish diplomat echoed his words:

We are the window to the West for Ukraine, as Germany is the window to the West for us. We would not like to become part of NATO if the price for that would be giving Ukraine back to Russia. Basically, they [the Ukrainians] say that bordering the Western system would be beneficial and would enhance their independence and security too—provided that NATO expansion would not be a deal with Russia that Poland gets in, but the dividing line is the Bug River, and Ukraine is on the wrong side.[37]

In this spirit Poland is conspicuously sponsoring Ukrainian entry into various central European regional groupings, and the two defense ministries are forming a joint peacekeeping battalion with English as the common language of command.

Perhaps most important in the long run, some Poles are even revisiting Polish-Ukrainian history to explain to their compatriots that Poles were also perpetrators—and not just victims, as the enduring myths would have it—in past Polish-Ukrainian clashes. "History in this part of the world plays an enormous role. As we learned in Yugoslavia so [disastrously], so here too, clearing up the historical problems is very important," observes one of the new breed of historians.[38]

In a similar spirit Ukraine and Romania have set aside their quarrel over Serpent Island. Poland and Lithuania have resolved feuds over the language and other rights of minority Poles in villages around Vilnius, and these two countries too are forming a joint peacekeeping battalion. Among themselves the Baltic states, besides joining Norway, Denmark, Sweden, and Poland in the Nordpol Brigade in Bosnian peacekeeping, are also fielding a joint "Baltbat" battalion—and are setting up "Baltnet," to monitor their airspace. Bulgaria, Romania, Greece, and Turkey have established a multinational Balkan force, with headquarters to be located in southern Bulgaria during the first four years and then rotated. Other joint peacekeeping units are proliferating in the region as well, on the models of the Eurocorps, the German-Dutch Corps, the Spanish-Italian Amphibious Force, and NATO's multinational AWACS surveillance-plane crews.[39] Germany, Denmark, and Poland have set up the Multinational Corps Northeast, with staff headquarters in Szczecin (but with no German or Danish troops stationed there, in accord with NATO promises to Russia). The Baltic states, and even Kyrgyzstan, Kazakhstan, and Uzbekistan, have all created joint army units for peacekeeping, and Estonia, Latvia, and Lithuania have also formed a common Baltic squadron. Poland, Hungary, and the Czech Republic, obliged to share their medium-term defense plans with NATO, even started showing them to each other before their induction. In varying degree the new democracies are being socialized to the West's culture of voluntary cooperation and the talking out of disputes.

Unresolved Issues

As of this writing, several alliance issues remain to be resolved: crisis management in Kosovo and Iraq and revision of NATO's strategic concept.

The Serbian province of Kosovo was the sleeper in Yugoslavia, the place that most observers had expected would be the first flash point. Revered by Serbs as the cradle of their civilization, it was the site of their epic defeat by the Turks in 1389 and is still the seat of the Serbian Orthodox Church.[40] Yet by the twentieth century the majority of Kosovo's population was ethnic Albanian, growing to some 90 percent today; Serbs are a small minority there.

In the 1970s the Croat-Slovene Josip Broz Tito, as part of his tactic to limit the power of the preponderant Serbs within Yugoslavia, gave autonomy within the Serbian Republic to both Kosovo to the south and Vojvodina to the north. After Tito's death in 1980, however, increasingly virulent nationalist Serbs rallied to redress alleged violations of Serbian rights and to restore full Serbian rule in Kosovo. In the late 1980s Slobodan Milosevic, then the little-known head of the Serbian Communist party, made the cause his own and rescinded Kosovan autonomy.

Still, it took until 1998 for the province to explode. By then, with the increasing polarization, the Kosovo Liberation Army (KLA) of a few thousand guerrillas overshadowed Kosovan moderates with its militant demand for full independence. Milosevic increased the number of Yugoslav army and paramilitary forces in the province to several tens of thousands in late 1997; by early 1998 they were torching ethnic Albanian villages accused of harboring KLA guerrillas. In what looked like a haunting repetition of Bosnia, civilians were massacred; some 400,000 refugees, or a fifth of the population, fled to Albania or to the woods. As risk grew that the conflagration might spread to the already unstable Albania and to ethnic Albanian areas of Macedonia, NATO threatened retaliation against Serbian military targets if Milosevic did not stop the bloodshed.

Once again Richard Holbrooke was called in to be the chief per-suader. Milosevic negotiated, and he calibrated his own show of force to stop just short of triggering NATO air strikes on Serbia. By October, after he had routed the KLA—and after NATO had run some pointed bombing simulations just outside Serbian borders—he did agree to draw his troops in Kosovo back down to their February levels and to talk with the Kosovans about a political solution. The gesture might have been a concession to NATO firepower, or it might have signaled only the Balkans' usual winter pause in fighting. Two thousand unarmed OSCE observers were sent into Kosovo to monitor the truce, backed up by a French-led, armed NATO "extraction force" of 1,800 offstage in Macedonia.

In trying to stop the savagery, NATO faced an acute dilemma. Unlike Bosnia after Western recognition of the Yugoslav successor states, Kosovo had no claim to being an independent land that was calling for external help against an outside aggressor; it was still recognized as an integral part of Serbia. Western military intervention in Serbia's internal affairs would set a precedent few really wanted to set and would certainly offend Moscow and jeopardize one of the main achievements of the Bosnian operation, Russian cooperation with NATO. Yet doing nothing would repeat the criminal negligence of the world community in the face of the Bosnian massacres.

In the end NATO did meddle in sovereign affairs, for the first time in its half century of existence. Had Milosevic not agreed to thin out his forces in Kosovo, the alliance was even prepared to ignore Russian and Chinese vetoes in the UN Security Council and use military force against Serbian targets. The operation left open as many questions as it answered—about exit strategy; about how NATO would react if either the Serbs or the KLA rebuilt over the winter or took monitors hostage in a further repetition of Bosnia; and about how much prior authorization would be required by the UN or OSCE to justify NATO strikes in case of violation of the Kosovo truce.

The same broad questions dogged Washington's efforts to deny Saddam Hussein nuclear, biological, or chemical weapons and hold him to serious monitoring by UN inspectors. If it came to that, the United States was prepared to bomb Iraqi targets in tandem with the

United Kingdom, without requiring any broader alliance participation. Washington asked of other allies only that they not criticize the United States for resorting to force in defense of the West's common interest. And the other allies, including the new center-left government in Germany, were prepared to promise this restraint. Indeed, so offensive was Saddam's defiance of world opinion in late 1998 that even the French—and most of Saddam's fellow Arab leaders—were ready to condone U.S. military action.

In addition to these urgent, concrete issues, NATO must agree on modernization of the alliance's overall "strategic concept" that is to be approved at the alliance's gala fiftieth anniversary summit in Washington in the spring of 1999. From 1995 to the present, NATO's adaptation to post–cold war Europe has been driven largely by pragmatic rather than theoretical considerations, by the exigencies of making peacekeeping in Bosnia (and Kosovo) work rather than by any ideal goal. Yet some conceptual coherence is needed, and the lines are not fully clear.

What is emerging is that the new strategic concept will be evolutionary rather than revolutionary. It will perpetuate collective defense on the territory of NATO members as the alliance's core task—but will describe crisis management in the turbulent periphery of Europe as an important second mission. To reconcile contradictions in the very different force structures required for these two tasks, it will note that NATO's flexible integrated command arrangement makes modules of units available both for any all-out defense and for lesser operations that require "rapid reaction"—and that might be implemented by exclusively European troops with U.S. intelligence and logistics support.

Beyond this, it is unlikely that the Europeans will agree to any of the code words Washington would like for a NATO commitment to act "out of area"—that is, in the Middle East. It is equally unlikely that the Europeans will specify, as Washington would like to do, that if a good-faith effort has been made and failed to get an explicit prior UN or OSCE mandate for NATO military action, the alliance is justified in proceeding with intervention without this imprimatur.

A more sublimated issue is that of the alliance doctrine on first use of nuclear weapons. Throughout the period of cold war deterrence against forward-massed Soviet-bloc forces with a large numerical superiority over the West in tanks, artillery, and other heavy ground weapons, NATO reserved the right, if it was losing territory, to offset Soviet conventional superiority by resorting to nuclear arms. German foreign minister Joschka Fischer, along with the Canadians, the Danes, and a number of other allies, wants to renounce this option. Fischer loosed the issue in talking with journalists about the government's coalition agreement between the Social Democrats and Greens—and was quickly repudiated by Social Democratic defense minister Rudolf Scharping on a conveniently timed trip to Washington. His cabinet colleague was merely thinking of the distant future, Scharping explained. The United States, letting sleeping dogs lie, quickly quashed the notion.

NATO–EU Synergy

NATO at the end of the 1990s, in part by methodical bureaucratic planning, in part by desperate improvisation under threat of self-destruction during the Bosnian crisis, has in fact established itself as the center of Europe's post–cold war security system. After the British vetoed French efforts to subsume the languishing Western European Union under the EU as the manifestation of an independent European security and defense identity (ESDI), the Europeans and Americans finally agreed in 1996 on a formula for developing ESDI within the NATO framework.[41] Under guidelines for "Combined Joint Task Forces," the WEU would borrow "separable but not separate" NATO assets for humanitarian, peacekeeping, or even peacemaking operations that the WEU wishes to conduct but the United States does not wish to participate in directly.[42]

NATO secretary-general Solana argues passionately that this should produce an ESDI that will give Europe more muscle and at the same time strengthen transatlantic security links by letting the Europeans share more of the burden of common defense. To the European and American defense elites he preaches, "Clearly, Europe is not yet the strategic actor it wants to be, nor the global partner the United States seeks. But these shortcomings do not result from 'too much United States,' as some still claim, but from 'too little Europe.' That is why the European integration process is not only relevant for Europe's own identity, but for a new transatlantic relationship as well."[43] What Europe needs now, he continues, is a wider "architecture based on different institutions acting toward shared strategic objectives," with each component open to taking in new members. He lauded as exemplary the cooperation in Bosnia among NATO, the UN, the EU, and the Organization for Security and Cooperation in Europe (the successor to the CSCE). And he anticipated that these overlapping organizations, along with the Contact Group and the WEU, would increasingly coordinate their crisis prevention, crisis management, and, if need be, peacekeeping and peacemaking in Europe.

Certainly in peacekeeping, as the former Yugoslavia demonstrates, NATO will be at the hub of Western responses because of its political cohesion, clear defense mission, integrated command, and ready forces. "Again NATO is the pole. It has the procedures, capabilities, philosophy that make all the difference," Solana declares. "Without the Article 5 command structure it would be impossible to do peacekeeping or peace enforcing. We have the [central organization], structure, and readiness. In thirty days we put 60,000 people into Bosnia. . . . Without [that] spine, it would be very difficult to be effective."[44] U.S. defense secretary William Cohen concurs, stating, "NATO–led Partnership for Peace operations will be the operational coalitions of the future."[45]

Internally, what initially seemed to be NATO's most difficult tasks—de-emphasizing nuclear deterrence, downsizing main forces that had been trained to repel a massed frontal attack and reorganizing them into more flexible rapid-reaction forces, and cutting the number of headquarters from sixty-five to twenty—went fairly smoothly.[46] The alliance's decades-old innovation of an integrated peacetime command with constant multinational rehearsals proved its value in readiness for unprecedented multinational operations at short notice under widely varied conditions. The byproduct of military transparency and trust in allies' intentions and capabilities resulting from shared medium-term planning provided reassurance to members. And NATO's core function of collective security and stability has been maintained in successive "strategic concepts" and extended to fill the old vacuum of Poland.

In addition, Spanish forces are now being fully integrated into the NATO command, ironically under a Spanish socialist secretary-general of NATO (Solana) who once opposed Madrid's entry into the alliance. The old Spanish-British quarrels over the Rock of Gibraltar, though they have not been resolved, are being finessed without detriment to NATO operations. And if the alliance is no closer to curing Greek-Turkish enmity, it is at least averting the worst danger by establishing rules to keep the two countries' navies and air forces apart in the Aegean Sea and coaxing them into joint maneuvers with NATO in 1998 for the first time in thirteen years.

By contrast, the thirty-year-old anomaly of Paris's withholding of French forces from NATO's integrated command remains. The initial gestures of rapprochement by President Jacques Chirac in the mid-1990s led nowhere as he demanded too much in insisting that a French general get the alliance's southern command, which includes the U.S. Mediterranean Sixth Fleet. The Germans, who hoped they might be able to mediate, started with some sympathy for Chirac, but lost it as his position hardened.[47]

NATO's various internal adaptations to the post–cold war world were perhaps commendable in their execution, but essentially predictable. What has been much more surprising, by contrast, has been the Cinderella Partnership for Peace. It began as an evasion of enlargement, but it has turned into both a preparatory school for that enlargement and a framework for organizing pan-European security space and softening the line between NATO and non–NATO Europe. An ongoing "Mediterranean Dialogue" is being conducted in this program, and Partners discuss common ways to fight terrorism and illicit arms trade. Increasingly, Partners, including Russia, not only take part in ad hoc exercises, but also station "Staff Elements" at the NATO military headquarters (SHAPE) in Mons, Belgium, and at regional commands; in the future they are expected to do so at subregional commands as well.

The military Partnership for Peace and its political companion, the Euro-Atlantic Partnership Council, which meets monthly at NATO headquarters in Brussels, are both immensely popular among the more than three dozen participants.[48] The alliance is a "magnetic pole," in Solana's words, and enables NATO "to shape the nature of security" in Europe.[49] "The Partnership can act as a catalyst for a common 'culture' of security cooperation which has never before existed in Europe," he declares.[50] Already it is expanding the stable western European peace, which is far more than a balance-of-power interregnum between wars; it approaches the Kantian concept of an international community.[51] In the same way that today's young French and Germans find it absurd that their great-grandparents took war between their two countries for granted, so should tomorrow's young Germans and Poles find war unthinkable—and the day after tomorrow's Serbs and Bosniaks, too. Far from drawing new east-west dividing lines in Europe, then, Solana contends, the developing system of an enlarged NATO and an extended Partnership for Peace is "erasing" these lines. "Dividing lines meant you were totally in or totally out. Nobody is totally out today."[52] Any division today is one of different standards of living, he suggests, not one of politics.

One further unexpected byproduct of the Partnership for Peace has been the increasing role played by the traditionally neutral countries. In the post–cold war world it is not obvious what neutrality might mean, but many citizens in these countries still remain attached to it. The Partnership program lets them cooperate with the Western alliance without committing themselves to a domestically controversial goal of membership. In varying degree Austria, Finland, Sweden, and even Switzerland thus feel comfortable in joining Partnership exercises, while their armies get the benefit of working directly with their first-rate foreign counterparts. Eventually Austria—and if Austria, then perhaps Finland and Sweden, too—might join NATO as a full member, but in the interim, all the neutrals find Partnership exercises a useful way to cooperate with NATO without compromising their neutrality. "Only the Alliance has force structures and decision-making mechanisms that are capable not only of providing for deterrence and collective defence but are also adaptable for robust crisis management and peace support operations," explains Finnish defense minister Anneli Taina.[53]

For all the improvisation, the fact remains that NATO today, as in the past, is generally appreciated for providing the security shield behind which the Europeans (and, by extension, the Americans in their transatlantic links) can pursue their happiness in tranquility. The cold war gap between the military-political NATO and the economic-political European Union has not yet disappeared, and there is no institutional coordination between the two Brussels-based organizations. Yet both are aware, as the Poles keep stressing, that they are the obverse sides of the same coin of keeping Europe as peaceful and united as possible. The enlargement of both to admit central European members is proceeding in parallel, and if the EU's first tranche of newcomers adds Estonia, Slovenia, (and Greek Cyprus) to NATO's list of Poland, Hungary, and the Czech Republic, this flexibility helps to avoid the disappointment and political backlash that might otherwise follow a hard and fast division between a smaller core of "ins" ready to join both organizations and a large number of "outs" pushed off to the distant future.

Instead, the permeability of the divide between ins and outs allows NATO and/or the EU to reward Estonia and Latvia with a faster track toward membership when they heed Western calls to ease restrictions on citizenship for ethnic Russians. It lets NATO extend implicit security protection to the Baltic states as they move closer to EU membership—without excessively damaging relations with Russia. And it lets NATO and the EU be effective in blackballing the Slovakia of Vladimir Mečiar's autocratic rule and thus persuade Slovaks to vote Mečiar out of office in 1998 and resume democratic development.

The upshot is that the alliance's attraction (and discipline) of potential members, its ability to build coalitions on its own military core—and, of course, its assurance of U.S. engagement—make western and central European governments regard NATO as the continent's indispensable policeman. Concerns remain, admits Paul Cornish, lecturer in Defense Studies at King's College, London—about the tricky "institutionalization of ad hoc cooperation," organizational details once the Combined Joint Task Force is actually called on to act, and, as usual, the cohesion of what is no longer an "alliance of necessity" but an "alliance of choice." Yet to his own surprise, he concludes that "[t]he U.S.-European security relationship is, remarkably enough, not too unhealthy. The prognosis is therefore good, although full recovery from the end of the Cold War will be delayed for as long as the patient chooses not to believe the diagnosis."[54]

CHAPTER FIVE

Present at the Second Creation: The EU and European Monetary Union

If NATO lurched into strategic evolution as it was confronted by the Bosnian crisis, the European Union marched into strategic evolution by provoking crisis—then extricating itself. At this game the Germans excelled. It was an unusual method of agenda management, especially for risk-averse Teutons. It was, however, the only approach possible for EU activists if they were to steer, and not just be buffeted by, the whirlwind of change.

Crisis, 1994

Certainly in the two years after Maastricht, Europe exuded crisis. "Europe is failing to prosper," sadly concluded an editorial in the *Financial Times*.[1] "Euro-gloom" was the topic of a six-page *Newsweek* special and "The Europe Question: Ill or Dead?" a headline in the *International Herald Tribune*.[2] "This is not just an ordinary Euro-cycle," warned The *Economist*," but an "identity crisis of a scale that is only beginning to become clear to its members." The Maastricht Treaty, it continued, is "an almost insulting irrelevance."[3] "Are all our creative energies exhausted?" asked George Steiner plaintively in the *Frankfurter Allgemeine Zeitung*.[4] And even true believer Peter Ludlow, at the Centre for European Policy Studies in Brussels, felt obliged to boost morale by asserting, "The post-Maastricht crisis is far from being terminal in character."[5]

In the face of this adversity, Kohl's approach, as usual, was to dismiss naysayers, continue on course, and wait. Once again he displayed his patience (as his staff preferred to call it), or his formidable capacity to do nothing for long periods (as adversaries saw it). He kept repeating that the German question could be laid to rest only by binding Germans "irreversibly" to Europe.[6] He doggedly pursued his defense against Bismarck's nightmare by encircling Germany with peaceful, friendly, and increasingly prosperous neighbors. And no matter how much the European enterprise might seem to pall, no matter how daunting the polls showing that two-thirds of Germans opposed giving up their lovely deutsche mark, he persisted. He continued to preach the need for strengthening the European institutions and building toward political unity, for enlarging the EU to admit central European members and remedying the "democratic deficit."[7] He insisted—at the time Germany was virtually alone in this—that deepening and widening were not only compatible, but complementary; widening would compel the deepening needed to escape paralysis, to keep the EU "handlungsfähig," or able to act.[8] It was a German vision of progress by crisis that would soon apply also to monetary and economic union.

Kohl's constant reiteration of his old positions was met with cynicism by those immersed in the contemporary malaise. But he never expected his words to inspire the public and mobilize it for European action. That kind of oratory he reserved for campaign exhortations to the faithful of the Christian Democratic Union (CDU). In between elections his rhetoric was much more of a holding action, keeping issues alive in a contrary climate while waiting for outside pressures to compel emergency solutions and create consensus for the policies he advocated. Now he waited for highly centralized France and Britain to discover the virtues of decentralization and devolve some of Paris's and London's concentrated powers to local or regional communities (like Germany's own practice of "federalism," with considerable powers reserved for the Länder, the constituent states). He waited for "cohabitation" to sort itself out, as he would soon wait for France's newly elected neogaullist president to decide, like the Socialists before him, that the only thing worse than being in lockstep with the Germans is not being in lockstep with them. He waited for French industrial lobbies to confront French peasant lobbies and trim anachronistic agricultural subsidies (and for a long enough break between Bavarian elections to do the same in Germany). He waited for Tony Blair to move into 10 Downing Street and cooperate with the City to marginalize the Tory Euroskeptics. He waited for Germans, if not to love the euro, then at least to resign themselves to its inevitability. And above all, he waited for the logic of events to persuade others that his course of action, if not brilliant, was probably less bad than any conceivable alternative.

Within Germany, then, there was no visible movement in European integration as Bonn took over the EU presidency in July of 1994. The one client Kohl wished to convince of the wisdom of monetary union was the Bundesbank. The main EMU drama was being played out behind the scenes in Frankfurt—until the "Lamers paper" hit the fan.

Multispeed Europe, 1994–96

On September 1, 1994, politicians were jolted out of their vacation reveries by a paper called "Reflections on European Policy," written by Wolfgang Schäuble, chairman of Kohl's conservative parliamentary caucus, and the caucus foreign policy spokesman, Karl Lamers.[9] Germans had waved goodbye the day before to their last Russian occupation troops. A court in Berlin was about to try the octogenarian East German secret police chief, Erich Mielke, for his role in the killing of hundreds of would-be escapees on the strip separating the German Democratic Republic from the Federal Republic. The German general election campaign was in its last weeks; the constitutional amendment on asylum had halved the influx of foreigners, and, it seemed, the appeal of the far right.

Economically, German growth was in the process of rebounding to 2.9 percent a year, but overall the EU share of world exports in manufacture had dropped by a fifth since 1980, with a particularly wide gap in high technology exports. EU unemployment was again up to mid-1980s levels of over 17 million, or some 11 percent, after having dipped to just 8 percent in 1990. The EU single market now applied, in the "European Economic Area" instituted at the beginning of 1994, to the EFTA countries of Austria, Finland, Iceland, Norway, Sweden,

Switzerland, and Liechtenstein, covering overall a population of 380 million and accounting for 43 percent of world trade. This made the European single market more populous than the U.S. single market—and persuaded most of the EFTA governments that if they were going to live under EU economic rules anyway, they should at least enfranchise themselves to help write those regulations by becoming formal members of the Union.

Surprisingly, at this point only half of the necessary national legislation for the single market had been passed by all twelve EU states; Germany was one notable sluggard, largely because of turf claims by the Länder. Nonetheless, the foreign ministry machinery was already humming with daily "coreu" memos requiring answers within twenty-four hours on a growing array of EU issues delegated down for bureaucratic decision. Secondment of young diplomats for tours in each other's ministries was also leading to novel pan-European meetings in which a German foreign service officer might well speak for the French delegation (though never would a Briton, however adroit at debating the other side, represent the Germans).[10]

In Frankfurt the European Monetary Institute was beginning its ninth month of operation under its Belgian chief, Alexandre Lamfalussy, and was starting to write detailed provisions for everything from the interconnection of large-value payments to the calculation of the sacred M3 money supply, for all the world as if it really expected a common currency to come into being.[11] The Banque de France, as required by the Maastricht Treaty as a precondition for handing over powers to the forthcoming European Central Bank, had been granted unprecedented independence a few months earlier. The French were still smarting from Sir Leon Brittan's steamrollering over their protectionism in the GATT negotiations. And Chancellor Kohl had cautiously joined his voice to those calling for more equitable sharing of EU costs.[12]

In part, the Lamers paper, as it was immediately dubbed, represented yet another prod to get things moving after the two-and-a-half years of conspicuous stagnation. Such an effort was familiar enough from the past, and relatively uncontroversial. What set off a storm of protest, however, was the paper's attempt to think through some basic conundrums. How, as new opportunity beckoned after the end of the cold war, could the deadlock be broken between those who wished to press forward toward "ever closer union" and those who adamantly opposed such deepening? And how could the fragile—and, apart from Poland, tiny—new democracies in central Europe be incorporated into the EU without bringing the Union machinery to a complete halt under ever more vetoes from its increasingly diverse members? As German foreign minister Klaus Kinkel again asked rhetorically, echoing his chancellor, "Should the convoy in future be held back by its slowest ship?"[13]

The German conservatives' answer to Kohl's and Kinkel's question was an unambiguous no. Those EU members who wished to do so should indeed proceed with greater integration among themselves in economic and monetary union, it proclaimed, as well as in fiscal, social, and foreign policy. A "strong center" should "counteract the centrifugal forces generated by constant enlargement and, thereby, . . . prevent a South-West grouping, more inclined to protectionism and headed in a certain sense by France, drifting apart from a North-East grouping, more in favor of free world trade and headed in a certain sense by Germany."[14] And the "strong center" must not let itself be held back by waiting for the laggards to join in.

The concept was hardly new; such differentiation had been explicitly written into the provisions for British opt-out from monetary union and the social charter in the Maastricht Treaty, as well as in the Schengen Agreement on open borders between consenting members. British prime minister John Major, eager not to be painted as the bad boy of Europe, had once again in the summer called for a "multi-speed, multi-track" Europe.[15]

Yet the Lamers paper immediately set off two firestorms. The first arose from the paper's indelicate identification by name of the presumed inner core of countries that should accelerate integration without regard for the hesitant. Only Germany, France, and the Benelux countries qualified. Italy—cofounder of the EC along with the other five, and host to the original Treaty of Rome—was not among them. Nor was newcomer Spain. Fearing that they might forever be excluded, Rome, Madrid, and the other "outs" reacted angrily.

The second protest was an objection to the whole notion of "concentric circles," "two- (or three-) speed Europe," "multitrack," "variable geometry," "core Europe," "flexibility," "differentiation," or "avant garde," as the various code words had it. The very purpose of the European Union was solidarity, ran this critique; inner cores would divide rather than unite Europe.[16] Lamers had made another suggestion a year earlier, in August 1993: that decisions in the EU (except on questions where a veto could be applied) be by a "super-qualified" or "double majority" of both member nations and the populations they represented. While this plan reassured the large states that they would not be forced into action, or payment, by the growing crowd of little partners, it aroused resistance among those small states whose disproportionate weight would be reduced.[17]

Moreover, behind the terse wording of the 1994 Lamers paper lay implicit German exasperation with the French; some French even suspected this was actually the main message of the exercise.

Formally, of course, the alliance within the alliance was operating smoothly. Joint French-German initiatives routinely set the agenda for Council summits. The two had solemnly celebrated the thirtieth anniversary of Charles de Gaulle's and Konrad Adenauer's Elysée Treaty in January 1993 and reaffirmed that their destinies were inextricably linked. Paris had finally agreed that the eighteen east German observers at the European Parliament could acquire full membership status with the next European-wide elections. To the relief of the Germans, the French were, for the first time in twenty-eight years, even taking part in a meeting of NATO defense ministers and looking as if they might finesse a face-saving formula for rejoining the unified military command.

Bilateral strains were growing, however. French officials were charging that the imminent accession of Austria and Scandinavia to the EU and the future accession of central European states would improperly augment German power. They were musing aloud about how much more they had in common with Britain than with Germany, both in defense issues and in the desire to avert a federal European polity of the sort Kohl seemed to want. Paris was advancing claims to EU financial aid for the French backyard of North Africa to match the claims of central Europe in Germany's backyard—with Bonn, as usual, tacitly understood as the designated paymaster. There were squabbles over defense procurement and the EU budget, which would require much higher contributions from Paris if Bonn paid less.[18] French fears that the EU was now shifting from its previous French domination (and constraint on Bonn) to a future German domination (and constraint on Paris) were fed by the increasing use of English, and not just French, inside the bureaucracy, by the imminent departure of Frenchman Jacques Delors from the Commission presidency, and by the promotion of Germany's top diplomat, Jürgen Trumpf, to become secre-tary-general of the European Council, a post second in power only to presidency of the Commission itself. This trend was only reinforced by the use of English as the primary and German as the secondary language in the European Monetary Institute (EMI), and by German provision of a third of the EMI's professional personnel. To be sure, the personalized French cabinet system rather than the more open German corporate culture still prevailed inside the Brussels bureau-cracy and frustrated German newcomers. Moreover, Trumpf's job change might just as well have been interpreted as a weakening of the German drive for political union, with decisions increasingly delegated upward to Brussels, and acceptance of the French "Europe of father-lands," in which Brussels would remain weak and every common European policy would have to be decided anew by agreement be-tween sovereign EU member nations. That was certainly not the French reading, however. As differences mounted, even the unflappable Ger-man foreign minister, Klaus Kinkel, was moved to note, "The time has come . . . when our interests and those of the French do not neces-sarily coincide."[19]

In this context the Lamers message to Paris was unmistakable. France should recall its own interest in "deepening the Union prior to en-largement" and the need "to integrate a powerful Germany into Eu-ropean structures," it lectured. All EU members should avoid "regressive nationalism" as a response to "the internal crisis of mod-ern society and by external threats, such as migration."[20] If this were not done, there would be less responsible nationalists waiting in the wings, the paper implied, Germany not excluded. Paris and Bonn in particular should make strenuous efforts to keep separate interests from pulling them apart. But there would have to be an open debate about the excessive French-inspired trade protectionism and farm sub-sidies in the EU. The European Parliament (despite French opposi-tion) should get more powers, to redress the democratic deficit. EU members must get beyond "intergovernmental cooperation, which might well encourage a trend towards a 'Europe a la carte.'" And Paris, like Bonn, would have to surrender more of its sovereignty to the common good.[21]

Most pointedly, if France did not stop playing its balance-of-power games against the Germans and end its ambivalence about political union, the paper implied, Bonn could yet respond in kind. For all of its European instincts, Germany, if provoked, might itself revert to the very go-it-alone policy that other Europeans feared. Therefore, France "must rectify the impression" that, despite its flowery words about European integration, "it often hesitates in taking concrete steps towards this objective—the notion of the unsurrenderable sovereignty of the 'Etat nation' still carries weight, although this sovereignty has long since become an empty shell." The study then warned laconically about the unfortunate "tendency, gaining ground once again especially among intellectuals, to seek a 'German special path.'"[22]

The *Frankfurter Allgemeine Zeitung* posed the challenge even more bluntly. Will France give up more sovereignty for the sake of Europe or not? it asked.[23]

Since the threat of a copycat German reversion to a policy of competitive national interest issued from Kohl's parliamentary party rather than the government, the chancellor could and did deny that it carried any official sanction. Yet this was a fiction that was meant to be seen through. Sometimes, noted one staff member dryly, the caucus needs to say things the government cannot.[24]

The French-German tension was of course not resolved by Lamers's démarche. But far more trenchantly than the media sensation of German recognition of Croatia and Slovenia had done, it put down a marker that unified, sovereign Germany was not to be merely the French horse.

For an answer to its challenge, Germany would have to wait at least until Mitterrand's successor was elected in the spring of 1995.[25] In the meantime, Germany and the EU proceeded with other, incremental business. Luxembourg's self-effacing Jacques Santer was selected to succeed the activist Delors as the new president of the European Commission. Germany, as EU president, institutionalized quietly—to avoid offending small states' sensitivities—close coordination on agendas with its immediate successor (France) and with France's next two successors (Spain and Italy) in order to make mid-term planning more coherent and enhance the capacity to generate consensus. This advance coordination indeed paved the way for subsequent decisions on expanding the EU to the east, on financial adjustments, and the new opening toward Mediterranean neighbors that Paris was seeking. Not coincidentally, it also instituted a new intensity of consultation among the larger EU countries.

In October Kohl's reelection ensured the chancellor a tenure of sixteen years, longer even than the term of founding father Konrad

Adenauer. Kohl's election campaign was fought on internal economic issues—increasing Germany's competitiveness was the main element of his platform—but his aura as the last European giant certainly helped reassure voters that he was the best guarantor of stability and predictability both in Germany and on the continent as a whole.

In December Germany steered the EU summit in Essen to avoid a transatlantic rift over Bosnia, to approve negotiation of European agreements with the three Baltic states, to invite central European leaders to audit selected sessions of Council meetings, and to replace the previous ad hoc approach toward central European applicants for membership with a somewhat more coherent policy. Building on Commission studies and on a previous French-German bargain promising aid for Mediterranean states beyond the existing cohesion funds, the Essen summit further asked the Commission to write a white paper on widening. This would give the central European applicants a "structured relationship" (rather than just bilateral accords) and would provide more recourse against piecemeal EU protectionist lobbying. At the same time, it would divide the acquis communautaire into unprecedented pre- and postaccession categories, with the latter class much more extensive than it was when Greece, Spain, and Portugal were admitted. This labeling was controversial, since it conceded implicitly that some parts of the acquis were more sacrosanct than others, by identifying some legislation as a precondition for membership and leaving other categories to a multiyear transition period after accession.

In the first half of 1995 the French assumed the delicate task of chairing the EU even as they staged their own presidential elections. The EU's easiest enlargement went ahead as planned, enrolling those rich EFTA members who now wished to become co-deciders inside the EU. In referendums the Swiss and Norwegians had rejected their governments' advocacy of membership. Austrians, however, now felt settled enough in their identity to join the Union without being submerged by Germany (and to begin, finally, to face their willing past collaboration with the Nazis). Swedes too, however strong their misgivings about letting Brussels regulate their snuff and Arctic farms, had narrowly approved membership, and the Finns gratefully seized the opportunity to slip further away from the compulsory deference to Moscow that they had endured for half a century.

In the spring the French finally, more or less, let the ten-year-old Schengen Agreement go into effect, abolishing frontier controls and authorizing mutual cross-border hot pursuit by police among seven of the nine signatories: France, Germany, the Benelux countries, Spain, and Portugal.[26] At the same time, the intrepid EU commissioner for agriculture, Austrian Franz Fischler, fired his first shot toward scaling down the expensive Common Agriculture Policy. Fischler now prepared the way for more radical cuts—even though the General Agreement on Tariffs and Trade (GATT) had just come into force, lowering EU external tariffs with cuts of more than a third in the value of subsidized EU farm exports.

At the same time, the German Bundesrat, or upper house, also fired its first shot aimed at European budget reform, approving Bonn's current contribution to the EU, but insisting that in the future Brussels must take less out of German wallets. Also in the spring, the European Commission issued its White Paper on Central European Accession, stressing the importance of establishing a robust legal and administrative infrastructure in the new democracies and depoliticizing many issues by snatching them away from politicians (and lobbies) and turning them over to technocrats for implementation. The white paper also relaxed social and environmental standards for the central Europeans by assigning them definitively to gradual postaccession transitions.

By far the greatest frisson of the season, however, was provided by the French election itself. The winner turned out to be neogaullist Jacques Chirac, no friend of Europe in the past. His partners soon found him to be considerably more erratic than his predecessor. He reduced French troops in the Federal Republic to token numbers, abolished military conscription with only minimal prior consultation with his close ally Kohl, and sought anachronistic grandeur by resuming unilateral nuclear tests. The new Scandinavian members of the EU berated Paris for the substance of the nuclear tests as well as for Chirac's conspicuous failure to confer with his friends on an existential nuclear issue; Kohl withheld any public criticism.[27]

Nonetheless, the French-German alliance recovered. After some shakedown months, President Chirac made the same Cartesian decision that President Mitterrand had made before him—that the only way to contain Germany was to embrace both Kohl and Kohl's policies of fiscal discipline and European integration. And he drew even more far-reaching conclusions from this premise than had Mitterrand, especially in security issues.[28] Paris did not abandon—but neither did it stress—its vision of "a Europe of fatherlands." And Kohl, for his part, drew back somewhat from both impossible goals of political union and institutional redress of the democratic deficit.

Kohl never retracted these goals publicly, but at some point they ceased to be a staple of his speeches. Gradually—the precise metamorphosis will no doubt occupy doctoral candidates for decades to come—Kohl reversed his priorities. No longer did he cite Winston Churchill's summons for a United States of Europe and portray political union as the necessary prerequisite for monetary union. No longer did he champion enhanced powers for the European parliament. The first was unreachable, the second perhaps less desirable as his political antennae assessed a debating club comprising, for the most part, neophytes and political pensioners who never strove to form a government or even to write a real budget.[29]

In their place, Kohl came to regard monetary and economic union as the centerpiece. Inexorably, the exigencies of EMU itself would "forcefully advance" political union in Europe, he contended.[30] In previewing the work of the 1996–97 Intergovernmental Conference that would prepare proposals on institutional reform for the next set of EU treaty amendments, Foreign Minister Klaus Kinkel echoed Kohl's new modesty.[31] And by the summer of 1998, Kohl would even be singing Britain's refrain about the need for more "subsidiarity" and convening a special summit on the subject.[32]

In the absence of clear signals of this shift in Kohl's own speeches, a few surrogates must be used to suggest the evolution of German policy. As early as the fall of 1993 one independent panel of German specialists on Europe concluded that a federal European state was no longer a realistic objective.[33] The Lamers paper of September 1994 did not address political union, but spoke only of the need "to deepen the Union in institutional and political terms before further enlargement."[34] Subsequently, Kohl's national security adviser, Joachim Bitterlich, was still hoping that Maastricht 2 would write a constitution spelling out federal and national competencies in the EU and increasing the powers of the European Parliament. A year later, however, a senior member of the foreign ministry policy planning staff set forth a German wish list for Europe that elevated "step-by-step evolution" with trial and error over any grander visions of political union.[35] By 1995, EMU was the name of the game.

EMU as an Engine

Under the Spanish EU presidency in the second half of 1995, bargaining about this most revolutionary of all the changes in the chaotic

1990s gathered pace. The issues now took shape that would frame the debate for the next three years, until the final decision to proceed with EMU in mid-1998.

On a theoretical level, the main question was whether monetary union would really unify Europe—or whether it would instead shatter the incremental integration already achieved.[36] On a policy level, the main point of contention was the strictness with which the criteria agreed on in Maastricht would be applied. The trick would be to devise some way to preserve both discipline and solidarity when the southerners, as it was thought, stood no chance of meeting the convergence criteria. The Maastricht Treaty had attempted to solve this riddle with enhanced transfers in the Cohesion Fund,[37] but four years later this no longer sufficed.

That EMU was a risky leap, everyone agreed. No previous monetary union on such a scale had ever endured without a political union to enforce it. And if EMU failed after half a dozen or a dozen countries had already abolished their centuries-old national currencies, there would be no simple return to the status quo ante. Far from unifying Europe, critics argued, a single currency would then blow apart what had already been achieved so painstakingly in European cooperation.

Moreover, even if it succeeded economically, it would divide Europe politically, opponents charged. If the specified majority of eight EU members (or even seven, if opt-out Britain was excluded from the count) defied expectations and met the criteria for monetary union by 1997, they would erect huge barriers between themselves and the others. And if a majority did not make the grade and a fallback minority proceeded in 1999, this would be even more divisive. It would set in cement the barriers between the elite nations of Germany, Austria, and the Benelux countries that already formed a deutsche mark zone—along with France, a guaranteed founding member in any case—and all those who were left out.[38]

In addition to these overarching issues, there were specific economic disputes. The broadest one focused on economist Robert Mundell's 1961 theory about what might constitute an optimum currency area. In size alone, the EU certainly qualified. Its population and economic output matched and somewhat surpassed those of the successful U.S. single-currency zone, and a case could be made that it was little more heterogeneous than a country in which per capita income in Rhode Island was twice that in Mississippi. Moreover, in terms of the foreign trade that would be crucial for exchange rates, the EU (excluding intra-EU trade) also matched and slightly surpassed the United States's tenth-plus of gross national product.[39]

The hitch came with two tools of adjustment to economic asymmetries that the United States had and Europe did not. The first was labor mobility and flexibility; the second was a system of financial transfers on a federal level to counteract uneven regional recessions. Europe's labor market was notoriously rigid, not only because its dozen languages and cultures made it hard for a laid-off east German riveter to seek work in a Spanish shipyard, say, but also because sheer stay-at-home habits—and high wages and related social insurance—discouraged people from moving. Redistribution transfers also were far more rudimentary within the EU than in the United States (or within each EU member state), despite the structural and cohesion aid for poorer member countries. With a total EU budget only a bit over 1 percent of Europe's gross production, and with half of this locked into farm subsidies, there was little discretionary money left. Nor were there instruments to compensate for the loss of differential monetary and, in practice, even fiscal adjustment.[40]

These economic dangers featured prominently in the common American dismissal of EMU, even as monetary union took on new life in 1995. Yet they played only a subordinate role in European calculations about what was far more a political than an economic undertaking. Even in Germany, the key country that had to be convinced to surrender its currency, the pro-EMU consensus of the political elite derived more from notions of good European citizenship than from calculations of economic feasibility. The German government expected economists to devise ways to make EMU work, not write treatises about why it could not. The economics-driven Bundesbank, in a sense, did both, but its main arguments were oriented more toward the narrow goal of maintaining a hard currency than toward broader economic efficacy. The bank realized full well that in the end it would be used by the government to justify monetary union, but it accepted this instrumentalization to maximize its own bargaining power in writing the rules of the system.

In mid-1995 the first cracks in the German consensus did begin to appear, but they remained no more than cracks. The premiers of Bavaria, Saxony, and Lower Saxony—Edmund Stoiber, Kurt Biedenkopf, and Gerhard Schröder—might express doubts about the risks or suggest that EMU be postponed to a more propitious time, but they did not oppose monetary union as such. That way, they could appeal to voters' continuing fear of EMU without actually blocking the union. Stoiber and the Bavarian Christian Social Union could play the usual game of running against the federal government (even though CSU finance minister Theodor Waigel in the Bonn coalition was one of the major shapers of EMU). Equally, "King Kurt" (Biedenkopf) could appeal to the local patriotism of Saxons in his east German redoubt, display his superior economic knowledge, and tweak the nose of the chancellor who had long ago fired him as Christian Democratic Union party chief in North Rhine–Westphalia. Premier Schröder, the chancellor in waiting and a Volkswagen board member because of Lower Saxony's large bloc of shares in the firm—could show that he was staving off any Italian exploitation of non–EMU exchange rates to undercut German car sales, while still not derailing the enterprise of the century. In the end, only Biedenkopf would actually cast a sole vote in the Bundesrat against EMU.[41]

Under the circumstances, the fundamental controversy about unifying or splitting Europe quickly merged into the concrete issue of the rigidity or flexibility of the Maastricht criteria.[42] Here the knights of strict interpretation were led by the Bundesbank; for good measure Bundesbank president Hans Tietmeyer kept reiterating as well that monetary union could hardly work without political union. As corollaries, the Bundesbank insisted that a "critical mass" of transactions—the figure of 90 percent was floated—must be conducted in the new European currency once it was introduced, that (in contrast to the position of the Bonn government) introduction of the new currency must be swift rather than gradual, that exchange rates must be fixed before adoption of EMU to minimize market turbulence,[43] and that data used to measure compliance with the convergence criteria must be actual performance rather than forecasts.[44] Finance Minister Theo Waigel, a close second to Tietmeyer in proclaiming that any budget deficit even a whisper over 3.0 percent would disqualify a candidate for EMU, happily exploited the Bundesbank's obduracy to strengthen his own hand in skirmishing with French, Italian, and Spanish colleagues—and with fellow German ministers, whose budgets he was slashing to meet the Maastricht criteria.

So obstinate was Waigel, in fact, that various foreign observers read into Germany's position a desire not only to exclude Italy, but also to wreck monetary union altogether by setting goals that not even Germany would be able to reach.[45] Some of these observers interpreted German declarations that Bonn would not pay more for EU enlargement—and that it needed more equity in EU dues in the next budget negotiation in 1999—to ask if Germany was not also abandoning enlargement and even tiring of the European project altogether.[46]

Not surprisingly, Germany and France were again the main gladiators as EU finance and economics ministers debated strict versus lax convergence at the first "Ecofin" meeting under the Spanish presidency in September. Bonn was striving to tighten the Maastricht criteria even more, and watching with some concern as the deutsche mark dropped to a nine-year low against the Swiss franc.[47] Paris, by contrast had both domestic and pan-European reasons to press for a looser interpretation of the criteria. In Paris the jobless were mounting noisy demonstrations, blaming the austerity and unemployment on EMU. And if France could set the hurdles low enough to nudge its Mediterranean allies, Spain and especially Italy, over the top, it could expect its patronage to produce confederates against German might inside the club and avert competitive devaluations by Madrid and Rome.

Paris and Bonn did, of course, patch up their quarrels enough to issue a joint wish list for the forthcoming meeting of experts on institutional reform. Their list included nomination of a high-ranking "Monsieur X" to guide efforts at formulating a common EU foreign and security policy; more transnational cooperation in fighting organized crime; more majority decisionmaking; and a year-long EU presidency rotating among the four largest members, representing two-thirds of the EU population—Germany, the United Kingdom, France, and Italy.[48]

In this period the one strong constituency that the German government could rely on to back monetary union was Europe's transnational industry and finance. The myriad of small banks that characterized Germany's unique financial landscape were less persuaded of the benefits they would accrue from a revolution that would entail high relative costs for them in a total change of currency. The famous family niche exporters to the world of everything from shoes to specialized machine tools in Baden-Württemberg were equally skeptical. But the large firms that accounted for a hefty share of the third of German GDP that goes into exports expected substantial savings in transaction costs and exchange-rate risks. The large banks also welcomed the long-term chance to become global players by creating Europe-wide financial markets that might eventually compete with the U.S. market in variety and liquidity. The same sentiment prevailed among Swedish and other transnational European concerns that saw themselves as the pioneers, well ahead of the politicians, in adapting to fast-moving globalization and the challenge of the Asian tigers that had outrun Europe in the 1980s. Already these companies were adopting pan-European strategies. Big business considered the days of national champions—and of national currencies—to be numbered.[49]

The German government thus had the full support of the Bundesbank and the large German industrial associations when it raised the ante in late 1995 and proposed a controversial "stability pact" to plug a major loophole in the Maastricht criteria. That loophole was the failure to specify what discipline would apply *after* monetary union came into existence. If wily candidate members manipulated their statistics for a few years to gain entrance, only to lapse back into inflationary habits once they were in the club, the Germans insisted, they should be forced to pay automatic fines, especially on excessive budget deficits. Again this smelled to some like a German plot to scuttle EMU altogether.[50]

The French were appalled.[51] Kohl, undeterred, spoke optimistically in the Bundestag before flying to the last European Council of the year. Again he warned of the "real fears about the size and strength of united Germany," but once more he celebrated "the great success story of our continent" in European integration. He hoped for progress in the near future in common European foreign policy and home affairs, in EU institutions, in reducing the democratic deficit, and, of course, in agreeing on a stability pact and making the unification process "irreversible."[52] But soon he too would scale down his expectations, saying that this conference was only Maastricht 2, and after that would come Maastricht 3, and 4, and 5.

In Madrid the Council tossed the hot potato of a stability pact back to the Ecofin, sensibly dropped the EMU target date of 1997 in favor of the fallback 1999—and acceded to the name Germany favored for the new currency, the "euro." In addition, it acceded to the Bundesbank demand in specifying that irreversible exchange-rate decisions for founding members would be made by early 1998 on the basis of actual 1997 performance rather than more manipulable forecasts.

In the background, the Dayton Agreement had just been signed, and the first IFOR troops were in Bosnia. Other signatories of the

Schengen Agreement were reluctantly accepting Paris's retreat from some of the agreed open-border provisions after a series of bomb explosions in France heightened security concerns there. Traditionally undisciplined Italy, by heroic effort, had ratcheted its budget deficit down 1.5 points from the previous year—but that still left it at 7.7 percent, or two and one-half times the Maastricht standard, and its inflation was still an unacceptable 5.4 percent. The EU feud over bananas was flaring up again.[53] Everybody was waiting for Tony Blair to get elected and move Britain out of its paralysis.

With some Schadenfreude, those who assumed the worst of Germany felt their judgments confirmed when Germany indeed failed to meet Waigel's own exacting standards for EMU in 1995—as it would again fail to do in 1996.[54] And they saw further confirmation of their suspicion that Bonn itself was turning anti-Europe as Germans began objecting more loudly to their bankrolling of a hefty 60 percent of the entire EU budget and as some Germans joined other Europeans in complaining that the European Court of Justice had arrogated too much power to itself.[55] Precisely because it did not want to fan voter resentment of the EU, the Kohl government gave out no official figures (nor did Brussels) analyzing Bonn's huge net contribution. But as the summit approached that was supposed to tidy up the Maastricht Treaty and set the EU's course for the future, Bonn did let its partners know that it could not continue such unequal net payments when the next apportionment fell due in 1999. While administration officials had before spoken publicly only about Bonn's reasonable direct assessment of 30.36 percent, they now began leaking statistics for the much larger 1 percent of value-added tax that went automatically to the EU.[56]

Under the circumstances, seasoned Anglo-Saxon observers Edward Mortimer, William Pfaff, and Brian Beedham thought, respectively, that monetary union was fading away, that the conflict of national interests in western Europe was the sharpest since World War II, and that Germany was pushing Europe too far too fast.[57]

Deepening and Widening, 1996–99

When the intergovernmental conference on EU institutional reform finally opened in March of 1996, it was sheer anticlimax. It had no competence in the most sensitive issues—EMU, agricultural reform, and renegotiation of EU financial assessments. And where it did have formal competence, it had been granted no real authority by heads of government who thought European policy was far too important to be left to diplomats. The conference beavered on for months to prepare for the Amsterdam summit, but it made no real progress in providing a framework for enlargement to the east or for writing the new EU "constitution" that it had originally been asked to produce. The one conclusion all participants drew from the experience was that the EU must never again stage a preparatory conference by civil servants that lasted longer than a day or two.

In what may have been his last try before giving up on the drive for political union, Chancellor Kohl declared a few weeks before the intergovernmental conference opened (and before another round of Länder elections took place in Germany), "European unification is in reality a question of war and peace in the twenty-first century."[58] In the spring of 1996, German voters, heeding his sentiment, rebuffed those Social Democrats who flirted with opposition to the euro—and confirmed Kohl's hunch that he could outlast popular reluctance to give up the deutsche mark. Indeed, Kohl's favorite pollster, Allensbach, said as much in pointing to the low salience of the issue despite its high negative rating.[59]

Kohl's apocalyptic words about war and peace found a less positive resonance in England. As usual, some chose to interpret them as a German threat.[60]

The French were not similarly upset by Kohl's abstract hyperbole. But they continued to be disturbed by the chancellor's persistent lobbying for a very down-to-earth stability pact. They cherished a vision that was just the reverse of Kohl's. In the ideal world of the Elysée— despite France's signature on the original Maastricht agreement that the European Central Bank would be as independent as the Bundesbank, and despite the Banque de France's own new-found liberation from the politicians—the central bank tail should not wag the government dog. The technocrats—and the Germans' grail of low inflation—should not be allowed to override political judgment and accountability, especially when 17 million Europeans remained out of work. Other critics also asked sardonically if the intent was to push struggling economies under by draining even more money from them when they were in recession—and, now that monetary policy was being taken from governments, to snatch away as well the one remaining instrument of fiscal policy. For a year Paris and Bonn sparred with each other over these questions, even as they continued to issue pious joint proposals before every Council and ministers' meeting.[61]

And then a funny thing happened. Those who were paying close attention observed that potential candidates for monetary union were in fact growing together. The fierce arguments about convergence of the 1970s were suddenly passé. Everyone (even maverick Greece was in the process of dropping its left economics) had internalized Bundesbank rectitude and the neoliberal orthodoxy. The new Scandinavian EU members, it turned out, were trimming their famed social welfare to the new financial realities and were even urging other EU members to aim for budget surpluses. Everyone was so intent on getting into the exclusive start-up club of EMU that the Maastricht convergence criteria had a preemptive halo effect, much as NATO's criteria for entry to the defense alliance modified central Europeans' behavior even before their countries became serious candidates.

Talking to visitors in Frankfurt's Eurotower in mid-1996, EMI president Alexandre Lamfalussy made no effort to hide his glee. France had achieved lower inflation than Germany for five years running, he pointed out; Spanish inflation was the lowest in forty years. Average EU inflation had been below 3 percent for two years. High debt was still a problem, but national long-term interest rates were also getting closer to one other. Exhibiting a skeptical *Wall Street Journal* editorial about EMU, Lamfalussy commented that all the newspaper's economic analysis was right on the mark—except that the paper had utterly failed to notice the most important development of all, the convergence that was happening before its eyes.[62]

As it turned out, there was even some hope in the air that the EU budget might be held in bounds despite all the new demands on it. The recipients of regional funds had prudently not drawn all the aid they were entitled to precisely because they were trying to slim down to qualify for EMU—and EU grants required matching appropriations by the beneficiary. The EU therefore had some 20 billion Ecu of unspent credits, or almost as much as its yearly allocations for the purpose.[63]

For the public, however, all of the experts' gathering optimism was upstaged by the spectacle unfolding during the summer, as Finance Minister Waigel—despairing of getting his desired DM50 billion ($34 billion) cuts in the budget deficit through parliament—tried to count

Bundesbank gold profits against the deficit. The Bundesbank, flexing its independence, vetoed Waigel on a practice that is routine in many countries, but not in Germany. The humiliated Waigel bounced back to block, along with Britain, an expensive plan for constructing Europe-wide transportation networks.[64] Italy announced, while northerners smirked, that it would return the lira to the European Monetary System.[65] The French floated a new idea, anathema to the Germans, for a G-7 type political club to steer EMU.[66] The European Commission started a major row in Germany by declaring illegal some subsidies that Saxony's premier Biedenkopf had granted Volkswagen.[67] John Major threatened to veto everything else until the continent lifted its embargo on diseased British beef.[68] The French engaged in yet an-other wrestling match about the "franc fort," which the politicians lost to the newly independent Banque de France under its strong-minded governor, Jean-Claude Trichet. The solid German burghers who always invested in predictable bonds suddenly made a rush for privatized Telekom shares and found they might like this sort of adventure after all. The *Economist* noted with satisfaction that the European Commission under Jacques Santer was making far fewer legislative proposals than it had under Delors.[69]

None of this persuaded American media or mainstream economists that EMU was anything but a pipe dream. In August 1996 a long article in the *New York Times* focusing on demonstrations against austerity in France and Italy noted that only Luxembourg, Denmark, and Ireland currently met the Maastricht criteria and concluded that nervousness about the project was growing.[70] In the fall, MIT eco-nomics professor Rudi Dornbusch debunked the "bad idea" of a "des-perate bid for a common money" for readers of *Foreign Affairs*. "Experimenting with a new money is a bad idea at a time when Eu-rope must face the tough realities of abolishing the welfare state, rein-tegrating millions of unemployed into a normal working life, deregulating statist-corporatist economies, cultivating the supply side of its economy, and integrating Central Europe," he lectured.[71] Lawrence H. Summers, Harvard economics professor turned deputy treasury secretary, was still dismissing the euro as a chimera.[72] Other U.S. commentators scolded the Europeans for giving priority to EMU while neglecting widening the EU to bring in the central Europeans.[73]

By the end of 1996, after a year of working over its allies, Bonn at last won its stability pact, albeit with changes, at the stormy Dublin summit. At the behest of the French—and after a screaming match between Kohl and Chirac—it was called a "stability and growth pact." Fines for budget deficits over 3 percent would not be automatic, but would be subject to decisions by the Council of Ministers. Some rules were further established for links between "ins" and "outs" to guard against competitive devaluations by outs. German finance minister Theo Waigel came away still championing a "culture of stability"; French finance minister Jean Arthuis came away still promoting "national sovereignty." And the French still urged creation of a political club to oversee the European Central Bank, plus enough leeway for euro devaluation to challenge the dollar in exports.[74] Sample euro coins and bills were unveiled, with their deracinated generic bridges and windows that would not favor one country's architecture over others. Germany itself still did not meet the Maastricht criteria, and its growth had slowed to 1.4 percent.

In the homestretch from Dublin to the final decision in May 1998 to proceed with EMU, the German approach of counting on crisis to force decisions truly came into its own. The underlying crisis was one of facts, as Kohl kept repeating; everyone knew that the global gun was at Europe's head to improve its competitiveness. Added to this was the manipulated crisis of deadlines as the tempo accelerated at each successive Council summit, and compromises were wrestled out at 2 or 3 or 5 a.m., before releasing exhausted negotiators—and letting a sovereign Kohl debrief exhausted journalists. To the casual observer it sometimes seemed that no question was ever really resolved and no settlement ever final. The French kept raising anew what the Germans considered obsolete dirigiste or Keynesian demands; the Germans kept tightening the screws on the French, as on the Italians and Belgians, to let the central bankers administer the neoliberal orthodoxy as a technical task without interference by the politicians. And through it all French and German officials kept issuing their periodic attestations of common European purpose—and the business world kept making its own adaptation, regardless of the political theater.

Thus in early 1997, Bonn and Paris jointly proposed an EU–wide tax code to eliminate unfair competition. The first euro-denominated bonds went on the market. The Germans reluctantly acceded to French insistence that a political "stability council" must parallel the European Central Bank to coordinate economic management—but blocked giving it real authority. The French kept pressing for more powers for the large states within the EU; the Germans kept arguing that it would be counterproductive to set up a directorate. Tony Blair won his election, pledged British adherence to the EU social charter, let the Schengen Agreement on border controls be included in the 1997 Amsterdam Treaty—and gave parliaments to Scotland and Wales. Jacques Chirac called snap elections, which he lost to Socialist premier Lionel Jospin, who promptly told other heads of government that he wanted job growth above all and was not bound by any previous EMU deals. His colleagues hastily wrote an "employment chapter" for the looming Amsterdam summit (while stipulating that it must not cost anything). Mr. Political Union himself, Kohl, under pressure from his Länder, vetoed majority voting on immigration issues at the summit.[75] The truncated Amsterdam Treaty promised to bring asylum and immigration policies under the first, community pillar and also to "communitize" justice and home affairs in five years. Though it had no claim left to being the promised EU constitution, it went out to the fifteen legislatures for ratification. Paris called for EMU to be postponed; Bavarian premier Edmund Stoiber seconded the motion. The *Economist* devoted a special section to Europe's mid-life crisis, speculated that monetary union was dead, and wondered if EU enlargement to the east might not now be pushed far into the twenty-first century. *Die Zeit* asked, "Can EMU still be saved?"[76]

In late 1997 the war of nerves continued—though the *Economist* revised its obituary of EMU to note that while it took Mitterrand two years to drop the old French litany, it took Chirac only six months and Jospin only one month to follow suit.[77] The deutsche mark hit an eight-year low of 1.88 to the dollar. The dispute over subsidies for Volkswagen dragged on, as did haggling over the EU banana regime. Like a deus ex machina, the EU statistical agency suddenly told Bonn that, by the way, hospital debt should not be counted against the public sector deficit—and Germany's 3.2 percent deficit magically shrank to Maastricht's requisite 3.0 percent. Deputy treasury secretary Summers began taking EMU seriously enough to testify to the Senate Budget Committee that the euro should be viewed positively.[78] European investors began showing a new, American-like interest in equities, especially as the EU forced national telecom monopolies to accept competition in January 1998 and power suppliers to do the same in February 1999. The phrase "shareholder value" joined "happy end" and other Anglicisms in the German vocabulary.

The sluggish European economy began picking up. The Asian crisis hit, and the four European members of the G-7 for the first time took an initiative in managing the world financial system by offering a second line of defense for South Korea. Chirac suddenly nominated (without talking to his friend Kohl beforehand) Banque de France governor Trichet as the first head of the ECB rather than Dutchman Willem F. Duisenberg, the candidate of the central banks and all other governments—and then floated the story that this deal had been quietly arranged with the Germans long before. The European Council met, wrestled its way through to a modified Dublin compromise all over again, and agreed to begin intensive accession negotiations in the spring of 1998 with Cyprus, Poland, Hungary, the Czech Republic, Estonia, and Slovenia.[79] The Council, none too tactfully, also told perennial candidate Turkey that it could join some day, but was not eligible even for the further waiting list of five central European states. Turkish officials, in fluent German, uttered rude remarks about Germans and said they would boycott the gala conference designed to make them feel better about their second-class status.

French-German quarrels continued to characterize Council meetings. But the following spring it was decided in conclave that a full eleven EU members, including Italy and Spain, met the Maastricht criteria. The biggest surprise of all was just how small a role creative accounting played in this judgment. None of the founding members-to-be had a budget deficit over 3 percent, at least officially, and five EU members even had a surplus. Their inflation was so low that most analysts ignored it.[80] Growth ranged from 2.4 percent in Italy to 8.2 percent in Ireland. Italy and Belgium had accumulated debts double the Maastricht 60 percent, but they were working assiduously, as Maastricht made allowance for, to bring them down.[81] Divergent short-term interest rates did pose a problem, but the average EU fiscal deficit had dropped from 6.1 percent in 1993 to 2.4 percent in 1997.[82]

Germany's "stability culture" had triumphed.[83]

CHAPTER SIX

Present at the Rebirth: Poland and Central Europe

To the east, the central European states that suddenly escaped Moscow's domination in the 1990s were playing catch-up, reclaiming a (western) European heritage and pursuing their impossible simultaneous political, economic, and social revolutions.[1] Their goal in every case was to win admission to both NATO and the European Union. And in order to qualify for one of the most complex and sophisticated polities in the world, that of the EU, they had to cram into a few years the kind of institution-building and formation of social trust that western Europeans had taken a leisurely two centuries to develop.

To be sure, the central Europeans had Western models and advice they could follow, and Western financial assistance to help them do so. But the democracies and market economies they now strove to emulate were still alien. Their own mentalities and whole life experience (except for those Czech octogenarians who might still remember President Thomas G. Masaryk) came from an authoritarian environment, both communist and precommunist. There was no foundation of a stable middle class or civil society in any conventional sense.

The strongest popular motivation for the palpable yearning to become Western was probably the desire to attain the West's prosperity rather than the West's freedom and demand for individual initiative. Yet for those with incomes only a third of the EU average, expectations of reaching a Western standard of living fast were bound to be disappointed. First would come social pain, as the once unitary communist structure disaggregated into separate political, economic, and social components; the state no longer took responsibility for jobs; low but reliable welfare subsidies were cut; and men and especially women were laid off from bankrupt industries. Social unrest and perhaps angry, frustrated nationalism were likely responses to the jolts of systemic change, to widespread impoverishment, and simultaneous exposure to the sudden riches of the unscrupulous or even simply those with a superior commercial instinct.

Until 1989, democracy and prosperity had been synonymous—and an unattainable abstract—for central Europeans. By the early 1990s, however, the concrete risk was that democracy might become equated instead with hardship and disorientation. The largest test case was Poland, with a population of 39 million settled on the historical crossroads of Europe's armies.

Extraordinary Politics

In the autumn of 1989, Leszek Balcerowicz, the unknown finance minister in the sudden Solidarity government, looked at the calendar and at the Polish industrial shambles. He had, he calculated, ten weeks in which to destroy the entire existing system so that firms would not simply fall into the habitual cycle and on January 1 grind out their accustomed, mindless central plans for yet another year.

"I remember every day, every night, every hour since September 1989," says one of his associates. Balcerowicz's team worked up to twenty hours a day, including Sundays. They had to fight not only the deadweight of old communists who still held the "power ministries," but also their own allies, most of whom urged caution and gradualness. "All the advisers and economists even were warning us: you are not prepared"; the hardships would be too great, and "people would revolt. [But] sometimes it is much better to make a decision in time even if it is not a perfect one. It is better than a perfect decision made too late."[2]

So Balcerowicz allied himself with the radical course advocated most famously by Harvard's Jeffrey Sachs. By December 29 his office had rammed twenty major laws and constitutional amendments through the Council of Ministers, the Sejm, and the Senate. By New Year's Day 1990, shock therapy was born.

It was the opening of what Balcerowicz christened a period of "extraordinary politics."[3] For a decade virtually the entire Polish population had been on patriotic strike against the communist government, which had outlawed the Solidarity trade union. When union hero Lech Walesa boldly converted a brokered Solidarity share in parliament into the communist world's first noncommunist government, voters were ready—for a time—to make sacrifices.[4] They would in any case not be consulted in parliamentary elections for several years.

Under these circumstances Balcerowicz determined to maximize the initial pain to get it over with as fast as possible, thus minimizing the total pain. He used the window of opportunity to free prices, slash government spending, privatize retail shops and services, make the zloty internally convertible—and kill the 640 percent hyperinflation of 1989.[5] Within weeks shortages and lines vanished. Red-cube kiosks sprouted on Warsaw's broad sidewalks to supplement the bazaars on the grounds of the Warsaw sports stadium and the Palace of Culture; there consumers could buy everything from Vietnamese fast food to shoes and jeans. But real prices rose from their subsidized level—by 40 percent for bread and 400 percent for electricity. Production plummeted. Unemployment grew. The standard of living dropped. Many union activists felt cheated as the very shipyards and factories that had been Solidarity strongholds proved to be uncompetitive in the harsh new market and lost their government handouts.

Nobody knew if this savage experiment with Schumpeterian destruction would really work.[6] Such a "leap into the abyss," as the Poles called it, had never before been attempted. Hungary was making the change more gently, having begun reforms twenty years earlier. Eastern Germany might be conducting the most massive privatization in history—but it was being absorbed into an existing and hugely successful free economy, that of western Germany. The Soviet Union would not collapse and start its reforms for another two years. That left it to the Poles to invent their own instant metamorphosis from central planning to chaotic market.

Transformation was made all the harder by the simultaneous disintegration of political and ecclesiastical authority. Walesa started his disastrous "war at the top," splitting Solidarity. As a result of this fracture, in the 1990 presidential elections, the unknown émigré demagogue Stanislaw Tyminski managed to defeat Solidarity prime minister Tadeusz Mazowiecki before losing to Walesa in the run-off. Even

Walesa himself sometimes conceived of noncommunist politics in the mold of Poland's 1920s autocrat Jozef Pilsudski and believed that the way to introduce tough reform was for the president or the government to assert special powers, bypassing parliament.

Right-wing, anti-European nationalist groups also sprang up. Tiny "couch parties"—all the members, it was said, could fit on one sofa—won seats in 1991 in proportional representation, splintering the Sejm into twenty-nine bickering factions. Even the venerable and rather medieval Roman Catholic Church—for centuries the surrogate for the nonexistent nation and then for the not fully sovereign nation under Soviet hegemony—plunged in prestige from 90 percent approval in 1989 to 50 percent by the early 1990s. The once-reviled police and army were left as the most respected institutions.[7] Cynicism about all politicians was rife.

Socially and psychologically, too, disorientation threatened disaster. Opinion polls revealed pessimism to be among the blackest in central Europe. Only 20 percent thought things were going in the right direction, while 58 percent were sure they were going in the wrong direction.[8]

"I wonder what would have been the fate of other countries," muses the associate of Balcerowicz, if Poland had not succeeded. "Now it is very easy to say what works—liberalization, stabilization, structural reforms. Then no one knew. We could have collapsed at least five to seven times."

He cited three perceived national traits that many were sure would disqualify the Poles from building a competitive market system. The first propensity was summed up in the pejorative phrase "Polish economy," slang for any mess. Second was the short attention span of the Poles, their enthusiasm for rushing on to a new "straw fire"—and their subsequent rush away a moment later. Third was their admirable penchant for heroic martyrdom—but their obverse distaste for compromise and the mundane work ethic. Fourth, he might have added from countless jokes, was a peasant envy that predisposed Poles to claw down anyone who begins to succeed rather than admiring and emulating him.[9]

Besides, after four decades of communist centralism, Poland had no experienced managers, economists, or civil servants to implement a new system. The country's bureaucratized enterprises were immune to market incentives, worried Solidarity's own newspaper, *Gazeta*

Wyborcza.[10] "I remember in 1989 many [ordinary] people and intellectuals said, 'Come on, you can't do it [carry out sensible economic reform] with Poles,'" relates the member of Balcerowicz's team.

Was shock therapy, then, a triumph of nurture over nature, the economists over the historians? Did it prove that if you can just change the economic system, even contrary human nature will respond rationally?

Yes, says the Balcerowicz ally in retrospect, though he was not altogether convinced at the time. Then, in the frenzy of constant crisis, he really considered the issue only twice—once when Soviet president Mikhail Gorbachev invited Balcerowicz to Moscow in September 1991, then again when Yegor Gaidar, the architect of Russia's post-Soviet economic reforms, solicited Balcerowicz's views in January 1992.

> We wanted to encourage them, [to persuade them] that the cultural and psychological aspects are secondary to the institutions and rules of the game. We made a quick review of various successful economic and political reforms, in South Korea, Hong Kong, Singapore, Chile, western Europe, and Germany, in so many diversified nations and cultures. When you introduced a consistently tough economic program, it worked, in three different cultures. It was clear for me after our two years [that the old mindset stereotypes] would not apply any more to Poles. At that time we were trying to strengthen ourselves morally, like soldiers on the battlefield. But now with hindsight I am sure it [really] is the case.[11]

Certainly success was not guaranteed. In the early 1990s polemicists still pointed to the Polish example as much to bury the whole notion of shock therapy as to praise it. In the first two years of the Balcerowicz plan, real wages declined 20 percent; unemployment climbed to 12 percent; GDP fell 35 percent; exports to the imploded Soviet Union dropped 90 percent.[12] Farmers' income halved as local factories closed and part-time workers returned to the inefficient tiny plots their parents had stubbornly clung to as they thwarted communist collectivization. Official figures categorized more than a third of Poles as living in poverty.[13] Nine million out of the 39 million population drew a normal, early, or disability pension—and devoured 15 percent of GDP. The budget deficit soared so far above guidelines that the World Bank suspended its $2.5 billion loan to Poland at the end of 1991.[14]

By mid-1992 the growing number of strikes had risen to 6,000 and threatened widespread social unrest. The newest of the shifting coalition governments threatened to substitute witch-hunts for policy. Early foreign investors encountered suspicious work forces that regarded them as exploiters out to destroy Polish jobs and competition. Surveys found that by now almost half of all Poles thought themselves worse off than before the changes; only 10 percent found their situation better; and less than a third approved the economic austerity.[15] The 3 million official jobless triggered memories of the pre–World War II gulf between urban, educated, and relatively well-off "Poland A" and the quarter of the population still stuck in rural, unskilled, deprived "Poland B."

The Turnaround

In retrospect observers identify 1993 as the turnaround year in which the Polish economy, the first in the region to recover from the systemic earthquake, grew by almost 4 percent, recording the fastest increase in Europe outside of Albania.[16]

On the ground, however, the view was still glum. In the early general election that fall, popular discontent with economic hardship punished the Democratic Union, Balcerowicz's party of old Solidarity intellectuals; it could not muster more than 11 percent of the vote. Two parties of the center right (in their nationalist Catholic politics though not in their statist, often anticapitalist economics) won another 11 percent in an election in which only 42 percent of those eligible participated. In the tradition of the "liberum veto" (by which seventeenth-century Polish nobles deadlocked their assemblies, allowing any representative to veto any legislation), the rest of the center and right split their 34 percent of the votes so badly that all failed to reach the new 5 percent threshold required to enter the Sejm. By default, with a combined 36 percent of the minority that actually went to the polls, the formerly communist Democratic Left Alliance (SLD) and the Polish Peasant party, a former communist clone, took two-thirds of parliamentary seats and formed the new government.

The victory of the former communists was widely treated in the United States as a resurgence of the old cadres, but this was a gross misreading. From the beginning Jozef Oleksy, who would be a prime minister in the "postcommunist" government, and Alexander Kwasniewski, the young mastermind of the SLD coalition, had cooperated quietly with the reforms. Unlike the Russian communists, the new Russian plutocrats, the Ukrainian socialists, or Vladimir Mečiar's Movement for a Democratic Slovakia, the SLD's leaders, at least, were already genuine social democrats. Under the top layer, various "stoneheads" remained—but the leaders ran the party. And it made perfect sense for them to support a system in which their advantages in education and experience in the ancien régime would predispose the old communist cadres to learn fast how to read markets and prosper as the heads of newly privatized or "commercialized" firms.

In fact, in one of those twists of history, it was the nationalist Catholic right, along with the noncommunist left—including numerous Solidarity chapters—that protested the most vociferously against disciplining the budget to affordable, noninflationary size by trimming subsidies and social welfare. And it was the SLD's coalition partner, the Peasant party, not the SLD itself, that insisted on protectionism for farmers and blocked sale of Polish soil to foreigners.

The outcome of the constant tug of war between the SLD and the Peasant party was that the government—although its campaign platform had demanded higher wages, pensions, and agricultural handouts—basically carried on the Balcerowicz plan. Technocrat finance minister Grzegorz W. Kolodko did some fine-tuning and repackaged the policy as his "Strategy for Poland."[17] The SLD–dominated government wielded its majority in a far more coherent Sejm of seven parties to get inflation down even further, to 38 percent, to decelerate the increase in pension payments, to halve the budget deficit to less than 3 percent, and to cut taxes sufficiently to begin hauling black-market operations back into the legal economy. It fudged on mass privatization by choosing an intermediate road, "commercializing" enterprises still held by the state—that is, leaving ownership unchanged while cutting subsidies and subjecting the firms to market constraints. But it kept its hands off the new small and medium-sized private firms that were becoming the engine of the economy. Already the private sector accounted for more than 92 percent of trade, 80 percent of construction, and 46 percent of industry. Overall, 1.8 million private firms employed 30 percent of the work force and produced 48 percent of output.[18] The fledgling market economy, various Western observers ventured, had already broken loose from dependence on politics and would now forge ahead, no matter what governments did or did not do.

Consumption took off, belying the official 16 percent unemployment and confirming those who said the important point in the exhaustive opinion polls was not the negative reaction to abstract policy, but the increasingly positive estimates of their own personal status by those interviewed. Auto and computer purchases soared. The subterranean kiosks in the passageways under Jerozolimskie Street in Warsaw got glassed in and gentrified (and began paying taxes). Upscale Polish traders now left the sports stadium exclusively to Russian and Ukrainian peddlers, whose annual $350 million in purchases made this single bazaar the fifth-largest exporter in Poland.[19] Thirty-five-year-olds put to work the trading skills they had acquired in a decade of dodging communist customs inspectors with cars full of sausages and shoes. Twenty-five-year-olds began snaring well-paid junior management jobs in Western companies. One mathematics professor, a fifth-generation Blikle, suddenly became manager of the renowned eponymous conditorei on Nowy Swiat—and to his surprise became fascinated by the game of matching pastry flows with customers. The Szczecin and Gdynia shipyards, turned over to private hands, actually began making profits and finally bought out the famous but bankrupt (and still state-owned) Gdansk shipyard.[20] Poles began thinking, in a sea change, that individual talents and drive were more important than personal connections for success. Sociologist Henryk Domanski discovered that every third Pole considered himself to be middle class, about on a par with findings in the United States in the 1950s.[21] Some 50,000 "third sector" volunteer groups began lobbying for everything from environmental cleanups to education for the handicapped. Imperceptibly, the psychology of relative deprivation yielded to the psychology of rising boats.

By 1995 both the new pain and the new hope helped the forty-one-year-old Kwasniewski to achieve the unthinkable and defeat the legendary Walesa in the next presidential election.[22] Warsaw still felt grateful enough to Walesa to appreciate his feistiness, overlook his proletarian manners and grammar, and approve him by a two-to-one margin. Rural and small-town dwellers, however, were anxious about the future and less touched by the promise of urban prosperity. They voted overwhelmingly for Kwasniewski, who had barnstormed in their villages, talked to them as if they really mattered, and represented a vanished tranquility. At the other end of the spectrum, 53 percent of all voters under thirty made the same choice. They identified not at all with the old-fashioned anticommunist electrician, but rather with the smooth-spoken yuppie who had willed away thirty-three pounds to fit into his Italian suits and now proclaimed an end to the polarization that Walesa still preached. The Polish "romantic-lyric approach to politics," suggested *Polityka* commentator Adam Krzeminski, succumbed to a new "Americanoid professional election machine."[23]

By now industrial production, and not just overall GDP, had recovered its 1989 levels. The zloty was holding its value so well that Warsaw never had to call on the Western-financed zloty protection fund, and the fund was rededicated to helping banks restructure and deal with bad debts and then recapitalize them. Poland had just graduated from IMF stand-by conditionality. Official purchasing power may have been only 75 percent of 1989 levels, but new car sales had reached an annual 275,000 and were increasing. Inflation, though still high at 28 percent, was falling. Some 62 percent of the work force was employed in the private sector. Infant mortality was down from 19.1 per thousand in 1989 to 13.4 in 1995. Trade, following Soviet disintegration, was already reoriented to the West, with 53 percent of Polish exports going to the EU, and 66 percent of imports coming from there.[24] Private Western banks, approving the trends, had followed the lead of creditor governments and forgiven half of the debt burden of $40-plus billion that the Republic of Poland had inherited from the People's Republic of Poland.

Kwasniewski's victory was a shock. Walesa could not even bring himself to attend his successor's inauguration. But the very normality of voting an icon out of office also suggested that the 68 percent of the electorate that voted this time was beginning to trust the new democracy and expected to influence it. The era of "extraordinary politics" was over.

Ordinary Politics

At this point Balcerowicz himself dipped into ordinary politics. He took over leadership of the Democratic Union party of old Solidarity intellectuals, now merged with the Liberal Democrats to become the Freedom Union. He set out a strategy for the next election that would eventually entail not only presenting his economic plan for the next stage, but also running boldly for the Sejm himself in Katowice, the heart of the iron-and-coal district that bore the brunt of mine closures and layoffs.

He did not glad-hand the man in the street in the Western style that Kwasniewski had mastered; instead, he still blended earnest appeals for long-term economic interest with the traditional Polish awe for intellectuals—and in set-piece stage appearances he was always respectfully introduced as "Professor Balcerowicz," never as "Leszek." He did make the rounds of local activists in a way no Freedom Union leader had ever done before, however. And he did learn to smile. "He has made it to fifteen seconds; he does Bill Clinton for fifteen seconds!" exulted one friend.

Simultaneously, the new generation of leaders in the labor-union wing of Solidarity mobilized for the next general election. They themselves had brought down the last Solidarity coalition government and handed the 1993 election to the former communists by refusing to work together. They were determined not to repeat that mistake. Marian Krzaklewski, Solidarity chairman and vehement Catholic critic of the new constitution for failing to accord God due deference, now pulled the fractious right together as Kwasniewski had pulled the somewhat less fractious left together. The stage was set for Poland's third fully free election in 1997.

The SLD, too—without Kwasniewski, who resigned from the party before taking his oath of office in order to be "president of all Poles"— began planning to expand its 20 percent share of votes in 1993 to 30 percent in 1997. It mediated compromises on abortion and on a new constitution that would be approved in referendum. It reaped the benefit of a continuing economic boom, as output averaged more than 6 percent from 1994 through 1997. It had negotiated the private debt relief. It had shepherded Warsaw into membership in the Organization for Economic Cooperation and Development, along with Prague and Budapest, and had seen Poland get a high enough maiden credit rating from Standard & Poor's and Moody's to borrow on capital markets at only 0.65 percent above the Bundesbank rate. Fast-growing labor productivity had brought average monthly wages up to $329.[25] Automobile sales were rising to an annual 478,000. By 1997 foreign direct investment stock was up to $16 billion, unemployment down to 12 percent, inflation down to 14 percent, public debt down to 53 percent, and the private sector's share up to 65 or even 70 percent of the economy. As exports picked up, net international reserves doubled in two years, reaching $22 billion. Deficit and debt figures met even the tough Maastricht criteria for European Monetary Union.[26]

Poland looked especially good in contrast to the Czech Republic, whose initially much-heralded economy fell into crisis in the spring of 1997 over stock manipulation, shortage of enterprise capital, and a soaring trade deficit. The more cautious Polish transparency and regulation of the stock exchange, and even the delay in privatizing large firms, turned out to be an advantage. Prague's early voucher privatization might have produced a nation of nominal shareholders overnight, but it neither restructured obsolescent industries nor gave them the necessary capital to start anew more rationally.[27] Nor did it give the atomized new "owners" any more say in running the companies, which continued to be controlled by the state-owned banks that managed the major investment funds. Instead, the distribution of shares allowed greater concentration of wealth in the hands of a few fund managers—Caribbean tax havens quickly gained new Czech residents—than did the sluggish Polish shift. It did not encourage the start-up of vibrant private small and medium-sized companies as, ironically, the Polish deadlock on large-scale privatization did. Nor—this was taken for granted—did Poland have the bandit capitalism of Russia, in which insiders bought privatized industries in sweetheart deals, stripped assets, and exported mineral wealth as millionaire rentiers, mixed inextricably with mafias, and reconverted their new wealth to become the political power brokers.

Warsaw's foreign policy also looked admirable to Polish citizens. Most important, their country was joining Hungary and the Czech Republic as the first eastern entrants both to NATO in 1999 and to the EU in the early 2000s.

Under these circumstances Poles became much more optimistic. EU Eurobarometer surveys in fall of 1997 showed approval rates (positive minus negative responses) of 42 percent for the market economy,[28] equal to popular enthusiasm when "extraordinary politics" began in 1990, and sharply improved from the trough of 26 percent in 1994. Satisfaction with "country direction" in general, while a much lower 19 percent (49 percent approval, as against 30 percent disapproval), still registered a notable improvement over the rank dissatisfaction from 1991 (minus 41 percent) to 1994 (minus 29 percent). Domestic

Polish surveys also showed 57 percent of families rating their financial position better than the previous year.[29] Correspondingly, 25 percent of households expected their financial situation to improve in the next year, while only 17 percent expected it to worsen; the gloomier figures in 1992 were 21 percent (better) and 34 percent (worse). The upbeat mood, suggested various analysts, indicated not only material improvement, but also an important psychological break from the old instinct to hide good fortune so as not to draw unwelcome attention to oneself.[30]

These happy conditions, the SLD hoped, would reward it with the most votes, enabling it to be the senior party in the coalition government. But they did not. On September 21 the party increased its share to 27 percent of the 48 percent that voted, but failed to gain a plurality; disappointed SLD strategists concluded that they had reached their peak and could not expect to overtake the center-right.[31] Their Peasant party partner fared worse, its vote halved to 7 percent. The top vote-getter, the new Solidarity Election Action (AWS), attracted all of the 34 percent of center-right voters who had disenfranchised themselves in 1993.

Balcerowicz also triumphed, bringing the Freedom Union share up to 13 percent and personally outpolling the more populist Krzaklewski in his rust-belt Katowice constituency. Economic success, at long last, vindicated the author of shock therapy in the eyes of the electorate. "I am voting for Freedom Union because I care about my wallet," commented a Katowice voter, one of Balcerowicz's many eighteen- to twenty-nine-year-old yuppie supporters. He and others perceived Balcerowicz as combining, unusually, both "honesty" and "efficiency," suggested Academy of Sciences sociologist Andrzej Rychard. They appreciated the efficiency of the SLD, while not trusting its honesty; they approved the "honesty" of the AWS's Polish Catholic values, while not trusting the efficiency of a party with no experience in government. Only Balcerowicz and the Freedom Union combined both virtues.

After seven turbulent years, it seemed, parliament had finally reached an equilibrium, with five relatively coherent parties reflecting real voter preferences. The AWS—though tempted ideologically to make common cause to the right with the reduced Peasant party and with the nationalist Catholic Movement for the Reconstruction of Poland, which also entered the Sejm with 6 percent—quickly chose a more centrist coalition with the Freedom Union. Despite the rivalry between Krzaklewski and Balcerowicz, Balcerowicz again became deputy prime minister and finance minister, under moderate AWS prime minister Jerzy Buzek, and got a relatively free hand in economic policy. Two of the Freedom Union's grand old Solidarity fighters, Bronislaw Geremek and Janusz Onyszkiewicz, took the posts of foreign and defense ministers.

Krzaklewski, the election's main victor, followed the path of the SLD's Kwasniewski four years earlier and chose a behind-the-scenes role, letting someone else take the brunt of criticism as prime minister and keeping himself out of the limelight, the better to run for the presidency in 2000. In the coalition deal, he secured a virtual ban on abortion, swift ratification of the languishing four-year-old Concordat with the Vatican, and a purge from the security services of anyone associated with the previous government.

Krzaklewski was a sometime firebrand whom Pope John Paul II reportedly had to restrain from calling for special nationwide masses to save the land from the godless left. A few months earlier he had called Freedom Union Sejm deputies "traitors" for not writing strong Catholic language into the constitution. With this deal, however, he took to cohabiting with these "traitors." The dozen AWS parliamentary deputies associated with the fundamentalist Catholic Radio Marija and the fifty-odd deputies at the right end of the broad AWS spectrum gritted their teeth and voted to cut the budget deficit to 1.5 percent. They accepted a Protestant as prime minister and a man of Jewish descent as foreign minister. And the AWS appointee to manage EU accession, Ryszard Czarnecki, stopped portraying the EU as the devil incarnate and vowing that Poland would not go to Brussels on its knees; now he insisted only that Polish farmers must get the same largesse in EU farm subsidies that French and German farmers got.[32] The old Solidarity workers at the Ursus tractor factory did burn EU flags in 1998 to protest their loss of subsidies in the new era—but they were the exception that proved just how little Poles scapegoated the EU and the West for the hardships of transition.

True to democratic theory, voting out the incumbents broke up some of the patronage networks that had started to regroup under the previous government. The SLD had been restrained in making personnel changes in the foreign ministry. Imitating Walesa, however, it had packed the television commission with its own cronies, and it had done the same on the boards of commercialized enterprises. For its part, the Peasant party had taken over many of the fiefs of voevod governors. And together, the two had passed laws to depoliticize the civil service, but they had set experience requirements so high as to penalize democratic newcomers and lock in the old nomenklatura.

The center-right coalition has its share of strains, but it stays together for lack of an alternative. The AWS has had too many fights with the Peasant party over provincial posts to allow any large new nationalist and protectionist coalition to form on the right. On the left, while SLD moderates would love to cooperate with the Freedom Union, memories of the titanic Communist-Solidarity clash of the 1980s are still too fresh for former Solidarity activists to bestow such sanction on the communists' heirs just yet. And at this stage, parliamentary mathematics precludes a center-left majority in any case.

The resulting political constellation has advantages, suggests sociologist Andrzej Rychard. He finds it helpful that society's splits in the present tumultuous transformation are reflected within the new government rather than polarizing views between inside winners and outside losers. The upshot, he hopes, will be an AWS that serves more as a bridge to trade unionists in foundering industries than as a populist rabble-rouser against economic reform. Despite confrontational rhetoric before the election, he points out, strikes were already decreasing, there was actually a good deal of pragmatic cooperation on the shop floor, and average wages that were shooting up 7 percent a year were creating their own constituencies for further liberalization. The AWS is acutely aware of the public mood as it shares the responsibility of government.[33]

Catholics and Jews

Nowhere is the assimilation of the nationalist right into the mainstream that Rychard describes better illustrated than in the gradual evolution of the Catholic Church. Less than a decade ago Pope John Paul II still hoped that devout Polish Catholics would save the secular West.[34] There were ample reasons for his hope. During the 123 years when Poland was partitioned, it was the church that kept the nation alive in the hearts of parishioners. Under Hitler's yoke, the church inspired resistance. In the communist era the church was the only moral authority in the country. For decades Poland exported its surplus of priests to less faithful lands. In 1978 it gave Rome its first non-Italian pope in 456 years, and John Paul's pastoral visit to his native soil in 1979 altered politics by spawning the Solidarity trade union that would shelter under the church and in ten short years shatter the Russian empire.

The church that had thrived under repression, however, seemed far less endearing to many when it returned to power in the early 1990s, reinstated virtually compulsory religious instruction in public schools, got abortion severely curtailed, laid claim to property taken from it as far back as the nineteenth century, tolerated anti-Semitic slurs by Lech Walesa's Gdansk priest and other prelates—and, often enough, instructed its flock to vote for right-wing nationalists. The church not only fell in prestige; in the 1993 and 1995 elections, it found that even village voters ignored the injunctions of their parish priests to vote against the pagan former communists.

Wounded, the Catholic Church withdrew from politics. By 1997 the hierarchy—apart from ten bishops acting on their own—did not tell Catholics how to vote in the May referendum on the new constitution, despite right-wing protests against the draft. Nor did the church back Krzaklewski in the constitutional referendum in opposing the surrender of some sovereignty to multinational organizations, as sanctioned in Article 90. Nor did it issue any recommendations from the pulpit for the parliamentary vote in the fall. This new modesty signaled retreat from the triumphalism that old-style Catholics had hoped would dominate Polish politics and even vanquish the West's atheism and hedonism.

Yet in one last policy area—the European Union—the church still broadcast its views. In one especially memorable sermon in August 1995, Primate Jozef Glemp portrayed the EU as an anti-Polish conspiracy that would bring pornography, divorce, and unbridled sex to the land. EU president Jacques Santer, from impeccably Catholic Luxembourg, immediately flew to Warsaw to invite the primate to visit Brussels—and, perhaps, to note that in the 1950s many western European Protestants opposed the fledgling European Community as a conspiracy of Catholic Europe.

It took two years and two months before the primate actually accepted the invitation. But in the meantime, some rethinking had begun within the hierarchy. A small colloquium on European integration was conducted for a year at the Catholic theological academy in Warsaw, with contributions by pro-European Catholic politicians. There was one discreet briefing on the EU by bishops from the much more liberal German Catholic Church. And in November 1997 a small group of Polish prelates was finally ready to visit Brussels to meet Santer and other EU officials there.

As the delegation departed from Warsaw, Cardinal Glemp declared, significantly, that the church is "not afraid of a united Europe. On the contrary, it is looking to the process with hope."[35] And on the group's return to Poland, Tadeusz Pieronek, the modernizing secretary-general of the bishops' conference, assured reporters that the church understands the pluralistic character of the EU—and, for its part, the EU respects the right of different faiths to make moral judgments on political and economic issues.[36] The church's change of heart was "the most important event of this past year," contended a west European diplomat in Warsaw. And even Ryszard Czarnecki, as the new head of Poland's Committee for Europe, praised the example of Catholic Ireland, which, he declared, integrated its economy into the EU without losing its soul or its identity. Radio Marija, shocked into silence, blacked out all news of the bishops' trip for its four million listeners.

Catholic attitudes toward Jews are also mellowing somewhat. There is no rush back to the open welcome that Prince Boleslaw extended in the remarkable thirteenth-century Statute of Kalisz forbidding discrimination against Jews in court, letting them swear their oaths on the Torah, and protecting their life and property. Three-quarters of world Jewry will never again, as in the eighteenth century, live in the land of the most infamous Nazi extermination camp of all, Auschwitz. Nor will the primate ever be enthusiastic in his pro forma requests that provocative crucifixes be removed from the environs of the Auschwitz concentration camp.[37]

Within the Polish Catholic Church there is, however, at least a grudging willingness to discipline prelates like Henryk Jankowski, Walesa's parish priest in Gdansk, for disparaging Jews from the pulpit and campaigning against Geremek's appointment as foreign minister, proclaiming that the country was not ready for a "minority" representative in the government.[38] By January of 1998, for the first time, it even joined celebrations for Judaism Day. Among the intellectual elite there is a growing awareness that the everyday folk anti-Semitism that has survived even the disappearance of most of Poland's Jews is not acceptable. And certainly in the government there is a desire to proceed with what may be the Poles' hardest reconciliation of all, more difficult even than Polish-German or Polish-Ukrainian rapprochement. Synagogues and cemeteries—though not private property—are being given back to the few Jews left in Poland. And in the capital a museum is to be opened shortly to show the prewar life of the third of Warsaw's population that was Jewish.

Any new chapter in relations will have to counter the terrifying memory of a genocide in which 3 million Polish Jews died, along with 3 million other Jews and 3 million other Poles. Periodically the deep animosity between the two has erupted into polemics, as, in the 1980s, over the movie "Shoah" and the novel *The Painted Bird*, and, in the 1990s, over commemoration of the dead in Auschwitz and restitution of Jewish property.

Both Claude Lanzmann's film "Shoah" and Jerzy Kosinski's novel *The Painted Bird* portrayed the Poles as willing abettors of the Nazi genocide. The movie unfairly blamed Poles more than Germans for the Holocaust, many Poles thought; it took no account of the Polish record of unparalleled resistance to the Nazis and of Poles' saving some Jewish lives despite the especially draconian penalty of the death sentence for such acts in Poland.[39] The novel, sold initially as the semiautobiographical account of Kosinski's own childhood persecution, presented the haunting metaphor of the villager who snared drab birds, dipped them in garish colors, then released them to be rejected and pecked to death by their own species. That the novel turned out to be "inauthentic," as Kosinski's oeuvre came to be described—the author's family had in fact been protected during the war by the Polish villagers he portrayed in the novel as anti-Semitic—did little to lessen its strong impact, especially on American readers.

Nor did disputes about Auschwitz in the 1990s help to lessen mutual hostility. President Walesa refused for more than a year to let a rabbi commemorate the fiftieth anniversary in 1995 of the liberation of Auschwitz and to lead prayers for the dead there, and the Polish Catholic hierarchy insisted on maintaining a cloister at the site of the extermination camp long after Jews first complained about it. Walesa then compounded the insult by stalling for weeks before disavowing even halfheartedly the derision of Jews in a sermon by Fr. Jankowski that he himself heard.

The first impulse for a new Polish-Jewish dialogue came in the Auschwitz anniversary year from Foreign Minister Wladyslaw

Bartoszewski. Bartoszewski, whose tree grows in Yad Vashem for the Jewish lives he saved as a member of the Polish underground, appointed a special ambassador to the Jewish diaspora (as distinct from the state of Israel), Krzysztof Sliwinski. The new ambassador had been a biology professor at Warsaw University during the communist anti-Semitic and anti-intellectual crackdown of 1968. He defended students who were ostracized as Jews and barred from continuing their education, then organized lectures on Jewish culture and rallied a few dozen volunteers to defy secret police harassment and clean up the desecrated Jewish cemetery in Warsaw. His writ includes advising the Sejm about legislation restoring communal property to Jewish communities; assisting in the revision of teaching about Jews in Roman Catholic seminaries; and serving as the channel for the efforts of the very active "Landsmannschaft" associations of American Jews to locate and restore Jewish cemeteries in their home towns. As he sees it, "Poland is trying to reach the level of mature Western democracies. It wants also to achieve international standards as far as minorities or different religions are concerned."[40]

Both Bartoszewski and Sliwinski defend the Poles against the more extreme accusations of anti-Semitism. "If there was an especially anti-Semitic mood in Poland, then why did three million Jews gather here?" asks Bartoszewski rhetorically. He points out that there were no state-fomented pogroms in Poland, as there were in Russia. And during the brutal German occupation, even though Poles were subject to house searches and summary death in a way Germans were not, an honorable few still did shelter Jews, as thirty trees in Yad Vashem confirm. There should have been more, but, in times of stress, "Few people think of anything other than their own survival. When the house is burning, you think about your own dwelling. Anyone who doesn't do so is exceptional."[41]

After his upset election in 1995, President Kwasniewski too endorsed the endeavor to improve Polish treatment of Jewish issues. He intervened to stop construction of a shopping center opposite the entry gate to Auschwitz. He also supported the first official investigation of the 1946 pogrom in Kielce, which admitted for the first time that Polish persecution of Jews in the 1940s was not just forced on Poles by their German occupiers. Kwasniewski's state secretary, Marek Siwiec, does not use the moral categories of a Bartoszewski or a Sliwinski in explaining why the new dialogue is important. But he does take it for granted that modernization of Poland must include rooting out old-fashioned anti-Semitism.

Siwiec hopes it will be possible to move beyond recrimination about the past to more forward-looking cooperation. "This Polish-Jewish dialogue must be directed more toward the future. We represent [a new generation]. We treat the ballast of history very seriously," he asserts, "but we would not like to create a Polish-Jewish dialogue only in terms of Polish anti-Semitism and the Holocaust, which is not creating [any basis for future cooperation.] If we invite thousands of Jewish youngsters [to visit Poland], we would like them to see not only camps, chimneys, and the ashes of their fathers or grandfathers. We want to show them Polish people who treat Jews like every other people."[42]

Some observers question the motivation behind the present quest for dialogue. "The record of Jewish affairs may affect our grades [from the United States] on politics, the economy, the market. Some people with satisfaction, some with regret, calculate that Jews are too powerful to be ignored," comments Andrzej Krzysztof Wroblewski, editor of *Polytika*. "I would like to believe it is sincere, but as well as being sincere, it is calculated."[43]

Whatever the motivation, contrition will not be easy. Return of Jewish cemeteries to the Jewish community is agreed in principle, but many of the burial grounds were destroyed in the past half century without a precise record of where they were located. Others have been covered over by buildings or roads, and fewer than half of the 1,020 Jewish cemeteries in existence before the war are still identifiable. Typically, in the very locality where the Statute of Kalisz was promulgated, one fight rages between the World Council of Orthodox Jewish Communities and local officials over a site that was once a cemetery but for three decades has been a sports field for a school for handicapped children.

Clearly, the biggest single battle will be joined over demands for restitution of Jewish private property seized by Germans and Poles in the early 1940s or by the communist government in the late 1940s. Individual descendants have claims for some 10 percent to 20 percent of these properties; various Jewish organizations contend further that the remaining 80-90 percent of property for which there are no identifiable heirs should be awarded to Jewish groups collectively. The Polish government maintains that it cannot restore these buildings and lands without opening a Pandora's box, since whatever provision it makes for Jews it will also have to make for Germans expelled from the western third of present-day Poland as the Soviet and Polish borders shifted west after German defeat in World War II. "The Jewish community will not get anything on private property. It will be a bone of contention. There is not going to be any reprivatization anywhere, but the issue will still be there," comments a senior Western diplomat.

Already this dispute has poisoned other intended areas of Polish-Jewish cooperation. Some potential American donors to the new Jewish museum in Warsaw have refused to give money unless property is restored. Artur Hajnicz, a Polish Jew who was instrumental in postwar Polish-German reconciliation—and who as a Senate adviser opposed restitution because of potential German claims—was so offended at being branded an anti-Semite by fellow Jews that he subsequently refused to have anything to do with a Polish-Jewish dialogue.

Beyond this concrete issue—and even harder to deal with—is the psychological confrontation. Is Polish good will going to solve the problem? asks the Western diplomat. "I doubt it seriously, because there is a deep, abiding anti-the-other-guy sense on both sides here. The world Jewish community cannot stand the Poles, and no doubt the level of anti-Semitism in this country is deep and pervasive, the taxi-driver approach. There is a generation, probably two generations of Jews, in the U.S. who think of Poland as the place where all evil was done. It rubs off on the Poles."

In this climate the shift from past to present that Kwasniewski's staff anticipates is far more easily said than done. It may even seem undesirable to many of the 40 percent or so of world Jewry descended from families that lived in Poland before they were driven out or killed. Their collective memory of the country is harsh. They do not want to forget the whiplash of both communist and anticommunist discrimination against Jews in Poland, the first clearly demonstrated in that anti-Semitic purge of 1968, the second in popular blame for hated communist rule on the many secularized Jews in the party and secret police.

Above all, they do not want to dilute remembrance of the Holocaust. Since the 1980s this memory is at the heart of a renewed sense of Jewish identity in the United States. For many—in Polish experience this is more true of American than of Israeli Jews, and more true of Jews who have never lived in Poland than those, say, who were expelled from Poland in 1968—a fixed part of Holocaust memory is anti-Semitism in the land of Auschwitz. They suspect that efforts to turn dialogue toward the future, or even to enshrine an extinct tradition in the planned Warsaw museum, could minimize the horror.

Sliwinski describes the psychology: "Polish-Jewish emotions are very strong. Therefore when you read anti-Semitic Polish press and, well, what is called anti-Polish Jewish press, when they are calling each other 'idiot' and 'murderer,' you have to understand and study the emotions underneath." He too now wants to clear the decks of old quarrels about which people were more victimized and move on to joint Polish-Jewish building for the future.

He sees some grounds for hope. On the Polish side he senses a healthy new interest in Jewish life and culture that goes far beyond a "superficial political" interest. Yiddish writer Isaac Bashevis Singer, who was ignored by Poles when he won the Nobel Prize in the 1970s, is now a best seller. Krakow sponsors popular Days of Jewish Culture every year and has had an influx of Jewish visitors since release of the movie "Schindler's List." Eighty master's theses and ten doctoral dissertations were written on Jewish themes in Poland in 1994, some 500 books in 1995. And in the mid-1990s the Polish-Israeli Friendship Society, which Sliwinski had helped found when it was still illegal, received 4,000 entries about local Jewish history from high school students hoping to win a trip to Israel.

Moreover, Sliwinski points out, the Polish media have become much more critical of anti-Semitic manifestations. Solidarity underground publications broke the taboo and wrote about the Kielce pogrom in the 1980s; in the 1990s the weekly *Wprost* dug out more information about the pogrom, and *Gazeta Wyborcza* unearthed anti-Semitism in the sacrosanct Home Army during World War II.

"One can go deep enough to know why it happens," observes Sliwinski about the Polish-Jewish love-hate relationship. "There is no other country except Poland which is so much present in living Jewish memory. For many, after Israel, it is still sort of the holy land, because here are the cemeteries of relatives, here is the history of the most horrible crime against the Jewish people. Now for [those] Jewish leaders who consider it important to have contact and practical dialog, I am coming with the message that Mother Poland is after thirty or forty years coming [to seek out] its Jewish daughters and sons."[44]

NATO and the European Union

"For over two hundred years, when foreign leaders put their signatures under documents concerning Poland, disasters were sure to follow," Foreign Minister Bronislaw Geremek reminded suddenly teary NATO ambassadors in late 1997 as they united on the simple protocol anticipating Polish, Czech, and Hungarian accession to the alliance. "History has been an unforgiving teacher to us," he continued. But "eight years ago we undertook to unlive the past, to restore Poland as a free, democratic and truly sovereign nation. We have since spared no efforts to return to the roots of our culture and statehood, to join the Euro-Atlantic family of democratic nations. We will not rest until Poland is safely anchored in Western economic, political, and military structures." On this occasion, he concluded, by contrast with the past, "Poland's friends" were signing "a document which is a source of joy, pride and hope for me and my compatriots."[45]

The fragile-looking, iron-willed medieval historian spoke for all those who preserved the idea of Poland when the nation was parceled out among Russia, Prussia, and Germany in the nineteenth century, for the 3 million victims of the Holocaust who were both Poles and Jews, for the intellectuals who rallied to the cause of Solidarity workers in 1980 and paid for their courage with years in jail—and for all Poles who now yearn for a normal "Western" life without the need for martyrdom. In the shorthand of naming NATO and EU membership as his goals, he summarized Warsaw's agenda for the new century.

To be sure, there is still business left over from Poland's reforms of the 1990s as well. The government is in the sometimes messy process of devolving significant powers to new regional and local governments. Secret police files from the communist years will finally, belatedly, be opened for individuals to read. The import surge must be restrained so that current accounts deficits do not imbalance the economy. Roads, rails, and other infrastructure must be built up. Various barriers to trade and capital flows must be phased out. In other actions less palatable to his AWS coalition partner, Balcerowicz is accelerating privatization of telecommunications, energy, railroads, banks, steel, chemicals, insurance, the national airline, and various other businesses to increase the private sector's share of GDP to 90 percent by 2000. Soon after that the government will divest itself of the rest of today's

4,000-odd firms still owned by the state. Corporate taxes will be streamlined and reduced, government spending will shift away from consumption toward investment, and pensions will be changed from pay-as-you-go to modern, self-funded schemes, following or speeding up plans already drawn up by the old government. Krzaklewski will have his hands full keeping the three dozen disparate AWS groups together as the government undertakes so many projects that confute Solidarity's statist reflexes.

By now, however, the still formidable reform tasks are all but taken for granted. They are seen less as ends in themselves than as means to fulfill the overriding aspiration articulated by Geremek as "unliving the past" and "joining the Euro-Atlantic family of democratic nations."

In that family, NATO will be the easy half. In essence, the alliance will free the Poles from being squeezed between Germans and Russians and reassure them that they can entrust their very new friendship with Germany to a postnational European and transatlantic framework.

That new friendship—the bedrock of peace and stability in central Europe—began when German and Polish bishops, against bitter opposition in both countries, issued a joint statement in the 1960s forgiving and asking to be forgiven for past cruelties. It continued with Chancellor Willy Brandt's kneeling in grief at the Warsaw Ghetto in the 1970s. It spread to the grass roots when millions of ordinary Germans sent packages of food and clothing to ordinary Poles after Solidarity was banned in the 1980s and Poles began to distinguish between democratic West Germans and East German "Prussians" (and Saxons). Rapprochement was formally sealed by bilateral treaties of friendship and recognition of borders between Poland and the newly united Germany in 1990 and 1991. Since then Bonn has been Warsaw's special champion in the EU and (along with the United States) in NATO— and has drawn France into regular consultations in the Weimar triangle. The crowning symbol of the special bilateral relationship was Poland's award to former chancellor Helmut Kohl of the Order of the White Eagle; it was the first time this honor was bestowed on a German after World War II. Janusz Reiter, now director of the Center for International Relations in Warsaw after five high-profile years as Polish ambassador to Germany, attributes the fact that Poland has "its friendliest and most intensive relations" with Germany to the recognition by both that they can maximize their roles as medium-size states in a

Europe of voluntary integration far better than in the old balance-of-power system.[46]

On this pattern, in conscious compliance with NATO norms, Poland is itself conducting an active good-neighbor policy as the largest country in central Europe. The old enemies of Poland and Ukraine cannot yet bring themselves to "forgive and ask to be forgiven" for past slaughter and forced migration, in the Polish and German bishops' trenchant formulation of the 1960s. But Warsaw has joined Western donor nations in contributing $10 million to help build a new sarcophagus around the Chernobyl nuclear power reactor, new Polish foreign ministers tend to make Kyiv their first port of call, and the joint peacekeeping battalion is beginning to take shape.

With Lithuania too—here the psychological gulf is not so great—Poland has sought rapprochement and mutual respect for the others' minority. The two nations are forming a joint military battalion, and Warsaw is providing helicopters, radar, and patrol boats to the start-up Lithuanian army.

President Kwasniewski, mindful of others' sensitivities, rejects in an interview the notion of Polish "leadership" in the region. He approves, however, the formulation of Nicholas Rey, former U.S. ambassador to Poland, who praised Poland for "exporting stability."[47] And he characterizes this key role of Polish foreign policy as ensuring that as Warsaw rejoins the West, no new East-West line of tension will arise on Poland's eastern border. To this end Warsaw is promoting entry of all central European states, including the Baltics, into the EU and (less volubly) into NATO. Here, too, Poland is following German precedents; Kwasniewski willingly accepts the analogy with current German promotion of Polish, Hungarian, and Czech membership in the West's two clubs.[48] In an effort that seems less likely to succeed, Poland is also trying to reconcile the EU demand for secure external borders with a visa-free Polish-Ukrainian boundary by urging Kyiv to police its borders to the east against traffic in drugs, contraband, and illegal immigrants.

Militarily, to qualify for entry into NATO, Poland has already redeployed its troops away from the massed preparation for attack to the west characteristic of the Soviet era to more even distribution throughout the country. In compliance with NATO transparency, it has already provided the alliance with Warsaw's first five-year defense plan. It has established civilian control of the military, depoliticizing both old generals who bonded with Russian counterparts in the Warsaw Pact and those who played partisan politics with Walesa. It has, without complaint, accepted an assessment of dues under which it will pay 2.48 percent of common NATO costs—more than Turkey, Greece, or Spain. (As the Poles calculate it, this will still be a bargain, since they will save money by pooling defense they would otherwise have to finance from national funds.)[49] It is putting officers through crash courses in English to meet the most rudimentary requirement for "interoperability" of forces. It has the first division commanders who have graduated from the German Bundeswehr Leadership Academy. It, along with Hungary and the Czech Republic, has participated actively in NATO's Partnership for Peace program with non–NATO members; the three nations have accounted together for 75 percent of the program's activity. It is offering the alliance large, unpopulated training grounds for the kinds of noisy exercises—including even the firing of live missiles, should NATO wish—that are by now taboo in Bavarian villages.[50]

More broadly, Poles also maintain that their gallant military history—from repelling the Turks in Vienna in the seventeenth century to Monte Cassino in the twentieth century—shows that they take their army very seriously. They contribute the largest contingent of troops to UN peacekeeping forces. And Defense Minister Janusz Onyszkiewicz highlights the 65 percent popular approval—in contrast to the inhibitions of voters in the United States, Germany, and every other NATO member state—for sending Polish troops abroad on any alliance missions. Typically, when the United States determined to bomb Iraq's chemical weapons plants in early 1998, Poland volunteered to send antibiological and chemical weapons specialists to the Gulf. Warsaw's zeal for the alliance, Western diplomats in Poland expect, will make it a staunch confederate of the United States in NATO's inner councils, by contrast to the French, who are allergic to American leadership, or even the Germans, who have a residual reluctance to put armed forces in harm's way.

For a country with purchasing power higher than Turkey's, but still only about half the level of Spain, Portugal, or Greece, preparing to join the EU will be far more difficult than preparing to join NATO.[51] Agriculture will have to be modernized and plots increased in size as economic growth absorbs more and more of the quarter of the work force that remains rural and produces only 6.5 percent of GDP.[52] Compliance with the EU's clean water regulations alone will cost an estimated $20 billion.[53] Moreover, since the EU is now in dynamic change, all the central Europeans will have to aim for a moving target in the acquis communautaire in a way that no previous entrants to the EU had to do. At best guess, Poland has already complied with 40,000 pages of the acquis, but it still has another 40,000 to go, including the Schengen agreement on open internal borders, which will require far better policing of Poland's now porous external borders to the east. It also must meet at some point the demanding criteria of European monetary union.

Yet Poles seem convinced that with long-term transition regimes to the EU's single market, they can survive and even thrive. With $30 billion foreign direct investment by 1998, they are already pulling in more new foreign capital than Russia is; and they expect their vibrant economy to attract still more money and lift the standard of living with the help of the EU.[54]

To be sure, out of deference to obsolescing steel workers, Warsaw dragged its feet on reducing tariffs on EU steel imports in 1999 as originally promised, from 9 percent to 3 percent, and won another extension. Poles complain that the EU finds some sanitary reason to bar Polish export of live animals whenever the season rolls around. Also, Warsaw has bargained hard for a generous EU interpretation of local content in the factories that Korean producers are establishing in Poland for future auto export to western Europe. So pugnacious are Polish negotiators that they sometimes goad their interlocutors into reminding them that Warsaw is, in fact, joining the EU, not vice versa.

Fundamentally, though, Poland is on its way to qualifying for membership. The 1997 Commission report card on candidates accorded Warsaw 4/5 on a scale of 5 in general democratic and market criteria, and 4 in its specific capacity to assume EU membership obligations. Poland is already a stable democracy, the report said, with institutions guaranteeing the rule of law, human rights, and respect for minorities.[55] It gets high marks from the British-based Penal Reform International for reforming its prisons in the early 1990s (perhaps because so many of the new officials had seen jails from the inside.)[56] Its Constitutional Tribunal, established unusually in the communist era in 1985, has proved itself in defending human rights and curbing abuse of power, whether by former communists or, in the early 1990s, by President Walesa.[57]

The Polish economy has been growing since 1992, with an average increase of more than 6 percent from 1995 to 1997 and more than 5 percent in 1998. The budget deficit has been cut to 1.5 percent. Inflation, running 18.5 percent in 1996, dropped to 13.2 percent in 1997 and a single digit in 1998.[58] The current accounts deficit on trade—two-thirds of which is already exchanged with the EU—is growing, but not dangerous. Some 70 percent of the investors in the Warsaw stock exchange of 300 companies are Poles, by contrast to 40 percent of Hungarians in Budapest and single digits of Russians in Moscow; this provides stability, keeps the money in the country even in turbulent times, and has so far enabled Poland to weather the impact of the Asian crisis much better than Russia. And substantial progress has been made in legislating EU standards on taxes, companies, intellectual property, accounting, and financial services.

What remains to be done, according to the Commission report, is improving the judicial system; combating corruption; applying EU norms in agriculture, environment, and transportation; liberalizing capital movements; opening up public procurement; reforming pensions and social security; finishing off the 75 billion zloty ($21 billion) sell-off to private buyers of state-owned telecommunications, refineries, steel plants, mines, and the national airline planned by the turn of the century—and, of course, modernizing agriculture.

With only eight short years of experience, then, the Poles are mastering the new terrain of democracy and a market economy. They are evolving Western institutions with consumer safeguards. They have invented instant governments, parties, civil society, watchdog media, parliaments with the wit and integrity to pass responsible budgets and legislate for an unfamiliar world, fledgling judiciaries independent of politics, subordination of security services to elected officials, ombudsmen, a functioning civil service, a framework for local self-government, civilian control of the military, and the habits of individual initiative and risk.[59] They have not, as in Russia and Ukraine, incurred wage arrears of billions of dollars. They have not surrendered their economy to robber barons who have gone straight from the ranks of the nomenklatura to become crony capitalists. They have not confined wealth creation to the glittering capital and a few favored regional cities, but are spreading prosperity and creating a stable middle class. Their initial faith that democracy brings affluence has been rewarded, after several years of interim doubt—and has fostered the further intuition that there is more to be gained by pooling sovereignty than by nationalist assertion. Their traditional fatalism has mutated even beyond a Germanic pessimism as a tool for action and now approaches an optimism that their cousins in Chicago would readily recognize.

Overall, Poland might well be judged the most successful of the new democracies and market economies in central Europe—but it is not thereby unrepresentative. Indeed, as the largest and arguably the most dynamic country in the region, Poland is the trailblazer, setting standards not only for its fellow western Slavs of the Czechs and Slovaks, but also for the Balts and other central Europeans.

Economically, its rapid resumption of sustained high growth after the shocks of 1990–92—based perforce initially on the motor of domestic investment by small and medium-sized firms (and on debt forgiveness)—has convinced both the market and mainstream economists that radical reforms really are the swiftest and least painful route to prosperity. With $30 billion so far, Poland now attracts the highest amount of foreign direct investment in the area (though it still lags behind Hungary, Estonia, and the Czech Republic per capita). Its exports are growing fast, even without being promoted by artificial devaluations, and are maturing out of the garden-dwarf and cherries stage to include far more sophisticated semifinished and finished goods, especially in light industry.[60]

In the particulars, Poland is at least beginning the cleanup—in part by imposing high polluters' fees—of the appallingly dirty air, water, and soil it inherited.[61] It has established a workable system of bankruptcy as a provider of the second chance.[62] It has shown that the incentives of legal protection and access to new investment can draw much of the black and gray sector into the taxpaying economy. Its infant courts are quickly gaining experience in adjudicating commercial law. Its corruption is episodic rather than a systemic part of intertwined governmental and criminal networks. The country has enormous problems—but they are the ordinary problems of an ordinary, working democracy.

Details would differ, but approximately the same case could be made as well for all the other first-tranche candidates for EU membership—Hungary, the Czech Republic, Slovenia, and Estonia.[63] They have certainly avoided the worst excesses of crony capitalism of either the Russian or the Asian varieties. They have been leapfrogging installed west European plants in telecommunications and computers and might just end up in a few years with information technology superior to much of western Europe. Their revised funded pension systems could turn into models for welfare reform in western Europe. And after the crash reorientation of trade away from the old Soviet bloc, the combined trade of all of central Europe with its leading west European trade partner, Germany, by 1994 already exceeded German-U.S. trade.[64]

Even for the first-cut central European states, convergence with the super-rich western European economies will still be, the OECD warns, "a matter of generations rather than of years."[65] But after a lag of centuries, even the prospect of reaching rough equivalence in four decades is a happy one. Those born today should, in their wanderlust years, enjoy the same opportunities for travel as their western colleagues. And they can expect that when their own children reach maturity, they can essentially match their western neighbors in becoming what today's Poles already feel like—middle-class citizens.

Politically, too, Poland, Hungary, the Czech Republic, Slovenia, and probably the Baltic states can already be counted as having achieved liberal democracy. Given the far shakier examples of new Latin American democracies—and illiberal central European history—this must be recognized as a major accomplishment. It owes much—as did the democratic transformation of Spain and Portugal after their dictatorships ended in the 1970s—to the example, encouragement, and financial aid of the EC/EU and to the carrot of membership in this elite club as a reward for good behavior.[66] Rule of law, separation of powers, checks and balances, tolerance, freedom of speech, assembly, religion, and property, and respect for minorities—whatever the individual challenges to these concepts—are the norm in the first-tranche candidates for EU membership and the declared goal in the later-tranche candidate countries. Free elections have already led to peaceful voting-out of incumbents in the region and to return of old incumbents the next time around. Armies, bureaucrats, and business magnates have respected these judgments, and often enough political newcomers have offered both coherent alternative policies and officials able to implement them. Parties are forming that articulate and aggregate interests. Independent judiciaries, media, and civil societies are being built, with varying degrees of robustness. Presidents do not rule as tsars, with powers of ukase and arbitrary manipulation of favors for courtiers and clans.[67]

In foreign policy, the central European states have also established a good record. Giving the lie to the many prognoses of widespread nationalist strife in the region that were bruited in the early 1990s, they have not reverted to pre–cold war patterns of armed conflict.[68] The Czech-Slovak divorce was a velvet one. The Slovenes fought their way to independence from Serb-dominated Yugoslavia, to be sure, but that war was brief and only a sideshow to the bloodletting in Croatia and Bosnia. As already noted, Hungary has foregone any irredentism or claims to represent Hungarians living abroad. Various populist politicians did exploit this theme in Budapest in the early 1990s, but their calls failed to stir the masses, and moderates prevailed in elections.

There are, of course, exceptions to the good overall picture in central Europe. Slovakia, long a laggard both in the practice of domestic democracy and in respect for its own Hungarian minority, paid the price (as of this writing) in being excluded from the first selection of new members for both the EU and NATO. To the south, Bulgaria and Romania are still struggling to catch up with the economic, political, and social reforms they failed to implement as governments run by the old nomenklatura persisted until the mid-1990s. And Albania, tucked between Yugoslavia and Greece, erupted into anarchy and tribal violence after half a decade of an elected illiberal leader—and a pyramid scam that sucked away the meager savings of thousands.

Yet the incentives to good behavior to win admission to the EU and NATO are taking hold, and their effect can be seen even in recalcitrant former Yugoslavia. Croatia is striving to prove itself tolerant enough of ethnic minorities and dissidents to qualify for EU aid. Voters elected more moderate Serbs in Srpska at least once in early 1998— and reaped the immediate reward of EU aid of 6 million Ecu ($6.5 million) and American aid of $5 million.[69] The EU's inducements, so ineffectual against the stoked passions of war in the early 1990s, proved more effective once the NATO–led coalition denied any prize for aggression and stopped the spiral of hate and bloodshed.[70]

In post–cold war Europe, then, the remarkable thing is not that old enmities flared into fighting on the Balkan and Caucasian fringes of the continent. Nor is it that the Balkan central European states of Romania and Bulgaria find it vastly more difficult to adopt democracy than do their northern neighbors or that the new market economies keep stumbling as they prepare themselves for world competition.

The astounding development is rather the dog that did not bark. Old enmities between Poles and Ukrainians, or between Romanians and Hungarians, have not flared into skirmishes. Populist Stanislaw Tyminski did not get elected president of Poland. Vladimir Mečiar, despite his control of the media and the security services, could not prevent Slovak voters from kicking him out in 1998. The old party command hierarchies have not disintegrated into rival marauding gangs of shake-down artists. Contracts are not enforced by murder. New robber barons have not hijacked politics. Vested interests have not blocked the breakup of their cozy monopolies as economies prepare for the onslaught of full, open competition with west European transnational giants. Western investments are not fleeing the area in the wake of the Asian crisis. Populations, whatever their initial hardships, have not lapsed into anarchy (outside of the Balkans). Poland did not collapse at any of the five to seven times that even Balcerowicz reformers thought it might. Western Europe and central Europe are knitting together.

Otto III and Boleslaw the Brave would surely be pleased.

CHAPTER SEVEN

Absent at the Rebirth: The Eastern Slavs

N ext door to the western Slavs in Poland, the eastern Slavs are *not* escaping from history, at least not in the Polish sense of becoming more European. For now the question of how far "Europe" extends to the east has been answered definitively. By its own choice the current generation of Russians, Belarusans, and Ukrainians has opted out of the Western democratic and market systems.[1]

Time of Troubles

The Russian crash of 1998 is only the most spectacular evidence of the rejection by the eastern Slav political and economic culture of the alien graft of democracy and the market. In retrospect, events have given the lie to the pious hope of Polish and Russian liberals in the early 1990s that these imported institutions might shape, more than be shaped by, the traditions they encountered. On the day of reckoning, August 17, 1998, the mounting conflicts between institutions and tradition brought default, devaluation, and a Russia recoiling from the macroeconomic stability, austerity, and restructuring that Moscow's "young reformers" had attempted. Political crisis followed. Even the country's treasure trove of mineral wealth could not ward off the debacle of the Russian pyramid scheme as ever-more short-term bonds were issued to cover long-term debt and interest payments. Finally, mathematical logic, the Asian economic crisis, and falling oil prices struck.

Previously, the West had been willing to profess belief in the Potemkin village of prettified facades, to pretend that the ballot box would turn Boris Yeltsin into a democratic president, no matter how much he ruled like a tsar, or tried to. Now, in the naked power struggles for the succession to the ill president, such pretense was no longer possible. It died when parliamentarian Galina Starovoitova, one of Russia's most beloved and fearless democrats, was assassinated on her doorstep in St. Petersburg at the end of 1998. What she herself called Russia's "democratic house of cards" collapsed. "The murder of Galina Starovoitova is . . . the start of a mass attack on what remains of the incomplete process of democratization," wrote Marina Salye in *Nezavisimaya gazeta*.[2]

West Europeans concur in this verdict. They are ready to live with whatever mix of political and economic authoritarianism and individual initiative the eastern Slavs now come up with and to hope that the resulting regimes will be as humane and stable as possible. They will be donating food and medicine to eastern Slav towns and villages to relieve shortages in the next several winters. And they will be willing to resume giving grants and low-interest credits to any of the three states when they again adopt anti-inflationary and growth policies and demonstrate the ability to channel outside money away from private pockets into economic development.

What the West is not prepared to do, however, is to call the interim eastern Slav economies and polities "European"—or to honor the importunate request of an unreformed Kyiv to be admitted to the EU club of market democracies.

To be sure, one could argue that the eastern Slavs did move in a fundamentally Western and more open direction when the Soviet Union collapsed and broke up the old Communist party monopoly on power, wealth, and truth. But this simply left the field open for the most ruthless of the second-tier nomenklatura to steal state property in sweetheart privatization deals, strip assets, and become billionaires in the worst Soviet caricature of capitalism—then buy back political power by funding Boris Yeltsin's and Leonid Kuchma's presidential campaigns. The IMF and Harvard theory—that if only you create property owners fast, without being too fastidious, the new robber barons will soon behave like economic rationalists and want to protect their riches by rule of law—proved to be a chimera. So did the notion that competing clans might turn into protoparties and generate rudimentary pluralism; instead, the ravaging gangs produced a new Time of Troubles.

In Russia the "virtual economy," under a malevolent invisible hand, actually subtracted rather than added value, and the demonetarized system was three-quarters dependent on barter.[3] What this economists' language meant in practice was that enterprises "borrowed" money by not paying their workers, their debts, or their taxes. They continued to provide some housing and social services—barely—and a base where employees could socialize when they were not off tending their crucial vegetable plots. It was a new, even more negative variation of the old communist social contract ("They pretend to pay us, and we pretend to work") that might be rendered as "They don't pretend to pay us, and we don't pretend to work."[4] GDP dropped by at least half in the 1990s, with some statistics showing a decline of more than 80 percent. Russian output is now no larger than Spain's; and Russia's 1998 grain harvest matched the country's record lows of the previous three decades.

Even worse, contagious diseases that had vanished have now returned in Russia and Ukraine. The elementary infrastructure of heat, running water, and food distribution, wretched as it was in Soviet times, has decayed further; as an example, 80 percent of cement casings for hot water pipes have fallen away in Russia, leaving lethal steamy mud pits for the burgeoning numbers of drunks to stumble into. Average real incomes fell at least 58 percent in the 1990s; arrears in wages mounted to $11 billion, and the country had one of the world's most unequal income levels, with the top decile 13.3 times richer than the bottom decile. At least a fifth—by some calculations half—of the population is living below subsistence level. At least 15 million are verging on starvation. Life expectancy for adult men is not only worse than in Soviet times, but even below the level a century ago. Births in Russia almost halved in the 1990s, from 2.2 million to 1.4 million a year, while deaths shot up almost 40 percent, from 1.6 to 2.2 million, for a net decrease (discounting immigrants) of 3.5 million, and a projected loss of another 10 million by 2010.[5]

Moreover, with the decomposition of the old order, a new arbitrary disorder has come to prevail. Bribes no longer guarantee protection, as various ethnically based mafias gun each other down for control of the different sectors of the economy. Crime has turned out to be less a parasite on the system than the system itself.[6] Contract murders are cheap, at a reported $2,000. Former deputy premier Boris Nemtsov declares that the KGB and other security services were "privatized by the Communists, Nazis, and oligarchic structures."[7] The West's

$58 billion of aid and credits (some reports put the outside world's total debt and equity exposure to Russia at $200 billion) had little visible impact on the economy, but joined mineral-export profits for a flight of capital totaling $66 billion into Swiss, British, Cypriot, and Israeli banks.[8] Russia had two successive years in which its stock exchange share prices doubled, but in 1998 its credit rating plunged to below that of Indonesia. The state is falling apart, even as 70 percent of the country's wealth continues to be concentrated in Moscow.

Everyone has a different list of culprits. Some IMF officials blame George Soros and the speculators and a West that was too stingy to top off its 1998 Russian bailout of $19 billion with another several-billion-dollar dollop just before the cataclysm.[9] Others blame the IMF and its "sadomonetarist" policies. Susan Eisenhower scolds an insensitive West for giving Russia enough money to coerce it into a heartless neoliberal straitjacket, but not enough to make a new system function.[10] More melodramatically, Walter Russell Mead condemns the West's policy of "discriminating" against Russia by "shut[ting] it out of both NATO and the European Union" as "a textbook case in how to drive a people to fascism."[11] Conversely, Clifford Gaddy and Barry Ickes censure the West for its credulity in pouring money down the black hole of the virtual economy.[12] Dmitri K. Simes, president of the Nixon Center, identifies the faults of the old Yeltsin house of cards as "capitalism without investment, the market without regulation or property rights and democracy without respect for the law and separation of powers."[13] Historian Richard Pipes blames Russian history and the absence of a Renaissance, individualism, and private property.[14]

The Chasm between the Poles and the Eastern Slavs

Whatever the proper apportionment of guilt, the lightning bolt of August 17, 1998, made it clear just how far away Russia is from fulfilling Gorbachev's aspiration to be part of the European house. The answer to the question—how far east does Europe extend?—is now obvious: Poland's Bug River. In eight years Warsaw created a virtuous circle, in which democracy and the market reinforce each other in a synergy that qualifies Poland, with continued hard work, for membership in the EU. In seven years Moscow, trying to follow the same recipe, recreated a vicious circle in which political disintegration leads to economic impasse, which increases political deadlock. Characteristically, Poland and Hungary have already generated one legally registered company per 10 persons, on a par with the industrialized West; Russia has generated only one per 55 persons, Ukraine one per 80— and these entrepreneurs are the very ones whose savings have been wiped out by the 1998 Russian default and resumption of inflation.[15]

In sum, in the categories of Ernest Gellner and Francis Fukuyama, Poland is succeeding in establishing that difficult civil society and social trust that are essential for democracy and an effective market economy. Russia, with no historical experience in the genre, has discovered just how hard it is "to create a Civil Society from above, by design *and in a hurry*."[16]

Under the circumstances, the Russian and Ukrainian publics, unlike the Poles, have come to equate the West's democracy and market with misery; politicians are applauded when they demonize the IMF and make it the scapegoat for the agonies of modernization.[17] Belarus, under its president and former collective farm chairman, Alexander Lukashenko, never tried to become more Western in any case, but reinstated central planning and authoritarian politics (and would have recreated the Soviet Union, had Moscow's reformers not recoiled from the cost).[18] In Poland, by contrast, the government has welcomed tough IMF (and EU) conditions as an additional pressure to make Warsaw do what it must anyway do for its own benefit.

Why the difference between Poland and Russia? What does Russia lack that Poland has? The Russian parliamentarian and would-be reformer Grigory Yavlinsky was asked this question two months before the Russian economic meltdown. Yavlinsky was a survivor who had come back from the grave, a healthy man who in the 1980s was consigned to death in a tuberculosis ward for his "dissidence" in recommending modest reform in the Soviet economy. In response to the question, he barked out a one-word reply: "Everything!"[19]

Wojciech Kostrzewa, young first deputy president of Poland's Bank Rozwoyu Exportu, perhaps shares Yavlinsky's despair about Russia, but he expresses himself circumspectly. "There is no one-dimensional answer. But I would prefer to explain it in terms of economics rather than history." His own formative years as an economist in the late 1980s were spent, not in a tuberculosis ward, but at the Kiel Institute of World Economics in Germany.

First, Kostrzewa explains, Poland came later to the smothering centrally planned economy than did Russia and left it earlier. In Poland "destruction of communism" began in the 1970s and 1980s, when Poles were allowed to travel abroad freely—and came back from Singapore and Taiwan with hard disks and chips they cobbled together to start the computer firms that are now listed on the Warsaw Stock Exchange. The corollary was that "the brightest" of the party nomenklatura understood from the imposition of martial law in 1982 "that a system that needs tanks and soldiers to keep people under control is close to its end." When 1989 came, they did not try to hang on to centralized planning and politics.

"Second, West Berlin was eighty kilometers from the Polish border, so with the removals of tariffs and nontariff barriers and introduction of internal convertibility, it was possible for traders to start importing [and exporting] goods on their own. They were not forced to wait until a big state organization imported the first bananas. So this part of shock therapy was visible; goods started to be available from one day to the next."

Third, he continued, "The radical opening of the Polish market happened at the very time when most of the monopolies were very weak as pressure groups" because of the total discrediting of the old party hierarchy in the Solidarity years. And this in turn meant that— "contrary to [what happened in] almost all of the former Soviet countries—the first government after 1989 was not driven by the ex-nomenklatura, which often in the former Soviet Union tried to delay the changes." This created far less high-level resistance to liberal reforms than Russia experienced—and it also did not allow Red managers to "privatize" their own plants and become the new oligarchs.

No, replies Kostrzewa, he does not think that Poland, Hungary, the Czech Republic, "and, I believe, even Slovakia" will repeat the old Latin American cycle of swinging back and forth between democracy and authoritarianism over a long period. Their "robust economic growth" is legitimizing democracy, and the "democratic system seems to overcome many childhood diseases of the system." These countries are building up their middle class and small and medium-sized firms, and they do not have, on the Russian pattern, "huge disproportions between the megarich and the megapoor." [20]

To be sure, Poland, like Russia and like Hungary, started its reforms in the early 1990s in the face of a skeptical to hostile popular mindset. As Hungarian philosopher G. M. Tamas summarized the situation at the time:

All the surveys and polling data show that public opinion in our region rejects dictatorship, but would like to see a strong man at the helm; favors popular government, but hates parliament, parties, and the press; likes social welfare legislation and equality, but not trade unions; wants to topple the present government, but disapproves of the idea of a regular opposition; supports the notion of the market (which is a code word for Western-style living standards), but wishes to punish and expropriate the rich and condemns banking for preying on simple working people; favors a guaranteed minimum income, but sees unemployment as an immoral state and wants to punish or possibly deport the unemployed.[21]

The western Slavs (with the perhaps temporary exception of the Slovaks) broke out of that rut; the eastern Slavs did not.

The Ukrainian Example

The best foil for exploring just why the East-West divide follows the Bug River is Ukraine. This was the one eastern Slav country that had a good chance, if its elites had really wanted to, to become more European and eventually, perhaps, become associated with the European Union. Its population of 50 million makes it a more manageable size than Russia's 147 million, and more comparable to Poland's 39 million (or France's 57 million). It does not have the extremes of a Russia, spread over the Eurasian continents. It is more homogeneous and less sprawling than Russia, with ethnic Ukrainians and Russians making up the large bulk of its population.

Moreover, many Ukrainians, both inside the country and in the large émigré communities in the United States and Canada, thought that Ukraine had been exploited by Russia in the Soviet Union and that it would flourish economically once it threw off its Muscovite masters and achieved independence.[22] In both the nineteenth and twentieth centuries, after all, the black Ukrainian earth was the primary source of grain for Russia. In Soviet times Ukraine was a center for manufacture of missiles, tanks, and sturdy turbines; and its skilled scientists and engineers were more oriented toward practical applications than their more theoretical Russian counterparts.[23] Its standard of living (partly because of privileges it enjoyed over three decades as the power base of Soviet leaders Nikita Khrushchev and Leonid Brezhnev) was higher than that in Russia. Besides, Kyiv could count on the secret weapon of the diaspora in North America. Throughout their generations in exile, the fiercely nationalist émigrés in Canada and the United States, who came from the part of western Ukraine that was not incorporated into the Soviet Union until after World War II, had nurtured the Ukrainian culture and mystique. They would bring investment and entrepreneurial and democratic expertise back to the land of their ancestors, it was thought.

So widespread was the conviction of Ukraine's economic advantage that an overwhelming majority of the population—including most of the 11 million ethnic Russians in the land—voted in favor of independence in the 1991 referendum.

Psychologically, too, the nationalist Ukrainians in the west around Lviv considered themselves much more Western than the Russians (or the Russian-speaking eastern Ukrainians, for that matter). Kyiv had brought Christianity to the eastern Slavs, after all, and, much later, imported whatever Enlightenment ideas came to the region. Western Ukraine had also been at different times part of the Austro-Hungarian Empire and of Poland, and its primary religious allegiance was not to the Orthodox Church, but to the Uniate Church under the pope in Rome. With this background, what could be more natural than for Ukraine to strengthen its weak sense of any identity as distinct from Russia, reclaim its unique heritage, assume a more Western character, and at the same time persuade the rich West to bolster its still fragile independence from Russia?

This indeed was the strategy of the policy elite around President Leonid Kuchma, the surprise winner in the 1994 presidential election. It looked promising.

To understand why the strategy succeeded brilliantly in foreign policy but in the end failed to establish any domestic and economic foundation for this policy, it is necessary here to look at the devil of details. The burden of tradition may suggest broadly why a Western course was even more difficult for Kyiv than for Warsaw. But history is not fate. Only by examining the interplay of the authoritarian inheritance with specific players and their shifting perception of policy choices can one come to an approximate explanation of events.

The account, then, begins properly with the new Ukraine's first president, Leonid Kravchuk. He was a communist apparatchik who had stolen the nationalists' clothes just in time to get elected by popular vote as the Soviet Union crumbled. He brought his old apparat with him to govern the new state. He introduced no Russian-style privatization—as late as 1994 there was not a single private bakery in Kyiv—but his cronies still managed to make personal fortunes in paler imitation of Russia's instant capitalists, buying petroleum and metals at old Soviet ruble prices for sale abroad at world dollar prices. No Ukrainian Boris Berezovsky or Mikhail Khodorovsky would make the Forbes list of billionaires, but, less flamboyantly, the Ukrainian nomenklatura also still preserved its power and converted its privilege into cash. Under the malign neglect, the economy went into a tailspin, with hyperinflation of 10,000 percent, a drop of 60 percent in GDP within three years, and what seemed at the time to be a peculiarly egregious arrears of several months' unpaid wages.

Despite the communist continuity and economic calamity, the West appreciated Kravchuk's initial consolidation of Ukrainian independence, which shut the door on any near-term Russian temptation to revert to imperialism. Russians of all political persuasions might still think that after three centuries of union Ukraine rightfully belonged to Russia and should return, but this union would not be restored unless Ukraine's many ethnic Russians and Russophile eastern Ukrainians wanted it. And if Russia did not reabsorb its Slavic soulmates in Ukraine, it was unlikely to have an undemocratic appetite whetted for reabsorbing other parts of the "near abroad." The longer the question of reassimilating Ukraine could be kept off the active agenda in Moscow, then, the better.

Kravchuk also won Western respect for the tolerance Ukraine showed its Russian, Polish, Romanian, Jewish, and other minorities. With this mix of peoples in a country lacking a tradition of nationhood, any ethnic concept of citizenship, rather than uniting the country, would have split it. It therefore made sense to strive for a civic concept; anyone living on Ukrainian territory on the day of independence was declared a citizen.

Finally, the West was grateful to Kravchuk for acceding to strong U.S. pressure over three years and forfeiting the nuclear weapons Ukraine had inherited from the Soviet Union. The informal quid pro quo was an American security assurance that was worded ambiguously enough so that Kyiv could interpret it as a hint of protection, while the United States could interpret it as a repetition of more general Organization for Security and Cooperation in Europe (OSCE) pledges.

In addition, once Kravchuk's successor started economic reform, Washington rewarded Kyiv with grants and credits that elevated Ukraine to the third-largest recipient of U.S. aid, after Israel and Egypt. Various Ukrainian-Canadian and Ukrainian-American businessmen flocked to the old country to start computer consultancies in Kyiv or supermarkets in Dnipropetrovsk. Compatriots explained the unique, flourishing system of ethnic Ukrainian financial cooperatives in the United States and Canada that might be adopted to channel a plethora of small savings into equitable investment. With funding from philanthropist George Soros, émigré educators also established a graduate school of public administration to rush civil servants through crash courses, while economists and political scientists advised parliament and government exhaustively on legislation and policy. North American lawyers helped educate fledgling jurists, compiled and translated a dictionary of Anglo-Saxon legal terms and concepts directly into Ukrainian (without the intermediation of Russian), published the corpus of (previously often secret) Ukrainian legislation, and computerized university law schools to give them on-line access to statutes.

With this start, Ukraine established its independence for the second time, following in the footsteps of the short-lived Ukrainian regime that emerged from World War I to be crushed by the Bolsheviks in brutal civil war. And it avoided the repeat civil war that the U.S. Central Intelligence Agency feared might break out.[24] Tension between ships of the Black Sea Fleet apportioned to the Russian and Ukrainian navies did escalate so far in the spring of 1994 that officers of the Russian vessel *Cheleken*—which had seized navigational equipment from the port of Odessa—gave orders to the 318th Division of the Russian fleet to fire on pursuing Ukrainian boats. The orders were never carried out, though, and the incident passed.

Similarly, although some leaders of the ethnic Russian majority on the Crimean peninsula agitated for secession to Russia once it became clear that the depressed Ukrainian economy would not pump money into their Black Sea resorts, no blood was shed there. (At least what blood was shed did not involve Ukrainians, but only Russians and those Tatars finally returning to their native Crimea after Stalinist exile in Siberia or the respective Russian and Tatar mafias in Crimea.) Nor was there in Kyiv any Russian-style shootout between president and parliament. There was no Chechen war, and Ukraine had no imperial ambitions. When Leonid Kuchma, an old industrial apparatchik who had managed what was touted as the largest missile factory in the world, was unexpectedly elected president over the incumbent in 1994, there was a peaceful succession, a test the Russians have yet to pass.

In his first years in office Kuchma finally introduced macroeconomic stabilization and rudimentary economic reforms. He reconciled eastern and western Ukrainians (with substantial help from Moscow, as the war in Chechnya made any Ukrainian return to union with Russia repugnant, especially to parents of draft-age sons). He displayed some unexpected political skills as well, courting individual members of parliament on key issues in a way Yeltsin never tried to do in Moscow, forging a power-sharing arrangement with a hostile parliament dominated by the old left, writing a constitution that many Ukrainians took as their nation's badge of maturity, and, under the stern eye of the central bank, introducing a new currency that stayed stable for several years. The United States and Germany, in particular—other Europeans focused on the former superpower of Russia to the exclusion of Ukraine—approved and supported Kuchma's efforts.

In his early reform period Kuchma followed the Russian model, timidly, rather than the Polish model. Warsaw might have offered Kyiv a helpful example, especially since Poland was already succeeding, economically and democratically, by the time Ukraine began its reforms. Some Poles, in fact, even urged the Ukrainians to use as a prototype the seventeenth-century Polish republic that Ukrainian lands had been part of and to build on that.[25] But the old Ukrainian peasant antipathies toward Polish landlords and memories of mutual butchery as recently as the 1940s remained too strong for that idea to be popular. In the early 1990s would-be Ukrainian reformers sometimes cited the rather inappropriate Estonian model of transformation as their ideal, but never the Polish. Ukraine never had the "bench depth" of successive sophisticated Polish finance ministers and economists in any case.[26] Despite all the top-down efforts to achieve Polish-Ukrainian reconciliation—and despite the availability in Kyiv of willing Polish economic advisers—Poland had little influence on its neighbor beyond spreading Western fashions through the bustling cross-border suitcase trade.

Russia's energetic young reformers in the mid-1990s also had little impact on Ukraine. The brain drain of ambitious Ukrainians over centuries to glittering Moscow had taken its toll; so had this century's four exterminations of Ukrainian elites in the Red-White civil war, induced famine, Stalin's purges, and World War II. There was no pack of hot-shot reformers in Ukraine with an education in basic market economics comparable to Anatoli Chubais and Boris Nemtsov and their colleagues in Moscow. And not even Grigory Yavlinsky had any desire to return to the small pond of his native Ukraine to become a politician there.[27]

For the North American diaspora, it was a surprise to find that western Ukrainians failed to become a strong transmission belt for modernization and Westernization in independent Ukraine. The émigrés certainly did not expect fraternization with the Poles by those Ukrainians who took over vacated Polish houses in Lviv in 1945, even as the expelled Lviv Poles took over the bombed-out cellars of German expellees in Breslau in western Poland as the postwar borders shifted. They did anticipate, however, that their Galician cousins would naturally think more the way Americans and Canadians thought. And they expected the Rukh movement in western Ukraine, which had agitated so effectively for independence in the 1980s, to have much more influence in the Ukraine of the 1990s than its minority vote ultimately accorded it. Yet the Galicians turned out to have little interest in pressing for a market economy—and their voice was in any case muffled by the atomization of politics in a country with little national consciousness and by the monopolization of Kyiv politics by the regional clans of Dnipropetrovsk and Donetsk.

The Death of Reform

These two old bureaucratic and geographical clans left over from communist days set the course of Ukrainian politics. The large majority of Kuchma's senior appointees came from Dnipropetrovsk, and originally he had a certain claim to leadership of that city's clan. By the time he lost interest in economic reform in 1996, though, Dnipropetrovsk's industrial and monetary power had essentially flowed to Petro Lazarenko, prime minister in the mid-1990s. Under the patronage of Lazarenko, the United Energy Systems empire quickly cornered some 80 percent of Ukraine's natural gas supply, then parleyed this near-monopoly into ownership of a network of other companies accounting for an estimated eighth of the country's GDP. Lazarenko and the Hromada party he founded (after he was fired as prime minister amid charges of corruption) clearly had no interest in changing a system that had been so good to them—nor did other political-business conglomerates.

In the new era of elections the Donetsk clan did form the Liberal party, but this was little more than the old power struggle in 1990s dress. The international liberal colleagues the Ukrainian Liberal party seemed to admire most were the Japanese Liberal Democrats, and their special attraction lay less in any distinct platform than in their enormous success in staying in power virtually uninterrupted for half a century.[28]

Under the circumstances, those Ukrainians in a position to profit from the new commerce generally focused their attention on making money today, at the expense of setting up durable institutions for tomorrow or doing the necessary nation-building in an infant state. And, unlike the Russian oligarchs, they preferred shutting out Western competition to attracting new investment that they might get a percentage of. No megadeals comparable to Russia's Caspian Sea energy projects were waiting to be made in any case, since Ukraine was less endowed with raw materials. But initially several smaller direct equity investors came in with the hope that Ukraine's ubiquitous chicanery, demand for bribes, taxes that often exceeded 100 percent of profits, and evershifting laws with arbitrary application were just temporary teething problems. Within a few years these companies had been chased away.

The British JKX Oil and Gas firm, for one, informed Kyiv that it could produce 20 percent of Ukraine's domestic gas needs from its Poltava fields and thus help correct the country's chronic trade deficits from imported energy. Yet it was barred by Ukrainian rivals from feeding its stock into the domestic pipeline. The sugar giant Tate & Lyle had to forfeit delivery contracts to Coca-Cola and other customers in Russia and close its Odessa refinery after Ukrainian bureaucrats suddenly banned import of sugar cane and export of the company's fine white sugar, apparently in a clumsy attempt to benefit domestic producers of lumpy, gray beet sugar. Similarly, Kiev Atlantic and other Western firms that had helped farmers finance seed, fertilizer, and other inputs nonetheless failed to get their contracted grain when the state abruptly expropriated harvests (at prices less than half the world price). In the telecommunications sector that is so crucial for the future,

Motorola finally wrote off its substantial initial investment on a contract for mobile phones after the rules and exorbitant fees for frequencies kept shifting, Ukrainian competitors were awarded prime wavelengths under opaque circumstances—and, according to one executive, Motorola refused to deliver a $1 million payoff.

One Canadian investor who abandoned projects in Kyiv and other graft-ridden cities and moved to what was then a better-run Odessa spoke for many of his colleagues in complaining that "former communists" who have hung on to bureaucratic posts "lie, do not tell the truth, deceive you, [and] tell you that they are working to assist your project, when in fact they work against you." This makes Ukraine "a very pathetic and sick place to do business."

More personally, a Ukrainian-American businessman in Kyiv recalls that he was not sure growing up whether he was American or Ukrainian, "but after one week here I knew I was American!"[29]

Even as the big-name companies, in frustration, pulled out close to half of the $2 billion that was all the investment Ukraine had been able to attract in the 1990s, there seemed to be little awareness in Kyiv that the sure penalty for killing the golden goose would be repulsion of potential future investors. On the contrary, there was a common feeling that the country had an innate right to foreign investment and a resentment of Westerners who willingly plowed money into the corrupt Philippines (as one of Kuchma's aides phrased it) but then cited corruption as an excuse not to invest heavily in Ukraine.[30] There was suspicion, in what was seen as a zero-sum game, that wily Westerners would use their unfair advantages in wealth and knowledge of capitalist rules of the road to cheat inexperienced Ukrainians. Often enough there was indignation at middle-level ranks when stingy foreigners would not cough up the few-thousand-dollar payoffs they so clearly could afford—or at higher levels when Westerners who had already made their bundle cited contract law to muscle out Ukrainians who just wanted to make their bundle too. In a government of low pay and high turnover, there was also an urge by various ministers and deputy ministers to line their own pockets fast, as their predecessors had done, before they got fired or lost access. The legal risk was negligible; as Vyacheslav Pikhovshek, director of the Ukrainian Center for Independent Political Research, pointed out, "There has not been a single trial in Ukraine for corruption."[31]

In this atmosphere, periodic anti-graft campaigns never flushed out the stables, but remained at the level of wars of sometimes true, sometimes false, accusations of corruption by rivals. The few officials who seemed intent on a real cleanup, like Justice Minister Serhiy Holovaty, soon found themselves out of office.

For a few years Ukraine's driving out of foreign direct investment did not seriously harm the country. Portfolio investment flowed in, eager to snap up undervalued firms as they privatized. When privatization also bogged down, however—and especially as the Asian and Russian crises made investors wary—the hot money flowed out again. The government repeatedly overshot its promised budget deficits, triggering suspension of IMF loans. It received from Moody's the lowest credit rating in all of eastern Europe and the former Soviet Union. When it launched its first Eurobonds in early 1998—just to raise money to service debt on the Western loans that had been heavily front-loaded in the advance vote of confidence in Kuchma—it had to offer a spread double that for Russian government paper. A month after Moscow defaulted on its debt in August 1998, Kyiv had to reschedule its domestic government debt. By then its hard-currency reserves were exceeded by debt coming due. Its wage arrears, like Russia's, now ran into billions of dollars.[32] Its pensioners were receiving $19 a month, if they got paid at all.[33]

The upshot was that Ukraine's shadow versions of Russia's oligarchs blocked both reform and Western investment, without any real battle. By 1996 reform was dead. The Ukrainian economy is still retracting, with one of the worst records in the region. Debts for Ukraine's profligate import of energy from Russia and Turkmenistan remain high. Land reform on the bankrupt collective farms has not begun, and grain harvests in this once-upon-a-time breadbasket are half what they used to be in the Soviet era. The old Communist party apparatchiks, who now call themselves businessmen, are still plundering the state. Structural reforms that are essential for the economy to start growing again are nowhere to be seen. The current arbitrary taxes are not being rationalized to draw the shadow economy into legitimacy. Russian and Ukrainian mafias, rather than imitating Italian or Colombian mafias in at least reinvesting their profits in the economies they leech, are diligently exporting more capital than their countries have been receiving in Western aid.[34] Gangland murders, while not on a Russian scale, are becoming more frequent.

Politically, there is no concept of government as a neutral provider of the common good or as umpire; instead, it is seen as the first in line to milk the state. The strongest incentives to getting elected to parliament or to taking government office still tend to be immunity from legal liability or having the inside advantage to manipulate licenses, contracts, and state credits. And Ukrainian, like Russian, business is both over- and underregulated—overregulated in the number of stamps (and therefore bribes) required for every franchise; underregulated in the lack of protection for the anonymous consumer or for honest firms.[35]

Moreover, in advance of presidential elections in 1999, fantastic rumors have become the grist of everyday politics. Kuchma, knowing he cannot win, will cancel the vote and override the new constitution to hang on to power, say some nationalists. No, retort presidential defenders; the real danger is that rival Evhen Marchuk, member of parliament, former prime minister, and former head of the Ukrainian KGB, will get money from Russia's Gazprom and the KGB successor organization, mobilize his own loyal secret service agents, impeach Kuchma, and return Ukraine to Moscow's suzerainty. No, no, chime in some European expatriates, sketching ominous geopolitical maps on paper napkins; the ultimate plot is a Russian-German conspiracy to conquer the world by getting a stranglehold on Caspian gas and oil.

Ironically, Kyiv's short-sighted and self-destructive domestic policy is coupled with a foreign policy that has been highly effective in enhancing Ukraine's security. Together, Kravchuk and Kuchma steered Ukraine through the fluid first years when rival Ukrainian politicians might have been tempted to make common cause with Moscow. Today, with new power bases solidified, no player would willingly trade his position even in a smaller, poorer Ukraine for a bit role in richer Russia—especially during Russia's current crisis. But beyond ensuring the sheer longevity by now of Ukraine's eight years of independence—the longest in the country's history—the two first presidents also managed to thwart Russia's attempt to marshal a common foreign policy and defense in a Moscow-led Commonwealth of Independent States—that is, the old Soviet Union minus the Baltic states. Ukraine initially declared itself "bloc-free," in a politically correct rubric for slipping out from the droit de regard Russia sought to exercise in the near abroad. Kuchma then went further in applauding Polish entry into NATO and even speculating that one day Ukraine, too, might join the alliance. Simultaneously, he outmaneuvered ethnic Russian politicians in Crimea who were trying to turn the peninsula's autonomy into accession to Russia; and he also wrested control of

Sevastopol away from the Russian military command, which had been running it de facto as a closed city. By 1995–96 Ukrainian officials were describing their overall policy choice as one between good (Western) integration and bad (Soviet/Russian) disintegration. Or they declared (by implicit contrast to Russia) that "Ukraine is European, and its future is European."[36] One Kyiv journalist was even blunter. "The U.S. should occupy Ukraine and teach it democracy the way America occupied Germany and taught Germany democracy!" he exclaimed.[37]

The official sentiment found some resonance among the Ukrainian policy elite.[38] And Russian nationalists inadvertently helped the progression by periodically claiming the naval port of Sevastopol and demanding as a right the indefinite berthing of the Russian Black Sea Fleet there. Repeatedly, the more strident Russian assertions forced even the Soviet loyalists in the very unreconstructed Ukrainian Communist party to swear their patriotism and steadfastness to Ukrainian sovereignty over Sevastopol.

Whatever back-handed help Kuchma had from Moscow, though, it was his own considerable accomplishment to effect the Western reorientation of foreign policy in an eastern Slav peasant land with an army, an ex-KGB security service, and a former communist hierarchy steeped in Soviet thinking. The fact that he brought off the shift so smoothly owed much to quiet U.S.-Ukrainian diplomacy and to the skill of a few key Ukrainian diplomats like Borys Tarasyuk, ambassador to Belgium and NATO in the mid-1990s and now foreign minister. By 1997 Kyiv had fulfilled the preconditions of resolving or neutralizing border disputes with Romania and other neighbors—without backlash from the old Ukrainian hierarchies. It was rewarded with the "distinctive partnership" with NATO that it sought—and this high-profile Western recognition of Ukraine at last jolted Yeltsin into recognizing Ukraine's borders.

Does this schizophrenia between a robust Western-oriented foreign policy and domestic entropy make any difference to Europe, or to the West as a whole? Yes, in two respects.

The first is that Ukrainian officials are pressing Germany hard to admit Kyiv into the European Union—and they do not seem to realize how remote they are from filling the EU's democratic, legal, and market requirements for membership. The Ukrainians have unrealistic expectations, and they are heading for a nasty shock when they finally realize that the EU means it when it says no.

The second cause for concern is the risk of domestic unrest in Ukraine (as in Russia) as the current hardships continue. So far both the Ukrainians and the Russians have been incredibly patient and have gone on strike only sporadically, usually in thinly veiled clan clashes rather than any spontaneous eruptions. And in the 1990s the Ukrainians seem to have shown more of a knack than the Russians for pulling back from the brink of violence. But as conditions get worse—and there is every sign that they will, especially given the drift until the 1999 Ukrainian presidential election—villagers and politicians could well start looking for scapegoats.

"The biggest enemy in Ukraine today is ourselves," confided Kuchma's closest adviser, Volodymyr Horbulin, to a Russian interviewer in 1997.[39] It was an apt verdict.

How Far East Will the West Go?

Among the central Europeans Poland, Hungary, the Czech Republic, Estonia, and Slovenia have all met enough of the democratic and competitive market conditions for membership in the EU and NATO, in the judgment of current club members, to be invited to join in the first admission of new entrants. At least they are well on their way. Or at least they are tiny enough, Poland excepted, for the EU and NATO to digest them without seriously altering the organizations' purpose, capabilities, equilibrium, and potential for evolution. Latvia, Lithuania, Bulgaria, and Romania show enough promise to be on the waiting list. Slovakia also is on the list, as an encouragement to it to shed any vestiges of Mečiar's authoritarianism and catch up with the other Visegrad states. Albania is also on the list because it was already there before a pyramid investment scheme exploded and loosed anarchy in the country.

Ukraine, the non-Baltic Soviet successor that once had the greatest potential for embracing a semi-Western identity, has, by tradition and default, chosen instead a non-Western path. It has implicit external security links with the West, but it does not have at all what EU members have started calling a "European vocation."

Russia—with residual claims to special influence in neighbor states, an exhilarating energy and volatility, a hybrid political system that is far more open than in communist times in requiring competing clans to pass the 1990s' hurdle of elections, and a hybrid economic system of bandit oligarchs and stranglehold mafias—has also chosen a non-Western path. It has more external links with the West than does Ukraine in its now institutionalized participation in the Contact Group, the Group of Seven (now Eight) "economic" annual summits, and the NATO–Russian Permanent Joint Council, and its oil, gas, nickel, and other raw-materials deals with Western corporations. It has a new relationship of regular summits with Germany and France; and it will always get more deference from the West than will less powerful non-nuclear nations. But it is unlikely to qualify, or want to qualify, for membership in the EU and NATO in this generation, or the next. Its security relationship with the West will remain an external one and will develop in large part through NATO-Russian contacts.

Western Russia, Ukraine, and Belarus are part of Europe geographically. But by self-selection they are not part of it economically or politically. As Europe is reborn, the eastern Slavs are bystanders.

CHAPTER EIGHT

Commencement de Siècle

The forces that impelled Europe's unprecedented integration were the deterrent horror of Auschwitz, the gulag, and the bomb; economic reconstruction; the magnetic attraction of a long peace and attendant prosperity; a globalized interdependence that has made statelets even as large as Germany far too small to cope alone with pollution and capital flows; German remorse and nightmares; and, in central Europe, a yearning for what is perceived as Western "normality."

Will these dynamics continue, now that the overarching Soviet threat and the post–cold war fluidity are both gone, displaced by Russian meltdown? Can capitalism's animal spirits of self-interest and personal gain that are now being called on continue to drive the European project further? And can this still delicate process be insulated against the Russian disorder?

Pessimists, the true conservators, argue from manifold lessons of history that the answer is no. To them it is obvious that the impulses to integration arose in a period of unusually mobile politics. That period is now over. Ordinary clashes of interest are back. And the new Russian Time of Troubles will only drive the EU back to a traditional Fortress Europe mentality.

Optimists, the true radicals, have a premonition instead that rationality, habit, and institutions can all prolong the new-found impetus to cooperation. In this view, the benefits of joint endeavor have already become so internalized that members will continue to pay the cost, however painful, of disciplined budgets and progressive loss of sovereignty. A new pragmatism reigns. If anything, the threat of chaos from the east will force (western and central) Europeans to accelerate their integration for their own protection. Put baldly, the institutions of monetary union and the EU Council, however imperfect, will have to succeed for sheer lack of any tolerable alternative.

It would be a mistake, optimists further suggest, to measure the six-year-old sapling of the European Union against the 200-year-old oak of the United States. The 1990s have made clear that the EU will continue to be a confederation-plus for decades to come—and despite Kohl's best efforts in the early 1990s, probably never will become a federation. Its genius, unlike the American genius—to judge from the evidence of the past decade—is expressed less in powerful competing institutions than in ongoing process. And as long as the U.S.-sponsored peace prevails in Europe, a consensual confederation process should suffice both to generate mutual commitments and to give member nations the confidence that they can maintain their own identities without being assimilated into a bland homogeneity that no one wants.

Indeed, the corollary of this rare social optimism is an equally rare mode of decisionmaking that projects the domestic consensus politics of Germanic Europe and the Benelux countries onto the European plane and makes it work—in many cases—even without the glue of national solidarity. This approach was manifest in the 1990s in treating crisis as opportunity, uncertainty as fluidity, and anxiety about the future in general and Germany in particular as an energizing disequilibrium. Repeatedly, compromise was tipped into mutual resolve rather than deadlock; interdependence led to pooling of sovereignty rather than scapegoating; inertia was turned into the kinetics of cumulative movement rather than inertness.

Above all, one of the most striking phenomena of the run-up to monetary union was that the Maastricht hurdles designed to exclude the unworthy became instead benchmarks for ratcheting up these poor performers. In 1992 the criteria were deliberately set so high as to shut out notoriously unstable Italy. But the Italian central bankers and finance ministers who had imbibed the Bundesbank's anti-inflation gospel exploited the requirements instead to force change on their crisis-ridden and almost bankrupt country—under penalty of Italian exclusion from the prestigious EMU founders' club if reform were rejected. So successful were they that when center-left prime minister Romano Prodi clashed with parliament over his 1997 budget cuts, the tables were turned. In any previous year in the past half century, an austerity that offended so many interlocking interests would have toppled the government in Rome. Yet this time, after gnashing of teeth, the tight budget was approved precisely because not to do so would have unseated the government and debarred Italy from the euro club. Remarkably, all this coincided with exposure of the "Tangentopoli," or "Bribesville," scandals, the conviction of one previous prime minister for fraud, the indictment of another for conspiracy with the mafia, and the flight of a third to North Africa to escape arrest.

Italian cabinet minister Beniamino Andreatta traces the metamorphosis to the 1992 crisis that expelled the lira from the European Monetary System. Successively minister of the treasury, foreign affairs, and defense, Andreatta was intimately involved in making "benchmarking" the 1990s shorthand for reversal of the axiom that bargaining among heterogeneous equals must degenerate to the lowest common denominator—and the more participants, the lower the commonality. In this reverse concept, instead, the *highest* common denominator became the "benchmark" or norm for lower performers to strive for and reach. Specifically, Andreatta, Finance Minister Carlo Ciampi, and like-minded colleagues insisted that the country's crony system of politics and economics had to end. They deemed modernization essential in any case for Italian exports to stay competitive in today's world, but the shame of ejection from the European Monetary System and the hope of qualifying for European Monetary Union gave them a tool of coercion. France might press for a slackening of the criteria to bring Italy and Spain into the EMU as a counterweight to German stringency; the Italians themselves would instead use the luster of "Europe" and the threat of rejection to compel their compatriots' conformity to the economic mores of that Europe.

Thus in the summer of 1993 an Italian social contract for moderate wage increases was concluded that fully deindexed pay for the first time since World War II (even if the price was a thirty-five-hour week in the name of job creation). The budget deficit was shaved from 9.6 percent in 1992 to 2.7 percent in 1997, inflation from 5.4 percent to 1.7 percent, matching German performance; bond yields dropped six points between 1995 and 1998, almost reaching German levels. The Banca d'Italia got full independence in 1992 in setting discount and Lombard rates and, with the zeal of a convert, controlled the money in circulation even more strictly than the Bundesbank.[1] A pension reform was introduced in 1997 that narrowed provisions for early retirement; comprehensive tax reform followed in 1998. Privatization and liberalization shed state companies and stocks worth some $38 billion in four years, allowed more part-time work so it cost less to create new jobs, pried open somewhat the closed shops of professional guilds, and let stores stay open longer. Segmentation of banks was broken down and transparency increased. Despite its continuing high debt ratio of almost 122 percent to GDP, Italy is now a net creditor.

There is a long way still to go, says Andreatta. Italy must also implement microeconomic reforms, liberalize and decentralize more, debureaucratize, cut the number of required licenses, continue tax reform, fully fund pensions for the 16 percent of the population now older than sixty-five—and write a new constitution. Ambitiously, Prodi—whose improvised Olive Tree government of Socialists, former Communists, and former Christian Democrats was among the longest serving since World War II—planned before he was unseated in 1998 to cut debt to 100 percent of GDP by 2003 and to the 60 percent required by Maastricht by 2016.[2]

Scarcely less dramatic is the role the EU has played in promoting modernization elsewhere in the poorer European periphery. Spain and Portugal attribute much of their successful transformation from authoritarian to democratic systems in the 1970s and 1980s to the aid and tutelage of the EC in general and of the German Social Democratic party in particular. They are also beginning to communicate with each other across a border that for 700 years divided rather than united them.[3] Greece, emerging from its long leftist ideological backlash to military rule, is finally following the same course. (Its earlier failure to do so and its concomitant economic stagnation were duly flagged by Poles in the early 1990s as a negative model to be eschewed.) And the self-confidence that Ireland acquired as it found in the EC an alternative orientation to England, moved into high-tech manufacture, and generated one of the fastest growth rates in Europe, was instrumental in boosting the Republic's self-image enough to end the cycle of killings in Northern Ireland in the 1998 peace settlement.[4]

This mutual benefit is repeated variously in the experience of virtually all EU members. Germans pay the most, but, as their political leaders keep reminding them, their exporters also profit greatly from the huge single market. The French National Assembly fumes about and defies the EU ban on shooting migratory birds during nesting season—but France owes it to the benign EC environment in the 1970s and 1980s that its per capita income today almost equals that of united Germany.

Such tangible progress is a powerful incentive for elites to continue and deepen integration, even at the cost of making some uncomfortable national concessions for the greater weal. It lets the Danes put up with the indignity of not getting their favorite little apples certified by Brussels, lets the French tolerate EU requirements that traded cheese be pasteurized, and forces the Germans to accept imported beer that does not meet their sixteenth-century purity standards.

Yet voters who take for granted the fruit of cooperation tend to ask politicians, "What have you done for me lately?" And in this century's fast-changing world, the answer to that question will depend on the answers to several clusters of further questions—about EMU, EU governance, Germany, the French-German connection, assimilation of the central Europeans, and security. In brief:

Can monetary union work economically? Or will it fail so spectacularly that it will blast apart the political integration achieved so far?

Will the Germans be able to make the necessary economic reforms to stay competitive in a globalized world? Or has a consensus system that is admirably suited to incremental change reached its natural limits and shown itself incapable of more radical metamorphosis?

Can the French-German special relationship survive the political departure of Helmut Kohl? How doggedly will France, now with the help of Keynesian German finance minister Oskar Lafontaine, try to claw back political control of the European (and French) central banks?

Will the EU knock heads together sufficiently to adapt institutions and rules for the six members to an EU of twenty-one and more members? Is the widespread premise that crisis impels change in fact correct? Will the Bavarians accept cuts in the Common Agricultural Policy? Will the French accept cuts in German contributions to the EU budget that Paris would have to compensate for? How can the sense of mutual benefit be sustained when the painful decisions are so often blamed on Brussels?

Will the central Europeans continue without political backlash, despite the agonies of transformation, on their course of crafting democracies and market economies?[5] Will they in fact provide a fresh raison d'être to a jaded western Europe? And how far east will the EU aura radiate into countries that will not soon qualify for double membership in the EU and NATO?

Finally, can some approximation of civility slowly be restored in the former Yugoslavia? Will armistice last long enough for European financial assistance to become an effective lever there? How can NATO, the WEU, and the OSCE together best contain or stop war in the Balkans? How, in short, can Europe export security rather than import insecurity?

EMU

In no decision was Europe's new activism more manifest than in the plunge into monetary union. It required surrender of some of the most cherished attributes of sovereignty—and even if a shrinking world had already made such surrender a fait accompli, it was remarkable that European leaders willingly ratified that accomplished fact in a new supranational institution. Monetary union presumed the instant conjuring up of a potent new European central bank, even when founding members' own central banks had evolved through trial and error over decades. It demonstrated faith that mutual commitments could be made and honored even in a period of severe recession—and faith that when the inevitable crises arose, European leaders would muster the wit and the unanimity to resolve them. It presupposed enough enlightened self-interest by the Germans for them to give up their most precious asset and symbol, the deutsche mark, and waive any claim to the first presidency of the European Central Bank (ECB), in the sheer confidence that whatever central banker took the post, his or her economic approach would reflect the German philosophy anyway. It trusted that the EU could juggle the overloaded agenda of monetary union on top of historic enlargement and administrative reform and reapportionment of EU finances.

Certainly no one knew whether monetary union would actually work or not. And everyone did know that if it failed, it would be a catastrophe that could bring down the whole edifice of the EU. It entailed extraordinarily high risk, in market probes, in the inevitable turf contests among institutions, and in strains over policy preferences among its eleven varied members.

In a world of liberalized capital movement, daily flows of $1.6 trillion—equal to the total foreign exchange holdings of the world's major central banks—overwhelm the capacities of central banks to stop any volatile run in inherently unstable financial markets. So far there has been little discussion of an ECB role as a lender of last resort, should any member nation's central bank come under mortal threat.[6]

In terms of institutions, a foretaste of brawls to come was offered at the European summit to launch the euro in May of 1998 as European central bankers, through the intermediary of German chancellor Helmut Kohl, confronted French president Jacques Chirac for a tense twelve hours. In this round "le Bulldozer" won a Pyrrhic victory, establishing the principle that government leaders rather than central bankers select the president of the European Central Bank—but failing to budge ECB policy, and losing the French monopoly on the presidency of the European Bank for Reconstruction and Development to German Horst Köhler in the process.[7] Conversely, the central bankers won what they suspected was also a Pyrrhic victory as their ECB nominee, Dutchman Willem F. Duisenberg, was in effect appointed for only the first half of the inaugural eight-year term. Duisenberg wiggled out of being held to a fixed date for resigning, however, and, in fact, his designated French successor, Jean-Claude Trichet, also subscribes to a tough antidirigiste, un-French approach. Bundesbank president Hans Tietmeyer demonstrated why his post pulls a higher salary than the federal chancellor's when he compelled this compromise, it was said, by threatening to resign otherwise (and thereby to scuttle monetary union altogether by withdrawing the Bundesbank's imprimatur). German commentary about the "dirty compromise" in naming the ECB chief was so negative that Kohl felt obliged to haul German president Roman Herzog before the cameras as stock markets opened the day after the Brussels summit to assure voters and investors that the euro was indeed a felicitous invention.[8]

As it turned out, the mid-1998 summit gave final approval to EMU in the only available window of opportunity. Russia had not yet collapsed economically, frightening Europeans away from any new experiments. And the rising European growth just before the Asian and Russian crises hit the continent's stock markets was producing economic cycles that were more synchronous for the eleven founders than they had been for decades. On the one hand, the solid rise in production, a current account surplus of 1 percent of GDP, and continental European bourses advancing 28 percent to Wall Street's 14 percent were gifts that no one had expected even a year earlier.[9] On the other hand, the convergence in low inflation, budget deficits, and long-term interest rates was the result of sheer political will and showed the normative power of the whole Maastricht project and its criteria. Member countries did remain far apart in unemployment, with Spain having double the high EU average, and Italy and Belgium having double the guideline in public debt. But the general correspondence gave the euro a favorable sendoff. Economists agreed in predicting at least short-term gains, a strong euro, and perhaps even appreciation against the dollar.[10]

For the European on the street there will clearly be an advantage in not having to carry six wallets on a holiday drive from Amsterdam to Venice, say, or to lose constantly in exchange fees. And even stay-at-home consumers should benefit as the transparency of listing prices everywhere in easily compared euros produces more open competition and forces automakers to charge the same in Italy as in Germany. Indeed, member governments are seeking to reinforce this message of a cheaper cost of living by urging banks not to charge fees for changeover when the time comes and pressuring towns not to "round up" bus and swimming-pool charges when they convert to the euro.

For exporters—and for foreign investors as well—transaction costs and exchange-rate risks will evaporate within what has already been nicknamed Euroland. This too should increase competition and efficiency, lower costs, improve allocation, and promote cross-border investment and trade. Indeed, the European Commission calculates that the removal of these trade barriers alone could provide a 0.5 percent fillip to GDP.[11]

Above all, however, it is investors and entrepreneurs who should benefit and stimulate the overall economy of what will be the world's largest exporter and largest single market of rich consumers. The advantages start with the very predictability of the currency; two-thirds of the increase in German wage costs in the past decade, for example, came from appreciation of the deutsche mark.[12] They should continue with the widely expected "Americanization" of European securities. Euro currency markets developed overnight, even before the euro was formally introduced, and euro zone bond markets should reach the American size of about $3 trillion in two or three years. Even the underdeveloped European equity markets should approximate their American counterpart within a decade or so, according to Deutsche Bank chief economist Norbert Walter.[13]

In the case of bonds, conservative insurance and pension funds that were previously confined to fragmented national markets to avoid exchange-rate risks will have much more choice and flexibility. They should therefore be able to find higher yields in a unified euro-de-nominated market, with early signs indicating that the German Bund will be the euro benchmark.[14] With EMU's stringent budgets, sovereign bond issuance will probably fall by $50 billion in the first year of the euro, but the underdeveloped category of corporate bonds—which currently fund only a third of business debt in the euro zone, compared with 80 percent in the United States—is expected to grow and fill any void.[15] As the volume increases and instruments become more varied and more liquid, the overall cost of debt should decrease, thereby aiding entrepreneurs seeking capital.

The European equity market will be slower to match its $139 trillion American counterpart. The euro-11 bourses have only a third, the EU-15 less than half that figure, since corporate financing on the continent has traditionally come much more than in the United States from in-house banks holding seats on borrowers' boards. Here, too, Europe is moving rapidly toward a pattern more like that of the United States, however. It will likely be driven by benchmarking on the North American capital market that, at least before the Russian and Latin American crises in the summer of 1998, had 35 percent higher returns than European securities.[16] Already the foundation for a Europe-wide stock market has been laid with the alliance between the London and Frankfurt exchanges and the likely accession to this alliance by the Italian, Spanish, and French bourses.[17] Economists anticipate that the evolving market—and the concomitant shift of focus from stakeholder to shareholder value—should even, at last, provide the kind of venture capital for start-ups that has been notoriously scarce on the continent.[18]

Regionally, as monetary union creates for the first time a true single market in which alternative costs can be easily measured by both consumers and entrepreneurs (including small as well as large businesses with greater analytical capability), the capital shakeup should encourage investment to flow to those EMU countries that have low wage scales and are most in need of development. Ireland and Spain are already attracting significant funds, with the result that Irish GNP per capita is higher than in Britain, and Spain is turning in its best economic performance in 200 years.[19] Central Europe also has begun to draw investment as manufacturers open plants in candidate member states for future sales within the EU single market.

On the negative side, analysts certainly agree on the costs and risks of monetary union, if not on the weight they should accord these dangers. Most immediately, countries suffering asymmetrical shocks will not be able to respond to these problems with differential exchange rates or changes in monetary policy because ECB technocrats will be fine tuning monetary policy for the single euro. The most glaring recent example of this—even before formal adoption of monetary union—was the high interest rate Germany generated in financing unification—and the prolongation of recession this transmitted to EMS partners with currencies pegged to the deutsche mark in the early 1990s. Moreover, fiscal policy also will be both formally and informally constrained under the EMU. That is the point of the stability pact that Germany insisted on, to rule out inflationary pump priming. And pressures are already growing, especially at the prodding of the new center-left government in Germany, for greater harmonization of tax, energy, wage, pension, and welfare regimes.[20]

In terms of policy, a one-size-fits-all approach from Portugal to Finland will therefore leave only two modes of adjustment to asymmetrical regional shocks, as in the United States: labor flexibility and substantial financial transfers to regions in recession.[21] Yet the first is curtailed in Europe, by linguistic and cultural barriers as well as by the otherwise admirable attachment to home communities and the comprehensive system of generous social welfare bound to locality.

The second tool of adjustment is similarly curtailed by the unwillingness of national governments to fund EU budgets beyond the present modest ceiling of 1.27 percent of GDP—and by the limited legitimacy of the EU in redistributing wealth across countries. A large increase in the EU budget was considered in the 1970s and then rejected, and the huge U.S. equalizers, fluctuating tax revenues and welfare payments, simply do not exist in the EU framework.

In a broad sense the issue of transfers has raised the most controversy so far. Spain has informally threatened to veto Polish accession unless the Mediterranean lands are guaranteed continuation of the EU largesse they currently enjoy—while Germany has barred any overall EU budget expansion. Strictly speaking, of course, the EU's existing structural and cohesion funds are intended to aid long-term development rather than short-term adjustment, and their amounts are miserly by comparison with normal domestic transfers through tax collection and social outlays. They do offer one small instrument that could be adapted to help counter asymmetric shocks, however.

And in practice the riddle of European-wide redistribution may be more easily solved than the problem of unemployment, since both EU assistance and private investment are rapidly spreading prosperity to the EU periphery. Tellingly, the Europeans who actively celebrated adoption of the euro were not the jaded French or Dutch at the heart of the European system, but the Italians, Spanish, and Finns at its fringes. Deutsche Bank economist Walter contends in any case that price shocks are more apt to affect all of Euroland than to hit different regions asymmetrically, given today's networks of company branches.

Beyond market probes of the value of the euro, then, the hardest test of EU and EMU solidarity may well be posed by unemployment. A clash within and among countries would seem inevitable when the first serious post-EMU recession hits. Surprisingly, given Europe's high unemployment, no European-wide protest a la Ross Perot has coalesced so far to complain about the great sucking sound of jobs being flushed south and east. In Germany the Kohl government deliberately compartmentalized EMU and unemployment questions; and Social Democratic chancellor Gerhard Schröder, whatever the tactical temptations, is compelled to be an exemplary European citizen and eschew making a scapegoat of the euro. Schröder's Social Democratic allies among the Länder premiers, even if not his finance minister, further share the U.S.–UK view that present unemployment is more structural than cyclical, that compulsory nonwage employment payments, which currently add 82 percent to wage costs in Germany, must be cut to induce job creation, and that passive welfare to the rustbelt jobless must be shifted to active training of them for modern employment in a high-tech era.

In France, by contrast, especially in the context of the ongoing battle to save French identity from the post–cold war domination of Europe by Germany and the United States, unemployment and the euro are often seen as potentially incompatible. Workers have repeatedly protested against EMU and associated austerity; and Chirac's own party refused to vote for ratification of monetary union. The contrary perceptions fueled all the old German-French spats pitting fiscal discipline against job promotion. And they make it much more difficult for France to carry out the painful economic modernization that both it and Germany urgently need.

Assessing the hazards, some renowned American economists in particular concluded early that the EMU, like the bumblebee, could not fly. Rudi Dornbusch, Martin Feldstein, and Milton Friedman all stressed the crucial barrier of European labor rigidity. Dornbusch concluded from this premise that the euro might trigger a severe recession. Feldstein feared that monetary union would remove competitive pressure on Europe and distract it from what should be its top priority of structural liberalization—and might even lead to war. James Tobin, Nobel Prize winner and adviser to Presidents Kennedy and Clinton, argued conversely that removing Keynesian stimuli could only increase unemployment.[22] Among big-name American economists, the guru of optimal currency areas himself, Robert Mundell, was one of the few in the runup to launch who thought the euro could work reasonably well and would be the most important monetary innovation since the dollar displaced the pound during World War I—or even since the rise of the gold standard in the 1870s.[23]

The answer to critics by mainstream European analysts—including some who began as scoffers—is to reverse the cause-and-effect relationship and to expect that EMU, far from diverting attention from the pressing need for more efficiency and competitiveness, will expose deficiencies and force their remedy. The code word for this is that monetary union will be a "catalyst." Its transparency will accelerate in Europe a decade later the kind of reform that globalization forced on the more responsive U.S. economy in the 1980s.[24] Conservative parliamentary caucus leader Wolfgang Schäuble says flatly, "EMU is the best answer to globalization"—and to overcoming German resistance to change.[25] It will compel politicians and businessmen to find ways to enable a shrinking work force to support a growing percentage of retirees and to augment funds to meet pension commitments that are running close to double GDP in Europe.[26] It will supplant broad social entitlements with means testing and shift income support toward investment.

Liberalization, privatization, and deregulation are already under way in Euroland, and they should pick up speed as younger generations (whether they call themselves right or left) inherit power. The portion of GDP controlled by the state should drop. Pensions will be trimmed. Pension funds will have to shift from pay-as-you-go to fully funded systems in any case as populations age. The heavy corporate and individual tax burden will be lightened, and it will become easier to fire workers—and to hire them, as nonwage labor costs are reduced. The social net of unemployment payments and universal health benefits will also be trimmed; full pay for sick Mondays and regular spa mudbaths is unsustainable. After a decade of airing these issues ad nauseam, the consensus for change is already present, even if politics is slow to follow. Typically, a country like the Netherlands, the main carrier in the 1970s of the "Dutch disease" of expansive socialist redistribution and wage costs 20 percent higher than Germany's, turned around fifteen years later to produce the "Dutch miracle" of flex-time work, job creation, and wage costs 20 percent lower than Germany's.[27] A footnote of history will surely record that one of the politicians who brought this about, as he himself changed from Keynesian to "pragmatic monetarist," is none other than the new ECB chief, Willem F. Duisenberg.

Despite all the reforms, however, Europe's emerging labor flexibility will never reach American levels of mobility, either geographically or financially. The bulk of Greeks, Italians, and Poles who flock to Germany for work will go back to their home countries as living conditions improve there—and they themselves will compound that advance with their savings and the small shops they start. And even Germans who live in Schwäbisch Gmünd will by and large want to stay there instead of moving to Frankfurt.

Besides, for all their admiration of American openness and exuberance, Europe's more homogeneous nations still value solidarity and regard America's extreme individualism as callousness toward life's unfortunates. Even the continent's conservative–social democratic consensus of the past decade had enough elements of the old social democratic–conservative consensus to ensure that while the social net could be slackened, it would not be torn down. Notably, Chancellor Kohl frequently made the point by asking American conservatives critical of "Rhine capitalism" if they really thought that Prime Minister Otto von Bismarck was a socialist when he introduced social payments a century ago.[28] Similarly, Sir Leon Brittan, the EU's trade commissioner, has long stressed to opponents of liberalization that Europe will not have to give up its social model. Instead, he turns the question around and asks how the continent could possibly afford to maintain decent social protection if it does not regain competitiveness and a healthy economy and end "the seduction of inflationary policies."[29] Warnfried Dettling, the conservative prophet of a new social contract above partisanship, argues that Germany can both modernize and attract investment because of its political stability, labor peace, and craftsmanship, and still defend the young, elderly, sick, and unemployed.[30] This devotion to basic social welfare is even stronger now in the overwhelmingly left-governed EU at a time of world recession.

Maybe this is wishful thinking. Maybe not. Given the fierce controversy among economists as to whether or not EMU can work, a layman is well advised to withhold judgment. As Wolfgang Münchau commented dryly in the *Financial Times*, "As a unique experiment, EMU will probably teach us more about economics than economics can currently teach us about EMU." In the end, he contended, it will be politics, not economics, that will determine whether monetary union works—and today's politicians assert that failure is simply not an option.[31]

Germany, France, and Britain

Clearly, the sanguine catalyst theory of EMU will be tested first and foremost in Germany and France. Germany has the third-largest economy in the world and is the main financier of the EU. France has an economy second only to Germany's in Europe and is the world's third-largest importer and exporter of capital and the fourth-largest trading nation, yet it is only a small net contributor to the EU budget. Paris would have to pick up any decrease in EU contributions that Germany managed to squeeze out of the European Council, and France feels itself the loser in monetary union as the Kohl government's preferences in bank locale, currency name, and operating rules all won the day. Moreover, even if France and Germany do not constitute a directorate, their bilateral policy clashes often reflect more general contradictions among EU members. If Paris and Bonn can reach satisfactory compromises, these often point the way to solutions that will be acceptable to others.[32]

Domestically, the French and especially the German economies are not as hopelessly encrusted as they might appear on the surface—as Germany's steady trade surpluses would suggest.[33] Dornbusch may fear that Europe will now be too fatigued by its epic fights over grand monetary union to muster the energy for the nitty-gritty of reform.[34] But out of the exhaustive public discussions of Europe's loss of competitiveness, a consensus seems finally to be emerging among German business, political, and labor elites—and in the French business, if not yet political and labor, elites—that there is no alternative to painful reforms.[35] Since 1996 trade unions in Germany have been accepting both lower pay hikes and more flexible localized wage settlements (rather than the once sacrosanct nationwide blanket deals), and, at least in western Germany, unit labor costs have fallen for three consecutive years, while relations at plant level have remained good. In manufacturing, if not in retailing and building, productivity, competitiveness, and profits have all risen in the past three or four years, and domestic demand is now joining the export boom (and weak deutsche mark) in promoting growth.[36]

Comprehensive reductions of taxes that currently run as high as 60 percent in the corporate sector—and evolution toward a funded pension system—were not possible before the German election in the fall of 1998, but they will be instituted in some form by the new Social Democratic–Green government.[37] Under the pressure of EMU budget constraints, the new government will gradually trim its exceptional $100 billion annual transfers to eastern Germany and bring the state share of GDP spending back below the 50 percent level it reached from 1993 to 1996 to the preunification "state quota" of 46 percent—and possibly further toward the British and American 40 percent.[38] It should also cut red tape; allow venture capital to be deducted from personal income, as in the Anglo-Saxon world; reduce the time it takes new companies to come onto the stock market from the present average forty years to something approaching the fourteen years that is the norm in the United States; and finally pass legislation to let German business report a profit-and-loss balance sheet that meets international standards of disclosure.[39] All in all, the 1998 report card on Germany by the OECD evaluated the country positively as being "in the process of substantial structural adjustment."[40]

The severest test of Germany's adaptability will come in the east, where the Federal Republic's newest citizens are squeezed between the high-productivity west Germans and the low-wage central Europeans, with, as many an Ossi (east German) sees it, the advantages of neither. Those cumulative west German transfers of almost $1 trillion may have brought east Germans well on their way to having some of the most modern telecommunications and just-in-time production in Europe. And the easterners' standard of living may have shot up from 23.7 Trabis per hundred in 1989 to 46.3 Volkswagens and Toyotas in 1997, from 17.6 telephones and 14.7 home computers per 100 middle-income households in 1991 to 90.5 and 39.7, respectively, in 1996.[41] Yet rising expectations have outpaced rising performance for easterners, whose gauge is less their own material improvement than the remaining gap between them and their west German cousins, who did not have to suffer under Soviet hegemony. And the greatest indignity, despite welfare payments, is eastern unemployment, which is double the German average (or even higher, counting hidden joblessness).[42]

The result is disorientation—and protest votes by more than a third of the electorate in Saxon-Anhalt in 1998 for a neonazi party and for east Germany's old communist cadres in the new Party of Democratic Socialism.

Given the democratic doubts in the east, the sluggishness of official reforms (as distinct from private-sector adjustments), and the often nasty politics of downsizing, numerous observers inside and outside the country ask whether slow consensus politics in Germany has finally reached its limits.[43] But those voices inside the country, at least, should be read not as proof of stagnation, but rather as contrary evidence that a consensus finally is building about the urgent need for change. Chancellor Schröder, however ambivalent he may have been in his election campaign about continuing liberal reforms, is committed to "modernization" of Germany's economy. His many business friends will certainly nudge him in the direction of completing structural reforms to maintain competitiveness. And Social Democratic control of both houses of parliament should enable him to carry out what Kohl, with his limited interest in economics, never pushed through.

Comparable slimming down will be much harder in France, not only because workers and peasants still insist that the state create jobs and keep out competing produce, but also because of French loss of historical certitude—and because "it is not easy being medium."[44] It is proving hardest for a country with one of the proudest histories in Europe to leave history behind. The initial French answer to the fall of the Berlin Wall was to lull itself with the assumption that the edifice of the EC and the French-German reconciliation would continue to let France be the star architect of Europe, as it had been for three decades. Instead, the changes transformed Bonn/Berlin into Europe's main collaborative architect. France turned "melancholy" and "morose," in Dominique Moisi's analysis, as globalization, unemployment, American supremacy, and European merger eroded French culture and identity. Prime Minister Lionel Jospin avoided ratifying the 1997 Amsterdam Treaty as long as possible because of the National Assembly's and Senate's aversion to surrendering French sovereignty on immigration. Chirac gave every indication of regarding adoption of the European Central Bank in the image of the Bundesbank as the final blow shattering the French illusion. The president might impose France's will on the fourteen other EU members once in naming the head of the ECB, but only at the terrible cost of Europe's mocking laughter. "On ne rit pas"[45]—as Chirac vainly lectured reporters in his post-midnight debriefing at the Brussels summit in May 1998—would be the epitaph for that French dream.

Nonetheless, at this point EMU in particular is forcing even Parisians to recognize how modern France has actually become by now, how much "more like the others." Prime Minister Jospin is both popular and pragmatic enough to lead reform, and he is aided by the present economic upswing and decline in unemployment. He has quietly dropped his campaign vow to stop privatization of France's large state sector and is proceeding to sell off chunks of France Telecom and Air France. He backed Air France's management against the 1998 strike by pilots. A senior German Finance Ministry official notes with approval that Jospin is stressing the need to offset the thirty-five-hour work week with flexibility. As in Europe as a whole, the political trick will be to get past the first, job-killing stage of restructuring as fast as possible to the second stage of releasing capital to generate new employment.[46]

How smoothly this process works in Europe at large will depend to a considerable extent on how well the French-German team continues to operate—and perhaps also on how fast Britain becomes a real player in the EU. The personal bruises in the relationship between Kohl and Chirac will not be transmitted to the next generation of leaders, but neither will the sense of special German obligation to France. With Kohl's electoral defeat, Paris lost "one of the best German chancellors the French have ever had,"[47] along with a national security adviser, Joachim Bitterlich, who was so pro-French as to provoke some concern on the part of Germany's American and British allies. Christian Democratic Union chairman Schäuble, from the Rhine region, has a natural affinity for France and will carry on this affection within the Christian Democratic Union. He will do so more coolly and with less emotion than Kohl, however, and he has differed openly with Paris in the past in stating that EMU or other inner circles within the EU must always remain open to accession by others. Chancellor Gerhard Schröder, unlike some of his fellow Social Democrats, has no special Gallic attachment, and before his election even said in Paris the same words about the ills of protectionism that he uttered in a more welcoming London. Joschka Fischer, the new Green foreign minister, finds it natural that France and Germany will have differing views because of their "opposite mentalities, histories, preconceptions, and interests." He goes on to say, however, that the duo "has worked astonishingly well," and that Schröder as chancellor will also give it top priority, simply because "with agreement with France we can do things better and take responsibility for the European process."[48]

Certainly Finance Minister Oskar Lafontaine is much more sympathetic than his predecessor was to the French Socialist wish ·to mold the euro-11 finance ministers into a political overseer of the European Central Bank.[49] He will not continue to press for rules requiring any budget surpluses in euro-11 countries to go for debt reduction (as the Kohl government did) rather than higher public-sector pay and social spending. If anything, he might even demand more pump-priming than Jospin currently does.

Bonn and Paris will clearly diverge on farm subsidies, however. Under the financial pressures of globalization and EMU, the Germans will pull away from the old bargain of high subsidies for French food and lesser subsidies for German industrial manufactures. Germany may avoid leading the present second round of trims in the Common Agricultural Program after the controversial first cuts in cereal and beef support in 1992. It will, however, cheer continuing efforts to cut the half of the EU budget that goes to farmers by shifting subsidies from the EU payments for dairy products, olive oil, tobacco, and wine into national support for maintaining village life and landscapes. This change is seen as a necessity by German policymakers if the European Union is not to bankrupt itself in extending its current 40 percent payment of the value of EU agricultural production to Poland's 10 million farmers.[50] Speeches by the Bavarian president of the German national farmers' association, Gerd Sonnleitner, already suggest that the German agrarian lobby is resigned to inevitable cuts in its handouts.[51] And Bavarian officials are already planning how to renationalize farm subsidies, paying income support rather than the EU's outdated price support—and probably making farmers richer in the process.[52]

Other bilateral quarrels will concern redistribution of member states' contributions to the EU budget; Paris's reluctance to privatize government defense holdings and let joint ventures with German firms proceed autonomously; liberalization of trade, and especially the goal of a transatlantic free-trade zone; treatment of Turkey; and privatization and liberalization of electricity providers.[53] Yet enough of a habit of bilateral coordination of European policies has built up in the past two decades to keep conflict over raw national interests in check. In September of 1998, France's European minister, Pierre Moscovici, finally admitted publicly for the first time that France could not indefinitely continue to pay only one-thirty-seventh of what Germany pays the EU.[54] The bilateral "entente elementaire," or basic alliance, as the French call it, will continue.[55]

The less predictable question is when and if the United Kingdom might choose to reengage in pan-European affairs and, possibly, expand the French-German duo to a trio. Even Britons who are not anti-European remain wary of having the British identity submerged in ever closer union.[56] But London City bankers do not want to be shut out of the financial single market, assuming it succeeds, and Prime Minister Tony Blair intends to lead the UK into the European Monetary Union with a referendum on the issue after the next election, assuming he wins. London appreciates Germany's waning of enthusiasm for more qualified majority voting and for that political union that is anathema to the British. It also welcomes the new German emphasis on the British precept of "subsidiarity" following European Commission restrictions on German industrial subsidies and corporate merger plans, and it approves the European Court of Justice rulings on the EU-wide applicability of health insurance, which now requires German firms to pay for eyeglasses bought in Ibiza, say, instead of Hamburg.[57] Businessmen like Martin Kohlhaussen of the Commerzbank Board openly call for the pragmatic British to join EMU and exert more influence in the sometimes overtheoretical European Union, and Bonn left the door of the euro-11 council more open to future British participation than Paris would have wished.

If Blair does get reelected and becomes a major player, German and British views will often coincide on trade and transatlantic issues— and could tip the EU balance away from French conceptions. Yet Germans, too, are wary. Including Britain in the inner circle would immediately trigger Italian and Spanish demands for inclusion, they say, and smaller members that now accept the usefulness of a French-German motor would not so readily accept what would be perceived as a French-German-British directorate.

Widening and Deepening

Whether or not Britain changes the character of the EU's inner leadership, the new central European members will definitely change the operation and even goals of the whole EU. In some ways EU tutelage of the new democracies to its east continues earlier EC tutelage of the new Spanish, Portuguese, and Greek democracies. But the assimilation of former Soviet-bloc countries is much more complex than was the incorporation of former dictatorships that already had capitalist economies. The sheer quantitative increase in members will also mutate quality, to produce gridlock—unless, as the French and Germans hope, this very threat compels enough streamlining to avoid impasse.[58]

Never before has the EU/EC taken in countries that were so much poorer than the Community average, and sensible environmental, trade, and other transitional regimes will have to be arranged to allow fair catch-up time for peasant farming and still-fragile industries. Obversely, the fast-track candidates for membership now face a moment of truth; they must prove that they are substantially meeting the moving target of 80,000 intricate pages of acquis communautaire. Furthermore, they will be expected sooner rather than later to meet even the Maastricht preconditions for monetary union. It is therefore exponentially harder for the double candidates of Poland, Hungary, and the Czech Republic to meet EU standards than to meet the much simpler NATO requirements.[59]

The current negotiations will tax the patience of both sides. Poland, the largest of the new applicants by far, with a population of 39 million, tends to think it has a right to EU membership because of its past suffering on the wrong side of the iron curtain and on the wrong side of history. Obversely, the EU inclines to exasperation over Polish stalling in complying with already agreed removal of steel import tariffs and lax accounting of EU aid moneys.[60] By and large, however, the Poles and other central Europeans are learning fast how to play the multilevel game of inner-EU negotiations and lobbying. A prime example is the growing skill of young Polish ecologists in circumventing the resistance of high-ranking bureaucrats in the Polish Environment Ministry; in time-honored EU fashion, they leaked negative data on pollution to the more sympathetic Polish Foreign Ministry for transmittal to EU evaluation teams.

Beyond the specific accommodations of the two quite different negotiating sides, the near-term accession of six new members from the vacuum between western Europe and the eastern Slavs—and the commitment to take in another five states in the medium term—will alter the self-image of the EU. Some hope that the central Europeans will even energize the European Union and give it a new sense of purpose in progressively unifying the continent.[61]

In institutions, even the optimists acknowledge that the necessary streamlining of the European Commission and the European Council has not yet begun. Large member countries still have two commissioners each, small countries one; a slate of thirty commissioners or more would be far too unwieldy. Rotation of the six-month EU presidency has been altered slightly to ensure that one large country is always among the steering troika of outgoing, present, and incoming presidents, but this is only a stop-gap measure. The formal voting weights that greatly favor small members must be revised to correspond better to political weights. Some system like a "double majority" of both member-nations and their populations must be introduced to keep the EU capable of reaching and implementing responsible decisions. And coordination in foreign policy and home and justice affairs must be regularized.[62]

All these reforms were scheduled to be addressed at the Amsterdam summit of 1997, but little was agreed on beyond a slight expansion of majority voting and "communitization" in principle of justice and home affairs within five years. More fundamental change got shunted aside by disagreement among members, by the all-consuming effort to start monetary union, and by the last-minute crisis of accommodating newcomer Jospin. Momentum will have to be regained, and a new overall balance will have to be struck between Commission and Council, as well as between the staff work of the Commission's secretary-general and the powerful Committee of Permanent Representatives (Coreper) of the personal envoys of heads of state or government. Later, democratic accountability will also presumably require greater transparency in the secretive Council deliberations and, eventually, a greater role for the European Parliament.

At least the fundamental theological dispute about elite inner circles is no longer a hot issue, since founding a large monetary union with eleven members has rendered the feud less relevant. In the end, EMU carved no new fissures in EU solidarity after all. Apart from Greece, all states that so desire are already in EMU. Greece and the three other remaining "outs" (or "pre-ins," in the preferred terminology) may join whenever they decide to do so and fulfill the criteria; and the incoming central European members of the EU are expected to strive to qualify within a decade or so. In practice, nonexclusive "concentric circles" are thus proving to be a way to keep momentum going, allowing the willing to proceed with further ad hoc integration like Schengen and EMU without being blocked by the unwilling—but leaving each new inner circle open to all other EU members in the future.

The second and third pillars established by the Maastricht Treaty—aiming at a common foreign and security policy and further pooling of justice and home affairs—will not be advanced by EMU and enlargement as institutional reform will be. The EU's new "high representative" for a common foreign policy and his tiny staff can write all the penetrating analyses they want to, but judgments about explicit and implicit committal of armed forces will for decades still be hammered out in national capitals or in ad hoc national bargaining within NATO or the Contact Group. The EU will not be the anvil; the Western European Union, as decided at the Amsterdam summit—where Britain joined the new neutral EU members to block incorporation of the WEU into the EU—will remain a subordinate mechanism.

Britain and some others will also postpone as long as possible the targeted "communitization" of home and justice affairs. France has strong misgivings whenever merging of police powers or other concrete measures are proposed. And the enthusiasm for these efforts on the part of the post-Kohl political generation in Germany is in doubt as well. In the early 1990s Europeanization of security and immigration policies looked to Kohl like a way to circumvent the popular German desire to abstain in most security issues and—by persuading allies to share the responsibility—to lighten the German burden of taking in more than half of all refugees and asylum seekers entering the EC/EU area. These motivations no longer exist, however. In the first case, the psychological shift to active German participation in peacemaking has already been accomplished. In the second, labeling immigration issues as European rather than national shows no prom-

ise of convincing EU partners that they should take foreigners off
Germany's hands.

Impetus and Consolidation

The original scorched memory of Hitler and Stalin and the craving
for obverse reconciliation no longer drive the process of European
integration as they once did. Nor do the tectonic upheavals that followed the end of the cold-war epoch.

Nor, after sixteen tumultuous years, is Kohl personally there to steer
Europe into the third millennium. So well did this century's longest-
lasting chancellor succeed in his quest to bind Germany irrevocably to
Europe that he made himself superfluous. By the 1998 election his
two jobs of unification were essentially finished. Monetary union and
German union were both fact, and, for all the complaints, both Germans and Europeans as a whole even had a soft landing. Germans felt
so comfortable with themselves that they no longer needed to hold
Kohl's familiar hand; they thought anybody could now deal with the
daily vicissitudes, even a Social Democrat who hardly bothered to
address European-wide issues in his campaign.

Looking back, Kohl must surely think that events justified his instinct that the next generation would have less of a compulsion than
his contemporaries had to unite Europe—and that he must therefore
lock Germany into irreversible monetary union while he still ruled.
Chancellor Schröder now accepts EMU as a given, but he would never
have toiled to produce it as Kohl did, and EMU would never have
been born without that German engagement. Speaking for those in
their fifties, Schröder says bluntly that the time has come for Berlin to
pursue its own national interest just as vigorously as Paris and London do. His generation is European, he adds, but this is a matter of
choice, not obligation.[63] This choice—with the corollary risk that
Germans might one day again make the wrong choice—is precisely
what Kohl wanted to ban forever.

With monetary union and the pan-European cooperative network
in place, though, Kohl has in effect won his gamble. He has precluded
any other option. As Luxembourg's premier, Jean-Claude Juncker, never
tires of saying, no divorce is possible out of EMU. Personally, Kohl's
successors may not reassure European allies of Germany's harmless-

ness as fully as he himself did. And they may not have the same innate regard for the sensitivities of the little Benelux countries just across the border from Kohl's native Palatinate. But the institutions Kohl established will render that assurance less necessary. Five decades of peace and prosperity in Europe have permanently redefined the way national interest is perceived in heartland Europe.

Much reconstruction remains to be done in the EU, of course. Its astonishingly low number of bureaucrats—30,000, or less than the administration of the single city of Cologne—can probably continue to run EU affairs without expanding greatly. But the number of allotted European commissioners must be slimmed down. Means must be found—possibly by shifting weights among its various directorates general—to decrease the Commission's vulnerability to special-interest pleading.[64] The European Council summits and ministerial meetings must have new voting rules that keep them supple enough to act—even if in practice participants have long since avoided votes and vetoes altogether as counterproductive. Some version of the Commission's "Agenda 2000" of institutional and agricultural reforms needed to facilitate the entry of central Europeans into the Union must be implemented.[65] Berlin must be relieved of the burden of paying 60 percent of net EU outlays if a new generation of Germans is not to rebel against this generosity.

Furthermore, parliamentary oversight of policies and actions must be strengthened, both in the European Parliament and in national legislatures. Transparency and democratic accountability must increase in a Union that, for an association of democracies, is shamelessly secretive in its decisionmaking and horse trading, and lacking in verifiable lines of responsibility. The chattering class may have exaggerated the popular backlash following the Maastricht summit and overlooked the fundamentally positive feeling for Europe below surface reactions. But the fact remains that enlargement to central Europe and, especially, monetary union are projects of the elites, not of the grass roots. The European Central Bank is doubly remote from citizens, both in its transnationality and in the deliberate depoliticization of monetary management. It is even more independent than the Bundesbank, which is even more independent than the U.S. Federal Reserve Bank. The ECB has inherited some of the Bundesbank's prestige, but its dearth of political accountability imposes a special need to prove itself to citizens, essentially by keeping the euro stable. National governments will similarly have to prove to voters that a Europe that is growing and overhauling its economy as a unit can produce jobs better than each country can do separately. If they fail, there will be a crisis not only of economics, but of overall legitimacy.[66]

Yet the blueprints for all of these alterations are already on the table. They do not have to be drawn up from scratch. However startling various innovations might have seemed when they were proposed at Maastricht in 1991, they are minor by contrast to the revolutions of monetary union and accession of the central Europeans to the European system. The required reconstructions will be accomplished step by step in the period of consolidation that now follows the convulsions. Their impetus will come from stimuli other than the familiar longing for reconciliation, the earthquakes at the end of the cold war, and the ardor of one German chancellor for exorcising the demons of the past.

In the new century, then, the impulse to further integration will essentially arise from the exigencies of interdependence and globalization, as reinforced by institutions and habit—and now from the threat of spillover from the Russian chaos. These could not have carried on the dynamics alone had the EC not awakened from its stagnation to shape the single European market in the late 1980s. But that single market was formed, with monetary union as its final target, in time to absorb the shocks of German unification and to embed that union in a sturdy European structure. In any number of crises, the only alternative to painful integration has been predictable disaster; the only solution has been, in the German phrase, to "flee forward." The successful habit of consultation has its own momentum, in any case, and institutions tend to perpetuate themselves. Pooling of sovereignty has brought tangible benefits to participants in the past, and there is a widespread expectation of common good to come, as well as a growing trust in the process itself. Monetary union, in order to function smoothly, will require much more intra-European economic coordination. And cooperation by finance ministers in the Euro Council will in turn require more prior cooperation by heads of government.

Combined, these forces of consolidation should continue to energize rather than enervate Europe, should provide synergy instead of entropy, benchmarks instead of lowest common denominators, mutual empowerment instead of scapegoating. Europe remains a work in progress. So far, it seems condemned to succeed.

CHAPTER NINE

Transatlantic Coopetition: The United States as a European Power

Europe, at least since the Bosnian debacle, knows it needs U.S. leadership—whatever the attendant frustrations. The United States, at least since the Asian crisis and Russian meltdown, knows it needs Europe to share the burdens of world economic leadership—whatever the attendant frustrations. Yet those inevitable frustrations will require sensitive handling if they are not to overpower the requisite cooperation in our age of globalization. The new Europe will test the transatlantic relationship in finance, economics, security policy, and psychology. Each side will have to respect the other as they improvise together the rules of the new game of mixed interdependence and rivalry that businessmen call "coopetition."

EMU

The United States has not yet made its peace with European Monetary Union. As the countdown to EMU accelerated in the fall of 1997, U.S. deputy treasury secretary Lawrence H. Summers finally broke Washington's skeptical silence with qualified praise. His careful litany, then and since, is: "If EMU is good for Europe, it will be good for us." His equally careful corollary is probably a fair summation of the wait-and-see skepticism in Washington: "EMU is a massive and ambitious project in many ways. Just the magnitude of the change involved is cause for concern that something could go wrong, but not reason to believe something will go wrong,"[1] The same noncommittal good wishes could be heard in President Clinton's hope, as Europeans concluded their EMU package in mid-1998, that monetary union would increase stability on the continent. "A strong and stable Europe, with open markets and healthy growth, is good for America and for the world," he declared.[2] Treasury Secretary Robert Rubin said virtually nothing.[3]

As approval goes, the official American endorsements were not, noted a senior German Finance Ministry official, altogether convincing.[4] But at least they were not negative. They were supplemented by the immediate leap to support the euro by America's multinationals, and by a few unofficial voices from the likes of former State Department counselor Robert Zoellick and C. Fred Bergsten, director of the Institute for International Economics. And at least the Treasury Department and the president were far ahead of the American media in finally realizing that this improbable renunciation of highly successful currencies in favor of an experimental new one was actually going to happen.

Other Americans have been less ready to give the euro the benefit of the doubt. Congressional staff members note that the euro, as of this writing, simply is not on the screen in Washington. It says volumes that former House Speaker Newt Gingrich thought he could get congressmen and senators who were less transatlantic-minded to pay attention to free trade issues (as his allies describe his ploy) only by declaring that EMU would enshrine the diktat of Frankfurt over Germany's neighbors and create crises that would feed European disunion—and that Britain should therefore join the North American Free Trade Area instead of EMU.

Harvard economist Martin Feldstein seems to believe his warning that EMU, rather than saving the whole European enterprise, might scupper it and even set Europeans to warring against each other once more. Foreign affairs guru Henry Kissinger certainly seems to believe that there are two equally gloomy possible outcomes from monetary union: an insolent European challenge to U.S. leadership, or, if EMU fails, a reactive, self-destructive nationalism.[5]

Besides the policy professionals, in and out of office, there are the constituencies of the American public and the media. The meager polling data that exist suggest that the public, while not knowing much about the euro, regards it favorably. Media coverage, however, before the final decision to proceed, was skeptical verging on hostile, as indicated in chapter 1; editorial and opinion treatment of EMU since then has been more neutrally skeptical, but has hardly provided an adequate base for politically interested readers to make informed judgments on the issues raised. On the one hand, there is little recognition that if the euro fails, the results could be as disastrous for the United States as for Europe. On the other hand, there is little discussion of the changes that would be required in American policies should the euro succeed quickly in establishing itself as a major world currency.

EMU failure is possible, of course, especially given the continuing uncertainties about how much more damage the Asian, Russian, and Latin American financial crises will do to the American and European economies. The European Central Bank's strict command to fight inflation could prove to be the wrong response in a period in which the chief danger may be global deflation. Interest rates that have been pushed down in the general monetary convergence could prove to be too low for the Mediterranean countries, generating bubbles there that would be waiting to burst. The peer pressure that has been so effective in impelling convergence could weaken as euro fatigue sets in and elections bring less committed politicians to office, especially in the southern tier. In the longer term, cyclical divergences and rigid labor markets could spin EMU members apart, if they do not quickly develop compatible tax, transfer, or other policy instruments to offset centrifugal pressures. The very success of the euro in getting started could induce complacence and neglect of the needed structural reforms, exacerbating rigidities under the single currency.[6] And in the short run, markets might test the euro mercilessly (though both the substantive convergence and the fastidious technical preparation seem to have precluded this hazard in the most delicate start-up phase).

If any of these failures occurred, two of the three motors of world growth would have sputtered out, and the American economy alone could hardly restart the other two engines, especially as its long expansion of the 1990s ends. Washington's policy would perforce be confined to limiting damage and trying to wall off North America against the tsunami waves from Asia, Europe, and Latin America.

In accord with the present German advance-through-crisis approach, however, Europe's key finance ministry regards the various risks not as autonomous mortal dangers, but as the prods that will stimulate the structural, institutional, and policy corrections that Europe sorely needs. This aspect is little addressed in American opinion columns. "We do not think through infinite scenarios about what could go wrong. That's American," comments the senior German Finance Ministry official dryly. "We have the basis. Now it's up to us. We are not objects, but subjects of the process, the active shapers of it."

Indeed, as monetary union makes its debut, economists are speculating not on a weak, but on a strong euro that will essentially build on the credibility of the deutsche mark and be its clone. It is thus Kissinger's first scenario—Europe's challenge to U.S. financial leadership—that the United States will probably have to deal with. German officials may dismiss French portrayals of EMU as a way of breaking free of U.S. dominance, but the fact remains that a euro that stayed strong would render impossible the kind of financial unilateralism the United States currently practices.

The most obvious effect would be use of the euro as a reserve currency parallel to the dollar. At present the deutsche mark and other European currencies account for 21 percent and the dollar, 63 percent, of reserve holdings around the world.[7] The IMF anticipates that the euro will attain international status only "in the medium to longer term."[8] But in Bergsten's analysis, there will be an initial one-off net flow from the dollar to the euro of between $500 billion and $1 trillion as some central banks make a deliberate switch and as Europeans shed the high dollar holdings they needed only in the era of multiple European currencies. In the absence of any countervailing factors, the dollar might then depreciate by between one-third and two-thirds. "A quantum leap in transatlantic cooperation" would be needed to avoid an increasingly volatile U.S.-euro rate, he suggests.[9] Yet neither the European Central Bank nor any other supranational authority is empowered to negotiate exchange rates.

Moreover, Bergsten believes that after a relatively short transition period the dollar and the euro could each account for a 40 percent share of world reserves. And this, in the common shorthand description, would mean that the United States could never again borrow in its own currency, inflate the dollar, and thus effectively tax its lenders to pay for another Vietnam War.

American officials reject such a scenario as a nonissue. With Washington's new antideficit consensus and first balanced budgets in decades, they say—and with the Defense Department's aversion to wars it is not guaranteed to win fast—the United States will neither want to wage expensive wars nor to pay for them by inflation. The new structural inability to do so should not therefore disadvantage Washington.

The more serious related question is how the United States will continue to finance its huge $200 billion-plus current account deficit—or $1.7 trillion cumulative deficit—when it can no longer do so without risk, in its own currency. One consequence for the world's largest debtor could well be de facto devaluation of the dollar, especially as European security markets and repatriation of the yen in the present market turmoil begin to absorb more of the vast Japanese funds that previously went to the United States in cumulative capital inflows of $1 trillion.[10] Having settled its own internal exchange rates, Europe will tend to neglect less important external exchange rates— as Washington regularly did in the past. Washington, by contrast, will necessarily become more concerned about dollar values. In the interests of stability of the world trading system, the European Central Bank and the Federal Reserve Bank will have to devise some coordinating mechanisms. And these two central banks, plus regional banks, the IMF, World Bank, and international regulatory agencies, will have to develop more effective surveillance of financial systems to identify potential crisis situations.[11]

Seignorage also is a real issue, but it is a lesser one. Sometimes described as an interest-free loan that has netted the United States an extra annual $10 billion-plus, seignorage is the technical name for fees paid by other countries for the use of dollar or other reserves that are not circulating as money in use. As the euro is increasingly utilized as an alternative to dollar reserves, some of the seignorage payments will flow to Euroland, leaving the United States with less income from this source.

A strong challenge to the United States will probably also arise as euro pricing increasingly supplements dollar pricing in international contracts. Until now, the dollar has been the preferred currency of convenience, covering half of world trade.[12] In the days of multiple national European currencies, dollar pegs avoided the risk of swings of exchange rates between, say, the Japanese yen and the Dutch guilder. And the predictability of the dollar was all the more important in long-term pricing of large deals in Saudi Arabian, Nigerian, or Siberian oil and gas.

As long as the dollar and euro keep their initial relative values, a shift of denomination from dollar to euro should not inconvenience the United States. But it will represent the loss of one more American financial lever. If the iron German stability culture in Europe outlasts America's new-found stability fashion, the United States will not again be able to export its own inflation to others with impunity.

A further unwelcome change for the United States (and probably also for Europe) will most likely occur within the prime international financial institutions—the International Monetary Fund and the World Bank—which the United States has hitherto dominated. Together, the Europeans contribute twice as much as the United States to the IMF— 35.4 percent as against 17.8 percent—yet they regularly defer to American financial direction. It was natural for Washington to take the lead in the Mexican financial crisis of the mid-1990s, of course—but all participants also took the American lead for granted in the Asian and consequent Russian crises of the late 1990s. To be sure, when the United States orchestrated the rescue of the Korean won through private banks, it depended on Europe's respective central banks to jaw-bone their commercial banks. But it was the U.S. Treasury that initiated and coordinated the strategy. Washington also was instrumental in the IMF's propping up of the yen.

In the future, such U.S. financial hegemony will not be as automatic as it has been in the past half century. The Germans are already laying the groundwork to bid for the next IMF presidency in 2002. And once Britain has joined monetary union, Europe will be far more inclined to assert its own interests in the international financial regime. With one currency, British, German, and other European interests are likely to be more congruent with each other than in previous decades. Europe will want to and will be increasingly able to speak with one voice on monetary issues and to demand that its influence reflect its invested share in the financial institutions. The United States will yield its position only grudgingly—and will certainly demand that Europe take on its full share of the burden of risks and initiative in managing global finance. Europeans in turn will find such responsibility uncomfortable. They have taken the lead in some cases in which they have had the most exposure—as German banks did in negotiating rescheduling of Poland's private debt in the early 1990s and Russia's in the late 1990s. They have not been ready to take initiatives on more remote Asian issues, however, and their slow consensus system mitigates against the swift decisions that are often needed in financial crises.

Especially if Congress slips into an inward-looking, America-first mood and restricts U.S. contributions to the IMF, then a transatlantic clash could develop over how to resolve the next international financial crisis. The greatest danger of all would probably come not from conflicting policy prescriptions, but from the absence of any leadership whatever as the United States limps under a lame-duck president, Japan flounders in its never-ending crisis, and Europe focuses on consolidating EMU and new EU institutional arrangements—and finds that it has forfeited macroeconomic and much microeconomic policy to the technocrats.[13]

Economy and Trade

In many ways, Europe and the United States are twins. Each generates a quarter of world output—about $8 trillion each—and exports more than a tenth of its GDP, accounting for 12.2 percent and 15.6 percent of world merchandise trade and 16.1 percent and 42.8 percent of commercial services, respectively. The EU has a population of 370 million (with another 120 million central Europeans waiting on its doorstep) to 265 million in the United States. Counting imports as well as exports, both depend on world trade for some 23 percent of their economies, even though this high figure would surprise most Americans.[14]

If anything, the similarities between the twins should increase as EMU introduces a continent-wide financial market in Europe, along with a corresponding altered investment mentality. Until now—in one enormous difference between the two sides of the Atlantic—the United States has been the sole superpower in financial instruments. U.S. stock, bond, and derivative markets are by far the biggest, most liquid, most flexible, and most complex in the world. They have neutralized the disadvantages the United States would otherwise have suffered from its huge trade imbalances and net debts by attracting huge offsetting European and especially Japanese investment. European bourses, by contrast—with the partial exception of Britain—have been small, segmented, and illiquid. They have been utterly incapable of absorbing and moving the sums of Japanese money accumulated from decades of export surpluses. Even taken together, they are only two-thirds the size of the U.S. stock market. Current German stock market capitalization is only 38 percent of GDP, by contrast to 138 percent in the United States and 163 percent in Britain; only 6 percent of Germans (though 17 percent of Britons and 35 percent of Swedes) own shares, as against 21 percent in the United States, or almost 40 percent if mutual funds are included.[15] While half of British private-sector financial assets were in equities in 1996, only 20 percent of private funds were similarly placed in more conservative Germany, France, and Italy.[16]

Soon the European modesty will change. EMU, as the final step in establishing the single market, is already acting as a catalyst in Europe's boardrooms and chancelleries. Within a decade—barring some euro catastrophe—Europe should become the second financial superpower, in accord with its wealth. Europe's thirty-plus segmented stock exchanges are beginning to merge and expand their scope. Even before British accession to EMU, the large London and small Frankfurt exchanges have begun an "alliance" that will allow shares to be traded at both locales, and the French, Italian, and Spanish bourses are waiting to join in.

Moreover, the Germans and French, and not only the British and Dutch, are rapidly developing an American-style equity culture. They are heeding the constant cry of their own liberal reformers that they must emulate American entrepreneurs. The characteristic continental capitalist model of in-house bank financing of corporations is giving way to less cozy (and cheaper) equity and loan flotations on the British and American model. Remaining regulatory barriers are slowly being pulled down; German banks are being permitted a wider range of investment activity; obsolescent German and French requirements that borrowers originate deutsche mark– or franc-denominated issues in their domestic market are falling by the wayside.[17] Italian mutual funds have begun to attract big money. Germany's logjammed tax reform will presumably pass the Bundestag soon and drop the bias that has previously rewarded investment in real estate over productive investment.[18] Deutsche Telekom itself was surprised by the enthusiastic reception of its stock issue in 1996 as it began privatizing.

So far Europe lacks the independently managed pension funds that are a mainstay of U.S. stock investment; pensions have been largely state-run, pay-as-you-go schemes, with legal restrictions more or less confining them to safe, low-yield domestic bond issues. This branch, too, should now develop rapidly as retirement pay adjusts to the demographic realities of aging populations and tight government budgets.

Governments are slower than entrepreneurs in adjusting to these realities, but even they are being forced to privatize national industrial champions. The rise of much of labor to a home-owning middle class is altering the terms of the social contract and turning trade unions into defenders of the status quo rather than militant fighters for those lacking jobs. In this atmosphere there is greater readiness all around to accept economists' analyses that half or three-quarters of Europe's unemployment arises from barriers to entrepreneurship, including the structural rigidity of entitlement welfare.[19]

These changes, and others, all follow from EMU's unification of European capital markets and forcing down of costs as the new transparency translates old lira and franc and peseta prices into the same easily compared euro prices, compelling companies to match the lowest price or else lose sales. Anticipating these shifts, industrial stalwarts like Hoechst, Veba, and BASF have already carried out aggressive cost-cutting and moved substantial manufacturing to cheaper central European, Asian, and Latin American factory sites. A wave of mergers and acquisitions paralleling the American trend has begun. Firms like the Swedish-Swiss ABB engineering conglomerate, which have thought globally for more than a decade, are seen as models. The national champions are becoming increasingly passé; transnational mergers are producing corporations in various sectors that will be able to hold their own on the world market.

Volkswagen—despite threatening to pull out of its new plant in eastern Germany if the European Commission enforced its ruling against excessive subsidies from the state government of Saxony—not only outbid BMW to purchase the venerable Rolls-Royce, but went on to buy the equally renowned Lamborghini, and this after having earlier bought the Czech Skoda and Spanish Seat. Airbus, with French, German, British, and Spanish participation, is turning into a major rival of Boeing.[20] Even defense industries are uniting across state borders—though more slowly, and with more French resistance. The new Eurofighter is a German-British-Italian-Spanish collaboration; Germany and Spain will shortly be producing joint tanks, Germany and Sweden joint missiles; the Nordics are buying helicopters together; and the threat that British Aerospace and Daimler-Benz Aerospace might merge without them has goaded the French to privatize Aerospatiale in order to join in.[21]

All told, Europe is currently experiencing its greatest economic ferment since Ludwig Erhard introduced Germany's social-market economic miracle in the 1950s.

The shakeout has not yet overturned small and medium-sized firms, the inner core of Germany's economic engine and the sector that must provide the jobs for redundant workers from the slimmed-down giants. But even here change is beginning—and will presumably be carried forward by the sons and daughters who are now inheriting post–World War II family businesses from their founding fathers and, less frequently, mothers. Venture capital is appearing even in risk-averse Germany, as the success of the country's thriving Neuer Markt, the exchange for innovative start-ups, attests. Germany's profusion of little banks is on the verge of consolidation to fewer, more efficient banks, with more solid capitalization.

More broadly, there is also a new openness to experiment as central European countries privatize telecommunications, energy, and other natural monopolies on their tabula rasa, or skip the pay-as-you-go stage of pensions in favor of full funding—then export these ideas back to western Europe. There is unprecedented curiosity about how Ireland shifted from a classic land of emigration to one of immigration, or how Poles, with a standard of living less than a third that of France, are financing those pension funds, or how Dutch employers and employees worked together to generate part-time jobs that please everyone.

To some extent the ongoing merger fever has pitted the United States and Europe against each other. The EU contested the terms of the Boeing-McDonnell fusion and is threatening to appeal other transatlantic disputes to the new World Trade Organization.[22] Yet to American businessmen, the striking thing about the new Europe is the opportunity it presents not only for European, but also for American investors, who have already put more foreign direct investment into Europe than anywhere else on the globe. Unlike Japan, Europe holds its economy open to outsiders, and some German officials argue that agile U.S. firms have profited even more from the developing European single market than have less supple European companies. Citibank, for one, has gained a leading position in Germany by pioneering functions that domestic banks have been slow to offer. U.S.-

based international accounting and management and even law firms are moving into, or expanding in, Europe. There is a widespread expectation that the most sensible rationalization in defense industries will turn out to be transatlantic rather than pan-European partnerships.[23] And the increasing number of Germans, French, and Swedes who attend Harvard Business School and return home to represent U.S. companies in Europe is growing by the year. The transatlantic CEO approach is increasingly homogeneous.

The current burst of restructuring and realignments already includes major transatlantic investment and mergers. Daimler-Benz was the first German company to be listed on the New York Stock Exchange—and to obtain the listing it was willing to adopt U.S. accounting standards and greater financial disclosure than the secretive German corporate world practices. It is producing automobiles in Alabama—and its rival BMW has assembly lines in South Carolina. Daimler-Chrysler will soon be a household brand in America. Bertelsmann, the world's third-largest media conglomerate, recently bought out Random House and now represents many of the top authors on best-seller lists in the United States.[24] The Star transatlantic (and transpacific) airline alliance is now competing with the "oneworld" transatlantic (and transpacific) alliance. The first transatlantic law firm merger brought Salans Hertzfeld Heilbronn Christy & Viener into being in 1999, with offices in Paris, London, New York, Warsaw, Moscow, and Almaty.

As European businessmen become more American—and as EMU's transparency, reduced transaction costs, and economies of scale take hold—European firms will also become more competitive with American firms. In theory, this is all to the good. Europe will be following the path the United States took in the late 1980s and early 1990s in streamlining, restructuring, and regaining the competitiveness it had lost to Asia. Europe's competitiveness will in turn drive the next round of innovation in the United States, and American and European consumers and investors alike will benefit from such benign rivalry.

In practice, however, the European rejuvenation is sure to distress North Carolina textile spinners, Indiana steel workers, and House Minority Leader Richard Gephardt. To American voters who listen to Sony Walkmans, wear jeans made in China, and use computer spreadsheets designed by Indian programmers but have never possessed a passport, the advantages of open world trade will not be as obvious as they are to Germans who buy summer houses in Tuscany or Greeks who run pizza parlors in Sweden. As the international slump takes its toll in the U.S. economy, resentment could lead to a protectionist backlash; aggrieved Americans could easily view themselves less as advantaged consumers buying bargain imports than as workers who have lost their jobs to "unfair" foreign competition. The precise political outcome may depend on just how many Tuscaloosa automobile assemblers train in Germany and come back with the sense that what is good for Europe is also good for America.

Before political America settles on its reaction, there may well be near–trade wars between the two sides of the Atlantic. Banana skirmishes flared up again in 1998–99, with the French-guided EU trying to escape World Trade Organization rulings against its quotas, and the United States threatening to impose unilateral sanctions on the EU rather than accept WTO arbitration. In the new round of international trade negotiations starting in 1999, the outstanding issues of agriculture and intellectual property are potentially so acrimonious—the Amsterdam EU summit refused to delegate to the European Commission the authority to negotiate on services and intellectual property—that European Trade Commissioner Sir Leon Brittan has proposed the prophylactic goal of a North Atlantic free-trade zone.[25] His aim is not only to cement good relations, but also to avoid some of the rancor of the past. He will need to deploy all of his considerable charm and arm-twisting to reconcile, in particular, the protectionist French and the protectionist U.S. Congress, which refused to extend the president's "fast-track" authority to negotiate reduced tariffs in the mid-1990s, then turned the issue into a political football.

Agriculture will, of course, be one of the thorniest issues. Even though real farm income in Europe grew 30 percent between 1990 and 1997, France will vigorously resist more trims on subsidies for EU food exports, especially given the late-1990s fall in cereal prices.[26] Video and entertainment will be another thorn, with the defenders of French culture confronting Hollywood's exuberant exports.

A further source of strain between the United States and Europe is sure to be the issue of American economic sanctions, which proliferated so much in the 1990s that at their height they applied to two-thirds of the world's population.[27] Here the bitterest protagonists will probably continue to be the U.S. Congress on the one hand and the major exporters of Germany, France, and (more quietly) Britain on the other. The origin of conflicts will be political differences in policy recommendations, but they will be aggravated by differences in evaluating the effectiveness of sanctions—and by European outrage over U.S. claims to "extraterritoriality," that is, Washington's writing of laws binding non-Americans. Europeans, while agreeing to withhold trade in cases of egregious violation of international norms like that practiced by Serbia, tend to doubt the efficacy of sanctions in less extreme or in prolonged cases. And they certainly resent being ordered about by the United States with no prior consultation—as in the case of congressionally mandated sanctions against trading with Iran and Cuba. So far the presidential administration and the Europeans have managed to find last-minute compromises that have averted an all-out trade war, but the problem will dog transatlantic relations.[28]

Security and CFSP

In security policy, there would seem to be no more warrant for expecting fundamental transatlantic clashes of interest now than there was at the close of the cold war. In the early 1990s there were indeed many predictions that newly sovereign Germany would kick off the American traces, or the United States would tire of playing sheriff if NATO allies did not actively join it in military operations in the Middle East; "out of area or out of business" was the catchy slogan.[29] So, too, at the end of the 1990s there were sporadic debates about whether the Europeans would or should shuck off overbearing American "hegemony."[30]

Yet the widely anticipated breach has not occurred in the decade since bipolarity ended and left every opportunity for rupture at only low apparent risk. In the United States, European and other foreign policy always comes in four-year segments anyway, and Clinton foreclosed any isolationist lurch in the aftermath of the cold war by vigorous reengagement in Europe. In essence, he chose reinforcement of the traditional NATO alliance over unilateralism and over the other alternatives of only ad hoc coalitions or a greater reliance on international institutions.[31] To put it another way, recognizing the advantages of coalitions in extended leverage and in cost savings in the post–cold war defense-spending squeeze, the United States decided to perpetuate NATO as the basis for future coalitions of the willing.

On the European side, the realities of interdependence—as well as the need for leadership by a superpower that upholds common values, has airlift and surveillance capability, and is far away and not German—have prevailed. The French may enjoy the intellectual game of baiting the U.S. hegemony, but except at moments of tactical exasperation, the Germans do not lose much sleep over U.S. dominance—and the Poles pray for as much U.S. hegemony as they can possibly persuade Washington to bestow on them.

There will be fierce transatlantic arguments about all joint Western policies, of course—but they will reflect no inherent incompatibility of interest, but will simply echo the robust interagency feuds as policy is hammered out within any administration in Washington. On both sides of the Atlantic advocates of military responses to acts of terrorism—or to third-world attempts to build missiles or nuclear, chemical, and biological weapons—will repeatedly confront advocates of more negotiation and tradeoffs. And in this increasingly intertwined world, activists in nongovernmental organizations will increasingly lobby foreign as well as their own national officials to press their various campaigns.[32]

Especially after each new terrorist attack on U.S. installations, American citizens will tend to define their interests as a hard line against Iran, say, and resent European attempts at continuing dialogue with Tehran. As U.S. policy itself shifts to explore dialogue, however, as at present, the issue will be seen not as bedrock national conflict, but rather as legitimate differences of perception on the domestic (transatlantic) spectrum of opinion.

In fact, asserts John Roper, associate fellow at London's Royal Institute of International Affairs and first director of the Western European Union's Institute for Security Studies from 1990 to 1995, the real security interests of Europe and the United States overlap. The allies all agree that their main threats today are economic and social, but that some agonizing cases (like Bosnia) require the application of military power.

Yet "the United States and Europe as a whole and as its individual countries have different priorities and different political formulations of their interests," Roper admits.[33] And the hard tests of transatlantic relations will be precisely those judgment calls on when to confront and when to compromise with changing regimes in the wider neighborhood—and how to deal with anarchic situations on the fringe of heartland Europe that would require foreign troops on the ground to stop carnage and restore rudimentary order. Here the two sides of the Atlantic will often have diverging instincts about what justifies a military response, for both philosophical and institutional reasons.

The United States, on the one hand, is used to acting as a superpower, to counter terrorism or aggression by rogue states, and to deter future threats. Besides, it can reach decisions rapidly, either on presidential authority or on a simple majority vote of the Senate. On the other hand, with the partial exception of Britain and France, medium-sized European states that for half a century depended utterly on the American nuclear guarantee are much more diffident. Any situation in which the United States threatens or uses military force unilaterally will thus reawaken some of the old European worry about Washington's cowboy reflexes and American resentment about unfair burden sharing.

Moreover, counsels Roper, tension arises from the U.S. inclination to regard "consultation" with allies as more or less automatic rallying of them to support causes Washington has already decided on. Europe's very "limited capacities for force projection" give the lie to any American vision of Europe as a kind of junior superpower. And if the U.S. idea of partnership is that Europeans "share in paying or providing ground troops, but not in designing the strategy or making the key decisions for their use," this simply will not work.[34]

The U.S. retort to this argument often is that Europeans who are richer than Americans can well afford to field armed forces that are more equivalent to U.S. forces in order to help Washington produce the common good of security for oil flows and security from terrorism.[35] The European riposte to this often is that EU members donate far more than the United States does to promote stability in the world through economic development and institution building and that this contribution to the common good also must be recognized. In particular, German diplomats suggest, the spreading zone of peace in a heartland Europe that was once the cauldron of wars is Europe's single most valuable sharing of the U.S. burden.

Structurally, Europe's reluctance to resort to force of arms is compounded, of course, by the EU's inability to speak with one voice on military commitments. In this realm the Maastricht Treaty's goal of a common foreign and security policy would seem to be a chimera.[36] The dividing line between low politics that the Europeans can agree on mutually and high politics that remain in the jealous domain of state sovereignty may be creeping constantly upward, but the level will certainly not rise very soon to include a nation's blood sacrifice. Nor can the EU's present consensus system, or any imaginable inter-governmental majority voting, legitimize grave life-and-death decisions within the loose EU framework. The Danes would not want to be sucked into any common military operation in the Balkans without a sovereign right of refusal. Nor would the British and French, with their own proud military traditions, countenance any EU limitation on the unilateral use of their armed forces. To this end, the British have successfully blocked any development outside the NATO alliance of the European Security and Defense Identity (ESDI) that the French champion. Neither Tony Blair's sudden warm words about the Western European Union in late 1998 nor the stationing of a European-only NATO extraction force in Macedonia altered this fundamental constellation.

Under the present consensus system, then, only some exercise of leadership echoing U.S. dominance in NATO could ever forge common European military policy, maintains Peter van Walsum, Dutch ambassador to Germany in the 1990s. "In NATO there has never been any discussion on decision making, but there have never been complaints about the organization's lack of ability to act either," he notes. "That is because NATO is blessed with a dominant partner. Decisionmaking [in general] is a matter of either qualified majority voting or leadership. If qualified majority voting is out because the [EU] structure is too solidly intergovernmental, leadership is all we have got."

Yet within Europe the largest nation, Germany, cannot assume such leadership because of its history, he continues, nor is the German-French tandem strong enough for the task. The only possibility for genuine pan-European military coordination would come if Tony Blair's Britain really joined Europe some day and expanded the French-German double engine to a triple motor for Europe. That kind of European defense identity and unity the United States would only welcome, he believes, "because it would be in conformity with existing NATO/WEU arrangements." Conceivably, it could finally commit Europe to share America's burdens in ways that would counter "the American perception of a Europe that lets the Americans pull Europe's chestnuts out of the fire."[37]

Not surprisingly, German diplomats strenuously reject the conclusion that the present-day EU is incapable of acting coherently on serious security matters. They cite as an example the speed with which Europe's consensus generated a financial aid package for the Srpska Republic after moderate Milorad Dodik was elected prime minister in 1998. They point out that the EU provided 80 percent of Western help to the Soviet successor states and three-quarters of the help given to the Palestinians. And they expect a process of incremental increase in common EU foreign policy in the early twenty-first century that will complement the increase in common financial policy in the 1990s.[38]

In the interim, before that hallowed state arrives, however, Washington will measure European unity precisely by this conspicuous area of security policy—and will find it sorely wanting. The definitive word will still be Henry Kissinger's sardonic question—What phone number do I call for Europe? Washington will welcome the chance to continue playing one European capital off the other—but it will also be frustrated whenever it tries to elicit a coherent European approach to common security problems. It will see a red flag every time German diplomats declare that, by contrast to the United States, Europe is a "civil power."

Despite these built-in strains, the Clinton administration and Europe have reached a certain modus vivendi over unilateral American military actions. The United States does what it feels compelled to do in the Mideast, with instant pledges of British military support and with quiet German logistics support on NATO bases in Germany. Especially when its precision missiles can pinpoint specific targets and inflict little collateral damage, Washington no longer tries to mobilize a multilateral coalition for joint operations. What it demands instead is just that allies not accept their free good of security, then criticize the provider of that free good. And even the German Social Democrats, in a swift seven-year transformation, now endorse that bargain.[39]

Regions of the world in which the modus vivendi will be put to the test will be the Mideast, the Balkans, and, if Russian society explodes, the former Soviet Union.

At the benign end of the spectrum, there is a running American-German dispute over whether and how fast Turkey should be admitted to the European Union. Washington, wishing to strengthen a secular Islamic state as a bulwark against Islamic fundamentalism (and to reward a loyal NATO member), pressed the EU to conclude a customs union with Ankara in 1995, and it now wants the EU to put Turkey on its preferred list of candidates. Germans, buffeted by the turbulence of their own unification, EMU, EU institutional reform, central European enlargement, and the fight over a new EU budget, retort that the EU cannot take on another huge challenge at this point without risking collapse. Turkey is too poor, too big, and too deficient in protecting human rights to qualify for the short list, they say—and they are irritated by American meddling on the issue.[40] Conversely, the United States gets irritated by Europe's "sleeping" through the Greek-Turkish impasse over Cyprus and the Aegean islands and sloughing the problem off onto the United States.[41]

Iran is much less of a transatlantic issue at the moment, since the Clinton administration has itself begun to seek dialogue with moderates in Tehran and has backed down from imposing extraterritorial penalties on European companies doing business with Iran. Differences over sanctions on Iraq are more serious, with a sometime U.S. tilt toward missile strikes of nuclear and chemical-weapons plants that Iraq will not open for inspection, and with a European tilt toward rewards for partial Iraqi compliance with inspections through partial lifting of trade embargoes. In the potentially most divisive regional issue of all, Europe disapproves of American tolerance of Israeli stonewalling on the peace process, seeing in increased Arab-Israeli polarization the greatest long-term threat to peace in the Mideast.[42]

In dealing with the Balkans, the alliance's problem is less a clash of opposing policy prescriptions than the dearth of promising prescriptions. The allies certainly agree that IFOR and SFOR troops have established enough of a truce in Bosnia for moderates to get a foothold there and in Montenegro. But as of this writing, there was no coalescing view about how to deal with the continued tension in Kosovo—or even how to convert military policing of the Bosnia peace accord into durable civilian governance. Here, too, U.S. and European instincts pull in different directions, with the United States giving strong priority to military, Europe to civilian, needs—and with Washington often inclined to simplify negotiations with fractious Yugoslav partners by dealing with them bilaterally rather than first coordinating joint Western positions.[43] So far, though, despite some showdowns inside and outside the Contact Group steering committee, at the end of the day the Western allies have come out with common policies. The successful SFOR operation has at least set the basic guidelines for future intervention.

Devising a common approach to a still nuclear-armed Russia with a weakening government and military discipline is potentially, of course, the most serious problem of all in transatlantic relations. The risk is not that Berlin will be tempted to live out the American nightmare of the 1980s that Germany might cut a secret Rapallo deal with a country that is now no more than an "Indonesia with missiles." In the judgment of Christoph Bertram, director of the Berlin think tank Foundation for Science and Policy:

> For the first time in 200 years, Russia is a marginal power in Europe, drifting along as the rest of Europe drifts westward. While Germans hope that Russia's democratic structures and economy will stabilize, theirs is more the attitude of an interested onlooker than a committed partner. Because of the tough lessons Germany learned this century and also because of Russia's reduced significance, the old debilitating German temptation to seek a place between East and West is now devoid of attraction.[44]

The much greater risk, though, is that the Russian financial collapse could degenerate into social and political disorder. Under these circumstances the United States and Germany in particular might well find themselves holding strong contrary views on such issues as intervention, refugees, and securing of the Polish border against spillover. A harbinger of this was the row between IMF deputy director Stanley Fischer, who wanted the Germans to ante up more billions for Moscow just before the Russian meltdown, and German officials, who protested that their generous government aid and obligation to cover most of the $30 billion exposure of government-insured German banks in Russia's de facto default was more than enough of a contribution.[45]

For its part, Europe is far more apt to be frustrated in the last years of this century by a lack of decisive leadership from a lame-duck president than by any American "hegemony." The very seriousness of a Russian political crisis (and continued crisis in Kosovo) should dwarf differences over Mideast policy, enhance the value to the United States of western Europe as a stabilizer on its own continent, and increase the pressure on Europe to fill the void in Western leadership. Yet in the absence of authoritative figures among European heads of government—and given Europe's preoccupation with the EU's unsettled institutional issues—the void is more likely to set off transatlantic recriminations than to accelerate a maturing of European leadership.

Most broadly, Europe, which has benefited enormously from its own progressive pooling of sovereignty and codification of common rules of the road in intra-European relations, seeks to replicate this development in some measure on an international plane. It has already taken more initiatives than the United States would like in negotiating treaties banning landmines, establishing an international war crimes court, and setting international ceilings on emission of greenhouse gases.[46] Various EU diplomats expect that Europe will have to take over from an ambivalent United States the leadership of the next round of world negotiations to cut tariff and nontariff barriers, establish the real authority of the young World Trade Organization to adjudicate disputes, and coordinate regulation and enforcement of competition policy. The overall aim, these diplomats say, is to produce an expanding corpus of international law and agreed standards of world behavior. Washington, while it would like rogue states held to international standards—and appreciates the enhanced reach and leverage that alliances provide—is wary lest either endeavor curtail its own freedom of action. Its defensiveness on these issues, combined with a circling of the wagons as its bull market turns into a bear market, could increase the temptation of protectionism.

So far a healthy American coalition of diplomatic fixers and a general public that likes to vacation in Europe has prevented exaggerated confrontations that serve neither side of the Atlantic.[47] Import of genetically altered meat, privacy in cyberspace, America's death sentence, cultural-political differences in dealing with Scientology's allure to young people, and even bananas may seize the headlines, but they are hardly the stuff of international showdowns. And, surprisingly, debate about NATO enlargement in Washington never led to any isolationist call for American withdrawal and divorce from Europe. With this history, both sides should be able to keep discrete spats under control. But as this century closes, they will have to work hard at it.

Coopetition

In core Europe, professional observers have long failed to see the woods for the trees. The abundant literature about all the dangers, while issuing useful warnings and calls to action, suffocates any celebration of the continent's extraordinary achievement and energy in the decade since the fall of the Berlin Wall. Yugoslavia smothers Poland. Yet the information age's casual globalization, pragmatism, and change of consciousness are leap years away from the more parochial instincts of the generation of even our grandfathers and grandmothers. Today's governments in heartland Europe simply do not expect to go to war with their neighbors, nor do they make any contingency plans for such an eventuality. They know viscerally (as the United States knows only intellectually) that they are too little to solve alone the problems of global warming, instant billion-dollar transfers, or Balkan savagery. And that emotional persuasion, instead of paralyzing them, has impelled them to an unwonted optimism, surrender of sovereignty, and now even relinquishment of national coinage.

"The very fact that a large number of countries have been willing to take the gamble is striking testimony to the political dynamism of the European Union. It is simply misleading to focus on and lament the difficulties experienced along the way and the relatively slow pace of innovation in other dimensions of European integration," suggests Pierre Jacquet, deputy director of the French Institute of International Relations. "EMU is a unique experiment in sharing a major attribute of sovereignty."[48]

"In a curious symmetry these changes [in Europe] have come partly as a result of a second thirty years' war: 1914–1945," concludes senior British diplomat Robert Cooper.[49] The first paroxysm led to rejection of Christianity or forms of Christianity as an organizing principle on the continent and to adoption instead of the state system as codified in the Peace of Westphalia of 1648. The second paroxysm, aided by the prod of globalization, has now led to another revolutionary systemic change in Europe based on reconciliation, postnational pooling of sovereignty, blurring of the distinction between domestic and foreign affairs, and hourly meddling in each other's business. A peculiar European Union has evolved that will never be a federation, but is vastly more than a confederation or even a concert of nations. This European Union is imperfect and therefore open to change. As Germans like to say, it is less an institution than a process. It is lean in bureaucracy and budget. Yet it still determines half of members' legislation, and interprets this body of law authoritatively in the European Court of Justice. And despite a consensus system that theoretically should ensure deadlock, it repeatedly wrestles out common positions on economic (if not yet on significant security policy) issues. It throws itself into crises that force it to "flee forward" as a less risky alternative to sticking with the status quo. It is flexible enough to allow for constant readjustment of the division of competencies and for a flow of authority back to states or regions as political moods shift. It bridges the political and technocratic by increasingly assigning economic decisions to experts. In tandem with NATO, the European Union rests its security on unprecedented acceptance of interdependence, transparency, and mutual vulnerability.[50]

The emerging European governance has nothing to do with a "new *world* order." It is a "postmodern," postnational island—albeit a large one—in a world that consists primarily of "modern" nation-states (like China, Iran, and the United States) and still "premodern" chaos, in Cooper's analysis.[51]

The interaction of this creature with a not-yet post-modern America that also takes pride in inventing itself every day will challenge the imagination and tolerance of both sides. Europe is certainly becoming more American, through the U.S. cultural and linguistic hegemony, the new economic orthodoxy of Anglo-Saxon neoliberalism, and the dominance on the continent of a Germany that grew up in the image of the United States. Yet Europe is also beginning to take on an American-like self-confidence, and it will increasingly wish to exercise its expanding financial power in ways that may impinge on the U.S. understanding of its own world leadership.

As the only military superpower, the United States, despite Vietnam, has not yet been compelled to internalize interdependence in the way Europe has had to. The United States still tends to want to establish rules of international law that will bind others, but not itself. It champions the cause of Chinese dissidents, but resents others' telling it not to convict and execute a Paraguayan immigrant who has not received adequate legal defense. Its boisterous ethnic and single-cause politics lead to national legislation that orders others to ban or limit their trade. Individual states set their own foreign policy in decreeing boycotts of Swiss banks that are judged too miserly in paying heirs to Jewish wealth confiscated by the Nazis. Yet Texas governors, after pro forma objections by Europeans as another death-row inmate is consigned to the electric chair, write retorts telling the Europeans to stop sticking their nose into other people's business.[52] Sharing sovereignty is not always America's first instinct.

Asymmetries will be all the more irritating for the United States when Washington feels that Europe expects it to do all the dirty jobs because it alone has the military capability and the worldwide network of political alliances to carry them out. And asymmetries will be all the more irritating for a reborn Europe as it grows financial muscle— but still requires American leadership to preserve its unprecedented peace and prosperity.

Yet such vexations should not overshadow recognition that American and European interests in an age of globalization are more congruent than they have ever been in the past. The two partners have far more to gain from the synergy they have practiced in the last half century than from confrontation. It is more than a cliché when American presidents proclaim, "Our destinies are joined. If Europe is at peace, America is more secure. If Europe prospers, America does as well."[53]

As Europe is reborn at this beginning of a new millennium, history has granted us the grace of miracles. Now it is up to the United States and Europe to live up to them. Transatlantic relations, too, are a work in progress.

Notes

Chapter One

1. Francis Fukuyama, *The End of History and the Last Man* (New York: Free Press, 1992). For the purposes of this book, "Europe" is most often used not in its geographic, but in its political, sense. It refers to the heartland Europe of the EU and the widening sphere of states in the region that share its democratic and market values, including Switzerland, Norway, and most of the central European states that are candidates to join the EU.

2. This book does not address the many arguments about the nature of globalization, but it assumes that in the computer age the phenomenon goes far beyond the high international capital flows and trade of the pre–World War I system of a gold standard and antagonism among still bellicist European nation-states. For an exploration of how globalization affects international relations, see Jean-Marie Guehenno, "Globalisation and Its Impact on International Strategy," paper presented at the International Institute for Strategic Studies (IISS) annual conference, Oxford, September 3–6, 1998.

3. Interview, Bonn, 1996.

4. Founding father Konrad Adenauer, in the midst of West Germany's economic miracle, won a unique absolute majority in 1957 with the simple slogan "No experiments." For four decades thereafter, as the mark rose and kept on rising, the Christian Democrats returned to this effective electoral appeal to the Germans' penchant for predictability.

5. See Robert Bideleux and Ian Jeffries, *A History of Eastern Europe: Crisis and Change* (New York: Routledge, 1998).

6. This concept appears in virtually every Kohl speech on Europe. See, for example, "Erklärung der Bundesregierung," Kohl speech in the Bundestag, December 12, 1996, in *Bulletin* no. 103, p. 1113, of the Press and Information Service.

7. Kohl used this phrase many times. The most famous occasion was in his speech in Louvain, Belgium, on February 2, 1996; excerpts in *Internationale Politik*, vol. 52, no. 8 (August 1996), p. 82.

8. Robert Cooper, *The Post-Modern State and the World Order* (London: Demos, 1996); interviews in February and May, 1998, and in May, June, August, and November 1997, when Cooper was deputy chief of mission in the British Embassy, Bonn.

9. Interview, November 1997.

10. Interviews, telephone, November 1997; Davos, January 1998.

11. Telephone interview, November 1997.

12. There are, in fact, formal restrictions on crossing the border. But virtually any Pole can get a three-month German visa for the asking. Anecdotal evidence suggests that most of the cleaning women in Berlin today are Poles who live in cramped rooms in the German capital during the week and return to their families in Poland on weekends. Even as far west as the Rhineland or Belgium there is a steady stream of Polish cleaning women, construction workers, and crop pickers who stay their three months, then pass their jobs on to cousins or friends in rotation.

13. Interview, Bonn, 1994.

14. The Maastricht conference of heads of government or state took place in December 1991; the treaty was formally signed February 7, 1992.

15. See, for example, John J. Mearsheimer, "Back to the Future: Instability in Europe after the Cold War," *International Security*, vol. 15, no. 1 (Summer 1990), pp. 5–56; John J. Mearsheimer, "The False Promise of International Institutions," Working Paper 10 (John M. Olin Institute for Strategic Studies, Harvard University, November 1994); Kenneth N. Waltz, "The Emerging Structure of International Politics," *International Security*, vol. 18, no. 2 (Fall 1993), pp. 44–79; Michael Mandelbaum, *The Dawn of Peace in Europe* (New York: Twentieth Century Fund Press, 1996); Charles A. Kupchan, "Reviving the West," *Foreign Affairs*, vol. 75, no. 3 (May/June 1996), pp. 92–104; Rudi Dornbusch, "Euro Fantasies," *Foreign Affairs*, vol. 75, no. 5 (September/October 1996), pp. 110–24; Tony Judt, *A Grand Illusion? An Essay on Europe* (New York: Hill and Wang, 1996); Milton Friedman, "Why Europe can't afford the euro. The danger of a common currency," *Times* (London), November 19, 1997; interview with James Tobin, "Ein schlimmes Beispiel," *Die Zeit*, March 28, 1998, p. 31; and virtually all of American media reporting on the EU Intergovernmental Conference of 1996/97.

Different though they are, these works all reflect the premises sketched here. Judt regards European cooperation from 1945 to 1989 as no more than a "parenthesis"—and notions of "Europe" as no more than a "mantra" to avoid facing real problems like unemployment. Mandelbaum mentions the European Union only three times in a 169-page text (excluding footnotes), once to point out its failure in Bosnia, the other two times to urge central European states' entry into the EU as a better alternative to NATO membership. Kupchan, while proposing a new institution of an "Atlantic Union" that would combine the functions of the EU and NATO, does so because he is convinced that the pursuit of the "cold war legacies" of NATO expansion, "monetary union, a common foreign and security policy, and centralized governance of Europe" will fail. Expectations of the worst from European monetary union on sheer economic grounds—especially the lack of regional adjustment by labor mobility—also predominate in the analysis of leading American economists like Dornbusch or Friedman.

Exceptions, curiously, to what the *Economist* identifies as the prevalent American "genre" of Europessimism ("Diplomatic baggage," *Economist*, November 15, 1997, p. 7 of review section) are two analysts who are more noted as eastern European than as western European specialists. Martin Malia flags the current steps toward European integration as the most significant since the time of Charlemagne ("A New Europe for the Old?" *Daedalus* (Summer 1997). Zbigniew Brzezinski, reflecting the Polish sensibility for western Europe, notes that while the European enterprise may be "lukewarm, lacking in passion and a sense of mission," it is nonetheless surging forward on the commitment of the French and German elites to it. Zbigniew Brzezinski, *The Grand Chessboard* (New York: Basic Books, 1997).

16. Interviews, Warsaw, 1996, 1995, 1994, 1993.

17. Wolfgang Schmale, *Scheitert Europa an seinem Mythendefizit?* (Bochum: Winkler, 1997).

18. Joseph S. Nye, *Bound to Lead: The Changing Nature of American Power* (New York: Basic Books, 1990).

19. This point is argued most cogently in Peter Katzenstein, ed., *Tamed Power: Germany in Europe* (Cornell University Press, 1998). In this book Katzenstein also proposes a theoretical synthesis of neorealism and neofunctionalism. While the theory of international relations is well outside the scope of the present book, it is worth noting that Katzenstein thus challenges the strong Euroskeptic bias of the neorealist school in the United States. See also Michael Mertes, "Germany's Social and Political Culture: Change through Consensus?" in Michael Mertes, Steven Muller, and Heinrich August Winkler, *In Search of Germany* (New Brunswick: Transaction, 1996).

20. Frank Umbach, "The Role and Influence of the Military Establishment in Russia's Foreign and Security Policies in the Yeltsin Era," *Journal of Slavic Military Studies*, vol. 9, no. 3 (September 1996), pp. 467–500; Bruce Blair, "Loose Cannon," *National Interest*, no. 52 (Summer 1998), pp. 87–98.

21. Martin Feldstein, "EMU and International Conflict," *Foreign Affairs*, vol. 76, no. 6 (November/December 1997), pp. 60–73.

22. John Newhouse, *Europe Adrift* (New York: Pantheon, 1997).

23. Philip Stephens, "Intellectual gulf," *Financial Times*, January 19, 1998, p. 14.

24. Irving Kristol, "Petrified Europe," *Wall Street Journal Europe*, February 2, 1998.

25. William Safire, "Alice in Euroland," *New York Times*, April 30, 1998.

In fairness, it should be noted that the United States was not altogether alone in its dismissal of EMU. In Britain, too, "Many politicians and financial commentators and most of the news media displayed an almost spectacular misjudgment of the events that ensured EMU's scheduled launch," according to Wolfgang Münchau. "Some of the more visceral critics totally misread the German institutions, in particular the Bundesbank and the German constitutional court, hoping that they might block the project at the last minute. They mistook German skepticism on EMU for a general Euroscepticism," and still "predict that the project will collapse." "Prepared for EMU? It's time to live with the euro," *Financial Times*, April 28, 1998, p. 3.

26. See, for example, Anne Swardson, "Europe Banks on A 30-Year Dream," *Washington Post*, April 28, 1998; and Richard W. Stevenson, "Euro Could Eventually Rival the Dollar," *New York Times*, April 28, 1998.

Chapter Two

1. Dean Acheson, *Present at the Creation* (New York: W. W. Norton, 1987), especially p. 231. See also Bark and Gress, *From Shadow to Substance: 1945–1963* (Oxford: Basil Blackwell, 1989), pp. 128–40; and Theodor Eschenburg, "Jahre der Besatzung, 1945–1949," DVA/Brockhaus *History of the Federal Republic of Germany* (Stuttgart/Wiesbaden: Deutsche Verlags-Anstalt/F. A. Brockhaus, 1981), vol. 1, pp. 265–69.

2. Cited in, among many other references, Dennis L. Bark and David R. Gress, *A History of West Germany's Democracy and Its Discontents*, vol. 2 (Oxford: Basil Blackwell, 1989), p. 460, citing *Der Spiegel*, September 10, 1984.

3. In a memo to British prime minister Anthony Eden on February 7, 1956. Cited in Hans-Peter Schwarz, *Die Ära Adenauer 1949–1957* (Stuttgart/ Wiesbaden: Deutsche Verlags-Anstalt/F. A. Brockhaus, 1981), p. 340.

4. In legal terms the council did not exist until it was formally identified at the Paris summit of October 1974. This merely codified already existing practice, however.

5. Fiona Hayes-Renshaw and Helen Wallace, *The Council of Ministers* (New York: St. Martin's, 1997), pp. 1, 211. The authors add dryly that the council is also the focus for the 800-strong Brussels press corps, "through which ministers address their domestic publics." For an ABC of the European Union, see Dick Leonard, *Guide to the European Union* (London: Economist, 1994/98).

6. See especially Schwarz, *Die Ära Adenauer*, pp. 94–118, 288–96.

7. Ibid., p. 289.

8. TREVI is an acronym for terrorism, radicalism, extremism, violence, and information.

9. Anthony Forster and William Wallace, "Common Foreign and Security Policy," in Helen Wallace and William Wallace, *Policy-Making in the European Union*, 3d ed. (Oxford: Oxford University Press, 1996), pp. 411–35.

10. Ibid., p. 61.

11. The bizarre transatlantic banana war of 1998–99 began in the early 1990s as a skirmish between the Germans, who dote on cheaper and tastier Latin American bananas and free trade, and the French, who dote on their former colonies and intervention in the market. The French won, and the EU, to encourage African and Caribbean imports of the fruit, set quotas on "dollar bananas" from Latin America. From 1993 on, African, Caribbean, and Pacific bananas could enter the EU duty-free, but dollar bananas had to pay a tariff of about 24 percent on the first 2 million tons, but more than 200 percent over this "quota." In its initial ruling, the European Court of Justice turned down a German government petition to declare the regime illegal, since the quota was flexible enough not to cause "serious and irreparable damage" to Germany. See Christopher Stephens, "EU Policy for the Banana Market," in Wallace and Wallace, *Policy-Making in the European Union*, pp. 325–51.

12. J. H. H. Weiler, "The Transformation of Europe," *Yale Law Journal*, vol. 100, no. 8 (1991), pp. 2403–83. See also Weiler's "A Quiet Revolution: The European Court of Justice and Its Interlocutors," *Comparative Political Studies*, vol. 26, no. 4 (January 1994), pp. 510–34; Andre Bzdera, "The Court of Justice of the European Community and the Politics of Institutional Reform," *West European Politics*, vol. 15, no. 3 (July 1992), pp. 122–36; Mary L. Volcansek, "The European Court of Justice: Supranational Policy-Making," *West European Politics*, vol. 15, no. 3 (July 1992), pp. 109–21; Karen J. Alter and Sophie Meunier-Aitsahalia, "Judicial Politics in the European Community," *Comparative Political Studies*, vol. 26, no. 4 (January 1994), pp. 535–61; Robert Rice, "States breaking EU laws may have to pay damages," *Financial Times*, November 29, 1995, p. 18; "France rapped over farmers," *Financial Times*, December 16, 1997, p. 10; and Josephine Shaw, *The Law of the European Union* (Basingstoke: Macmillan, 1996).

13. For complaints about the Court see Andrew Adonis and Robert Rice, "In the hot seat of judgment," *Financial Times*, April 3, 1995, p. 15; Robert Rice, "German judge attacks European court," *Financial Times*, August 21, 1995, p. 2; editorial, "European law in the dock," *Financial Times*, August 21, 1995; Robert Rice, "EU liability ruling turns spotlight on Court," *Financial Times*, November 29, 1995, p. 2; Günter Hirsch, "Keine Integration ohne Rechtseinheit," *Frankfurter Allgemeine Zeitung*, October 9, 1996, p. 15; Uwe Wesel, "Ausgerechnet Bananen," *Die Zeit*, April 4, 1997, p. 44; "Biased referee?" *Economist*, May 17, 1997, pp. 35f; and "Bonn to defy European Court," *Financial Times*, June 6, 1998, p. 2.

14. Brigid Laffan and Michael Shackleton, "The Budget," pp. 71–96; and

Helen Wallace and Alasdair R. Young, "The Single Market: A New Approach to Policy," pp. 125–55, in Wallace and Wallace, *Policy-Making in the European Union.*

15. David Allen, "Competition Policy: Policing the Single Market," pp. 157–83; Janne Haaland Matlary, "Energy Policy: From a National to a European Framework?" pp. 257–77; and Stephen Woolcock and Michael Hodges, "EU Policy in the Uruguay Round," pp. 301–24, in Wallace and Wallace, *Policy-Making in the European Union.*

16. Interviews. See also Alberta Sbragia, "Environmental Policy: The 'Push-Pull' of Policy-Making," in Wallace and Wallace, *Policy-Making in the European Union*, pp. 235–55.

17. Interviews. See also Dominique Moisi, "End in sight for Mr Eternity," *Financial Times*, March 10, 1998, p. 18; and Gilbert Ziebura, *Die deutsch-französischen Beziehungen seit 1945* (Stuttgart: Günther Neske, 1997).

18. On Mitterrand's efforts to forestall unification, see Elizabeth Pond, *Beyond the Wall* (Brookings, 1993); Horst Teltschik, *329 Tage* (Berlin: Siedler, 1991); and Philip Zelikow and Condoleezza Rice, *Germany Unified and Europe Transformed* (Harvard University Press, 1995); Kohl's affection for Mitterrand shines through the laudatio for this "great European" that he gave *Le Monde* on Mitterrand's retirement from office on May 11, 1995. German Government Bulletin 41 (May 1995), pp. 356f.

19. See Pond, *Beyond the Wall*, pp. 33–55, 65–68; and Catherine McArdle Kelleher, *The Future of European Security* (Brookings, 1995), pp. 57–63.

20. See Valerie Guerin-Sendelbach, "Ein Tandem für Europa? Die deutsch-französische Zusammenarbeit der achtziger Jahre," Working Paper on International Relations 77 (Bonn, German Society for Foreign Policy, September 1993).

Chapter Three

1. The East German Politburo had intended to allow much freer travel outside the German Democratic Republic, but only later and only with official exit stamps. An ambiguous televised press conference during prime-time evening news led many East Berliners to think they could suddenly visit West Berlin at will, however, and they quickly massed at the crossing points. Border guards initially blocked their way, but—without orders—finally chose to let the East Berliners through rather than shoot. See Elizabeth Pond, *Beyond the Wall* (Brookings, 1993). For an account of the Leipzig demonstration a month earlier that established the precedent that East German security forces would not shoot demonstrators, see David Schoenbaum and Elizabeth Pond, *The German Question and Other German Questions* (London: Macmillan, 1996), pp. 146–49.

2. Patricia Clough, *Helmut Kohl* (Munich: DTV, 1998); Klaus Dreher, *Helmut Kohl* (Stuttgart: Deutsche Verlags-Anstalt, 1998).

3. Kai Diekmann and Ralf Georg Reuth, *Kohl: Ich wollte Deutschlands Einheit* (Berlin: Propyläen, 1996), p. 483.

4. For some Anglo-Saxon premonitions of the pending French revaluation, see Richard Bernstein, "The French Revolution: Right or Wrong?" *New York Times Book Review*, July 10, 1988, pp. 1ff.; and the *Economist* section on the French Revolution, December 24, 1988, pp. 119ff.

5. For evaluations of the bilateral relationship in this period see Valerie Guerin-Sendelbach, *Ein Tandem für Europa?* (Bonn: Europa Union Verlag, 1993); Ingo Kolboom and Ernst Weisenfeld, eds., *Frankreich in Europa* (Bonn: Europa Union Verlag, 1993); Patrick McCarthy, ed., *France-Germany 1983–1993* (New York: St. Martin's, 1993); and Philip H. Gordon, *Die Deutsch-Französische Partnerschaft und die Atlantische Allianz* (Bonn: Europa Union Verlag, 1994).

6. For a sampling of the flood of literature in this vein predicting or advocating the demise of NATO after the collapse of the Berlin Wall, see Ronald Steel, "NATO's Last Mission," *Foreign Policy,* vol. 76 (Fall 1989), pp. 83–95; Christopher Layne, "Superpower Disengagement," *Foreign Policy*, vol. 78 (Spring 1990), pp. 3–25; and Richard H. Ullman, *Securing Europe* (Princeton University Press, 1991).

7. See especially Lily Gardner Feldman's chapter, "The European Community and German Unification," in Leon Hurwitz and Christian Lequesne, eds., *The State of the European Community, 1989–90* (Boulder, Colo.: Lynne Rienner, 1991); Lily Feldman, "Germany and the EC: Realism and Responsibility," *Annals of the American Academy* (January 1994), pp. 25–43; and Helen Wallace and Alasdair R. Young, "The Single Market," in Helen Wallace and William Wallace, *Policy-Making in the European Union*, 3d ed. (Oxford: Oxford University Press, 1996), pp. 125–55.

8. French finance minister Dominique Strauss-Kahn summarized this strategy in Craig Whitney, "Euro-Ready France Pleases a Guide with Vision," *New York Times*, April 19, 1998.

9. This reading is based on interviews, consistency with Kohl's later positions on EMU, and the dynamic of allied acceptance of German unification. The received wisdom is that Kohl agreed to give up the deutsche mark as payment for unification. However, this version was categorically denied by Wilhelm Schönfelder, the Foreign Ministry's point man in the issue from the mid-1980s on and currently head of the EU division in the ministry, in interviews in 1997 and 1998; by Dietrich von Kyaw, German ambassador to the EU Committee of Permanent Representatives, in interviews in 1998; and by Horst Teltschik, national security adviser to Kohl during the process of German unification, in interviews in 1990 and 1997. Their interpretation—that Kohl supported EMU, but only under stringent conditions—is in any case

more consistent with Kohl's later fierce defense of EMU than is the view that his opposition inexplicably turned to advocacy as the going got tough. Finally, it is clear from other evidence that the shift of initial French and British resistance into acquiescence to unification reflected less an EMU tradeoff than American pressure on Paris and London to accede to the inevitable. *Der Spiegel* purported to show from official minutes of a Kohl meeting with Secretary of State James Baker in early 1990 that the chancellor thought then that monetary union would run counter to German national interest—but the magazine omitted the sentence after its chosen quote that made clear Kohl was referring to the arguments of those in the Bundesbank and elsewhere that he would have to refute to win EMU. See Hanns Jürgen Küsters and Daniel Hofmann, eds., *Deutsche Einheit. Sonderedition aus den Akten des Bundeskanzleramtes. Dokumente zur Deutschlandpolitik* (Munich: R. Oldenbourg, 1998), document 120, pp. 636–41; and an article by the political scientist who has written the first history of the economic aspects of German unification based on the opened documentation, Dieter Grosser, "Der Euro war nicht der Preis für die deutsche Einheit," *Welt am Sonntag*, May 17, 1998, p. 9.

See also Wilhelm Schönfelder and Elke Thiel, *Ein Markt—Eine Währung* (Baden-Baden: Nomos, 1996); Thomas Hanke and Norbert Walter, *Der Euro* (Frankfurt: Campus, 1998), p. 18; Reimer von Borries and Wolfgang Glomb, *Beck-Ratgeber Euro-Währung* (Munich: C. H. Beck, 1997), p. 29; Peter Norman, "EMU's broody hen," *Financial Times*, May 2, 1998, p. 7; Joachim Bitterlich, "Anfangs frostig, später europäisch," *Die Zeit*, May 7, 1998, p. 4; Thomas Hanke and Wolf Proissl, "Die Dolchstosslegende," *Die Zeit*, May 7, 1998, p. 5; and, for the American role in unification, Philip Zelikow and Condoleezza Rice, *Germany Unified and Europe Transformed* (Harvard University Press, 1995); and Pond, *Beyond the Wall*, pp. 138ff. Most English-language literature, by contrast, accepts the conventional wisdom. See, for example, the analysis by Loukas Tsoukalis, "Economic and Monetary Union," in Wallace and Wallace, *Policy-Making in the European Union*, p. 293; and Anne Swardson, "Europe Banks on a 30-Year Dream," *Washington Post*, April 28, 1998, p. A1. For one last polemic against the euro on the eve of its adoption, see Rudolf Augstein's argument that EMU is a "chimera in the desert" and cannot work unless one changes human nature. "Neue Menschen, neue Menschen," *Der Spiegel*, April 27, 1998, pp. 102f.

10. Reinhard Bettzuege, ed., *Aussenpolitik der Bundesrepublik Deutschland. Dokumente von 1949 bis 1994* (Bonn: German Foreign Ministry, 1995), pp. 776ff. The phrasing is taken from Kohl and Mitterrand's summary of their April meeting to the Italian president of the EC on December 6, 1990.

11. Bettzuege, *Aussenpolitik*, pp. 729ff.

12. See, for example, Timothy Garton Ash, "Germany's Choice," *Foreign Affairs*, vol. 73, no. 4 (July/August 1994), pp. 65–81.

13. Europol was in fact not launched until 1998.

14. Bettzuege, *Aussenpolitik*, pp. 846ff.

15. Group interview with the German-American Workshop, May 1998, Bonn.

16. December 5, 1991.

17. For one example of the economic argumentation against EMU, see Manfred J. M. Neumann, "Die Mark ist ein Wohlstandsfaktor," *Die Zeit*, October 16, 1992, p. 32.

18. Kolboom and Weisenfeld, *Frankreich in Europa*, p. 75.

19. As translated from the German translation in ibid., p. 79.

20. Strictly speaking, this was not in the same league as Adenauer's flouting of public opinion, since more nuanced polls in the 1980s in Germany, unlike those in the Netherlands, never showed a majority against the deployment. See Pond, *Beyond the Wall*, chapter 4.

21. See, for example, "From Here to EMU," *Economist*, October 23, 1993, pp. 29ff.

22. Lionel Barber, "EU warned budget cannot grow to pay for expansion," *Financial Times*, October 23, 1995, p. 1; and Rudolf G. Adam, "Wo ein Wille ist, gibt es viele Wege," *Frankfurter Allgemeine Zeitung*, December 5, 1995, pp. 16f. The Visegrad states—the name derives from the city where they first met to try coordinate their approaches to the West—were originally Poland, Hungary, and Czechoslovakia. After Czechoslovakia split into the Czech Republic and Slovakia, there were four members of the group.

23. After Austria, Belgium, Denmark, and Luxembourg, and only slightly above France and the Netherlands, as measured in purchasing power parity in the annual pamphlet "OECD in Figures." One indicator of the sensitivity of this issue was the unavailability for many years of any official EU figures for net contributions. Through the mid-1990s even many senior German officials accepted at face value Bonn's assessment of a far more modest 30.36 percent of the EU budget, without factoring in the 1 percent of national value-added taxes going automatically to the EU, or other EU revenues.

24. Representative discussions from the ubiquitous contemporary coverage of the phenomenon include the insert section entitled "Politikverdrossenheit" in *Das Parlament*, July 30, 1993, and "Doch wie Weimar?" *Der Spiegel*, December 20, 1993, pp. 38ff.

25. Elizabeth Pond, "After Gulf War, a Drive toward European Unity," *Boston Globe*, March 31, 1991.

26. See, for example, Andrei Markovits and Jürgen Hoffmann, "Ein amerikanischer Jude und eine deutsche Friedensrede," *Frankfurter Rundschau*, February 16, 1991, p. 6; Rainer Erd, "Deutsche Linke an die Front?" *Frankfurter Rundschau*, February 20, 1991, p.4; Andrei Markovits, "Eine ernüchternde Erfahrung," *Die Zeit*, February 22, 1991; "An der deutschen Heimatfront," *Der Spiegel*, March 4, 1991, pp. 238–45; "Die Linke gibt es nicht—und sie gibt es doch," *Frankfurter Rundschau*, March 7, 1991, p. 6;

Henryk Broder, "Unser Kampf," *Der Spiegel*, April 29, 1991, pp. 255–67; and Wolf Biermann, *Der Sturz des Dädalus oder Eizes für die Eingeborenen der Fidschi-Inseln über den IM Judas Ischariot und den Kuddelmuddel in Deutschland seit dem Golfkrieg* (Cologne: Kiepenheuer & Witsch, 1992).

27. Hans-Dietrich Genscher, one of the Liberals' grand old men and foreign minister for almost two decades, had held to the party's long-standing interpretation that the constitution forbade sending German troops outside the NATO area. His successor in the early 1990s, Klaus Kinkel, took the case to the constitutional court as a way to get a decisive legal ruling and break with the past interpretation. For the habit of constitutional appeal of political issues in the Federal Republic, see especially Donald P. Kommers, "The Federal Constitutional Court in the German Political System," *Comparative Political Studies*, vol. 26, no. 4 (January 1994), pp. 470–91.

28. See, for example, David Marsh, *Germany and Europe: The Crisis of Unity* (London: William Heinemann, 1994).

29. Wallace and Wallace, *Policy-Making in the European Union*, pp. 375f.

30. Ibid., p. 371.

31. Deutsches Institut für Wirtschaftsforschung weekly report, "Bananenfestung Europa," April 8, 1992, pp. 175–79; Wallace and Wallace, *Policy-Making in the European Union*, 1996, chapter 13.

Chapter Four

1. According to megahistorian Paul Johnson, the present peace is the longest in history. He maintains that "the fifty years of peace between the Great Powers is a significant landmark in human history. Never before, and indeed never since there have been great powers to fight each other, has a general peace lasted so long. . . . As a historian, I can confidently say that this is unique: There is no precedent in world history for war being ruled out of forward calculations at such a high level." "World War II and the Path to Peace," *Wall Street Journal Europe*, May 8, 1995, p. 6. Some commentators, ignoring the Crimean War, alternatively identify the period between the Congress of Vienna in 1814 and the Franco-German war in 1870 as the longest peace. See also John Gaddis, *The Long Peace* (Oxford: Oxford University Press, 1987).

It would go well beyond the scope of this book to address the broader academic debate about the thesis that democracies tend not to go to war with other democracies. This controversy can be followed in Michael Doyle, *Ways of War and Peace* (W. W. Norton, 1997); in the fall 1994 edition of *International Security*, vol. 19, no. 2; and in Pierre Hassner, "Beyond the Three Traditions: The Philosophy of War and Peace in Historical Perspective," *International Affairs*, vol. 70, no. 4 (October 1994). What is indisputable, however, is that war in western Europe is now unthinkable.

2. See, for example, Ian Davidson, "Atlantic Alliance Fails to Read the Writing on the Wall," *Financial Times*, July 12, 1990, p. 2; Daniel T. Plesch and Daniel Shorr, "NATO, Down and (Soon) Out," *International Herald Tribune*, July 24, 1992; and even John Lukacs, *The End of the Twentieth Century and the End of the Modern Age* (New York: Ticknor and Fields, 1993).

3. Robert Mauthner and Lionel Barber, "U.S. seeks EC defence pledge," *Financial Times*, November 8, 1991, p. 1.

4. Vera Tolz measures the shift in Yeltsin's dropping of the adjective "Rossiiskaya" to revert to the traditional "Russkaya" for "Russian." The latter refers to common blood, the former, in 1990s usage, to a nation united instead by common institutions. This analysis was presented in "What Is Russia: Post-Communist Debates on Nation-Building," at the annual conference of the British Association for the Advancement of Slavic Studies, Cambridge, April 5, 1998.

5. Frank Umbach, "The Role and Influence of the Military Establishment in Russia's Foreign and Security Policies in the Yeltsin Era," *Journal of Slavic Military Studies*, vol. 9, no. 3 (September 1996), pp. 467–500.

6. See Anatol Lieven, *Chechnya: Tombstone of Russian Power* (Yale University Press, 1998).

7. NATO London Declaration, Press Communiqué S-1(90)36, July 6, 1990.

8. Laura Silber and Allan Little, *Yugoslavia: Death of a Nation* (New York: TV Books, 1996), p. 159.

9. See Susan L. Woodward, *Balkan Tragedy* (Brookings, 1995); Silber and Little, *Yugoslavia*; Warren Zimmermann, *Origins of a Catastrophe* (New York: Times Books, 1996); Richard Holbrooke, *To End a War* (Random House, 1998); David Rohde, *Endgame* (New York: Farrar, Straus and Giroux, 1998); and Mark Danner, series of articles in the *New York Review of Books* on November 20, 1997, December 4, 1997, December 18, 1997, February 5, 1998, February 19, 1998, March 26, 1998, and April 23, 1998. For a rather different European perspective on the "endgame" in Bosnia, see Carl Bildt, "The search for peace" (review of Holbrooke's book), *Financial Times*, July 2, 1998, p. 16.

10. Silber and Little, *Yugoslavia*, p. 201.

11. Probably the most influential book to view the Yugoslav bloodletting as an outbreak of ancient ethnic hatreds—it was famously read by President Clinton in the early 1990s—was Robert Kaplan's *Balkan Ghosts* (New York: Vintage, 1994). For refutation of this view, see the books on Yugoslavia already cited, plus Michael Ignatieff, "The Politics of Self-Destruction," *New York Review of Books*, November 2, 1995, pp. 17ff; and Brian Hall, "Rebecca West's War," *New Yorker*, April 15, 1996, pp. 74–83.

12. Holbrooke, *To End a War*, pp. 65–68.

13. Ibid., p. 67.

14. "NATO beyond Bosnia," Congressional Research Service Report for Congress 94-977 S (December 7, 1994).

15. The atmosphere in Dayton was captured in one sputtering British cable from the airbase that began, according to an American diplomat who saw it, "The Americans let the animals out of the cage today." "Animals" refers to all the non-Americans and their perceived treatment by Holbrooke.

16. Countries participating under Partnership for Peace were Albania, Austria, Bulgaria, the Czech Republic, Estonia, Finland, Hungary, Latvia, Lithuania, Poland, Romania, Russia, Slovakia, Slovenia, Sweden, and Ukraine. Additional IFOR personnel came from Argentina, Egypt, Ireland, Jordan, and Morocco.

17. See the summary in the International Institute for Strategic Studies, *Strategic Survey 1993–1994* (London: Brassey's, 1994), pp. 117–25.

18. Volker Rühe, "Shaping Euro-Atlantic Policies—a Grand Strategy for a New Era," Alastair Buchan Memorial Lecture at the International Institute for Strategic Studies, London, March 26, 1993; copy distributed by German Defense Ministry.

19. Interviews with Onyszkiewicz, February 1998 (Munich) and February 1997 (Warsaw).

20. Geremek speech in Aachen on May 21, 1998, provided by the Polish Embassy in Cologne. For the current state of the special Polish-German relationship, see especially Roland Freudenstein, "Poland, Germany and the EU," *International Affairs*, vol. 74, no. 1 (January 1998), pp. 41–54. For earlier descriptions, see Dieter Bingen, *Die Polenpolitik der Bonner Republik von Adenauer bis Kohl: 1949–1991* (Baden-Baden: Nomos, 1998); Roland Freudenstein, ed., *VII. Deutsch-Polnisches Forum* (Bonn: Europa Union Verlag, 1993); Hans-Adolf Jacobsen and Mieczeslaw Tomala, eds., *Warschau-Bonn* (Cologne: Wissenschaft und Politik, 1990); and Michael Ludwig, *Polen und die deutsche Frage* (Bonn: Europa Union Verlag, 1990.)

21. Interviews; James Goldgeier, "NATO Enlargement: Anatomy of a Decision," *Washington Quarterly*, vol. 21, no. 1 (Winter 1998), pp. 85–102; and Jonathan Eyal, "NATO's enlargement: Anatomy of a decision," *International Affairs*, vol. 73, no. 4 (October 1997), pp. 695–719.

22. A striking feature of the American debate was the overwhelming opposition to enlargement among columnists and opinion writers. The crusade was led by Thomas L. Friedman of the *New York Times*. See, for example, his "Gulf of Tonkin II," *New York Times*, March 31, 1998, and numerous other columns; Jim Hoagland, "From NATO to the Real World," *Washington Post*, May 3, 1998; Charles A. Kupchan, "Expand NATO—And Split Europe," *New York Times*, November 27, 1994; Michael Mandelbaum, "Preserving the New Peace," *Foreign Affairs*, vol. 74, no. 3 (May/June 1995), pp. 9–13; John Lewis Gaddis, "The Senate Should Halt NATO Expansion," *New York Times*, April 27, 1998, and "History, Grand Strategy and NATO Enlarge-

ment," *Survival*, vol. 40, no. 1 (Spring 1998), pp. 145–51; William Pfaff, "European Security Isn't Broken. So Why Try to Fix It Now?" *International Herald Tribune*, February 18, 1997, p. 8. See also "Expanding NATO: Will It Weaken the Alliance?" (transcript of a debate between Richard C. Holbrooke and Michael E. Mandelbaum at the Council on Foreign Relations in New York), December 9, 1996.

23. The pro-enlargement campaign was spearheaded initially by RAND Corporation analysts in a flurry of articles. See, for example, Ronald D. Asmus, Richard L. Kugler, and F. Stephen Larrabee, "Building a New NATO, *Foreign Affairs*, vol. 72, no. 4 (September/October 1993), pp. 28–40; and Ronald D. Asmus, Robert D. Blackwill, and F. Stephen Larrabee, "Can NATO Survive?" *Washington Quarterly*, vol. 19, no. 2 (spring 1996), pp. 79–101. See also NATO's own "Study on NATO Enlargement, " September 1995. For a discussion of civilian-military relations in the candidate countries, see Reka Szemerkenyi, "Central European Civil-Military Reforms at Risk," Adelphi Paper 306 (December 1996), International Institute for Strategic Studies.

24. Strobe Talbott, "Why NATO Should Grow," *New York Review of Books*, August 10, 1995, pp. 27–30. See also Richard C. Holbrooke, "America, a European Power," *Foreign Affairs*, vol. 74, no. 2 (March/April, 1995), pp. 38–51.

25. See, for example, her "Bringing New Democracies Into the NATO Fold," *International Herald Tribune*, July 8, 1997, p. 8.

26. Obversely, Kaliningrad was a special concern of Poland and Lithuania in the early 1990s because of the concentration there of Soviet troops that were withdrawing from eastern Germany and Poland. For German interest in helping to develop the Kaliningrad special economic zone as a link between Russia and the West rather than a bone of contention, see Heike Dörrenbächer, *Die Sonderwirtschaftzone Jantar' von Kaliningrad (Königsberg)* (Bonn: Europa Union Verlag, 1994).

27. Jonathan Eyal, "NATO's enlargement," specifies that the Baltics could be defended only if there were prepositioning of materiel there. Prepositioning would be seen as so provocative by Russia that it is not a serious NATO option.

28. Interviews with Onyszkiewicz, February 1998 (Munich) and February 1997 (Warsaw). Other Poles argued as well that it was only after NATO finally decided to admit Poland to membership that the Russians began talking to Poles directly and seriously about their bilateral relationship, rather than expecting to negotiate with the West about Poland over the heads of the Poles.

29. Bartolomiej Sienkiewicz, "A Gentle Russia," *Gazeta Wyborcza*, July 1, 1998; English translation in David Johnson List #2251 available from <davidjohnson@erols.com>.

30. "The Baltic Revolution," *Economist*, April 18, 1998, pp. 30ff.

31. Interview, February 1997.

32. Olga Alexandrova, "Perzeptionen der auswärtigen Sicherheit in der Ukraine," paper for the Federal Institute for Eastern Studies, Cologne, August 1993.

33. Interview, Warsaw, 1995.

34. The delimitation of bilateral borders has not yet been completed, and numerous Russian politicians still speak of the "inherent" unity of the two nations. The two presidents were trying to coordinate their responses to their common economic crisis, however, and there was no climate of confrontation.

35. The best analyses of Ukrainian security issues and the Russian-Ukrainian agreements have been written by James Sherr and Sherman Garnett. See James Sherr, "Russia-Ukraine Rapprochement?" *Survival*, vol. 39, no. 3 (Autumn 1997), pp. 33ff; James Sherr, "Russia and Ukraine: Towards Compromise or Convergence?" CSRC, Royal Military Academy, Sandhurst, August 1997. <gopher://marvin.nc3a.NATO.int/00/secdef/csrc/f60all.txt%09%09%2B>; Sherman W. Garnett, *Keystone in the Arch: Ukraine in the Emerging Security Environment of Central and Eastern Europe* (Washington: Carnegie Endowment for International Peace, 1997); Stephen A. Cambone, "NATO Enlargement: Implications for the Military Dimension of Ukraine's Security," *Harriman Review*, vol. 10, no. 3 (Winter 1997), pp. 8–18; and Christian F. Wehrschütz, "Die ukrainisch-russischen Beziehungen: Ungewisse Partnerschaft," AP 3066 Stiftung Wissenschaft und Politik (April 1998).

36. Interview, Brussels, June 1998.

37. Interviews in Kyiv and Warsaw, March 1997.

38. Interview, Warsaw, 1996.

39. The Eurocorps began in the late 1980s as a French-German brigade and then added Belgian, Spanish, and Luxembourg troops.

40. The cult of 1389 was itself actually the nineteenth-century invention of Serbian nationalists, however, Noel Malcolm reveals in *Kosovo: a Short History* (Basingstoke: Macmillan, 1998); and the Albanian participants of the famous battle mostly fought on the side of the Serbs. Moreover, the patriarchate did not originate in Kosovo, but moved there from central Serbia, abandoned the site in the late eighteenth and nineteenth centuries, and moved back to Kosovo only in the 1920s.

41. The WEU was born in 1948—before NATO existed—as the Brussels Treaty Organization of Britain, France, and the Benelux countries. It was intended as a defense pact against any return to German aggression, and when it admitted Germany and Italy as members in 1954, it barred Bonn from acquiring certain classes of weapons; these restrictions would not be lifted until the 1980s and 1990s. The WEU ceased to have any serious function once NATO was founded, but it was revived as part of the renewed French-German rapprochement in the 1980s. Its ten current full members include

also Portugal, Spain, and Greece. The eighteen others in the organization are associate members Iceland, Norway, and Turkey; associate partners Poland, Hungary, the Czech Republic, Slovenia, Estonia, Slovakia, Latvia, Lithuania, Bulgaria, and Romania; and observers Austria, Denmark, Finland, Ireland, and Sweden. For discussion of ESDI, see Michael O'Hanlon, "Transforming NATO: The Role of European Forces," *Survival*, vol. 39, no. 3 (Autumn 1997), pp. 5ff.

42. See Charles Barry, "NATO's Combined Joint Task Forces in Theory and Practice," *Survival*, vol. 38, no. 1 (Spring 1996), pp. 81–97; and Philip H. Gordon, "Europe's Uncommon Foreign Policy," *International Security*, vol. 22, no. 3 (Winter 1997/98), pp. 74–100.

43. Solana speech at the annual Munich security conference, February 1998.

44. Interview. Article 5 of NATO's 1949 founding treaty designates an attack on any NATO member as an attack on all alliance members; this is the basis for the "spine" of NATO's continuous political consultations and the integrated command that was activated in Bosnia.

45. Speech at NATO's Defense Planning Committee, June 11, 1998, NATO press release.

46. For an overview of the shrinking of commands, see Thomas-Durell Young, ed., *Command in NATO after the Cold War: Alliance, National, and Multinational Considerations* (Carlisle Barracks: Strategic Studies Institute, U.S. Army War College, 1997).

47. For overviews of the aborted French–NATO rapprochement, see Bruno Racine, "Für ein transatlantisches Gleichgewicht. Frankreich, NATO und europäische Verteidigungspolitik," *Internationale Politik*, vol. 53, no. 2 (February 1998), pp. 19–24; Jonathan Marcus, "Adjustment, Recrimination: Franco-U.S. Relations and the New World Disorder," *Washington Quarterly*, vol. 21, no. 2 (Spring 1998), pp. 17–32; and Gilles Andreani, "Frankreich und die NATO," *Internationale Politik*, vol. 53, no. 7 (July 1998), pp. 27–32.

48. The Euro-Atlantic Partnership Council replaced the North Atlantic Cooperation Council after the Soviet Union split into fifteen states.

49. Interview.

50. Solana speech at the University of Warsaw, April 18, 1996; NATO press release.

51. James Goodby, citing Alexander George and Kenneth Boulding, explores the difference between stable peace, conditional peace, and precarious peace in "Europe Undivided," *Washington Quarterly*, vol. 21, no. 3 (Summer 1998), pp. 191–207. He also notes Hedley Bull's distinction between the Hobbesian view of international politics as a state of war, the Kantian view of it as a potential community of mankind, and the Grotian view of it as relations within an international society.

52. Interview.

53. Interview, Brussels, 1996.

54. Paul Cornish, *Partnership in Crisis: The U.S., Europe and the Fall and Rise of NATO* (London: Royal Institute of International Affairs, 1997). See also the upbeat assessment after NATO bit the bullet in Bosnia and hammered out a CJTF agreement in Stanley Sloan, "Negotiating a new transatlantic bargain," *NATO Review*, vol. 44, no. 2 (March 1996), pp. 19–23. For a contrary argument that NATO will "be reluctant to use force to manage or settle disputes that do not involve its members' territories"—and that this "would be politically embarrassing and ultimately perhaps dangerous for NATO," see Joseph Lepgold, "NATO's Post–Cold War Collective Action Problem," *International Security*, vol. 23, no. 1 (Summer 1998), pp. 78–106. Lepgold advocates instead a "decentralization" of the alliance that would push military planning and responsibility further down the chain of command and devolve more responsibility and accountability onto Europeans.

Chapter Five

1. "Germany's Europe," *Financial Times*, April 28, 1994.

2. Scott Sullivan, "Down in the Dumps," *Newsweek*, April 12, 1993, pp. 10–15; *International Herald Tribune*, April 20, 1994.

3. John Andrews, Survey of "The European Union: Family frictions," *Economist*, October 22, 1994.

4. George Steiner, "Sind unsere Kräfte erschöpft?" *Frankfurter Allgemeine Zeitung*, August 27, 1994.

5. Peter Ludlow, "Beyond Maastricht: Recasting the European Political and Economic System," Centre for European Policy Studies Working Document 79 (Brussels, July 1993). See also Stanley Hoffmann on Europe's "serious crisis" in "Goodbye to a United Europe?" *New York Review of Books*, May 27, 1993, pp. 27ff; Stanley Hoffmann, "Europe's Identity Crisis Revisited," *Daedalus* (Spring 1994), pp. 1–23; and Hans Arnold, *Europa am Ende?* (Munich: Piper, 1993).

6. Kohl's speeches from 1996 to 1998 are available on the internet at <http://www.bundesregierung.de>. Earlier Kohl speeches are available in the regular print issues of the government "Bulletin."

7. The "democratic deficit" is the conspicuous lack of direct accountability to voters in all the EU institutions. The European Commission and the European Council cut their deals behind closed doors in a kind of secrecy that no national parliament would tolerate. The toothless European Parliament is not in a position to force disclosure or transparency on either.

8. For a discussion of the conflict between widening and deepening, see the survey of the European Union in The *Economist*, October 22, 1994. For one of the earliest statements of the German position—even before the fall of the Berlin Wall—see Michael Mertes and Norbert J. Prill, "Der verhängnisvolle

Irrtum eines Entweder-Oder," *Frankfurter Allgemeine Zeitung*, July 19, 1989, p. 8. For a discussion of it in the post-Maastricht period, see Rudolf Seiters, deputy chairman of the Christian Democratic Union/Christian Social Union (hereafter CDU/CSU) parliamentary caucus, "Welches Europa wollen wir?" *Frankfurter Allgemeine Zeitung*, April 28, 1995, pp. 8f.

9. CDU/CSU Parliamentary Group, "Reflections on European Policy," September 1, 1994. Quotations here are from the CDU's English translation.

10. For one study of these exchanges, see Guido Hartmann, *Sozio-kulturelle Probleme deutsch-französischer Ministerialkooperation* (Berlin: Wissenschaftlicher Verlag, 1997).

11. For Lamfalussy's own summation of EMI activity, see his interview, "Der Weg wird noch unruhig," *Die Zeit*, December 22, 1995, p. 19; and Andrew Fisher and David Wighton, "EMI sets out options on euro," *Financial Times*, January 11, 1997, p. 1.

12. Quentin Peel, "Kohl warns on EU contributions," *Financial Times*, May 18, 1994, p 2.

13. Kinkel speech at the German Society for Foreign Policy, August 24, 1994; cf. Kohl speech at the thirtieth-anniversary celebration of the Elysée Treaty, January 21, 1993; Reinhard Bettzuege, ed., *Aussenpolitik der Bundesrepublik Deutschland. Dokumente von 1949 bis 1994* (Bonn: German Foreign Ministry, 1995), pp. 1081–86 and 899–902.

14. CDU/CSU, "Reflections on European Policy."

15. "Back to the drawing-board," *Economist*, September 10, 1994.

16. David Marsh argued in *Die Zeit*, for example, that the whole experiment in monetary union in fact threatened to split Europe wide open. Sardonically, he predicted that a single currency would indeed come—and that it would probably be called the deutsche mark. "D-Mark für alle?" *Die Zeit*, September 23, 1994; and "Spaltpilz Einheitswährung," *Die Zeit*, March 1, 1996. See also Ian Davidson, "Chord of Disunity," *Financial Times*, October 2, 1996, p. 2.

17. Karl Lamers, "Germany's Responsibilities and Interests in the Field of Foreign Policy," paper presented to the CDU/CSU parliamentary caucus executive committee, August 23–24, 1993.

18. For differences over joint plane production, see, for example, Bernard Gray and David Buchan, "France pulls out of air project," *Financial Times*, February 24, 1996, p. 1; and Michael Lindemann and Andrew Jack, "Germany, France to discuss military transport," *Financial Times*, August 8, 1996, p. 2.

19. See Wernhard Möschel, "Europapolitik zwischen deutscher Romantik und gallischer Klarheit," *Aus Politik und Zeitgeschichte*, B 3-4/95 (January 13, 1995), pp. 10–16; and Stanley Hoffmann, "French Dilemmas and Strategies in the New Europe," in Joseph S. Nye, Robt O. Keohane, and Stanley Hoffmann, eds., *Europe after the Cold War* (Harvard University Press, 1993).

20. CDU/CSU, "Reflections on European Policy."

21. Ibid.

22. Ibid.

23. "CDU und CSU wollen Kerngruppe in der EU stärken," *Frankfurter Allgemeine Zeitung*, February 9, 1994, p. 1.

24. See also the tracing of Kohl's fingerprints on the paper in "Kinkel widerspricht Europa-Konzept," *Frankfurter Allgemeine Zeitung*, September 3, 1994, p. 1; and "Verstimmung über Europapapier der Unionsfraktion," *Frankfurter Allgemeine Zeitung*, September 6, 1994, p. 1.

25. For a plea for continued French-German coordination just before the election, see Deutsche Gesellschaft für Auswärtige Politik and others, *Handeln für Europa* (Opladen: Leske + Budrich, 1995).

26. The other two signatories were Austria and Italy. Greece later acceded to the accord as well.

27. For suppressed German irritation over these and other surprises, see, for example, "Kohl will mit Chirac über Frankreichs Atom-Politik sprechen/ Bonner Unbehagen," *Frankfurter Allgemeine Zeitung*, July 11, 1995, p. 2; "Deutsch unerwünscht," *Frankfurter Allgemeine Zeitung*, November 3, 1995, p. 6; "Millon verspricht Abstimmung mit Bonn," *Frankfurter Allgemeine Zeitung*, February 21, 1996, p. 5; Günther Nonnenmacher, "Auf dem Weg zur Berufsarmee," *Frankfurter Allgemeine Zeitung*, February 23, 1996, p. 1; "Unklarheiten in der deutsch-französischen Sicherheitspolitik," *Frankfurter Allgemeine Zeitung*, March 2, 1996, p. 1; "Französiche Soldaten verlassen Deutschland bis 1999," *Frankfurter Allgemeine Zeitung*, July 18, 1996, p. 1; "Diesmal ohne Jubel," *Frankfurter Allgemeine Zeitung*, July 18, 1996, p. 1.

28. For one of the clearest expositions both of the French logic and of the breach with the past that this decision required, see Michel Rocard, "Wir sollten mehr auf die anderen hören," *Die Zeit*, September 6, 1996, p. 8. See also the interview with Jean-Pierre Chevènement, "Angst vor Deutschland?" *Die Zeit*, August 2, 1996, p. 39. For a sampling of media coverage tracing Chirac's evolution, see, for example, David Buchan, "Schengen stand ignites French Euro debate/Doubts grow over Pres. Chirac's commitment," *Financial Times*, July 1, 1995, p. 2; "Chirac becomes Balladur," *Economist*, November 4, 1995, p. 45; David Buchan, Andrew Jack, and John Ridding, "France backs Germany on EMU penalties plan," *Financial Times*, November 13, 1995, p. 20; David Buchan, "France and Germany gear up for next IGC," *Financial Times*, December 2, 1995, p. 2; "Verworrene französische Maastricht-Debatte," *Neue Zürcher Zeitung*, February 3, 1996, p. 3; "Die Handlungs-fähigkeit der Europäischen Union verbessern," *Frankfurter Allgemeine Zeitung*, December 8, 1995, p. 1; Erik Hoffmeyer, "Bystanders at the infighting," *Financial Times*, February 9, 1996, p. 22; "Juppé-bekenntnis in Bonn zur Europäischen Währungsunion," *Frankfurter Allgemeine Zeitung*, February 13, 1996, p. 13; David Buchan, "EMU back on French lips," *Financial Times*,

February 20, 1996, p. 2; David Buchan, "France wants to rein in non-EMU states," *Financial Times*, February 21, 1996, p. 2; Peter Norman, "Paris and Bonn agree EU foreign policy opt-out pact," *Financial Times*, February 28, 1996, p. 2; David Buchan, "Paris-Bonn accord on EMU 'ins' and 'outs,'" *Financial Times*, March 27, 1996, p. 2; Klaus Kinkel and Hervé Charette, "Es muss eine echte europäische Identität entstehen," *Frankfurter Allgemeine Zeitung*, March 29, 1996, p. 7; "Staatsminister besucht Slowakei," *Frankfurter Allgemeine Zeitung*, July 1, 1996, p. 2; Werner Hoyer and Michel Barnier, "Gemeinsam zu europäischen Zielen," *Die Zeit*, July 12, 1996, p. 8; and "Kohl und Chirac planen für ein Europa des 21. Jahrhunderts," *Frankfurter Allgemeine Zeitung*, September 2, 1996, p. 1. So much has been published on this and other issues discussed in chapters 5 and 8 especially that notes can only be indicative.

29. Compare, for example, Kohl's evocation of Churchill on April 29, 1991, and June 18, 1992, with Kohl's statement on October 5, 1993, that he would no longer use Churchill's formulation because of "misunderstandings" it aroused. "Im Bewusstsein der europäischen Idee als Werte- und Kulturgemeinschaft," Federal Press Office Documentation Bulletin, April 29, 1991; and "Helmut Kohl. Bilanzen und Perspektiven" (Bonn: Federal Government Press and Information Service, 1997), pp. 60, 192.

30. "Kohl beschwört die Unumkehrbarkeit der europäischen Integration," *Frankfurter Allgemeine Zeitung*, December 8, 1995. Compare Kohl's repetition of this theme before a Bundestag committee on the eve of final Bundestag approval of the EMU. "Kohl empfiehlt Zurückhaltung bei Deutschlands Rolle in Europa," *Frankfurter Allgemeine Zeitung*, April 21, 1998, p. 2.

31. See "Bonn und Paris rufen nach europäischer Identität," *Frankfurter Allgemeine Zeitung*, March 29, 1996, p. 1; "Die letzte Entscheidung bleibt bei den Regierungen," interview with Kinkel, *Süddeutsche Zeitung*, March 7, 1996.

32. Robert Graham, "Paris, Bonn seek to bring EU institutions closer to citizens," *Financial Times*, May 8, 1998, p. 2; and Lionel Barber, "A punctured image," *Financial Times*, June 15, 1998, p. 17.

33. Karl Kaiser and Hanns W. Maull, eds., "Die Zukunft der europäischen Integration: Folgerungen für die deutsche Politik," Working Paper 78 (Bonn: Research Institute of the German Society for Foreign Policy, October 1993).

34. CDU/CSU, "Reflections on European Policy."

35. Rudolph G. Adam, "Wo ein Wille ist, gibt es viele Wege," *Frankfurter Allgemeine Zeitung*, May 12, 1995. For subsequent recognition of this shift, see also "Reality dawns in Tralee," editorial, *Financial Times*, September 9, 1996, p. 17; Neil Buckley, "Dehaene to present EMU budget," *Financial Times*, September 30, 1996; "'Der euro ist mehr als eine Münze," *Die Zeit*, interview with Lamers, September 5, 1997, p. 7; and "Goodbye, federal Europe," *Economist*, November 15, 1997, pp. 27ff.

36. The most sensational formulation of this concern was the book by a British employee of the European Commission who was subsequently disciplined, Bernard Connolly, *The Rotten Heart of Europe* (London: Faber and Faber, 1995). More sophisticated and qualified concern was expressed by Timothy Garton Ash, "Back to Europe," *Prospect* (June 1996), p. 25.

37. Ludlow, "Beyond Maastricht," p. 43.

38. See, for example, Holger Schmiedling, "Price worth paying," *Financial Times*, December 19, 1995, p. 12.

39. For Mundell's own evaluation as it became clear that EMU would proceed, see his articles, "Great Expectations for the Euro," *Wall Street Journal Europe*, March 24, 1998, p. 10; "Great Expectations for the Euro-Part II," *Wall Street Journal Europe*, March 25, 1998; and "Making the Euro Work," *Wall Street Journal Europe*, April 30, 1998. The United States exports 11.4 percent of its GDP, as calculated from 1996 statistics in the brochure "OECD in Figures," 1998 edition, supplement to *OECD Observer*, no. 212, June/July 1998.

40. For an overview of this and other issues, see the 26-page "EMU" survey in the *Economist* of April 11, 1998; and the insert section, "The Birth of the Euro," in the *Financial Times*, April 30, 1998.

41. "Scharping verzichtet auf 'Manifest'/Schröder: Währungsunion als nationales Thema der SPD," *Frankfurter Allgemeine Zeitung*, October 30, 1995; Peter Norman, "Schroeder upsets SPD euro consensus," *Financial Times*, October 30, 1995, p. 2; Alan Friedman, "Vision of a Single EU Currency Collides with German Politics," *International Herald Tribune*, October 31, 1995, p. 1; "Stabilität ist nicht alles," interview with Schröder, *Der Spiegel*, December 25, 1995; "Mover and shaker," interview with Schröder, *Financial Times*, March 17, 1997, p. 16; Peter Norman, "Pressure mounts on Bonn to delay EMU" [with subsequent correction identifying the quotes in the story as coming from Bavarian Premier Edmund Stoiber, not Finance Minister Theo Waigel], *Financial Times*, July 7, 1997, p. 1; Ralph Atkins, "EMU divisions hit Kohl's party," *Financial Times*, July 29, 1997, p. 1; "Ein Tausch von Sicherheit gegen Hoffnung," *Handelsblatt*, April 22, 1998, p. 3; and Günter Bannas and Hans-Jörg Heims, "Im Zweifel lieber doch keinen Putsch," *Süddeutsche Zeitung*, April 24, 1998, p. 3. Tellingly, a more frontal German dissent had to come from outside the country, from Lord (Ralf) Dahrendorf in Oxford, in an interview in *Der Spiegel*, "Alle Eier in einen Korb," November 12, 1995, pp. 27ff.

42. For an overview of the criteria from the German perspective, see "Wie wichtig sind die finanzpolitischen Konvergenzkriterien?" *Deutsches Institut für Wirtschaftsforschung Wochenbericht* (hereafter *DIW*), February 8, 1996, pp. 93–99.

43. Tietmeyer, group interview, Gütersloh, March 1995; Oliver Schumacher, "Kulturkampf der Geldhüter," *Die Zeit*, November 17, 1995, p. 25.

44. Lionel Barber and John Kampfner, "Germany sets hard terms for EMU deal," *Financial Times*, December 13, 1995, p. 1. See also "Die Debatte um den EU-Haushalt," *DIW*, October 2, 1997; "'Wir müssen den Spielraum beschränken,'" interview with Otmar Issing, *Der Spiegel*, January 15, 1996, pp. 85–87; "Gut für Deutschland," *Der Spiegel*, January 15, 1996. pp. 84f; Robert Chote, "Tietmeyer warns on one currency," interview, *Financial Times*, February 3, 1996, p. 2; "Tietmeyer nennt die Europäische Währungsunion 'im wirtschaftlichen Sinne nicht absolut notwendig,'" *Frankfurter Allgemeine Zeitung*, March 21, 1996, p. 5; Andrew Fisher and Peter Norman, "Bundesbank outlines plans for EU currency stability," *Financial Times*, April 11, 1996, p. 10; Tietmeyer interview, "Finding way through ins and outs," *Financial Times*, April 11, 1996, p. 2; Reimut Jochimsen, "Der Euro verzeiht keine Tricks," *Die Zeit*, April 19, 1996, p. 6; Peter Norman, "'Pöhl cautions on cost of EMU 'mistakes,'" *Financial Times*, April 19, 1996, p. 2; Andrew Fisher, "Issing warns on euro and competitiveness," *Financial Times*, December 18, 1996, p. 3; Nina Grunenberg, "Prediger der harten Mark," *Die Zeit*, January 24, 1997, p. 3; Samuel Brittan, "How Bundesbank sees EMU," *Financial Times*, February 12, 1997, p. 18; Peter Norman and Andrew Fisher, "German row over EMU deepens," *Financial Times*, May 30, 1997, p. 1; and Hans Tietmeyer interview, "Der Euro—ein entnationalisiertes Geld," *Die Zeit*, December 12, 1997, p. 24.

45. See, for example, Ian Davidson, "A divisive destiny," *Financial Times*, January 24, 1996, p. 12; *Die Zeit* shared this suspicion: Oliver Schumacher, "Unter mittelständischen Unternehmen in Deutschland grassiert die Angst vor der europäischen Währungsunion," *Die Zeit*, January 29, 1995, pp. 21f. See also Tom Buerkle, "A European Slowdown Chills Prospects for Single Currency," *International Herald Tribune*, November 23, 1995, p. 1; "A dying deadline?" *Economist*, January 20, 1996, p. 31; John Schmid, "Can Bonn Pass EMU Test? 2 Reports Raise New Doubts That It Will," *International Herald Tribune*, January 27, 1996, p. 1; Tom Buerkle, "Maastricht Criteria on Ropes," *International Herald Tribune*, January 27, 1996, p. 9; Terence Roth, "Economic Woes Oblige Bonn to Consider Delay in EU Single Currency," *Wall Street Journal Europe*, February 5, 1996, p. 1; and Tom Buerkle, "Skittish, Europeans Won't Part With Their Money," *International Herald Tribune*, February 19, 1996, p. 1.

46. "Bonn sind die Ausgaben für Brüssel zu hoch," *Frankfurter Allgemeine Zeitung*, July 25, 1995, p. 11; Marcell von Donat, "Europa braucht einen Plan," *Die Zeit*, August 12, 1995, p. 16; Joseph Fitchett, "Good for Germans, Good for Europe," *International Herald Tribune*, December 5, 1995, p. 1; Tom Buerkle, "An Apparent Dead End for European Centralization," *International Herald Tribune*, December 6, 1995, p. 5; Alan Friedman, "Devotion to DM Dictates Europe's Sacrifice," *International Herald Tribune*, December 6, 1995, p. 5; George Graham, "Payment system hurries the pace in debate on EMU," *Financial Times*, July 19, 1996, p. 2; "Grössere Ausge-

wogenheit angestrebt," *Frankfurter Allgemeine Zeitung,* July 22, 1996, p. 5.

47. Emma Tucker, "Schengen group backs France," *Financial Times,* September 6, 1995, p. 2; Peter Norman, "Germany urges measures to guarantee EMU discipline," *Financial Times,* September 12, 1995, p. 1; "Eurosceptic markets," editorial, *Financial Times,* September 16, 1995, p. 8; Emma Tucker, "Market turmoil over EMU fear," *Financial Times,* September 22, 1995, p. 1; Lionel Barber, "Europe in new currency split," *Financial Times,* September 29, 1995, p. 1; Lionel Barber, "Bonn sets agenda for monetary union," *Financial Times,* October 2, 1995, p. 2; Lionel Barber, "EMU hits stumbling block," *Financial Times,* October 6, 1995, p. 22; "Vor 'Maastricht Zwei' eine deutsch-französische Initiative," *Frankfurter Allgemeine Zeitung,* October 9, 1995, p. 4; and Tom Buerkle, "A French-German Feud Festers on Currency Plan," *International Herald Tribune,* November 27, 1995, p. 1.

48. "'Monsieur X' für die EU-Aussenpolitik?" *Frankfurter Allgemeine Zeitung,* September 13, 1995; Quentin Peel, "Germans seek 4-year agenda on EU reform," *Financial Times,* September 13, 1995. For the companion wish list of the Reflection Group, which was writing the official agenda for the forthcoming Intergovernmental Conference, see Peter Hort, "Materialsammlung für eine EU–Reform an Haupt und Gliedern," *Frankfurter Allgemeine Zeitung,* September 8, 1995, p. 9.

49. See, for example, Dr. Ludolf von Wartenberg, director-general of the Federation of German Industry, writing in *Financial Times,* August 24, 1994, "UK needed at the heart of Europe"; and the interview with Percy Barnevik, chief executive officer of the Swedish-Swiss ABB engineering firm, "The Moment of European Truth," *Time,* September 19, 1994, pp. 40f.

50. Peter Norman, "Waigel spells out plan for EMU stability," *Financial Times,* November 8, 1995, p. 2; "Stabilitätspakt soll die Währungsunion sichern," *Frankfurter Allgemeine Zeitung,* November 11, 1995, p. 13; and Peter Norman, "Germany proposes fines to regulate EMU states," *Financial Times,* November 11, 1995, p. 1.

51. "In Paris keimt Unbehagen über Deutschland und die Währungsunion," *Frankfurter Allgemeine Zeitung,* November 11, 1995, p. 18. Beyond specific policy differences, there was a basic philosophical difference in the two countries' approach to democracy. For the Germans there are some issues that are exempt from populist decision; over the decades the pursuit of low inflation had become one of those sacrosanct areas. This violated the principles of the more republican heirs of the French revolution, who regarded every issue as subject to political choice.

52. "Federal Government Statement," Bulletin 103 (December 1995), pp. 1011–15.

53. For one of the many episodes in the long-running banana opera, see Frances Williams, "US to seek WTO ruling on EU banana plans," *Financial Times,* July 24, 1998, p. 6.

54. No one took this statistical shortfall as a serious breach of financial

rectitude by model Germany; everyone understood that it was a temporary deviation in the 1990s brought about by Bonn's assumption of East Berlin's debts and the $100 billion a year transfers to the east. This lapse by the preacher of strictness was, however, embarrassing. See Terence Roth, "Economic Woes Oblige Bonn to Consider Delay in EU Single Currency," *Wall Street Journal Europe*, February 5, 1996, p. 1; Robert Chote, "Germany and France may miss Maastricht targets," *Financial Times*, June 21, 1996, p. 14; and Peter Norman, "Bonn increases deficit forecast to 2.9 percent," *Financial Times*, January 27, 1997, p. 1.

55. See Robert Rice, "German judge attacks European court," *Financial Times*, August 21, 1995, p. 2; Andrew Adonis and Robert Rice, "In the hot seat of judgment," *Financial Times*, April 3, 1995, p. 15; Manfred Zuleeg, "Ein Gericht jenseits von Gesetz und Recht?" *Frankfurter Allgemeine Zeitung*, March 17, 1994, p. 13; and J. H. H. Weiler, "A Quiet Revolution: The European Court of Justice and Its Interlocutors," *Comparative Political Studies*, vol. 26, no. 4 (January 1994), pp. 510–34.

56. In the absence of official figures, publications had to make their own calculations. Christian Reiermann, "Ende der Spendierlaune," in *Focus*, July 22, 1996, pp. 20ff, calculated Germany's share of EU funding as 62 percent. The *Economist*, "Who pays for it?" November 23, 1996, pp. 39f, calculated just short of 60 percent. The Centre for European Policy Studies calculated 58 percent in Dick Leonard, "The price that must be paid for friendship," *Financial Times*, September 17, 1998, p. 14. The two other sources of EU revenue, in addition to the value-added tax and contributions based on GDP, are customs duties and agricultural levies. See also "Grössere Ausgewogenheit angestrebt/Auch Kinkel und Lafontaine für niedrigeren EU-Beitrag Deutschlands," *Frankfurter Allgemeine Zeitung*, July 22, 1996, p. 5; "Nachdenken über gerechte Lastverteilung in der Europäischen Union," *Frankfurter Allgemeine Zeitung*, August 29, 1996, p. 14; "Blockade des EU-Haushalts erwogen," *Frankfurter Allgemeine Zeitung*, August 12, 1996; and Peter Norman, "Germany to seek ceiling for contributions to EU," *Financial Times*, September 9, 1996, p. 3. Budget assessments are given in Helen Wallace and William Wallace, *Policy-Making in the European Union* (Oxford: Oxford University Press, 1996), p. 86.

57. Edward Mortimer, "The wrong priority," *Financial Times*, January 17, 1996, p. 10; William Pfaff, "Progress Doesn't Just Run Ahead, You Have To Help It," *International Herald Tribune*, January 2, 1996, p. 6; and Brian Beedham, "Germany Has a Plan for Europe, That Goes Too Far Too Fast," *International Herald Tribune*, January 9, 1996, p. 8.

58. Speech in Louvain, Belgium, February 2, 1996. This was a theme he would repeat again and again, as, for example, when he quoted Mitterrand to Lower Saxony voters in early 1998: "Nationalism—that is war." (Christian Wernicke, "Der euro-fighter," *Die Zeit*, April 29, 1998.) Actually, although

Kohl's use of the phrase set off the greatest public commotion, German connoisseurs point out that German president Roman Herzog used it before Kohl did, and that Mitterrand was the "real inventor" of it in one of his last speeches before the European Parliament. Officials on Kohl's staff were surprised by the commotion set off by the repetition of a phrase that Kohl had often used before. They attributed the reaction to the fact that Kohl was speaking in Belgium; the Brussels reporters covering his speech had not previously heard his one-liner.

Substantively, it should be noted here that various German civil servants who have been working the issue of European integration contest the interpretation that Kohl gave up the goal of political union at all. They ask what political union actually is and argue that the possible spectrum is so wide that that concept of "giving up" on it is meaningless. Nonetheless, it should also be noted that Kohl's rhetorical shift was sufficient to raise British hopes of a common German-British understanding on the issue.

59. Renate Köcher, "Kühle Realisten," *Frankfurter Allgemeine Zeitung*, November 15, 1995. She observed, "A good 90 percent are not especially interested in the topic." Resignation that the euro was going to come anyway was growing, she pointed out. See also "96 percent gegen Bonn/Hände weg von unserer Mark," *Bild*, December 7, 1991; "Umfrage: Wir wollen unsere Mark behalten," *Bild*, June 20, 1992; and Herbert Kremp, "Mit der DM verlören die Deutschen mehr als ihre Währung," *Welt an Sonntag*, November 5, 1995, pp. 24–25.

60. Ian Davidson, "Beyond the catcalls," *Financial Times*, February 7, 1996, p. 10.

61. Including, most strikingly, a joint appeal by parliamentary majority leaders Wolfgang Schäuble and the same Philippe Seguin who had branded Bonn's Maastricht negotiators worthy successors of Hitler. Other examples were the joint statements by the two foreign ministers and the two defense ministers. See, for example, Kinkel and Charette, "Es muss eine echte europäische Identität entstehen"; Peter Norman, "Paris and Bonn agree EU foreign policy opt-out pact"; "The Helmut and Jacques show," *Economist*, April 6, 1996, pp. 29f; "Frankreichs Staatspräsident Chirac besucht Bundeskanzler Kohl," *Frankfurter Allgemeine Zeitung*, May 11, 1996, p. 2; "Kohl und Chirac vereinbaren gemeinsames Vorgehen," *Frankfurter Allgemeine Zeitung*, June 7, 1996, p. 1; David Buchan, "Kohl and Chirac plan to push EU," *Financial Times*, June 7, 1996, p. 3; Peter Norman, "Paris and Bonn vow to meet EMU date," September 18, 1996, p. 1; and "Paris und Bonn," editorial, *Frankfurter Allgemeine Zeitung*, December 9, 1996, p. 1. For a German insider's view of the stability pact, see Wilhelm Schönfelder and Elke Thiel, "Stabilitätspakt und Euro-X-Gremium—Die stabilitätspolitische Untermauerung der WWU," *Integration* (Bonn) vol. 21, no. 2 (April 1998), pp. 69–76.

62. Group interview, June 1996. Other convergence statistics are given in "Europäische Währungsunion: Reale Konvergenz unentbehrlich," *DIW*, August 1, 1996, pp. 515–24.

63. Lionel Barber, "EU nations underspend on regional aid by $24bn," *Financial Times*, July 29, 1996, p. 1.

64. Lionel Barber and Robert Graham, "UK, Germany block financing for EU transport networks," June 25, 1996, p. 16; Robert Chote, "Germany isolated over IMF gold sales," *Financial Times*, June 26, 1996, p. 4; and "Cut and grow—hope and woe," *Economist*, July 27, 1996. pp. 25f.

65. Andrew Hill, "Italian PM begins preparing lira's re-entry into ERM," *Financial Times*, June 11, 1996, p. 1.

66. Peter Norman, "France wants G7-style club for single currency, *Financial Times*, June 18, 1996, p. 14; and Robert Chote, "Welcome for EMU policy 'club' proposal," *Financial Times,* June 20, 1996, p. 2.

67. Neil Buckley, "Brussels fury over cash for VW," *Financial Times*, July 31, 1996; "Ein Rechtsbruch als Antwort auf einen Rechtsbruch?" *Frankfurter Allgemeine Zeitung,* July 31, 1996, p. 4; "Bonn und Brüssel wollen den Streit um die VW-Subventionen beilegen," *Frankfurter Allgemeine Zeitung,* September 4, 1996, p. 15; Wolfgang Münchau, "VW aid fight part of wider battle," *Financial Times*, September 6, 1996, p. 12.

68. For an overview, see Joe Rogaly and others, "Britain: The rogue piece in Europe's jigsaw," *Financial Times*, June 12, 1996, special section. The ban would not be lifted until the end of 1998.

69. "In Santer's style," *Economist*, July 1, 1996, p. 32.

70. John Tagliabue, "European Monetary Union Hits New Snags," *New York Times*, August 30, 1996.

71. Rudi Dornbusch, "Euro Fantasies," *Foreign Affairs*, vol. 75, no. 5 (September/October 1996), pp. 110–24.

72. Carola Kaps, "Die Währungsunion ist ein Vorhaben ohne ökonomische Vernunft," *Frankfurter Allgemeine Zeitung*, December 18, 1996, p. 18. For U.S. skepticism about visions of EMU in the early 1990s, see Mark N. Nelson, "Transatlantic Travails," *Foreign Policy*, vol. 92 (Fall 1993), pp. 75–91.

73. See, for example, John Newhouse, *Europe Adrift* (New York: Pantheon, 1997).

74. Lionel Barber and Neil Buckley, "Germany pushes EU into tough pact over euro," *Financial Times*, December 14, 1996, p. 1; Lionel Barber, "France and Germany struggle to turn their European dreams into reality," *Financial Times*, December 14, 1996, p. 2; "EMU after Dublin," *Economist*, December 21, 1996, p. 15; Lionel Barber, "The cracks appear," *Financial Times*, April 29, 1998, p. 14.

75. For a sophisticated reading of the Amsterdam outcome in social policy and subsidiarity, see Carl Lankowski, ed., "Break Out, Break Down or Break In?" AICGS Research Report No. 8 (Washington, 1998), especially

Lankowski's own essay, pp. 39–52. For a study of the *Länder* use of their new constitutional voice in European policy, see Michael J. Baun, "The *Länder* and German European Policy: The 1996 IGC and Amsterdam Treaty," *German Studies Review*, vol. 21, no. 2 (May 1998), pp. 329–46.

76. John Peet, special section, "Europe's mid-life crisis," *Economist*, May 31, 1997; Robert Leicht, "Kleinmut vor dem grossen Sprung," *Die Zeit*, June 6, 1997, p. 1; "Is Europe's currency coming apart?" editorial, *Economist*, June 7, 1997, pp. 15f. Special section, "Towards EMU/Kicking and screaming into 1999," *Economist*, June 7, 1997, pp. 21–25; "Amsterdam is no Maastricht," editorial, *Financial Times*, June 14, 1997, p. 6; and "Euro-divisions," *Economist*, June 14, 1997, pp. 33f.

77. "France still trapped," *Economist*, July 5, 1997, pp. 23f.

78. "Advent of EMU means Europeans must make reforms," October 21, 1997; text provided by U.S. Embassy, Bonn.

79. Malta was originally on this short list, but the newly elected Labour party withdrew its application for membership in 1996. When the Nationalist party returned to power in 1998, it reinstated the application.

80. Average EU inflation in mid-1998 was a negligible 1.4 percent.

81. "Keeping up the pace in the EMU race," *Financial Times*, March 26, 1998, p. 2.

82. "The verdict on EMU members," *Financial Times*, March 26, 1998, p. 11.

83. Theo Waigel's speech in the Bundestag euro debate; excerpts in *Frankfurter Allgemeine Zeitung*, April 24, 1998, p. 6.

Chapter Six

1. As used here, "central Europe" refers to the ten central European states that have "Europe agreements" promising membership in the EU—Poland, Hungary, the Czech Republic, Slovakia, Bulgaria, Romania, Slovenia, Estonia, Latvia, and Lithuania—plus Albania, which has a trade and cooperation agreement with the EU. It thus includes the Baltics, but excludes other Soviet successor states as well as the Yugoslav successor states other than Slovenia.

2. Interview, October 1997.

3. Leszek Balcerowicz, "Fallacies and other lessons," *Economic Policy*, December 1994, p. 47. See also his article "The Interplay between Economic and Political Transition," *Polish Quarterly of International Affairs* (Summer/ Autumn 1996), pp. 9–28.

4. When the Polish communist leadership softened somewhat and entered "round table" talks with Solidarity representatives in the spring of 1989, the two sides agreed on a free election for a new upper house and for 35 percent of the seats in the lower house, the Sejm. To the astonishment of both sides,

opposition candidates won all but one of the contested seats. The communists then offered to give some less-important cabinet posts to Solidarity nominees, but in a move that electrified the Soviet bloc, Walesa scrapped the brokered deal and got small parties that had previously been satellites of the communists to give Solidarity a majority for forming a new government. In the resulting coalition the communists held onto the military and police ministries, but Solidarity's Tadeusz Mazowiecki became prime minister in fact as well as in name. It was the first time in seventy years that communists had surrendered power peacefully in any country.

5. Polish statistics and IMF estimates given in Stanislaw Gomulka, "The IMF–Supported Programs of Poland and Russia, 1990–1994," Center for Social and Economic Research Studies and Analyses Working Paper 36 (Warsaw), p. 33.

6. See Joseph A. Schumpeter's classic *Capitalism, Socialism, and Democracy* (1942; reissued in 1976 by Allen and Unwin, London); plus Larry Diamond and Marc F. Plattner, eds., *Capitalism, Socialism, and Democracy Revisited* (Johns Hopkins University Press, 1993). One of Schumpeter's central points was the need for creative destruction of inefficient economic structures to make way for efficient capitalist ones.

7. Interviews at CBOS (Centrum Badania Opinii Spolecznej) polling organization, 1993 and 1994. For essays about the Catholic Church in the early years of Polish transition, see Leszek Nowak, "Essay on the Church," and Andrzej Gierech, "Will Messianism Reduce Our Distance to Europe?" in *Polish Western Affairs* (Poznan), vol. 33, no. 1 (1992), pp. 3–11, 13–26.

8. Commission of the European Communities, *Central and Eastern Eurobarometer no. 2* (Brussels: February 1992). In answers to the more concrete check question about the coming year, only 17 percent expected things to improve; 32 percent thought things would get worse; and 33 percent expected no significant change from their current discomfort.

9. For discussion of the Polish mindset, see Stanislaw Gomulka and Antony Polonsky, eds., *Polish Paradoxes* (London: Routledge, 1990). For a sociological analysis of the choices in the transition, see Andrzej Rychard, *Reforms, Adaptation, and Breakthrough* (Warsaw: IFiS, 1993).

10. Cited in Richard F. Staar, ed., *1990 Yearbook of International Communist Affairs* (Stanford: Hoover Institution Press, 1990), p. 374.

11. Interview with Balcerowicz associate, October 1997.

12. Ben Slay, "The Polish Economic Transition," *East-Central European Economies in Transition*, Joint Economic Committee, 103 Cong. 2 sess. (Government Printing Office, 1994), pp. 463–79; Ben Slay, "The Dilemmas of Economic Liberalism in Poland," *Europe-Asia Studies*, vol. 45, no. 2 (1993), pp. 237–57.

13. The OECD notes both the shallowness of Polish poverty—that is, the large number of those in the category who fall just under the line set—and the resulting discrepancy in results of between a tenth and a quarter of the popu-

lation classified as poor, depending on the method of calculation. *OECD Economic Surveys: Poland 1997* (Paris, 1996), p. 89f.

14. Even Balcerowicz lost his nerve for fiscal and monetary rigor in mid-1990, charged his deputy Marek Dabrowski, and tried "to bend the economy to fit promises of imminent relief after six months of shock therapy." Quoted in Ben Slay, "The Dilemmas of Economic Liberalism in Poland," *Europe-Asia Studies,* vol. 45, no. 2 (1993), p. 241. Subsequent statistics are taken from Gomulka, "The IMF–Supported Programs of Poland and Russia"; Slay, "The Polish Economic Transition"; *OECD Economic Surveys: Poland 1997*; "Poland," *Business Central Europe,* Annual, 1997/98, p. 26; John Hardt, "External Economic Relations with Particular Focus on Regional Cooperation," Janima Witkowska, "Foreign Capital as a Factor of Structural Changes in the Polish Economy," and Zofia Wysokinska, "Evaluation of Structural Changes in Polish Industry and in Foreign Capital Flow to Poland in the Period of Systemic Transformation," from the NATO Economic Colloquium, Brussels, June 25–27, 1997; World Bank "Transition" newsletters; and Grzegorz W. Kolodko and D. Mario Nuti, "The Polish Alternative," paper prepared for the United Nations University World Institute for Development Economics Research in Helsinki in March 1997.

15. Cited in Brooke Unger, "Against the grain: a survey of Poland," *Economist,* April 16, 1994, p. 5.

16. Kolodko and Nuti, "The Polish Alternative," table 1.

17. This assessment summarizes the mainstream Western evaluation to be found in, among others, Deutsche Bank Research, "Eastern Europe: Heading for Reform: Issue 4: Poland," (1993); Jeffrey D. Sachs, *Poland's Jump to the Market Economy* (MIT Press, 1993); OECD, *OECD Economic Surveys: Poland 1997*; Slay, "Polish Economic Transition," pp. 463f; and Stanislaw Gomulka, "The IMF-Supported Programs of Poland and Russia, 1990–1994," Studies and Analyses 36 (Warsaw: Center for Social and Economic Research, 1995). Kolodko, a severe critic of Balcerowicz, rejects this characterization, maintaining that while Balcerowicz's shock therapy led to severe recession and relatively high inflation until mid-1993, his own strategy for Poland led to the sustained growth since 1993. See Kolodko and Nuti, "The Polish Alternative"; Grzegorz Kolodko, *From Shock to Therapy* (Oxford: Oxford University Press, forthcoming); and Kolodko, "Russia Should Put Its People First," *New York Times,* July 7, 1998. For an analysis that argues that Poland's growth derived from an evolutionary process growing out of the old communist system rather than a revolutionary scrapping of it, see Kazimierz A. Poznanski, *Poland's Protrected Transition* (Cambridge: Cambridge University Press, 1996).

18. Kolodko and Nuti, "The Polish Alternative," table 1; and *East-Central European Economies in Transition.*

19. OECD, *OECD Economic Surveys: Poland 1997*, p. 153. Although the bazaars are declining in importance as wealth spreads, the fifteen largest ba-

zaars still accounted for turnover of $2.2 billion in 1997, according to official figures. "Poland: Cross-Border Trade with Neighbors Declines," *RFE/RL Magazine,* July 16, 1998 <http://www.rferl.org/nca/features/>.

20. Simon Johnson and Gary W. Loveman, "State Enterprise Restructuring: A Tale of Two Shipyards," in Simon Johnson and others, *Starting Over in Eastern Europe: Entrepreneurship and Economic Renewal* (Harvard Business School Press, 1995).

21. Domanski interviews, Warsaw, February 1997; 1995.

22. See Elizabeth Pond, "The Polish Election," *Harriman Review*, vol. 8, no. 4 (December 1995), pp. 35–40.

23. Interview, Warsaw, November 1995.

24. Kolodko and Nuti, "The Polish Alternative," table 1 and p. 39; Christopher Bobinski, "Poland finds feel-good factor," *Financial Times*, February 5, 1996, p. 2.

25. *Business Central Europe* annual 1997/98.

26. Ibid.; Kolodko and Nuti, "The Polish Alternative," pp. 6, 30.

27. For a study proposing that the Czech insider deals, exclusion of foreign competition, and resulting "culture of dishonesty" also played a major role in the Czech debacle, see Mitchell Orenstein, "Vaclav Klaus: Revolutionary and Parliamentarian," *East European Constitutional Review* (Winter 1998), pp. 46–55. Orenstein concludes that Klaus's legacy is likely to be less that he once built the strongest neoliberal party in central Europe, but rather that he demonstrated "the limits of neoliberal economics in practice."

28. European Commission, *Central and Eastern Eurobarometer no. 8* (Brussels, March 1998).

29. Cited in Kolodko and Nuti, "The Polish Alternative," p. 7.

30. Eurobarometer questionnaires further revealed that popular evaluation of the overall "direction of the country" was far more positive than it had been five years earlier, with 40 percent judging their direction "right" and 33 percent "wrong" (1995 surveys), as against only 20 percent "right" and 58 percent "wrong" verdicts in 1991, the worst evaluation in the nine countries polled (including Czechoslovakia, Hungary, the three Baltic states, Albania, Bulgaria, and Romania).

31. Interviews, Warsaw, just after the election.

32. Within less than a year Czarnecki would be dropped from his post after an exasperated EU canceled a PHARE grant to Poland—the only time it has ever taken such a drastic step—for lack of proper use of the money to prepare Poland to meet EU entry requirements. The PHARE program ("Poland Hungary: Aid for the Reconstruction of Economies" at its inception in 1989, later expanded to cover all of central Europe) had a pilot function, since the EU was the coordinator for all western aid to central Europe; by the late 1990s PHARE itself was devoted solely to preparing candidates for EU membership. The EU disciplinary action, along with the public EU statement

that the first-tranche candidates might not be the first entrants after all if they did not meet requirements, was a warning to the AWS that was quietly cheered by its Freedom Union coalition partners. If Poland sloughed off and kept postponing the tough adjustments needed, the EU action further implied, Poland might also find loans from the European Bank for Reconstruction and Development curtailed. For background on EU aid to central Europe, see Ulrich Sedelmeier and Helen Wallace, "Policies Towards Central and Eastern Europe," in Helen Wallace and William Wallace, *Policy-Making in the European Union*, 3d ed. (Oxford: Oxford University Press, 1996), pp. 353–87; and Barbara Lippert and Peter Becker, eds., *Towards EU-Membership: Transformation and Integration in Poland and the Czech Republic* (Bonn: Europa Union Verlag, 1998). For accounts of Polish–EU negotiations before and after their spat, see Klaus-Peter Schmid, "Ein netter Starrkopf," *Die Zeit*, March 26, 1998, p. 2; and Lionel Barber, "The Poles' position," *Financial Times*, July 30, 1998, p. 12.

33. Interviews, Warsaw, September 1997.

34. Malachi Martin, *The Keys of This Blood: The Struggle for World Dominion between Pope John Paul II, Mikhail Gorbachev and the Capitalist West* (Simon and Schuster, 1990.)

35. Polish newspaper reports November 4–7, 1997, carried in English translation in the Polish News Bulletin.

36. Pieronek was replaced in 1998, but the shift did not change church policy on the EU.

37. For ongoing coverage of Jewish-Polish strains, see especially coverage in the *New York Times* and *Washington Post*, and in the Radio Free Europe/Radio Liberty daily *Newsline*, at <http://www.rferl.org/newsline/search/>. Examples are Jane Perlez, "A Polish Playgound Has Plenty of Ghosts to Go Around," *New York Times*, June 24, 1998; Christine Spolar, "Settling the Right to Poland's Jewish Past," *Washington Post*, April 22, 1998, p. A27; Bogdan Turek, "Tension Rises Over Crosses In Auschwitz," *RFE/RL Magazine*, August 10, 1998; and Peter Fink, "Dispute over Auschwitz Crosses Roils Polish-Jewish Relations," *Washington Post*, September 6, 1998, p. A29. In the summer of 1998 the Polish Association of War Victims, vociferously backed by Radio Marija, erected more than a hundred crosses next to the death camp in an explicitly anti-Semitic gesture. The Polish government put pressure on the church hierarchy to order removal of the crosses. The church suspended priest Ryszard Krol for putting up one of the crosses, but otherwise moved very slowly.

38. The church suspended Jankowski for a period. While this hardly muzzled him, Poles took the action as serious discipline.

39. See Elizabeth Pond, "'Shoah stirs painful memories for Poles," *Christian Science Monitor*, December 13, 1985, p. 1.

40. Interview with Sliwinski, 1996.

41. Telephone interview, November 1997.

42. Interview, Warsaw, 1996.

43. Ibid.

44. Ibid. See also Elizabeth Pond, "The Polish-Jewish Dialogue," *Harriman Review,* vol. 9. no. 3 (Summer 1996), pp. 65–68; Andrew Nagorski, "'Schindler's List' and the Polish Question," *Foreign Affairs,* vol. 73, no. 4 (July/August 1994), pp. 152–57; Piotr Wrobel, "Double Memory: Poles and Jews after the Holocaust," *Eastern European Politics and Societies,* vol. 11, no. 3 (Fall 1997), pp. 560–74; and H. H. Ben-Sasson, ed., *A History of the Jewish People,* English trans. (Harvard University Press, 1976).

45. Text provided by the Polish Embassy, Cologne.

46. Interviews with Reiter and others in Warsaw, Poznan, Wroclaw, Bonn, and Berlin. See also the interview with Polish foreign minister Bronislaw Geremak, "Heimweh nach Europa," *Die Zeit,* July 30, 1998, p. 7. Although German-Polish rapprochement was initially top-down, driven by the two governments and disliked by much of their populations, by the late 1990s it was taken for granted by ordinary citizens as well. One CBOS survey found that Germans surpassed even Americans when Poles were asked whom they most liked to work with in business and in politics: Germans ranked 77 percent and 74 percent respectively, Americans 58 percent and 67 percent. Cited in Steve Crawshaw, "Germany Looks East," *Prospect* (January 1997), pp. 50–53. The best single source on post–World War II German-Polish relations is Dieter Bingen, *Die Polenpolitik der Bonner Republik von Adenauer bis Kohl 1949–1991* (Baden-Baden: Nomos, 1998). See also Josef Füllenbach and Franz J. Klein, *Bonn und Warschau* (Bonn: Europa Union Verlag, 1977); Hans-Adolf Jacobsen and Mieczyslaw Tomala, *Bonn Warschau 1945–1991* (Cologne: Verlag Wissenschaft und Politik, 1992); the English-language journal *Polish Western Affairs* published by the Institute for Western Affairs in Poznan; issue on "The New Germany, Poland, and the Future of all-European Cooperation," *Polish Review* (New York), vol. 37, no. 4 (1992); Ewa Kobylinska, Andreas Lawaty, and Rüdiger Stephan, *Deutsche und Polen, 100 Schlüsselbegriffe* (Munich: Piper, 1992); Thomas Urban, *Deutsche in Polen* (Munich: C. H. Beck, 1993); Stephen E. Hanson and Willfried Spohn, eds., *Can Europe Work?* (University of Washington Press, 1995); Krzysztof Skubiszewski, "Deutschland: Anwalt der MOE-Staaten," *Internationale Politik* (February 1997), pp. 29–33; and Elizabeth Pond, "A Historical Reconciliation with Poland," *Transition* (Prague), February 9, 1996, pp. 9ff.

47. Interview with Rey, February 1997.

48. Interview with Kwasniewski, Davos, Switzerland, January 1998.

49. Czech president Vaclav Havel also calls NATO membership "the least expensive way to guarantee security." See the *Annual Survey of Eastern Europe and the Former Soviet Union: 1997* (Armonk: M. E. Sharpe, forthcoming 1999).

50. For a more reserved view of the status of the armed forces of NATO candidates in central Europe, see James Sherr's four-part series on "Armed Forces in Central Europe: Reform without Direction," June 1996, Conflict Studies Research Center, Royal Military Academy, Sandhurst. <gopher://marvin.nc3a.nato.int/00/secdef/csrc/g53.1%09%09%2B> for the first essay.

51. OECD, *OECD Economic Surveys: Poland 1997*, p. 120. The OECD also notes, however, that if the measure is consumer durables, then Poland is just about equal to Greece.

52. Ibid., p. 147.

53. Interview with Werner Hoyer, member of Parliament and state minister in the German Foreign Ministry, Salzburg, June 1998.

54. Investment figure from Stefan Wagstyl and Christopher Bobinski, "West is the way to eastern promise," *Financial Times*, October 27, 1998, p. 1 of special section "Poland: Finance and Investment."

55. European Commission's "opinions concerning the applications for membership in the European Union presented by the ten candidate countries," summarized in the World Bank's *Transition*, vol. 8, no. 4 (August 1997), p. 5–7.

56. Ben Partridge, "The East: Prisons: Polish System Serves as a Model," Radio Free Europe/Radio Liberty magazine, October 1, 1998 <http://www.rferl.org/nca/features/>.

57. Herman Schwartz, "Eastern Europe's Constitutional Courts," *Journal of Democracy*, vol. 9, no. 4 (October 1998), pp. 100–14.

58. "Polish inflation down to one digit," Radio Free Europe/Radio Liberty Newsline, November 18, 1998 <http://www.rferl.org/newsline/search/>.

59. For an assessment that gives high grades to the vigorous Polish press, see Wojciech Sadurski, "Freedom of the Press in Postcommunist Poland," *East European Politics and Societies*, vol. 10, no. 3 (Fall 1996), pp. 439–56.

60. OECD, *OECD Economic Surveys: Poland 1997*, p. 19. For a projection of the likely impact of entry into the EU on the Polish economy, see Zenon Wisniewski, "Effekte des EU–Beitritts auf den Arbeitsmarkt in Polen," *Osteuropa-Wirtschaft*, vol. 42, no. 3 (September 1997), pp. 293ff.

61. OECD, *OECD Economic Surveys: Poland 1997*, pp. 132f.

62. Ibid., p. 67.

63. Cyprus and Malta, with their unique geography and circumstances, are not included in this survey of central European states.

64. Two-way trade for 1994 was worth more than DM150 billion. "Kräftiger Zuwachs im Osthandel," *Frankfurter Allgemeine Zeitung*, March 31, 1995; "Osteuropa erreicht als deutscher Handelspartner das Niveau Amerikas," *Frankfurter Allgemeine Zeitung*, April 8, 1995.

65. OECD, *OECD Economic Surveys: Poland 1997*, p. 120.

66. The EU's financial aid to central Europe is modest—$3.3 billion a year for the entire region to help speed adjustment in the pre-accession period.

This is only a fraction of the $100 billion a year that western Germany has been pouring into eastern Germany. The assistance, unlike Germany's, is not intended as investment or consumer subsidies, however; the EU sees the only effective way to organic growth in the region as creating the conditions to attract private investment, as Poland, Hungary, and the Czech Republic have done.

For lessons from the Iberian transformation about what builds or destroys democracies, see Juan J. Linz and Alfred Stepan, *Problems of Democratic Transition and Consolidation* (Johns Hopkins Univerity Press, 1996); Guillermo O'Donnell, Philippe C. Schmitter, and Laurence Whitehead, *Transitions from Authoritarian Rule* (Johns Hopkins University Press, 1986), especially in that book Philippe C. Schmitter, "An Introduction to Southern European Transitions from Authoritarian Rule: Italy, Greece, Portugal, Spain, and Turkey," pp. 3–10, and Adam Przeworski, "Some Problems in the Study of the Transition to Democracy," pp. 47–63; and Adam Przeworski, *Democracy and the Market: Political and Economic Reforms in Eastern Europe and Latin America* (Cambridge University Press, 1991). For other general studies of the difficulty of introducing democratic systems, see Ernest Gellner, *Conditions of Liberty: Civil Society and Its Rivals* (New York: Penguin, 1994); Giuseppe Di Palma, *To Craft Democracies* (University of California Press, 1990); and Robert D. Putnam, "Bowling Alone," *Journal of Democracy* (January 1995), pp. 65–78. The *Journal of Democracy* consistently carries essays exploring the hard work required to turn formal elections into real liberal democracies, especially in light of the repeated failure to do so in South America. *East European Politics and Societies*, vol. 10, no. 3 (Fall 1996) also explores this issue in articles by Vladimir Tismanean, "The Leninist Debris or Waiting for Peron," pp. 504ff; and Daniel Cirot, "Why East Central Europe Is Not Quite Ready for Peron, but May Be One Day," pp. 536ff. See also Martin Krygier, "Virtuous Circles: Antipodean Reflections on Power, Institutions, and Civic Society," *East European Politics and Societies*, vol. 11, no. 1 (Winter 1997), pp. 36–88; Stephen Haggard and Robert R. Kaufman, *The Political Economy of Democratic Transitions* (Princeton University Press, 1995); Mary Kaldor and Ivan Vejvoda, "Democratization in Central and Eastern European Countries," *International Affairs*, vol. 73, no. 1 (1997), pp. 59–82; Josef Novak, "The Precarious Triumph of Civil Society," *Transition*, January 10, 1997, pp. 11ff; Fareed Zakaria, "The Rise of Illiberal Democracy," *Foreign Affairs*, vol. 76, no. 6 (November/December 1997), pp. 22–43; Ellen Comisso, "Is the Glass Half Full or Half Empty?" *Communist and Post-Communist Studies*, vol. 30, no. 1, pp. 1–21; Jakob Juchler, "Probleme der Demokratisierung in den osteuropäischen Transformations-Ländern," *Osteuropa*, vol. 47, no. 9 (September 1997), pp. 898–913.

For broad early studies of the transformation in central Europe, see John Pinder, *The European Community and Eastern Europe* (New York: Council on Foreign Relations Press, 1991); John R. Lampe, ed., *Creating Capital Markets in Eastern Europe* (Washington: Woodrow Wilson Center Press, 1992); Bundesinstitut für ostwissenschaftliche und internationale Studien (Cologne), *Aufbruch im Osten Europas* (Munich: Carl Hanser, 1993); Jerzy Hausner and Grzegorz Mosue, eds., *Transformation Processes in Eastern Europe: Western Perspectives and the Polish Experience* (Krakow: Friedrich Ebert Stiftung and Polish Academy of Sciences, 1993); A. E. Dick Howard, ed., *Constitution Making in Eastern Europe* (Washington: Woodrow Wilson Center Press, 1993); Romuald Holly, ed., *Political Consciousness and Civic Education during the Transformation of the System* (Warsaw: Polish Academy of Sciences, 1994); and Joan M. Nelson, ed., *Precarious Balance* (San Francisco: Institute for Contemporary Studies, 1994).

67. The classic checklist of minimal democratic requirements is to be found in Robert A. Dahl, *Democracy and Its Critics* (Yale University Press, 1989).

68. For a thoughtful discussion of "Ethnic Conflict and International Security" as viewed at the height of the atrocities in the former Yugoslavia and before NATO intervention there, see the whole issue of *Survival*, vol. 35, no. 1 (Spring 1993).

69. Interview with Wolfgang Ischinger, political director in the German Foreign Ministry, January 1998; David Buchan, "U.S. planning reward for Milosevic," *Financial Times*, February 23, 1998, p. 2.

70. The fragile nature of gains was illustrated, however, when more ultra-nationalist Serbs won subsequent elections in September 1998.

Chapter Seven

1. Andrei Piontkovsky, head of the Moscow Center for Strategic Studies, makes this point explicitly in "Window of Opportunity: How Russia Might Fit into the International Scheme," in the Jamestown Foundation's Prism 22, part 2, November 13, 1998, carried in David Johnson List #2479, November 16, 1998, available from <davidjohnson@erols.com>.

2. Timothy Heritage, "Analysis: What Next for Russia after Starovoitova?" Reuters, Moscow, November 24, 1998.

3. Clifford Gaddy and Barry Ickes, "Beyond a Bail-Out: Time to Face Reality about Russia's 'Virtual Economy,'" (Brookings, 1998) <http://www.brook.edu/fp/w-papers/gaddy/gaddick1.htm>.

4. Geoffrey Hosking, "We Must Stop Demanding of Russians What We Would Never Tolerate Ourselves," *Independent*, August 29, 1998, in David Johnson List #2322, August 29, 1998.

5. These statistics are all taken from Brown University's Stephen Shenfield, in "On the Threshold of Disaster: The Socio-Economic Situation in Russia," in David Johnson List #3245, July 2, 1998.

6. President Yeltsin told a conference on crime in February 1993 that two-thirds of private companies and 40 percent of businessmen were involved in corruption. Viktor Ilyukhincho of the Duma Security Committee said in May 1994 that 55 percent of capital was in mafia hands. Cited in James Sherr, "Russia, Geopolitics and Crime," CSRC, Royal Military Academy Sandhurst, <gopher://marvin.nc3a.nato.int/00/secdef/csrc2.1%09%09%2B>. The *Economist* of July 4, 1998, identified "criminal infiltration of state bodies that have the power to snoop and confiscate" as "one of the most sinister developments in Russia." ("The Russian mafia means business," p. 64.) And Transparency International, on the basis of questionnaires to international businessmen and others, ranked Russia just behind Nigeria as second worst on its list of corruption in 1996; Russia improved on Transparency International's 1998 list for a ranking of tenth worst.

For representative discussions of the intertwined criminal, economic, and political worlds and some comparisons with Poland, see also Antoni K. Kaminski, "The New Polish Regime and the Specter of Economic Corruption," Woodrow Wilson Center paper, April 3, 1996; Dieter Bingen, "Zwischen Raum und Wirklichkeit," *Internationale Politik*, vol. 52, no. 1 (January 1997), pp. 69–72; Kurt Schelter, "Bedrohung durch die russische Mafia," *Internationale Politik*, vol. 52, no. 1 (January 1997), pp. 31–36; and David Satter, "The Rise of the Russian Criminal State," *Jamestown Foundation Prism*, September 4, 1998, <brdcast@mx.jamestown.org>; Ol'ga Kryshtanovskaya, "Russia's Illegal Structures," in Klaus Segbers and Stephan De Spiegeleire, eds., *Post-Soviet Puzzles* (Baden-Baden: Nomos, 1995), vol. III, pp. 591–614; Igor' Sundiev, "Criminological Components of the Current Social Dynamics in Russia," in Segbers and De Spiegeleire, *Post-Soviet Puzzles*, pp. 615–34; and Donald N. Jensen, "How Russia Is Ruled—1998," <http://www.rferl.org/nca/special/ruwhorules/index.html>.

7. Fred Hiatt, "Russia's Iron Lady," *Washington Post*, November 16, 1998.

8. Clay Harris and Jeremy Grant, "World's exposure exceeds $200bn," *Financial Times*, August 28, 1998, p. 3.

9. "Wäre George Soros nicht gewesen, hätten wir es in Russland geschafft," *Frankfurter Allgemeine Zeitung*, August 24, 1998, p. 17.

10. Susan Eisenhower, "A Summit for Listening," *Washington Post*, September 1, 1998, p. A19.

11. In the October 1998 issue of *Esquire*, cited without headline in David Johnson List #2394, September 24, 1998.

12. Gaddy and Ickes, "Beyond a Bail-Out."

13. Dmitri K. Simes, "Don't Mess with Russia's Self-Rule," *Newsday*, September 23, 1998.

14. Richard Pipes, "Russia's Past, Russia's Future," *Commentary* (June 1996), pp. 30ff.

15. Anders Åslund, "Post-communist report card," *Financial Times*, August 5, 1998, p. 10.

16. Ernest Gellner, *Conditions of Liberty: Civil Society and Its Rivals* (New York: Penguin, 1994), p. 148 (emphasis in the original). Examining why the Enlightenment notion of civil society was revived among humanist dissidents in central Europe in the 1980s, Gellner defines the phenomenon as "that set of diverse non-governmental institutions which is strong enough to counterbalance the state and, while not preventing the state from fulfilling its role of keeper of the peace and arbitrator among major interests, can nevertheless prevent it from dominating and atomizing the rest of society" (p. 5). See also Francis Fukuyama, *The Social Virtues and the Creation of Prosperity* (New York: Free Press, 1995); and Bronislaw Geremek and others, *The Idea of a Civil Society* (Research Triangle Park, N.C.: National Humanities Center, 1992).

17. John Thornhill, "Moscow mayor blames IMF advice for Russia's woes," *Financial Times*, September 24, 1998, p. 2.

18. See David Marples, "Belarus: An Analysis of the Lukashenka Regime," *Harriman Review* (Spring 1997), vol. 10, no. 1, pp. 24ff; Kathleen J. Mihalisko, "Belarus, Moldova, and Ukraine," in Karen Dawisha and Bruce Parrott, eds., *Democratic Changes and Authoritarian Reactions in Russia, Ukraine, Belarus, and Moldova* (Cambridge: Cambridge University Press, 1997), pp. 223–81; running RFE/RL Newsline reports.

19. Exchange in Salzburg, June 1998.

20. Interview, Warsaw, September 1997.

21. G. M. Tamas, "Socialism, Capitalism, and Modernity," in Larry Diamond and Marc F. Plattner, *Capitalism, Socialism, and Democracy Revisited* (Johns Hopkins University Press, 1993), p. 67.

22. The earliest serious economic study to reach this conclusion was Ivan Koropeckyj, ed., *The Ukraine within the USSR: An Economic Balance Sheet* (New York: Praeger, 1977).

23. George Gamota, "Science, Technology and Conversion in Ukraine," MITRE, March 1993.

24. See Daniel Williams and R. Jeffrey Smith, "U.S. Intelligence Sees Economic Plight Leading to Breakup of Ukraine," *Washington Post*, January 25, 1994, p. 7.

25. Interviews, Antoni Kaminski, Warsaw, March 1997 and earlier.

26. The U.S. ambassador to Poland, Nicholas Rey, used this image about football teams with good substitute players in February 1997 as one excellent finance minister was suddenly succeeded by another in Warsaw.

27. To be fair, Yavlinsky does not regard his choice as only one between being a big fish in a provincial pond or a small fish in the more exciting Russian pond. He explains that as a Jewish politician he would be targeted as a scapegoat for hardship in Ukraine in a way that he is not in Russia.

28. Interview in Donetsk with Vladimir Shcherban, then Donetsk governor, head of the Liberal party, and member of parliament, 1996.

29. Interviews, Kyiv, February and March, 1997.

30. Interview with presidential chief of staff Yevhen P. Kushnariov, Kyiv, February 1998.

31. Interview, Kyiv, September 1997.

32. One of the more bizarre comparisons is that wage arrears account for only 35 percent of GDP in Russia but well over 100 percent in Ukraine.

33. Peter K. Cornelius and Patrick Lenain, eds., *Ukraine: Accelerating the Transition to Market* (Washington: International Monetary Fund, 1997), p. 98. See also Michelle Riboud and Hoaquan Chu, "Pension Reform, Growth, and the labor market in Ukraine," World Bank Policy Research Working Paper 1731, February 1997; and TACIS, *Ukrainian Economic Trends*, quarterly issues and updates (Brussels: European Commission, August 1998).

34. See Louise Shelley, "The Price Tag of Russia's Organized Crime," *Transition* 8 (World Bank, February 1997), pp. 7f; and Kevin Done, "Investors give E Europe a miss," *Financial Times*, April 15, 1997, p. 2.

35. See Elizabeth Pond, "Letter from Kiev: Crisis, 1997 Style," *Washington Quarterly*, vol. 20, no. 4 (Autumn 1997), pp. 79–87; Ilya Prizel, "Ukraine between proto-democracy and 'soft' authoritarianism," in Dawisha and Parrott, *Democratic Changes and Authoritarian Reactions*, pp. 330–69; F. Stephen Larrabee, "Ukraine's Balancing Act," *Survival*, vol. 38, no. 2 (Summer 1996), pp. 143–65; the whole issue of *Harriman Review*, vol. 10, no. 3 (Winter 1997) on "Ukrainian National Security"; and Taras Kuzio, *Ukraine under Kuchma* (Basingstoke: Macmillan, 1997).

36. Volodymyr Mukhin, chairman of the Defense and Security Committee of the Ukrainian Supreme Rada, on a visit to Bonn in 1996.

37. Conversation, Kyiv, 1995.

38. For an analysis of the most focused elite opinion poll, see Evgenii Golovakha, "Elites in Ukraine: Evaluation of the Project's Elite Survey" in Segbers and De Spiegeleire, eds., *Post-Soviet Puzzles*, pp. 167–241.

39. Interview in *Nezavisimaya gazeta*, February 5, 1997; translated into English in Foreign Broadcast Information Service, February 6, 1997.

Chapter Eight

1. The Lombard rate is one of the rates for banks to get overnight loans from the central bank.

2. Andreatta at the German-Italian Colloquium on "Europe and the Challenge of Globalization," Bonn, April 1, 1998. See also Friedhelm Gröteke, "Märchen von Alice im Wunderland," *Die Zeit*, April 23, 1998, p. 28; the interview with Italian finance minister Ciampi, "Problem erkannt," *Die Zeit*, April 23, 1998, p. 29; James Blitz and Martin Wolf, "Ciampi defies odds on monetary union," *Financial Times*, May 7, 1998, p 3; "Promoted to Europe's premier league," *Financial Times*, June 15, 1998, p. 1 of

survey of Italy; "Italy's government soldiers on, but for how long?" *Economist*, July 4, 1998, pp. 25f.

3. David White, "New connections start to bring change to an ancient frontier," *Financial Times*, June 16, 1998, p. 3.

4. Fintan O'Toole, "Peace in Northern Ireland Moves into the Realm of the Possible," *Washington Post*, April 12, 1998, p. C1.

5. Giuseppe Di Palma, *To Craft Democracies* (University of California Press, 1990).

6. Ernst-Moritz Lipp, member of the Dresdner Bank board, and Hans-Olaf Henkel, president of the Federal Association of German Industry (BDI), at the German-Italian Colloquium, Bonn, April 1998; Jeffrey Sachs, "The Last Resort," *World Link*, March/April 1998, pp. 6f.

7. Until then, the EBRD had been a French fief, and Chirac expected it to continue as such. The other nations that set up the bank in the early 1990s were sufficiently angered by Chirac's stonewalling, however, that they demonstratively left the post vacant for more than half a year and finally appointed Köhler.

8. "The euro could hardly have had a worse start," scolded Eberhard Wisdorff in "Schwere Hypothek," *Handelsblatt*, May 4, 1998, p. 2. The leaders "gambled away a chance to convince citizens that the new money will be hard," asserted Peter Hort in "Schatten auf der Währungsunion," *Frankfurter Allgemeine Zeitung*, May 4, 1998, p. 1. Kohl "leaves the Eurobattle defeated," and the decision "gives German Euroskeptics [a] boost," concluded Andreas Oldag in "Schwere Geburt," *Süddeutsche Zeitung*, May 5, 1998, p. 4. The boulevard *Bild* joined the chorus in "Euro: The dirty compromise," May 4, 1998, p. 1—but kept the proper perspective by placing this story below its announcement of the simultaneous, ignominious fall of Cologne's First Football Club into the second league. In the event, German markets seconded *Bild*'s priority and rose helpfully, despite what Kohl called his "dogfight" with Chirac. See also Lionel Barber, "Wim-Claude Trichenberg," *Financial Times*, May 4, 1998, p. 15; "The euro: single currency, multiple injuries," *Financial Times*, May 5, 1998, p. 2; and Michael Stabenow, "Nur Santer und Blair können beim Familienfoto mühelos lächeln," *Frankfurter Allgemeine Zeitung*, May 4, 1998, p 3. For unconvincing denials that Tietmeyer ever threatened to resign, see "Bundesbank dementiert Tietmeyer-Rücktritt," *Süddeutsche Zeitung*, May 6, 1998, p. 30; and Christian Wernicke, "Der Sündenfall von Brüssel," *Die Zeit*, May 7, 1998, pp. 2f. A few days later, Chirac apologized to Kohl at their own bilateral summit, saying, according to one German official, he had not realized his implicit veto against the fourteen other EU heads of government would bring such domestic political trouble for Kohl. The French president is "an unguided missile," asserted another German official in an interview in May 1998, fastidiously quoting the *Economist*.

9. Barry Riley, "Aim for bourse without borders," *Financial Times*, May 18, 1998, p. 15.

10. On this topic the literature is so vast and burgeoning that no attempt is made to provide references beyond a few general surveys: Barry Eichengreen, *European Monetary Union: Theory, Practice, Analysis* (MIT Press, 1997); Kathleen R. McNamara, *The Currency of Ideas: Monetary Politics in the European Union* (Cornell University Press, 1998); Paul R. Masson, Thomas H. Krueger, and Bart G. Turtelbloom, *EMU and the International Monetary System* (Washington: International Monetary Fund, 1997); statements by C. Randall Henning, "American Interests and Europe's Monetary Union," before the U.S. Senate Committee on the Budget, October 21, 1997, and "Europe's Monetary Union, the United States, and International Cooperation," before the U.S. House of Representatives Subcommittee on Domestic and International Monetary Policy, April 18, 1998; Daniel Gros and Niels Thygesen, *Economic Monetary Integration* (Harlow: Longman, 1992/98); Thomas Hanke and Norbert Walter, *Der Euro—Kurs auf die Zukunft*, 3d ed. (Frankfurt: Campus, 1998); Reimer von Borries and Wolfgang Glomb, *Beck-Ratgeber Euro-Währung* (Munich: C. H. Beck, 1997); Albert Bressand, ed., *Strategic Conversations on the Euro at the Vanguard of Global Integration* (Paris: Prométhée and Ernst & Young, 1998); *Financial Times*, special section on "The Birth of the Euro," April 30, 1998; and Pierre Jacquet, "EMU: a worthwhile gamble," *International Affairs*, vol. 94, no. 1 (January 1998), pp. 55–71.

11. John Peet, "An Awfully Big Adventure," special section, *Economist*, April 11, 1998.

12. Estimated by the Federal Association of German Industry [BDI]; cited in Hanke and Walter, *Der Euro*, p. 116.

13. Telephone interview, April 1998.

14. Edward Luce and Vincent Boland, "Retreat from Moscow takes investors back to German safe haven," *Financial Times*, September 1, 1998, p. 2.

15. Simon Davie, "Powerful force for change," *Financial Times*, euro special section, April 30, 1998, p. 6.

16. Ernst-Moritz Lipp, member of the Dresdner Bank board, at the German-Italian Colloquium, Bonn, April 1998; and Werner Seifert, CEO of the Deutsche Boerse, at the World Economic Forum, Davos, January 1998.

17. George Graham and Simon Davies, "London and Frankfurt exchanges set for alliance," *Financial Times*, July 8, 1998, p. 1; Vincent Boland, David White, and Paul Betts, "Madrid and Milan back pan-Europe exchange," *Financial Times*, November 19, 1998, p. 1.

18. Hugo Dixon, "EMU's capital consequences," *Financial Times*, April 30, 1998, p. 17. For the portrait of a rare German venture capitalist of the new breed and his pioneer listing on the new Neuer Markt for innovative companies, see Ralph Atkins, "An upwardly mobile star," *Financial Times*,

April 30, 1998, p. 14. For the broad German shift away from family-owned and bank-financed firms to equity financing, see Graham Bowley, "Corporate Germany reaping the rewards of risk-taking," *Financial Times*, August 11, 1998, p. 14.

19. John Murray Brown, "Eve of an emerald era," *Financial Times*, September 22, 1998, p. 1 of special section on Ireland.

20. "An uncommon market," *Economist*, July 4, 1998, p. 80.

21. See, for example, Horst Siebert, "Monetary carrots and fiscal sticks," *World Link*, March/April 1998, pp. 4f.

22. Dornbusch, "Euro Fantasies," *Foreign Affairs*, vol. 75, no. 5 (September/October 1996), pp. 110–24; Feldstein, "EMU and International Conflict," *Foreign Affairs*, vol. 76, no. 6 (November/December 1997), pp. 60–73; Milton Friedman, "Why Europe can't afford the euro. The danger of a common currency," *Times* (London), November 19, 1997; interview with James Tobin, "'Ein schlimmes Beispiel,'" *Die Zeit*, March 28, 1998, p. 31. However, Dornbusch in person was much more relaxed about EMU prospects at the Davos Economic Summit in January 1998, telling journalists that he had meant only that EMU would not solve unemployment, not that inflexible labor would sabotage the unified European economy. For two other fiercely negative American readings shortly before final adoption of EMU plans in 1998, see Irving Kristol, "Petrified Europe," *Wall Street Journal Europe*, February 2, 1998; and William Safire, "Alice in Euroland," *New York Times*, April 30. 1998. For a critical German view that EMU cannot work without changing human nature, see Rudolf Augstein, "Neue Menschen, neue Menschen!" *Der Spiegel*, April 27, 1998, pp. 102f.

23. Robert A. Mundell, "The International Impact of the Euro and Its Implications for the Transition Countries," paper at the fourth Dubrovnik Conference on the Transition Economies, June 23–26, 1998. See also Martin Wolf, "Euro's world test," *Financial Times*, July 7, 1998, p. 16. Others who held a positive view of EMU were Fred Bergsten and Randall Henning of the Institute for International Economics.

24. See, for example, Martin Wolf, "Strange love/Or how I have not stopped worrying but learned to love the euro," *Financial Times*, May 5, 1998, p. 20.

25. German-Italian colloquium, Bonn, April 1998.

26. World Economic Forum, Davos, February 1998.

27. World Economic Forum, Davos, February 1998.

28. Wolfgang Streeck, "German Capitalism: Does It Exist? Can It Survive?" in Colin Crouch and Wolfgang Streeck, eds., *Modern Capitalism or Modern Capitalisms?* (London: Francis Pinter, 1995).

29. "Sir Leon Brittan," *World Link*, March/April, 1998, pp. 12f.

30. Warnfried Dettling, "Koalition der Ideen," *Die Zeit*, May 7, 1998, p. 11.

31. Wolfgang Münchau, "Prepared for EMU? It's time to live with the euro," *Financial Times*, April 28, 1998, p. 3.

32. Interviews, Bonn. See also "Franco-German fractures," editorial, *Financial Times*, May 6, 1998, p. 13.

33. *OECD Economic Surveys, Germany* (Paris, 1998). Germany's visible trade surplus hit record highs in 1997 and 1998 of more than $60 billion; its 1998 current accounts deficit was heading down toward only about $1 billion as of this writing.

34. Dornbusch at the Davos Economic Forum, January 1998.

35. See, for example, the consultants' report on competitiveness written for the European Commission in 1998. It found that GDP per capita in Europe is a third lower than in the United States because of the failure to create service jobs. Emma Tucker, "Europe outpaced by US on competition, says report," *Financial Times*, November 16, 1998, p. 18. See also the widely noted speech by German president Roman Herzog at the Hotel Adlon in Berlin on 26 April, 1997, available at <http://www.bundespraesident.de/txt/vi-00.htm>. Within the CDU, Kohl, who is no economist, never displayed much interest in restructuring. Among conservatives Schäuble has been the point man for reform.

36. Graham Bowley, "Europe looks to Germany to provide shield from emerging markets fall-out," *Financial Times*, September 1, 1998, p. 20.

37. The 60 percent figure is cited by businessmen who are campaigning for its reduction. It includes the 45 percent federal tax on undistributed profits (distributed profits are taxed 30 percent), plus a roughly 15 percent local tax on large businesses. There are, however, so many loopholes that critics charge that many of the richest Germans and companies escape paying taxes altogether. The highest federal income tax category is 53 percent (with no local income tax); to this is added an 8 or 9 percent church tax on the tax levy, plus a 5.5 percent "solidarity surcharge" to finance reconstruction in east Germany.

38. Wolfgang Schäuble at the German-Italian Colloquium, Bonn, April 1998. German Finance Ministry figures from 1996 show an estimated 48 percent state share of GDP for 1998, and a targeted 46 percent for 2000.

39. Ernst-Moritz Lipp at the German-Italian Colloquium, Bonn, April 1998. For a sampling of other discussions about the need for Germany and Europe to shake up their rigidities, but also of the problems this will trigger in social security, see Robert Taylor, "New strategies called for," *Financial Times*, April 30, 1998, special section, p. 2; Dirk Meyer, "The Provisions of the German Charitable Welfare System and the Challenge of the Free Market," *German Studies Review*, vol. 20, no. 3 (October 1997), pp. 371–98; and Jürgen von Hagen, "Von der Deutschen Mark zum Euro," *Aus Politik und Zeitgeschichte Beilage zu Das Parlament*, B24, June 5, 1998, pp. 35–46.

40. *OECD Economic Surveys.*

41. German Federal Statistical Office.

42. For an eloquent portrayal of the view that east Germans are the ones who are being sacrificed to the euro and global competitiveness, see Irwin L.

Collier Jr., "The Twin Curse of the Goddess Europa and the Economic Reconstruction of Eastern Germany," *German Studies Review*, vol. 20, no. 3 (October 1997), pp. 399–428. For the authoritative refutation of a "Mezzogiorno-scenario," see "Gesamtwirtschaftliche und unternehmerische Anpassungsfortschritte in Ostdeutschland" (18th combined economics institutes' report), *Deutsches Institut für Wirtschaftsforschung Wochenbericht*, vol. 65, no. 33 (August 13, 1998).

43. Editorial, "Goldilocks on speed," *Financial Times*, April 25, 1998, p. 6.

44. Dominique Moisi, "The Trouble with France," *Foreign Affairs*, vol. 77, no. 3 (May/June 1998), pp. 94–104; Dominique Moisi, "A fresh direction," *Financial Times*, May 11, 1998, p. 14; Robert Graham, "France cuts working week to 35 hours," *Financial Times*, May 20, 1998, p. 2.

45. "It's no laughing matter."

46. See Robert Graham, "Dose of realism for France," *Financial Times*, August 17, 1998. Graham cites the annual report of the Bank of France by Jean-Claude Trichet in late 1998 as pressing for a reduction of the 54.1 percent share of public spending in GDP toward the EU average at 48.2 percent and the G-7 average at 38.3 percent.

47. "Franco-German fractures," editorial, *Financial Times*, May 6, 1998, p. 13.

48. Group interview, April, 1998. For an assessment of bilateral relations before German unification, see Julius W. Friend, *The Linchpin: French-German Relations, 1950–1990* (Washington: CSIS, 1991). For evaluations in the 1990s, see Patrick McCarthy, ed., *France-Germany 1983–1993* (New York: St. Martin's, 1993) and David P. Calleo and Eric R. Staal, eds., *Europe's Franco-German Engine* (Brookings/SAIS, 1998).

49. For the traditional German point of view fiercely defending the independence of the ECB against any encroachment by the euro-11 finance ministers, see Wilhelm Schönfelder and Elke Thiel, "Stabilitätspakt und Euro-X-Gremium-Die stabilitätspolitische Untermauerung der WWU," *Integration* (Bonn), vol. 21, no. 2 (April 1998), pp. 69–76.

50. OECD figures, given in The *Economist*, August 8, 1998, p. 87. See also Lionel Barber, "Brussels sees EU eastward expansion without budget rise," *Financial Times*, June 26, 1996, p. 1.

51. He spoke in this vein, for example, at the EU Commission representation office in Bonn, December 3, 1997.

52. For an overview of EU farm policy, see K. A. Ingersent, A. J. Rayner, and Robert C. Hine, eds., *The Reform of the Common Agricultural Policy* (Basingstoke: Macmillan, 1998).

53. *Financial Times* editorial, "Franco-German fractures," May 6, 1998, p. 13.

54. "Frankreich muss mehr in EU-Kasse einzahlen," *Süddeutsche Zeitung*, September 17, 1998, p. B1.

55. Klaus Hänsch, "Zwei Konzepte für ein Europa?" *Frankfurter Allgemeine*

Zeitung, April 24, 1998, p. 11; Gerald Braunberger, "In der Wagenburg," *Frankfurter Allgemeine Zeitung*, April 22, 1998, p. 17. See also the warnings in the whole issue of *Internationale Politik* devoted to "Deutschland-Frankreich: Tandem auf Schlingerkurs," September 1998.

56. Timothy Garton Ash, "Europe's Endangered Liberal Order," *Foreign Affairs*, vol. 77, no. 2 (March/April 1998), pp. 51–65; and Mitsuko Uchida, "Chalk and cheese," *Prospect*, February 1998, pp. 124–28.

57. Eberhard Wisdorff, "Bonn fordert strikte Anwendung der Subsidiarität/ Kohl und die Kompetenzen der EU," *Handelsblatt*, May 6, 1998, p. 2; "Freier Markt für Europas Patienten," *Süddeutsche Zeitung*, April 29, 1998, p. 1.

58. For two studies of the connections—and some concern that the EU may use failure to agree on deepening as an alibi to postpone widening—see Christopher Preston, *Enlargement and Integration in the European Union* (London: Routledge, 1997); and Heather Grabbe and Kirsty Hughes, *Enlarging the EU Eastwards* (London: Royal Institute of International Affairs, 1998).

59. In this sense the repeated American criticism of the EU for trailing NATO in taking in new EU members would seem to be overdrawn. U.S. Treasury secretary Robert Rubin, for example, reiterated this complaint on the eve of the G-8 summit in 1998. "G8 minister urged to reform and widen horizons," *Financial Times*, May 9. 1998, p. 1.

60. Michael Smith, "Steel obstacle on Poland's road to EU," *Financial Times*, November 28, 1998, p. 3; Christopher Bobinski, "EU tussles with Poland over aid," *Financial Times*, May 12, 1998, p. 3; Janusz Tycner, "Vom Leben im Türrahmen," *Die Zeit*, May 14, 1998, p. 51.

61. See Alan Mayher, *Recreating Europe: The European Union's Policy toward Central and Eastern Europe* (Cambridge: Cambridge University Press, 1998).

62. Fiona Hayes-Renshaw and Helen Wallace, *The Council of Ministers* (New York: St. Martin's, 1997).

63. Peter Norman and Ralph Atkins, "Schröder proposes alliance to cut German joblessness" (p. 1), and "Germany's modernizer" (p. 14), *Financial Times*, May 11, 1998.

64. On lobbying by the estimated 13,000 "interest representatives" already in place in Brussels, see Helen Wallace and William Wallace, *Policy-Making in the European Union* (Oxford: Oxford University Press, 1996); Sonia Mazey and Jeremy Richardson, eds., *Lobbying in the European Community* (Oxford: Oxford University Press, 1993); Helen Wallace and Alasdair Young, eds., *Participation and Policy-Making in the European Union* (Oxford: Clarendon, 1997); Justin Greenwood and Mark Aspinwall, eds., *Collective Action in the European Union: Interests and the New Politics of Associability* (London: Routledge, 1998); Justin Greenwood, *Representing Interests in the European Union* (Basingstoke: Macmillan, 1997); Claus Schnabel and Rüdiger Tiedemann, "Brüsseler Spitzen—gefragt wie nie," *Frank-*

furter Allgemeine Zeitung, February 11, 1995, p. 13; Lionel Barber, "Lobbyists in search of a fast Ecu," *Financial Times*, January 27, 1997, p. 8; R. Pedler and M. C. P. M. van Schendelen, eds., *Lobbying the European Union* (Aldershot: Dartmouth, 1994); H. Randall, ed., *Business Guide to Lobbying in the EU* (London: Cartermill, 1996); and "The Brussels lobbyist and the struggle for ear-time," *Economist*, August 15, 1998, p. 25.

65. European Commission, "Agenda 2000: Überblick über die Legislativvorschläge der Europäischen Kommission," March 19, 1998.

66. Martin Wolf, "Union that defies modern taboos," *Financial Times*, April 30, 1998, special section, p. 3.

Chapter Nine

1. Testimony before the Senate Budget Committee, October 21, 1997, "Europe's Monetary Union and Its Potential Impact on the United States Economy," October 21, 1997, Government Printing Office, pp. 6–18.

2. Clinton statement, May 3, 1998. Text provided by the U.S. Embassy, Bonn.

3. A long profile of Rubin in the *New York Times Magazine* suggested by omission that, a half year before launch, European Monetary Union was not yet on the policy agenda in Washington. While the yen, the won, and the peso all figured in the article, the euro was not mentioned once. See Jacob Weisberg, "Keeping the Boom from Busting," July 19, 1998.

4. May 1998.

5. Henry Kissinger, "Chance und Risiko der Währungsunion," *Welt am Sonntag*, May 10, 1998, p. 34.

6. This warning was issued in the IMF *World Economic Outlook* special section, "EMU and the World Economy," October 1997.

7. IMF figures for 1996 cited in the *Economist* special section, April 11, 1998; Vicki Barnett, "Watch out, dollar," *Financial Times*, April 23, 1997, p. 19.

8. IMF, *World Economic Outlook*, October 1997.

9. C. Fred Bergsten, "The Dollar and the Euro," *Foreign Affairs*, vol. 76, no. 4 (July/August 1997), pp. 83–95; *Economist* special section on EMU, April 11, 1998; Charles Grant, "Fixed fortunes," *WorldLink*, May/June 1998, pp. 6f; Richard W. Stevenson, "Euro Could Eventually Rival the Dollar," *New York Times*, April 28, 1998. Bergsten does not himself set a figure on the likely size of dollar depreciation beyond saying that it would be "substantial."

10. The cumulative figures are as calculated by Robert A. Mundell in "The International Impact of the Euro and its Implications for the Transition Countries," paper presented at the Dubrovnik Conference on Transitional Econo-

mies, June 22–24, 1998, p. 13. Mundell ascribes the difference between American current account deficits and net capital inflows to foreign use of $700 billion as dollar reserves. See also Lexington column, "Dow and out," *Financial Times*, September 1, 1998, p. 18; and Simon Kuper, "Dollar becomes casualty of turmoil," *Financial Times*, September 1, 1998, p. 29.

11. Erik Peterson, director of studies at the Center for Strategic and International Studies (CSIS), at the World Economic Forum in Davos, January 1998.

12. EU president Jacques Santer at the World Economic Forum in Davos, January 1998.

13. Richard Waters, Gerard Baker, and Philip Coggan, "Severe and risky correction," *Financial Times*, September 2, 1998, p. 11.

14. The precise share of the United States and the EU varies according to the year, the calculation, and the exchange rates used. Yves-Thibault de Silguy, "Now for the real test," *Financial Times*, May 4, 1998, p. 14, puts the share at one-fifth of world output. *Financial Times* editorial page, in "A world in turmoil," August 29, 1998, p. 6, sets it at 30 percent. See also *OECD in Figures*, 1998 edition; Bergsten, "The Dollar and the Euro"; and "Welcome to Euroland," *Financial Times*, April 30, 1998, p. 4, of the "Birth of the euro" special section.

15. Andrew Fisher, "Listening—and learning," *Financial Times*, June 24, 1998, special section on German banking and finance, p. 3.

16. Hugo Dixon, "EMU's capital consequences," *Financial Times*, April 30, 1998, p. 17. Put another way, OECD figures show equities as constituting almost 39 percent of personal sector net wealth in the United States, but only 8 percent and 13 percent in Germany and France, respectively. Waters, Baker, and Coggan, "Severe and risky correction."

17. Edward Luce, "A cloud over Frankfurt's ambitions," *Financial Times*, June 24, 1998, special section on German banking and finance, p. 2.

18. Andrew Fisher, "Euro offers promise of bright new horizons," *Financial Times*, June 24, 1998, special section on German banking and finance, p. 1.

19. Undersecretary of State Stuart Eizenstat, speech at Johns Hopkins University, May 4, 1998.

20. Charles Goldsmith, "Powerful Updraft at Airbus Creates Turbulence at Boeing," *Wall Street Journal Europe*, March 16, 1998, p. 1.

21. See Alexander Nicoll, David Owen, and Robert Graham, "France bites a bullet," *Financial Times*, July 24, 1998, p. 15; and Charles Grant, "Europe Outgunned," *World Link* (March/April 1998), pp. 38ff. Both the British-German negotiations on an aerospace merger and the London-Frankfurt stock exchange "alliance" have been flagged by younger Germans as a sign that their generation no longer shares the guilt that made their fathers cling to a special German-French relationship.

22. The EU's zealous antitrust commissioner, Karel van Miert, it should be noted, is just as tough on intra-European or even intra-German mergers and also blocked the planned union of the Bertelsmann media giant with movie magnate Leo Kirch.

23. See U.S. Defense Under Secretary Jacques S. Gansler's paper, "Changes in Technology and Warfare," at the annual IISS conference, September 1998. More surprisingly, many U.S. defense industry executives also share Gansler's preference for transatlantic cooperation over the old "Buy American" approach in defense procurement. At the annual Munich security conference in February 1998 Vance D. Coffman, CEO and vice chairman of Lockheed Martin Corporation, noted the post–cold war downsizing of defense spending and urged on the U.S. "an unprecedented willingness to be dependent on others— even close and trusted allies—for some of the means to protect our security." For one example of a U.S. defense corporation buying into European producers, see Peter Marsh, "European strategy pays off for Textron," *Financial Times*, September 15, 1998, p. 29.

24. "Deutschland über alles?" *Economist*, July 4, 1998, pp. 63f.

25. He initially called it the New Transatlantic Marketplace, then, when he ran into staunch French resistance to the idea, rechristened it the less offensive Transatlantic Economic Partnership. See Christian Wernicke, "Atlantischer Zündstoff/Die Europäische Kommission will den Handel mit den VS weitgehend liberalisieren," *Die Zeit*, March 12, 1998, p. 35; and the special section on "The world trade system at 50," *Financial Times*, May 19, 1998. In interviews German officials maintain that the exclusion of services and intellectual property from Sir Leon's writ is formal only and that he will be able to negotiate on these issues, too.

26. Santer at CDU convention in Düsseldorf, April 1997.

27. Nancy Dunne, "Sanctions overload," *Financial Times*, July 21, 1998, p. 15; Christian Tenbrock, "Knüppel aus dem Sack," *Die Zeit*, August 13, 1998, p. 22; Dieter Buhl, "Die verwundbare Weltmacht," *Die Zeit*, August 13, 1998, p. 2.

28. For a critical look at the U.S.-European truce on penalties under the Iran-Libya Sanctions Act, see the editorial "Transatlantic relations," *Financial Times*, May 19, 1998, p. 19.

29. Richard G. Lugar, "NATO: Out of Area or Out of Business," press release, June 24, 1993.

30. On American hegemony, see, for example, Robert Kagan, "The Benevolent Empire," and Charles William Maynes, "The Perils of (and for) Imperial America," in *Foreign Policy*, vol. 111 (Summer 1998), pp. 24–48; U.S. newspaper coverage of the NATO summit in Madrid in summer 1997; and David P. Calleo's classic *Beyond American Hegemony* (New York: Basic Books, 1987).

31. These are the four choices outlined by Richard Haass in *The Reluctant*

Sheriff (New York: Council on Foreign Relations, 1997). For a different slant on the options in terms of U.S. forces planning, see the alternative "prudent," "innovative," "cooperative," and "balanced" defense proposals put forward in John Hillen, *Future Visions for U.S. Defense Policy* (New York: Council on Foreign Relations, 1998).

32. Amy Smithson, senior associate of the Henry L. Stimson Center in Washington, for example, openly asks allied governments to "démarche the U.S." and hold its feet to the fire in establishing a reliable inspection regime for monitoring chemical weapons proliferation.

33. John Roper, "A European Comment," in David C. Gompert and R. Stephen Larrabee, eds., *America and Europe* (Cambridge: Cambridge University Press, 1997), pp. 218–30.

34. Ibid.

35. The RAND Corporation is the most articulate promoter of this viewpoint. See especially the contributions by Ronald D. Asmus and David C. Gompert in Gompert and Larrabee, *America and Europe*.

36. See Philip H. Gordon, "Europe's Uncommon Foreign Policy," *International Security*, vol. 22, no. 3 (Winter 1997–98), pp. 74–100; and John Peterson and Helene Sjursen, eds., *A Common Foreign Policy for Europe?* (London: Routledge, 1998). A number of European diplomats privately argue that there was more foreign policy coordination under the intergovernmental "European Policy Cooperation" of the 1970s and 1980s than there is today under a more centralized "common foreign and security policy."

37. Interview, August 1998, and paper by Ambassador van Walsum at the conference on "Germany and Its Neighbors" in Amsterdam, November 28–29, 1997.

38. For one plea for the United States to grant the Europeans more leeway in defense, see Alyson Bailes, "Europe's Defense Challenge," *Foreign Affairs*, vol. 76, no. 1 (January/February 1997), pp. 15–20.

39. Contrast the Social Democrats' criticism of American actions in the Gulf War of 1991 with party foreign policy expert Rudolf Scharping's response to the 1998 U.S. strikes on Sudan and Afghanistan. His support of Washington was fully as cordial as Christian Democratic chancellor Kohl's. Deutschlandfunk interview in the "Fünf nach Zwölf" program, August 21, 1998, c. 12:15 p.m. The Social Democrats' other foreign policy expert, Günter Verheugen, was more reserved in his approval of the American strike—as, significantly, were the foreign policy spokesman for the German conservatives' parliamentary caucus, Karl Lamers, and British Foreign Secretary Robin Cook. See "Die Bonner Koalition und die SPD billigen das Vorgehen Washingtons," *Frankfurter Allgemeine Zeitung*, August 22, 1998, p. 2; and Robert Peston, "Blair 'too hasty' in backing U.S. strike on Sudan," *Financial Times*, August 27, 1998, p. 6.

40. See Stephen Kinzer, "U.S. Presses European Union to Be More Friendly

to Turkey," *New York Times*, May 1, 1998; and American Institute for Contemporary German Studies, "The Parameters of Partnership: Germany, the U.S. and Turkey" (Washington, October 24, 1997).

41. In early 1996 Richard Holbrooke famously criticized the Europeans for "sleeping through the night" on Greek-Turkish conflicts. Under the barrage of European protests he subsequently softened his comment to say that the "institutional structure . . . makes it hard for Europe to use its full moral, political, and diplomatic authority in a coherent and consistent way." Richard Holbrooke, *To End a War* (Random House, 1998), pp. 331f.

42. See Rosemary Hollis, "Europe and the Mideast: power by stealth?" *International Affairs*, vol. 73, no. 1 (January 1997), pp. 15–29; and Robert D. Blackwill and Michael Stürmer, *Allies Divided: Transatlantic Policies for the Greater Middle East* (MIT Press, 1997).

43. The Germans objected, for example, to Richard Holbrooke's failure to inform them for two days about his deal on Kosovo with Milosevic in the fall of 1998. For other European views that the United States has neglected and/ or tried to hog the civilian side of peace enforcement in Bosnia, see Pauline Neville-Jones, "Dayton, IFOR and Alliance Relations in Bosnia," paper presented at the annual IISS conference in Dresden, September 1–4, 1996; and Carl Bildt's understated review of Holbrooke's book on the Dayton settlement, "The Search for Peace," *Financial Times*, July 2, 1998, p. 16. For a general discussion of civil-military relations, see Michael C. Williams, "Civil-Military Relations and Peacekeeping," IISS Adelphi Paper 321, August 1998, especially pp. 53–76.

44. Christoph Bertram, "Germany Moves On," *Foreign Affairs*, vol. 77, no. 4 (July/August, 1998), p. 190.

45. See the interview with Stanley Fischer, "Wäre George Soros nicht gewesen, hätten wir es in Russland geschafft," *Frankfurter Allgemeine Zeitung*, August 24, 1998, p. 17; and Peter Norman and Stephen Fidler, "Clinton discusses Moscow summit," *Financial Times*, August 27, 1998, p. 2.

46. In the most extreme signal of displeasure, U.S. defense secretary William Cohen even threatened to pull U.S. troops out of Germany if Germany kept insisting on lobbying for "universal jurisdiction" for the court, according to Alessandra Stanley, "U.S. Presses Allies to Rein in Proposed War Crimes Court," *New York Times*, July 15, 1998.

47. See the broad public support for alliance with Europe in John E. Rielly, ed., "American Public Opinion and U.S. Foreign Policy 1995," Chicago Council on Foreign Relations, 1995; and Steven Kull, "A New World Order," *Christian Science Monitor*, September 18–24, 1998, p. 11.

48. Pierre Jacquet, "EMU: a worthwhile gamble," *International Affairs*, vol. 74, no. 1 (January 1998), pp. 55–71.

49. Robert Cooper *The Post-Modern State and the World Order* (London: Demos, 1996), p. 8. Jessica Mathews draws the same contrast to reach the

related conclusion that power is now seeping away from states to nongovernmental organizations. She notes, "The absolutes of the Westphalian system—territorially fixed states where everything of value lies within some state's borders; a single, secular authority governing each territory and representing it outside its orders; and no authority above states—are all dissolving." "Power Shift," *Foreign Affairs*, vol. 76, no. 1, p. 50.

50. For much gloomier interpretations of present-day Europe, see Mark Mazower, *The Dark Continent: Europe's Twentieth Century* (Harmondsworth: Penguin, 1998); Vladimir Tismaneanu, *Fantasies of Salvation: Democracy, Nationalism, and Myth in Post-Communist Europe* (Princeton University Press, 1998); and Christian Graf von Krockow, *Der deutsche Niedergang* (Stuttgart: Deutsche Verlags-Anstalt, 1998).

51. Cooper, *The Post-Modern State*, p. 33.

52. This missive was received by Hubertus von Morr, German consul in Texas in the mid-1980s.

53. Bill Clinton, speech in Berlin on the fiftieth anniversary of the Berlin Airlift, May 13, 1998; text provided by U.S. Embassy, Bonn.

Suggestions for Further Reading

Books

Acheson, Dean. *Present at the Creation* (New York: W. W. Norton, 1987 reissue).

Alestalo, Matti, and others. *The Transformation of Europe* (Warsaw: IFiS, 1994).

Anderson, Benedict. *Imagined Communities* (London: Verso, 1991).

Åslund, Anders. *How Russia Became a Market Economy* (Brookings, 1995).

Åslund, Anders, and Richard Layard, eds. *Changing the Economic System in Russia* (London: Pinter, 1993).

Bail, Christoper, Wolfgang H. Reinicke, and Reinhardt Rummel, eds. *EU–US Relations: Balancing the Partnership* (Baden-Baden: Nomos, 1997).

Baldwin, Richard E. *Towards an Integrated Europe* (London: Centre for Economic Policy Research, 1994).

Bark, Dennis L., ed. *Reflections on Europe* (Stanford: Hoover Institution Press, 1997).

Begg, David, and others, eds. *EMU: Prospects and Challenges for the Euro* (Malden, Mass.: Blackwell, 1998).

Ben-Sasson, H. H., ed. *A History of the Jewish People*, English trans. (Harvard University Press, 1976).

Bettzuege, Reinhard, ed. *Aussenpolitik der Bundesrepublik Deutschland. Dokumente von 1949 bis 1994* (Bonn: German Foreign Ministry, 1995).

Bideleux, Robert, and Ian Jeffries. *A History of Eastern Europe: Crisis and Change* (London: Routledge, 1998).

Biermann, Wolf. *Der Sturz des Dädalus oder Eizes für die Eingeborenen der Fidschi-Inseln über den IM Judas Ischariot und den Kuddelmuddel in Deutschland seit dem Golfkrieg* (Cologne: Kiepenheuer & Witsch, 1992).

Bingen, Dieter. *Die Polenpolitik der Bonner Republik von Adenauer bis Kohl 1949–1991* (Baden-Baden: Nomos, 1998).

Black, Stanley W., ed. *Europe's Economy Looks East: Implications for Germany and the European Union* (Cambridge: Cambridge University Press, 1997).

Blejer, Mario I., and Marko Skreb, eds. *Macroeconomic Stabilization in Transition Economies* (Cambridge: Cambridge University Press, 1997).

von Borries, Reimer, and Wolfgang Glomb. *Beck-Ratgeber Euro-Währung* (Munich: C. H. Beck, 1997).

van Brabant, Jozef M. *Industrial Policy in Eastern Europe* (Dordrecht: Kluwer, 1993).

Bressand, Albert, ed. *Strategic Conversations on the Euro at the Vanguard of Global Integration* (Paris: Prométhée and Ernst & Young, 1998).

Brown, J. F., and others, eds. *Western Approaches to Eastern Europe* (New York: Council on Foreign Relations, 1992).

Brown, Michael, and others, eds. *Nationalism and Ethnic Conflict* (MIT Press, 1997).

Brzezinski, Mark. *The Struggle for Constitutionalism in Poland* (New York: St. Martin's, 1997).

Brzezinski, Zbigniew. *The Grand Chessboard* (New York: Basic Books, 1997).

Buchan, David. *Europe: The Strange Superpower* (Aldershot: Dartmouth, 1993).

Bukkvoll, Tor. *Ukraine and European Security* (London: Pinter for Royal Institute of International Affairs, 1997).

Bulmer, Simon, and William Paterson. *The Federal Republic of Germany and the European Community* (London: Allen and Unwin, 1987).

Bundesinstitut für ostwissenschaftliche und internationale Studien. *Aufbruch im Osten Europas. Jahrbuch 1992/93* (Munich: Carl Hanser, 1993).

Cable, Vincent. *Globalization: Rules and Standards for the World Economy* (London: Pinter for RIIA, 1998).

Calleo, David. *Beyond American Hegemony* (New York: Basic Books, 1987).

Calleo, David P., and Eric R. Staal, eds. *Europe's Franco-German Engine* (Brookings, 1998).

Centre d'Information et de Recherche sur l'Allemagne Contemporaine, Paris, Deutsche Gesellschaft für Auswärtige Politik, and others. *Handeln für Europa. Deutsch-französische Zusammenarbeit in einer veränderten Welt* (Opladen: Leske + Budrich, 1995).

Clark, Bruce. *An Empire's New Clothes* (London: Vintage, 1995).

Clough, Patricia. *Helmut Kohl* (Munich: Deutscher Taschenbuch Verlag, 1998).

Colchester, Nicholas, and David Buchan. *Europower* (Times Books, 1990).

Connolly, Bernard. *The Rotten Heart of Europe* (London: Faber and Faber, 1995).

Cooper, Andrew, ed. *Niche Diplomacy: Middle Powers after the Cold War* (Basingstoke: Macmillan, 1997).

Cooper, Robert. *The Post-Modern State and the World Order* (London: Demos, 1996).

Cornish, Paul. *Partnership in Crisis: The US, Europe and the Fall and Rise of NATO* (London: Pinter for RIIA, 1997).

Coulson, Andrew, ed. *Local Government in Eastern Europe* (London: Edward Elgar, 1995).

Crampton, R. J. *Eastern Europe in the Twentieth Century* (London: Routledge, 1994).

Crawford, Beverly, ed. *Markets, States, and Democracy* (Boulder, Colo.: Westview, 1995).

Dahl, Robert. *Democracy and Its Critics* (Yale University Press, 1989).

Dawisha, Karen, and Bruce Parrott, eds. *The Consolidation of Democracy in East-Central Europe* (Cambridge: Cambridge University Press, 1997).

———. *Democratic Changes and Authoritarian Reactions in Russia, Ukraine, Belarus, and Moldova* (Cambridge: Cambridge University Press, 1997).

Deutsche Bundesbank. *The monetary policy of the Bundesbank* (Frankfurt: Deutsche Bundesbank, March 1994).

Diamond, Larry, and Marc F. Plattner, eds. *Capitalism, Socialism, and Democracy Revisited* (Johns Hopkins University Press, 1993).

Doyle, Michael. *Ways of War and Peace* (New York: W. W. Norton, 1997).

Dreher, Klaus. *Helmut Kohl* (Stuttgart: Deutsche Verlags-Anstalt, 1998).

Dunay, Pal, and others., eds. *New Forms of Security* (Aldershot: Dartmouth, 1995).

Eichengreen, Barry. *European Monetary Union: Theory, Practice, and Analysis* (MIT Press, 1997).

European Commission. *Agenda 2000: For a Stronger and Wider Union* (Brussels: European Commission, 1997) .

Falk, Richard, and Tamas Szentes, eds. *A New Europe in the Changing Global System* (Tokyo/New York/Paris: United Nations University Press, 1997).

Freudenstein, Roland, ed. *VII. Deutsch-Polnisches Forum: Deutschland und Polen im veränderten Europa* (Bonn: Europa Union Verlag for the German Society for Foreign Policy, June 1993).

Friend, Julius. *The Linchpin: French-German Relations, 1950–1990* (New York: Praeger, 1991).

Frydman, Roman, and others. *The Privatization Process in Russia, Ukraine and the Baltic States* (Budapest: Central European University Press, 1992).

Fukuyama, Francis. *The End of History and the Last Man* (New York: Free Press, 1992).

Fullbrook, Mary, ed. *National Histories and European History* (London: UCL Press, 1993).

Garnett, Sherman. *Keystone in the Arch* (Washington: Carnegie Endowment for International Peace, 1996).

Gellner, Ernest. *Conditions of Liberty: Civil Society and Its Rivals* (New York: Penguin, 1994).

Genscher, Hans-Dietrich. *Erinnerungen* (Berlin: Siedler, 1995).

Goldman, Marshall I. *Lost Opportunity: Why Reforms in Russia Have Not Worked* (New York: W. W. Norton, 1994).

Gompert, David C., and F. Stephen Larrabee, eds. *America and Europe: A Partnership for a New Era* (Cambridge: Cambridge University Press, 1997).

Goodby, James E. *Europe Undivided: The New Logic of Peace in U.S.-Russian Relations* (Washington: U.S. Institute of Peace Press, 1998).

Gordon, Philip. *NATO's Transformation* (Lanham, MD: Rowman & Littlefield, 1997).

Grabbe, Heather, and Kirsty Hughes. *Enlarging the EU Eastwards: Prospects and Challenges* (London: Pinter for RIIA, 1998).

De Grauwe, Paul. *The Economics of Monetary Integration* (Oxford: Oxford University Press, 1997).

Greenwood, Justin. *Representing Interests in the European Union* (Basingstoke: Macmillan, 1997).

Greenwood, Justin, and Mark Aspenwill, eds. *Collective Action in the European Union* (London: Routledge, 1998).

Gros, Daniel, and Niels Thygesen. *European Monetary Integration* (Harlow: Longman, 1992/98).

Haass, Richard N. *The Reluctant Sheriff: The United States after the Cold War* (New York: Council on Foreign Relations, 1997).

Hanke, Thomas, and Norbert Walter. *Der Euro—Kurs auf die Zukunft* (Frankfurt: Campus, 3d ed., 1998).

Hardt, John P., and others, eds. *Parliamentary Responsibility for Economic Transition in Central and Eastern Europe* (Washington: U.S. Government Printing Office for Congressional Research Service, rev. ed., 1996).

Hausner, Jerzy, and Grzegorz Mosur, eds. *Transformation Processes in Eastern Europe: Western Perspectives and the Polish Experience* (Krakow: Polish Academy of Sciences and Friedrich Ebert Stiftung, 1993).

Hayes-Renshaw, Fiona, and Helen Wallace. *The Council of Ministers* (New York: St. Martin's, 1997).

Heuser, Beatrice. *Transatlantic Relations* (London: Pinter for RIIA, 1995).

Hill, Christopher, ed. *National Foreign Policies and European Political Cooperation* (London: Allen and Unwin, 1983).

Holbrooke, Richard. *To End a War* (Random House, 1998).

Howard, A. E. Dick, ed. *Constitution Making in Eastern Europe* (Washington: Woodrow Wilson Center Press, 1993).

Hrbek, Rudolf, and others, eds. *Die Europäische Union als Prozess* (Bonn: Europa Union Verlag, 1998).

Huntington, Samuel. *The Third Wave* (University of Oklahoma Press, 1991).

Hutchings, Robert, L. *American Diplomacy and the End of the Cold War* (Washington: Woodrow Wilson Center Press, 1997).

Ignatieff, Michael. *Blood and Belonging* (London: BBC Books, 1994).

Ingersent, K. A., A. J. Rayner, and Robert C. Hine, eds. *The Reform of the Common Agricultural Policy* (Basingstoke: Macmillan, 1998).

Islam, Shafiqul, and Michael Mandelbaum, eds. *Making Markets* (New York: Council on Foreign Relations, 1993).

Johnson, Simon, and others. *Starting Over in Eastern Europe: Entrepreneurship and Economic Renewal* (Harvard Business School Press, 1995).

Jopp, Mathias, Andreas Maurer, and Otto Schmuck, eds. *Die Europäische Union nach Amsterdam* (Bonn: Europa Union Verlag, 1998).

Judt, Tony. *A Grand Illusion? An Essay on Europe* (New York: Hill and Wang, 1996).

Karp, Regina Cowen, ed. *Central and Eastern Europe* (Oxford: Oxford University Press for SIPRI, 1994).

Kennedy, Ellen. *The Bundesbank: Germany's Central Bank in the International Monetary System* (New York: Council on Foreign Relations Press, 1991).

Keohane, Robert O., and Stanley Hoffmann. *The New European Community* (Boulder, Colo.: Westview, 1991).

Kohl, Helmut, with Kai Diekmann and Ralf Georg Reuth. *Ich wollte Deutschlands Einheit* (Berlin: Propyläen, 1996).

Kolboom, Ingo, and Ernst Weisenfeld, eds. *Frankreich in Europa* (Bonn: Europa Union Verlag for the German Society for Foreign Policy, 1993).

Kornai, Janos. *The Road to a Free Economy* (New York: W. W. Norton, 1991).

Küsters, Hanns Jürgen, and Daniel Hofmann, eds. *Deutsche Einheit: Sonderedition aus den Akten des Bundeskanzleramtes 1989/90. Dokumente zur Deutschlandpolitik* (Munich: R. Oldenbourg, 1998).

Kuzio, Taras. *Ukraine under Kuchma: Political Reform, Economic Transformation and Security Policy in Independent Ukraine* (Basingstoke: Macmillan, 1997).

Lampe, John R., ed. *Creating Capital Markets in Eastern Europe* (Washington: Woodrow Wilson Center Press, 1992).

Larres, Klaus, and Torsten Oppelland. *Deutschland und die USA im 20. Jahrhundert: Geschichte der politischen Beziehungen* (Darmstadt: Wissenschaftliche Buchgesellschaft, 1997).

Layard, Richard, and John Parker. *The Coming Russian Boom* (New York: Free Press, 1996).

Larrabee, F. Stephen. *East European Security after the Cold War* (Santa Monica: RAND, 1993).

Läufer, Thomas, ed. *EG—Polen—Ungarn: Die Vertragstexte von Maastricht und die Europa-Abkommen* (Bonn: Europa Union Verlag, 1993).

Leonard, Dick. *Guide to the European Union* (London: Economist, 1994/98).

Lieven, Anatol. *Chechnya: Tombstone of Russian Power* (Yale University Press, 1998).

Linz, Juan J., and Alfred Stepan. *Problems of Democratic Transition and Consolidation: Southern Europe, South America, and Post-Communist Europe* (Johns Hopkins University Press, 1996).

Lippert, Barbara, and Peter Becker, eds. *Towards EU-Membership* (Bonn: Europa Union Verlag, 1998).

Ludwig, Michael. *Polen und die deutsche Frage* (Bonn: Europa Union Verlag for the German Society for Foreign Policy, December 1990).

Lundestad, Geir. *"Empire by Integration": The United States and European Integration, 1945–1997* (Oxford: Oxford University Press).

McAuley, Mary. *Russia's Politics of Uncertainty* (Cambridge: Cambridge University Press, 1997).

McCarthy, Patrick, ed. *France-Germany 1983–1993* (New York: St. Martin's, 1993).

McGuire, Steven. *Airbus Industrie: Conflict and Cooperation in US–EC Trade Relations* (Basingstoke: Macmillan, 1997).

McNamara, Kathleen R. *The Currency of Ideas: Monetary Politics in the European Union* (Cornell University Press, 1998).

Malcolm, Neil. *Soviet Policy Perspectives on Western Europe* (New York: Council on Foreign Relations Press, 1989).

Malcolm, Noel. *Kosovo: A Short History* (Basingstoke: Macmillan, 1998).

Mandelbaum, Michael. *The Dawn of Peace in Europe* (New York: Twentieth Century Fund, 1996).

Marsh, David. *Germany and Europe: The Crisis of Unity* (London: William Heinemann, 1994.

Masson, Paul R., Thomas H. Krueger, and Bart Turtelboom, eds. *EMU and the International Monetary System* (Washington: International Monetary Fund, 1997).

Mayhew, Alan. *Recreating Europe: The European Union's Policy toward Central and Eastern Europe* (Cambridge: Cambridge University Press, 1998).

Mazey, Sonia, and Jeremy Richardson, eds. *Lobbying in the European Community* (Oxford: Oxford University Press, 1993).

Miall, Hugh. *Shaping the New Europe* (London: Pinter for RIIA, 1994).

Michalski, Anna, and Helen Wallace. *The European Community: The Challenge of Enlargement* (London: RIIA, 1992).

Michta, Andrew A. *The Soldier-Citizen* (New York: St. Martin's, 1997).

Müllerson, Rein. *International Law, Rights and Politics* (London: Routledge, 1994).

Muravchik, Joshua. *Exporting Democracy* (Washington: American Enterprise Institute, 1991).

Nelson, Joan M., ed. *A Precarious Balance: Democracy and Economic Reforms in Eastern Europe*, vol. I (San Francisco: Institute for Contemporary Studies and others, 1994).

Newhouse, John. *Europe Adrift* (New York: Pantheon, 1997).

Open Media Research Institute. *Building Democracy Annual Survey 1995* (Armonk: M. E. Sharpe, 1996; 1997 edition to be issued 1999).

O'Donnell, Guillermo, Philippe C. Schmitter, and Laurence Whitehead. *Transitions from Authoritarian Rule* (Johns Hopkins University Press, 1986).

Di Palma, Giuseppe. *To Craft Democracies* (University of California Press, 1990).

Pedler, R. and M. C. P. M. van Schendelen, eds. *Lobbying the European Union* (Aldershot: Dartmouth, 1994).

Peterson, John, and Helene Sjursen, eds. *A Common Foreign Policy for Europe?* (London: Routledge, 1998).

Piening, Christopher. *Global Europe: The European Union in World Affairs* (Boulder, Colo.: Lynne Rienner, 1997).

Pinder, John. *The European Community and Eastern Europe* (New York: Council on Foreign Relations for the Royal Institute of International Affairs, 1991).

Polish Academy of Sciences. *Political Consciousness and Civic Education during the Transformation of the System* (Warsaw, 1994).

Pond, Elizabeth. *Beyond the Wall: Germany's Road to Unification* (Brookings, 1993).

Poznanski, Kazimierz Z. *Poland's Protracted Transition: Institutional Change and Economic Growth 1970–1994* (Cambridge: Cambridge University Press, 1996).

Pridham, Geoffrey, and Tatu Vanhanen, eds. *Democratization in Eastern Europe* (London: Routledge, 1994).

Przeworski, Adam, ed. *Democracy and the Market: Political and Economic Reforms in Eastern Europe and Latin America* (Cambridge: Cambridge University Press, 1991).

———. *Sustainable Democracy* (Cambridge: Cambridge University Press, 1995).

Randall, H., ed. *Business Guide to Lobbying in the EU* (London: Cartermill, 1996).

Regelsberger, Elfriede, and others, eds. *Foreign Policy of the European Union: From EPC to CFSP and Beyond* (Boulder: Lynne Rienner, 1997) .

Rohde, David. *Endgame: The Betrayal and Fall of Srebrenica* (New York: Farrar Straus & Girous, 1997).

Rouget, Werner. *Schwierige Nachbarschaft am Rhein* (Bonn: Bouvier, 1998).

Rueschemeyer, Dietrich, Marilyn Rueschemeyer, and Bjorn Wittrock, eds. *Participation and Democracy East and West: Comparison and Interpretations* (Armonk: M. E. Sharpe, 1998).

Sbragia, Alberta M., ed. *Euro-Politics* (Brookings, 1992).

Schoenbaum, David, and Elizabeth Pond. *The German Question and Other German Questions* (London/New York: Macmillan/St. Martin's, 1996).

Schönfelder, Wilhelm, and Elke Thiel. *Ein Markt—eine Währung* (Baden-Baden: Nomos, 1996).

Schöpflin, George. *Politics in Eastern Europe 1945–1992* (Oxford: Blackwell, 1993).

Schumpeter, Joseph A. *Capitalism, Socialism, and Democracy* (1942; reissued in 1976 by Allen and Unwin, London).

Serfaty, Simon. *Taking Europe Seriously* (New York: St. Martin's, 1992).

Shaw, Josephine. *The Law of the European Union* (Basingstoke: Macmillan, 1996).

Siedenberg, Axel, and Lutz Hoffman, eds. *Ukraine at the Crossroads: Economic Reforms in International Perspective* (Heidelberg: Springer, 1998).

Silber, Laura, and Allan Little. *Yugoslavia: Death of a Nation* (New York: TV Books/Penguin, 1995 and 1996).

Simon, Jeffrey. *Central European Civil-Military Relations and NATO Expansion* (Washington: National Defense University McNair Paper 39, April 1995).

Smith, Bruce L. R., and Gennady M. Danilenko, eds. *Law and Democracy in the New Russia* (Brookings, 1993).

Thomas, William I., and Florian Znaniecki. *The Polish Peasant in Europe and America*, ed. Eli Zaretsky (1918; Urbana: University of Illinois Press, 1996).

Thurow, Lester. *Head to Head* (New York: Warner Books, 1992).

Ullman, Richard H. *Securing Europe* (Princeton University Press, 1991).

Wallace, Helen, and William Wallace. *Policy-Making in the European Union*, 3d ed. (Oxford: Oxford University Press, 1996).

Wallace, Helen, and Alasdair Young. *Participation and Policy-making in the European Union* (Oxford: Clarendon, 1997).

Wallace, William. *Regional Integration: The West European Experience* (Brookings, 1994).

Walter, Norbert and Thomas Hanke. *Der Eurokurs auf die Zukunft* (Frankfurt: Campus, 1997).

Walzer, Michael, ed. *Toward a Global Civil Society* (Providence: Berghahn for the Friedrich-Ebert-Stiftung, 1995).

Weidenfeld, Werner, ed. *Maastricht in der Analyse* (Gütersloh: Bertelsmann Foundation, 1994).

———. *Demokratie am Wendepunkt* (Berlin: Siedler, 1996).

Weidenfeld, Werner, and Josef Janning, eds. *Europe in Global Change* (Gütersloh: Bertelsmann Foundation, 1993).

Weidenfeld, Werner and Wolfgang Wessels, eds. *Jahrbuch der Europäischen Integration 1996–97* (Bonn: Europa Union Verlag, 1998).

———. *Jahrbuch der Europäischen Integration 1997–98* (Bonn: Institut für Europäische Politik, 1998).

Wilson, Andrew. *Ukrainian Nationalism in the 1990s* (Cambridge: Cambridge University Press, 1996).

Woodward, Susan L. *Balkan Tragedy: Chaos and Dissolution after the Cold War* (Brookings, 1995).
Young, Thomas-Durell, ed. *Command in NATO after the Cold War: Alliance, National, and Multinational Considerations* (Carlisle Barracks, PA: U.S. Army War College, 1997).
Zelikow, Philip, and Condoleezza Rice. *Germany Unified and Europe Transformed* (Harvard University Press, 1997).
Zimmermann, Warren. *Origins of a Catastrophe* (Times Books, 1996).

Articles and Papers

For the purposes of this book, the *Financial Times*, with its superb coverage of European issues, served as the newspaper of record. Except for special sections, articles from newspapers and weeklies cited in footnotes are too numerous to list here.

Andrews, John. "The European Union: Family frictions," survey in the *Economist*, October 22, 1994.
Broder, Henryk. "Unser Kampf" *Der Spiegel*, April 29, 1991, pp. 255–67.
Christian Democratic Union/Christian Social Union Bundestag Caucus. "Reflections on European Policy" (the "Lamers paper"), September 1, 1994.
Collier, Irwin L., Jr. "The Twin Curse of the Goddess Europa and the Economic Reconstruction of Eastern Germany," *German Studies Review*, vol. 20, no. 3 (October 1997), pp. 399–428.
Collingnon, Stefan, and Susanne Mundschenk. "Die internationale Bedeutung der Währungsunion," *Integration*, vol. 21, no. 2 (April 1998), pp. 77–85.
Danderstädt, Michael. "EU–Osterweiterung: Wirkungen, Erwartungen und Interessen in den Beitrittsländern, *Integration*, vol. 21, no. 3 (July 1998).
Dornbusch, Rudi. "Euro Fantasies," *Foreign Affairs*, vol. 75, no. 5 (September/October 1996), pp. 110–24.
Ebel, Robert E. "The Oil Rush in the Caucasus," *Current History* (October 1997), pp. 331ff.
Economist. "From here to EMU," October 23, 1993, pp. 29ff.
Erd, Rainer. "Die Linke an die Front?" *Frankfurter Rundschau*, February 20, 1991, p. 4.
Feldstein, Martin. "EMU and International Conflict," *Foreign Affairs*, vol. 76, no. 6 (November/December 1997), pp. 60–73.
Financial Times editorial. "Germany's Europe," April 28, 1994.
Freudenstein, Roland. "Poland, Germany and the EU," *International Affairs*, vol. 74, no. 1 (January 1998), pp. 41–54.

Gaddy, Clifford G., and Barry W. Ickes. "Beyond a Bailout: Time to Face Reality About Russia's 'Virtual Economy,'" Brookings paper, 1998 <http://www.brook.edu/fp/w-papers/gaddy/gaddick1.htm>.

Garnett, Sherman. "Speaking the Truth to a Friend: Al Gore in Ukraine," July 21, 1998, in David Johnson List #2278, 23 July, 1998 <davidjohnson@erols.com>.

Garton Ash, Timothy. "Europe's Endangered Liberal Order," *Foreign Affairs*, vol. 77, no. 2 (March/April 1998), pp. 51–65 .

Goldgeier, James. "NATO Enlargement: Anatomy of a Decision," *Washington Quarterly*, vol. 21, no. 1 (Winter 1998), pp. 85–102.

Gomulka, Stanislaw. "Economic and Political Constraints During Transition," *Europe-Asia Studies*, vol. 46, no. 1 (1994), pp. 83–106.

Gordon, Philip H. "The Transatlantic Allies and the Changing Middle East," Adelphi Paper 322, International Institute for Strategic Studies, 1998.

―――. "Europe's Uncommon Foreign Policy," *International Security*, vol. 23, no. 2 (Winter 1997–98), pp. 74–100.

Henning, C. Randall. Statements before the U.S. Senate Committee on the Budget, October 21, 1997, "American Interests and Europe's Monetary Union"; and before the House of Representatives Subcommittee on Domestic and International Monetary Policy, April 18, 1998.

Hoffmann, Stanley. "Goodbye to a United Europe?" *New York Review of Books*, May 27, 1993, pp. 27ff.

Jacquet, Pierre. "EMU: a worthwhile gamble," *International Affairs*, vol. 74, no. 1 (January 1998), pp. 55–71.

Jensen, Donald N. "How Russia Is Ruled in 1998," RFE/RL special report, August 1998 <http://www.rferl.org/nca/special/ruwhorules/index.html>.

Journal of Democracy, special issue on Schumpeter, July 1992.

Kohl, Helmut, interview. "'Was hat der denn geleistet?'" *Focus*, April 6, 1998, pp. 21ff.

Kohl, Helmut. Major excerpts from speeches between 1982 and 1994 in Bettzüge, Reinhard, ed. *Aussenpoltik der Bundesrepublik Deutschland. Dokumente von 1949 bis 1994* (Bonn: Verlag Wissenschaft und Politik for German Foreign Ministry, 1995); government declarations since then as distributed by the German Information and Press Service.

Kupchan, Charles A. "Reviving the West," *Foreign Affairs*, vol. 75, no. 3 (May/June 1996), pp. 92–104.

Lindner, Rainer. "Die Ukraine zwischen Transformation und Selbstblockade" (Ebenhausen: Stiftung Wissenschaft und Politik, March 1998).

Ludlow, Peter. "Beyond Maastricht: Recasting the European Political and Economic System," Centre for European Policy Studies Working Document No. 79, Brussels (July 1993).

Markovits, Andrei. "Eine ernüchternde Erfahrung," *Die Zeit*, February 22, 1991; and "Die Linke gibt es nicht—und sie gibt es doch," *Frankfurter Rundschau*, February 20, 1991, p. 4.

Markovits, Andrei, and Jürgen Hoffmann. "Ein amerikanischer Jude und eine deutsche Friedensrede," *Frankfurter Rundschau*, February 16, 1991, p. 6.

Marples, David. "Belarus: An Analysis of the Lukashenka Regime," *Harriman Review*, Spring 1997, pp. 24ff.

"Marshall Plan and Its Legacy," special section, *Foreign Affairs*, vol. 76, no. 3 (May/June 1997), pp. 157–221.

Mathews, Jessica. "Power Shift," *Foreign Affairs*, vol. 76, no. 1 (January/February 1997), pp. 50–66.

Mearsheimer, John J. "Back to the Future: Instability in Europe After the Cold War," *International Security*, vol. 15, no. 1 (Summer 1990), pp. 5–56.

———. "The False Promise of International Institutions," Working Paper 10 (John M. Olin Institute for Strategic Studies, Harvard University, November 1994).

Meyer, Dirk. "The Provisions of the Charitable Welfare System and the Challenge of the Free Market," *German Studies Review*, vol. 20, no. 3 (October 1997), pp. 371–98.

Moisi, Dominique. "End in sight for Mr Eternity," *Financial Times*, March 10, 1998, p. 18.

Neville-Jones, Pauline. "Dayton, IFOR and the Future of Bosnia" paper at the IISS annual conference in Dresden, September 1–4, 1996.

Orenstein, Mitchell. "Vaclav Klaus: Revolutionary and Parliamentarian," *East European Constitutional Review* (Winter 1998), pp. 46–55.

Parlament, Das. Special section on Politikverdrossenheit, July 30, 1993.

Pond, Elizabeth. "After Gulf War, a Drive Toward European Unity," *Boston Globe*, March 31, 1991.

———. "International Politics, Viewed from the Ground," *International Security*, vol. 19, no. 1 (Summer 1994), pp. 195–99 (letter and response from Kenneth N. Waltz).

———. "Letter from Bonn: Visions of the European Dream," *Washington Quarterly*, vol. 20, no. 3 (Summer 1997), pp. 53–72.

———. "Letter from Kiev: Crisis, 1997," *Washington Quarterly*, vol. 20, no. 4 (Autumn 1997), pp. 79–87.

———. "The Escape from History," *WorldLink* (January/February 1998), pp. 64–68.

Putnam, Robert D. "Bowling Alone," *Journal of Democracy* (January 1995), pp. 65–78.

Schönfelder, Wilhelm, and Elke Thiel. "Stabilitätspakt und Euro-X-Gremium-Die stabilitätspolitische Untermauerung der WWU," *Integration*, vol. 21, no. 2 (April 1998), pp. 69–76.

Schwartz, Herman. "Eastern Europe's Constitutional Courts," *Journal of Democracy*, vol. 9, no. 4 (October 1998), pp. 100–14.

Sherr, James. "Russia, Geopolitics and Crime," Conflict Studies Research

Centre (CSRC), Royal Military Academy Sandhurst, February 1995, <gopher://marvin.nc3a.nato.int/00/secdef/csrc/csrc2.1%09%09%2B>.

———. "Russian Great Power Ideology: Sources and Implications," CSRC, RMA Sandhurst, July 1996, <gopher://marvin.nc3a.nato.int/00/secdef/csrc/f54.txt%09%09%2B>.

———. "Russia and Ukraine: Towards Compromise or Convergence?" CSRC, RMA Sandhurst, August 1997, <gopher://marvin.nc3a.nato.int/00/secdef/csrc/f60all.txt%09%09%2B>.

Spiegel, Der. "An der deutschen Heimatfront," March 4, 1991, pp. 238–45.

Spiegel, Der. "Doch wie Weimar?" December 20, 1993, pp. 38ff.

Sullivan, Scott. "Down in the Dumps," *Newsweek*, April 12, 1993, pp. 10–15.

Thiel, Elke. "German Politics with Respect to the European Economic and Monetary Union," paper presented at the American Institute for Contemporary German Studies, Washington, May 18, 1995.

Tolz, Vera. "What is Russia: Post-Communist Debates on Nation-Building," paper presented at the annual conference of the British Association for the Advancement of Slavic Studies, Cambridge, April 5, 1998.

Umbach, Frank. "The Role and Influence of the Military Establishment in Russia's Foreign and Security Policies in the Yeltsin Era," *Journal of Slavic Military Studies*, vol. 9, no. 3 (September 1996), pp. 467–500.

U.S. Senate Budget Committee Hearing. "Europe's Monetary Union and its Potential Impact on the United States Economy," October 21, 1997, including statement by U.S. Treasury Deputy Secretary Lawrence H. Summers.

Thygesen, Niels. "Why Economic and Monetary Union Is an Important Objective for Europe," *SAIS Review*, vol. 14, no. 1 (Winter-Spring 1994), pp. 17–34.

Wagner, Helmut. "Perspectives on European Monetary Union," American Institute for Contemporary German Studies Research Report No. 7, 1998.

Walt, Stephen M. "International Relations: One World, Many Theories," *Foreign Policy*, vol. 110 (Spring 1998), pp. 29–46.

Waltz, Kenneth N. "The Emerging Structure of International Politics," *International Security*, vol. 18, no. 2 (Fall 1993), pp. 44–79.

Interviews
(Partial List)

The month is given for those interviews conducted in 1997 and 1998. Earlier interviews since the fall of the Berlin Wall are given by year only. The city is indicated only when it was not otherwise obvious. When the author was not the sole interviewer, this is indicated. The names of those who requested that their interviews not be listed are omitted

Aden, Hans
    First secretary, Swedish Embassy, Kyiv: 1995, 1996, February 1997
Appatov, Semyon
    Chairman, Department of International Relations, Odessa University: 1996
Arnot, Alexander
    German ambassador to Ukraine: 1994, 1995, 1996
Asher, Jim
    Agricultural consultant, Kyiv: March and August 1997
Åslund, Anders
    Senior associate, Carnegie Endowment for International Peace: 1994, 1995, 1996, (Kyiv) March 1997, (Washington) November 1997
Bagger, Hartmut
    Lt. Gen., Bundeswehr general-inspector: (group) 1996
Bahr, Jerzy
    Polish ambassador to Ukraine: March 1997
Balcerowicz, Leszek
    Polish finance minister and vice prime minister, member of Parliament: 1995
Bandler, Donald
    U.S. diplomat in Paris and Bonn, later senior director for European Affairs, U.S. National Security Council: 1992, 1993, October 1997
Bartoszewski, Wladyslaw
    Polish foreign minister: 1995, (group) 1996, (telephone) November 1997

Bergsdorf, Wolfgang
Minister-director, German Interior Ministry: 1996
Biedenkopf, Kurt
Minister-president of Saxony: 1991, 1992, 1995
Bielecki, Jan Krzysztof
Polish prime minister, member of Parliament, and leader of the Liberal Democratic party in the early 1990s: 1992, 1993
Bindenagel, J. D.
U.S. diplomat in Bonn and East Berlin, later chargé, U.S. Embassy to Germany, later senior coordinator, Trans-Atlantic Agenda, German Marshall Fund of the United States: 1989, 1990, 1992, 1993, 1994, 1995, 1996, 1997, 1998
Bingen, Dieter
Poland specialist, Federal Institute for Eastern and International Studies, Cologne: 1994
Black, David
U.S. Agency for International Development, Kyiv: February 1997
Blakely, Pollard
Agricultural attaché, British Embassy, Kyiv: 1996
Blankert, Jan Willem
European Union Embassy, Warsaw: January, September, and November 1997
Boden, Johan
General director, South Foods (Kakhovka, Ukraine): August 1997, October 1998
Bogdan, Angela
First secretary and consul, Canadian Embassy, Warsaw: 1995
Bressand, Albert
Director, Prométhée, Paris: January 1998
Broomfield, Nigel
British ambassador to Germany: 1993, 1994, 1996
Broukhovetsky, Viatcheslav
President, Kyiv Mohyla Academy, Kyiv: February 1997
Brümmer, Claus
Coordinator for German Business Counsel, Kreditanstalt für Wiederaufbau, Kyiv: 1994
Brzezinski, Ian
Security advisor in parliamentary Council of Advisors, Ukraine, later adviser to U.S. Senator William V. Roth: 1994, 1995
Brzezinski, Zbigniew
Former U.S. national security adviser: 1996
Burns, Nicholas
U.S. National Security Council senior director for Russia, Ukraine and

Eurasia Affairs 1990–95; State Department spokesman 1995–97: 1994, 1995, 1996

Buteiko, Anton Denisovich
Ukrainian first deputy foreign minister: 1995

Bylynskyj, Markian
Director of Field Operations, Pylyp Orlyk Institute for Democracy, Kyiv: 1994, 1996, August 1997

Cameron, Fraser
Adviser, Directorate General I.A, European Commission: 1993, 1994, January 1997

Campbell, Robert
Economics professor, University of Indiana and Kyiv Mohyla Academy: February 1997

Chornovil, Viacheslav
Ukrainian member of Parliament: 1994

Chrobog, Jürgen
German ambassador to the United States: 1995, 1996, October 1997

Cieslik, Miroslaw
Chargé, Polish Embassy, Kyiv: March 1997

Cimoszewicz, Wlodzimierz
Polish prime minister: (group, Salzburg) 1996

de Clercq, Willi
Member of European Parliament: (group, Strasbourg) 1996

Constantinescu, Emil
Romanian president: (conversation, Davos) January 1997

Cooper, Robert
Counselor, British Embassy, Bonn: 1994, 1995, 1996, May, June, August, and November 1997, February, May, and June 1998

Czaplinski, Kazimierz
Professor of History, Wroclaw University, and chairman in the 1970s of Club of Catholic Intellectuals, Wroclaw: 1994

Czyzewski, Adam B.
Economist, World Bank Representation, Warsaw: February 1997

Dabrowski, Marek
Economist, World Bank: 1995

Davis, Jim
Agricultural and opera consultant, Kyiv: March 1997, October 1998

Dijckmeester, Alexander
EU ambassador to Poland: 1993, 1995

Domanski, Henryk
Sociologist, Polish Academy of Sciences: 1995, February 1997

Dubovka, Nina
Head of the regional teachers' trade union, Odessa: 1996

Dulnev, Lev
    Deputy general director, Windenergo Ltd., Kyiv: 1994
Earle, Hobart
    Conductor of the Odessa Philharmonic: 1996
Ebel, Robert E.
    Director, Energy and National Security, CSIS: November 1997
Elbe, Frank
    Director, Office of German foreign minister Hans-Dietrich Genscher: 1992
Eppinger, Monica
    Diplomat, U.S. Embassy, Kyiv: March, June, and October 1997
Falenski, Hans-Joachim
    Head of staff, foreign policy section, CDU-CSU Parliamentary Group,
    Bundestag: 1993, 1994, 1995, 1996, January, March, and May 1997, January and May 1998
Fischer, Joschka
    Member of the Bundestag, later German foreign minister: (group) April 1998
Fishel, Gene
    Ukrainian Desk, Intelligence and Research, U.S. State Department: 1994, 1995, 1996
Flyaks, Alexander
    Vice president, Parus-Bearbrook supermarket, Dnipropetrovsk: 1994
Freeland, Halyna
    Director, External Relations, Ukrainian Legal Foundation: 1995, 1996, March 1997, October 1998
Freudenstein, Roland
    Director of the Konrad Adenauer Foundation, Warsaw: 1996, November 1997
Freytag, Dirk
    Chief of staff for Alexandre Lamfalussy, EMI: (group) 1996
Frick, Helmut
    Minister in the German Embassy, Warsaw: April and September 1997
Fried, Daniel
    Political counselor, U.S. Embassy, Poland 1990–93; National Security Council Director for European Affairs 1993–95; National Security Council senior director for central and eastern Europe 1995–97; U.S. Ambassador to Poland from 1998: 1993, 1994, 1995, 1996
Frishberg, Alex
    Partner, Law Offices Frishberg & Partners, Kyiv: 1994
Fritsch, Conrad
    Project manager, Agricultural Land Share Project, RONCO Consulting Corporation, Kyiv: March and August 1997
Garnett, Sherman
    Senior associate, Carnegie Endowment for International Peace: 1995, 1996, October 1997, March and October 1998

Hunter, Robert
U.S. ambassador to NATO: 1993, 1996
Ischinger, Wolfgang
Political director, German Foreign Ministry: 1989, 1990, 1993, 1994, 1995, 1996, January 1998, (group) May 1998
Jankowski, Maciej
President, Solidarity Trade Union, Mazowsze region: (Warsaw) 1993, 1995
Jaresko, Natalie
Head of Economics section, U.S. Embassy, Kyiv, later executive vice president, Western NIS Enterprise Fund: 1995, October 1998
Jaruzelski, Wojciech
Last president of the Polish People's Republic: 1992
Jarzembo, Georg
Member of European Parliament: (group) 1996
Kaiser, Karl
Professor, Bonn University, and director of studies, German Foreign Policy Association: 1995, (group) September 1998
Kaminski, Antoni
Professor, Warsaw Institute of International Relations: 1992, 1994, 1995, March 1997
Kapeliushniy, L. V.
Editor-in-Chief, *Slovo*, Odessa: 1996
Karkoszka, Andrzej
Polish deputy defense minister: 1994, 1996, February and November 1997
Kaufmann, Daniel
World Bank resident representative, Kyiv: 1995, 1996
Kavalski, Jan
World Bank resident representative, Warsaw: September 1997
Kharchenko, Ihor
Head of Planning Staff, Ukrainian Foreign Ministry, later ambassador at the United Nations: 1995, 1996, February and March 1997
Khmara, Stepan
Ukrainian member of Parliament: 1994
Kimmett, Robert
U.S. ambassador to Germany: 1992
Kinach, Jaroslav B.
Resident representative, European Bank for Reconstruction and Development, Kyiv: August 1997
Kiselyov, Stanislav
Founder, Radio Glas, Odessa: 1996
Klaiber, Klaus Peter
Head, Policy Planning Staff, German Foreign Ministry, later deputy secretary-general, NATO: (Bonn) March 1997, (Brussels) January 1998

Kosminski, Jerzy
Polish ambassador to theUnited States: October and December 1997, October 1998

Kwasniewski, Alexander
Member of Sejm, later president of Poland: 1993, (group) 1996, (Davos) January 1998

von Kyaw, Dietrich
German Foreign Ministry, deputy director-general for Economic and European Community Affairs, later German chancellor's permanent representative to Coreper: 1989, 1990, 1991, 1992, 1993, 1994, 1995, 1996, January and June 1998

Lambsdorff, Otto Graf
Bundestag Member: (group) May 1998

Lamers, Karl
European spokesman for the Christian Democratic/Christian Social Union parliamentary group in the Bundestag: (group) January and September 1998

Lamfalussy, Alexandre
Director, European Monetary Institute: (group) 1996

Landau, Jean-Pierre
Former undersecretary for foreign affairs, French Economics Ministry: (group, Washington), 1996

Lavrynovych, Oleksandr
Member of Ukrainian parliament: September 1997

Lenain, Patrick
IMF senior resident representative, Kyiv: August 1997, October 1998

Lendvai, Paul
Intendant, Austrian Broadcasting: June 1997, June 1998

Lyschynski, Roman
Counselor in Canadian Embassy, Kyiv, later head of the NATO office, Kyiv: 1994, August 1997

Luczywo, Helen
Editor in chief, *Gazeta Wyborcza*, Warsaw: 1992

Mallaby, Christopher
British ambassador to Germany: 1992

Marchuk, Yevhen
Ukrainian prime minister, then member of Parliament: 1996

Matussek, Thomas
Counselor, German Embassy, Washington: 1994, 1995, 1996, November 1997

Mertes, Michael
Director-general, Social and Political Analysis and Cultural Affairs in Helmut Kohl's chancellery: 1991, 1992, 1996, February, March, May, June, November, and December 1997, February and August 1998

Meyer-Landrut, Andreas
  Chief of the German president's office, later Daimler-Benz representative in Moscow: 1990, 1991, 1992
Miller, Bowman
  Director, Office of Analysis for Europe and Canada, Bureau of Intelligence and Research, U.S. State Department: 1990, 1991, 1992, 1996, March, October, and December 1998
Miller, William
  U.S. ambassador to Ukraine: 1995, 1996, March 1997
Millotat, Christian, Brig.-Gen.
  Deputy chief of staff, Eurocorps: (group) 1996
Minchev, Emil
  Counselor, Bulgarian Embassy to Germany: September 1997
Moisi, Dominique
  Deputy director, French Institute for International Relations: 1990, 1991, (telephone) November 1997, (Davos) January 1998
Möllers, Felicitas
  German Economic Advisory Group, Kyiv: March 1997, October 1998
Moore, Lou
  Agricultural adviser, USAID, Poznan: 1994
Moroz, Oleksandr
  Member and former Speaker of Supreme Rada, Kyiv: October 1998
Müller, Wolfgang
  Ukrainian section, German Economics Ministry: 1996
von Münchow-Pohl, Bernd
  Head of Ukrainian section, German Foreign Ministry: 1995, 1996, February 1997
Murphy, Richard
  Senior associate, Center for Security and International Studies, Washington: October 1997
Nanivskaya, Vera
  World Bank Mission, Kyiv: 1996
Naumann, Klaus, Maj. Gen.
  Inspector-general of the Bundeswehr, later chairman, NATO Military Committee: 1990, 1992, 1994, January 1998
Nemtsov, Boris
  Governor, Nizhnii-Novgorod: (Davos) 1995, (Salzburg) 1996
Nowina-Konopska, Piotr
  Democratic Union, Sejm, later deputy head of European Integration Committee: 1992
Nyberg, Jan
  Counselor, Swedish Embassy to Poland: September and November 1997
Nyberg, Rene
  Deputy director general, Finnish Ministry of Foreign Affairs: September 1998

Onyszkiewicz, Janusz
   Member of the Sejm, later Polish defense minister: 1992, 1993, 1994, 1995, 1996, February 1997, February 1998
Papadiuk, Roman
   Former U.S. ambassador to Ukraine: (Washington) 1995
Parmentier, Guillaume
   Adviser, French Defense Ministry: 1996
Parrish, Capt. C. A. M.
   Defense attaché, British Embassy, Kyiv: 1994
Pieronek, Bishop Tadeusz
   Spokesman for Polish Episcopate: 1995, 1996
Pikhovshek, Vyacheslav
   Director, Ukrainian Center for Independent Political Research: 1994, 1995, 1996, February, March, and September 1997, October 1998
von Ploetz, Hans-Friedrich
   State secretary, German Foreign Ministry: 1989, 1993, 1994, 1995, 1996, January, February, and May 1998
Poettering, Hans-Gert
   Member, European Parliament: (group) 1996
Ponomarenko, Anatoliy
   Ukrainian ambassador to Germany: December 1997
Rau, Karin
   Representative of German business in Kyiv: 1994, March 1997
Redman, Charles
   U.S. ambassador to Germany: 1994, 1995
Reilly, Tim
   External affairs director, JKX Oil and Gas, Kyiv: March and August 1997
Rejt, Jerzy
   Chairman, Union of Ukrainians in Poland: 1995
Regulski, Jerzy
   Director, Foundation in Support of Local Democracy, Warsaw: 1992
Reiter, Janusz
   Polish ambassador to Germany, later director, Center for International Relations, Warsaw: 1994, 1995, 1996, February and April 1997, (telephone) September 1997
Rewald, Roman
   Lawyer, Weil, Gotshal, and Manges, Warsaw: April 1997
Rey, Nicholas
   U.S. ambassador to Poland: 1994, 1995, 1996, February and September 1997
Rodlauer, Markus K.
   IMF resident representative, Warsaw: 1996, September 1997
Ruban, Volodymyr
   Editor, *Den'*; later, editor, *Vseukrainskie Vedemosti*, Kyiv: (group) 1996

Rubin, Eric
Chief of the political section, U.S. Embassy, Kyiv, later assistant press secretary for Foreign Affairs, U.S. National Security Council: 1996, October 1997
Rühe, Volker
Christian Democratic Union general secretary, later German defense minister: 1992
Rühl, Lothar
State secretary in German Defense Ministry, later columnist for *Die Welt*: 1996
Rychard, Andrzej
Professor of Sociology, Polish Academy of Sciences: 1994, 1995, September 1997
Rzepka, Anna
Director, local self-government Sejmik in Kielce, Poland: 1993
Rzhimeshevsky, Konstantyn
Director of Foreign Economic Relations, Odessa: 1996
Saryusz-Wolski, Jacek
Polish undersecretary of state for European Integration and Foreign Assistance, Council of Ministers, later vice rector, College of Europe, Natolin: 1992, 1996
Schäuble, Wolfgang
Majority parliamentary leader in Bundestag until September 1998: 1992, 1994, 1996, (group) December 1997
Scharping, Rudolf
Bundestag deputy, later German defense minister: (group) May 1998
Schönfelder, Wilhelm
Chief of EU Division, German Foreign Ministry: 1993, 1994, 1995, 1996, March, May, and December 1997, May 1998
Seiters, Rudolf
Deputy Bundestag CDU/CSU leader: (group) 1996
Shcherban, Vladimir P.
Member of Ukrainian Parliament: 1996
Shcherbak, Yuriy
Ukrainian ambassador to the United States: 1996
Shea, Jamie
NATO spokesman: 1993, 1994, 1995, 1996, January, February, and May 1997, February and June 1998
Shpek, Roman
Ukrainian National Agency for Reconstruction and Development: 1996, March 1997
Simons, Thomas
U.S. ambassador to Poland: 1992, 1993, 1994
Siwiec, Marek
State secretary in Polish president's office: 1996, February and September 1997

Sliwinski, Krzysztof
Ambassador to the Jewish Diaspora (outside Israel), Polish Foreign Ministry: 1996
Sloan, Stanley
NATO specialist, Congressional Research Service: 1995, 1996, March and October 1998
Smeshko, Ihor, Maj. Gen.
Military attaché in Ukrainian Embassy to the United States, later director of Strategic Planning and Analysis in the President's Office, Kyiv: 1995
Snelbecker, David
Associate director, Project on Economic Reform in Ukraine: 1994
Solana, Javier
NATO secretary-general, June 1998
Stark, Jürgen
State secretary, German Finance Ministry, later vice president, Bundesbank: (group) May 1998
Staudacher, Wilhelm
Chief of staff to German president Roman Herzog: 1996
Stechel, Walter
Head of Section on Ukrainian economy, later on Russian economy, German Foreign Ministry: 1996, February 1997
Stoecker, Volkmar
Minister, German Embassy in Warsaw, then head of the U.S. section in German Foreign Ministry: 1995, 1996, June 1998
Stolzman, Maria
Member of Polish Parliament and director of the Water Supply Foundation: 1993
Stomma, Swiatoslaw
Warsaw: 1992
von Studnitz, Ernst-Jörg
Deputy Head of West German representation office in East Germany, later ambassador to Russia: 1989, 1990, 1992, 1993, 1994, 1995, 1996
Sturen, Carl
General director, South Foods, (Kakhovka, Ukraine): March and August 1997, October 1998
Szlajfer, Henryk
Senior deputy director, Polish Institute of International Affairs: 1993, 1994, 1995, 1996, April, September, and November 1997
Szmajdzinski, Jerzy
Member of Parliament, Warsaw: 1994, 1995, 1996
Szczypiorski, Andrzej
Novelist, Warsaw: 1992

Tabachnyk, Dmytro
   Chief of staff to Ukrainian President Kuchma, later member of Supreme Rada: August 1997, October 1998
Talbott, Strobe
   Deputy secretary of state: 1994
Tarasyuk, Borys
   Ukrainian ambassador to NATO, later foreign minister: 1995, 1996, January 1997
Teltschik, Horst
   Foreign policy adviser to Chancellor Kohl, later director of Bertelsmann Foundation; currently member of BMW board: 1989, 1990, 1991, 1992
Teriokhin, Serhii
   Member of Parliament, Ukraine: September 1997
Tietmeyer, Hans
   President, Bundesbank: (group) 1995
Tindemanns, Leo
   Member of European Parliament: (group) 1996
Tomala, Mieczyslaw
   Professor, Polish Institute of International Affairs: 1992
Towpik, Andrzej
   Undersecretary of state, Polish Foreign Ministry: 1996, September and November 1997
Tsok, Nadiya
   Adviser to member of Parliament Ivan Zayets: 1994
Veldkamp, Caspar
   Dutch diplomat, Warsaw: February 1997
Verheugen, Günter
   Foreign policy coordinator of the German Social Democratic parliamentary caucus: (group) May 1998
Vershbow, Alexander
   Senior director for European Affairs, U.S. National Security Council, later U.S. ambassador to NATO: 1993, 1994,1995, 1996, June 1998
Vogel, Wolfdietrich
   Minister, German Embassy to Poland: 1992, 1993, 1994, 1995, 1996
van Walsum, A. Peter
   Dutch ambassador to Germany: March 1997, August 1998
Walter, Norbert
   Head of Research, Deutsche Bank: (telephone) April 1998
Washchuk, Roman
   Counselor, Canadian Embassy, Kyiv: 1996, February and August 1997
Wasylyk, Myron
   Advisor to the chairman, State Property Fund of Ukraine: 1994, 1995

Weise, Hans Heinrich
Planning Staff, German Defense Ministry: 1990, 1991, 1992, 1993, 1994, 1995, April 1997
Weisser, Ulrich
Chief of the Planning Staff, German Defense Ministry: 1994, 1995, 1996, January 1997, February 1998
Wetteke, Ernst
President, Hessen Central Bank: (group) 1996
Whitehead, Cynthia
Environmental consultant, Brussels: 1994, 1995, 1996, April 1998
Williams, Selma
Adviser to International Media Center, Kyiv: February and March 1997
Winiecki, Jan
President, Adam Smith Research Center, Warsaw: 1994
Wolff-Paweska, Anna
Director, Western Institute, Poznan: 1994
Wolthers, Pieter Jan
Counselor in Dutch Embassy, Warsaw: 1995, 1996, April, September, and November 1997
Wroblewski, Andrzej Krzysztof
Deputy editor, *Polityka*, Warsaw: 1996, February, March, and April 1997
Wziezinski, Wojciech
Rector, University of Wroclaw: 1994
Yavlinsky, Grigory
Member of the Duma: (Davos) January 1998
Zayets, Ivan
Ukrainian member of Parliament: 1994
Zoellick, Robert
Undersecretary of State, U.S. State Department, later executive vice president, Fannie Mae, then president, Center for Strategic and International Studies: 1991, 1992, 1994, 1995, 1996, September 1998

Other diplomats, officials, editors, and journalists in Bonn, Warsaw, Kyiv, Lviv, and Odessa

Index

38; labor market, 172; Lamers paper crisis, 88–95; Maastricht goals, 44, 45–47, 55; military policy, 52–53; monetary union policy, 33–34, 38, 43–44, 49, 55, 97–100, 101, 103–04, 105–06, 163, 167, 168; movement for European integration, 3, 11–12, 158; Poland and, 3, 10, 15–16, 66, 130–31, 236n46; Polish workers in, 207n12; postnational consciousness, 7; postwar experience, 25, 26; private-sector restructuring, 191–92; public opinion on integration, 40; public opinion toward monetary union, 9, 47, 48–49; recession of 1990s, 51, 52, 54–55; refugees, 52; reunification. See German reunification; tax system, 172, 246n37; on Turkey EU candidacy, 200; U.S. perceptions of Russia and, 201; U.S. relations, 196. See also Kohl, Helmut
Gingrich, Newt, 184
Giscard d'Estaing, Valéry, 31, 47
Glemp, Jozef, 122, 123
Gorbachev, Mikhail, 15, 24, 37, 57, 112
Greece, 76, 82, 161, 179; in EC, 31
Gulf War, 52, 59

Hajnicz, Artur, 127
Havel, Vaclav, 67
Herzog, Roman, 164
History of Europe: cold-war cooperation in West, 27–29, 219–20n41; context of current developments, 14–15; current European outlook and, 13, 14; European perceptions of, 4; motivation toward integration, 158; Poland, 65–66, 129; Polish Jewry, 123–28; post–cold war expectations, 10–11; postwar

experience, 24–27; stereotyped U.S. perceptions, 20–23
Holbrooke, Richard, 64, 78
Holovaty, Serhiy, 152
Horbulin, Volodymyr, 156
Hungary, 144–45; NATO candidacy, 69, 72, 74–75; post–cold war accomplishments, 135–36, 137; Romanian border dispute, 74–75; self-perception, 8
Hussein, Saddam, 59, 78–79

Ickes, Barry, 142
Immigration, 52, 106, 179–80
Interest rates, 48
International Monetary Fund, 142; implications of EMU for, 188–89
Iran, 200
Iraq, 78–79, 200
Ireland, 161, 166
Italy: domestic reform for EMU qualification, 159–61; EMU qualification, 107; Lamers paper crisis, 89; recession of 1990s, 51; trends toward integration, 7

Jacquet, Pierre, 203
Jankowski, Henryk, 123
Jaruzelski, Wojciech, 24
Jospin, Lionel, 106, 174

Kennedy, John F., 29
Kharchenko, Ihor, 75
Khrushchev, Nikita, 29
Kinkel, Klaus, 91, 95
Kissinger, Henry, 184
Kohl, Helmut, 24, 92–93, 130; accomplishments of, 4–5, 180–81; Chirac and, 94, 164, 174; in evolution of single market, 34–35, 38; German reunification policies, 39–40; intellectual style, 36, 39–40; Maastricht goals, 45–47; Mitterand and, 36–37; monetary union policy, 43, 95,